SC...

AND HIS WORLD

OTHER PRINCETON UNIVERSITY PRESS VOLUMES

PUBLISHED IN CONJUNCTION WITH

THE BARD MUSIC FESTIVAL

Brahms and His World
edited by Walter Frisch (1990)

Mendelssohn and His World
edited by R. Larry Todd (1991)

Richard Strauss and His World
edited by Bryan Gilliam (1992)

Dvořák and His World
edited by Michael Beckerman (1993)

Bartok and His World
edited by Peter Laki (1995)

Schumann
and His World

—

EDITED BY
R. LARRY TODD

PRINCETON UNIVERSITY PRESS

Copyright © 1994 by Princeton University Press

Published by Princeton University Press, 41 William Street
Princeton, New Jersey 08540
In the United Kingdom: Princeton University Press, Chichester, West Sussex

Library of Congress Cataloging-in-Publication Data

Schumann and his world / edited by R. Larry Todd.
p.   cm.
Includes bibliographical references and index.
ISBN 0-691-03697-7 (CL). — ISBN 0-691-03698-5 (PA)
1. Schumann, Robert 1810–1856.   I. Todd, R. Larry.
ML410.S4S323   1994
780′.92—dc20   94-9686

This book has been composed in Baskerville
by The Composing Room of Michigan, Inc.

Music typeset by Don Giller

Princeton University Press books are printed on acid-free paper and meet the
guidelines for permanence and durability of the Committee on Production
Guidelines for Book Longevity of the Council on Library Resources

Printed in the United States of America

3   5   7   9   10   8   6   4   2

Designed by Laury A. Egan

Contents

CONTENTS

Preface

Writing at the middle of the nineteenth century, the American Beethoven scholar Alexander Wheelock Thayer pondered the difficulties of the music of Robert Schumann and his need to be "ranked as an original thinker." Thayer juxtaposed Schumann with Wagner and suggested that "there is a something within them—great, grand, mighty, huge, or mean and insignificant—what it is matters not—but a something which they feel the musician's longing to produce musically, while the musical forms in use—the means hitherto sufficient for the purposes of others, do not and will not give the expression they desire."[1] This unusual pairing of the two composers dates from May 1853, less than a year before Schumann's attempted suicide, and only a few months before Schumann published his celebrated "Neue Bahnen" manifesto, in which he championed the young Brahms and distanced himself from the "New German" movement of Wagner and Liszt (the movement openly endorsed during the 1850s by the *Neue Zeitschrift für Musik*, the very journal that Schumann had founded in 1834).

In endeavoring to identify a particular difficulty with Schumann's music, Thayer enunciated an idea that recurs in Schumann reception history: in Schumann, Thayer wrote, "the reflective and imaginative faculty may be stronger than the so called creative—really producing—genius, which clothes the thought so that the next man can comprehend it; and the music, which he *would* write, may only be found in Hawthorne's cabinet of a virtuoso, or be heard in that hall in the clouds, where the Man of Fancy met his strange guests. Schumann may be all wrong—but if so I believe honestly."[2] In essence, the force of Schumann's imagination could not be contained by the traditional molds of musical forms, so that in Schumann's music the tension between form and content could create untoward difficulties for the listener. Indeed, as early as 1844, in an extended review of Schumann's piano music, Carl Koßmaly noted the composer's penchant for bizarre mannerisms and technical demands;[3] and a not uncommon complaint from Schumann's publishers was that the music was simply too difficult, for performer and listener alike. By the later 1840s, Schumann began to offer some accommodation to this criticism and began to write piano music more responsive to the growing market of *Haus-musik*.[4] Certainly works such as the *Album für die Jugend*, Op. 68, or the *Waldscenen*, Op. 82, breathe an air of accessibility; now absent are the formal experiments of the Fantasy, Op. 17 (a work whose dedicatee, Franz Liszt, chose not to perform publicly[5]), the dramatic *in medias res* beginning of the *Kreisleriana*, or the fragmentlike arabesques of the *Carnaval*.

There is a certain irony that later history reversed the significance of this accommodation and judged more favorably the corpus of Schumann's *early* piano music. The works that Koßmaly and others struggled to understand are now generally viewed as visionary romantic masterpieces, along with, of course, the great song cycles, where Schumann joined word and sound to enable music, in effect, to become a higher form of poetry. But if we look beyond the piano music and the Lieder, Schumann's other music has met with at best a mixed reception. Unlike Wagner, who chose not to embrace the symphony, Schumann attempted to fill that classical genre with new contents, an endeavor that preoccupied him through much of his later career. If Schumann could detect veiled symphonies in Brahms's early piano sonatas,[6] later generations faulted Schumann's symphonies for their pianistic underpinnings and did not hesitate to offer substantial retouchings in their orchestration. Like his contemporary Mendelssohn, Schumann continued to explore the realm of chamber music, though this predilection became viewed as a classicist tendency not fully consistent with the aesthetic and cultural aims of Germany after the 1848 Revolution. And, most significantly, in his efforts at dramatic composition, Schumann fell victim to the inevitable comparisons with Wagner. *Genoveva*, Schumann's sole opera, failed after three performances, and his other dramatic works were viewed as curious experiments that remained in the shadows of Wagner's titanic music dramas: for instance, *Manfred*, conceived as a melodrama (which Liszt endeavored to stage at Weimar in 1852); and the generically ambiguous "oratorio, though not for the oratory," *Das Paradies und die Peri*, which Mendelssohn highly praised and which enjoyed some popularity in the United States during the nineteenth century.

The issue of Schumann's mental collapse further compounded his reception. During the waning days of his position as music director in Düsseldorf, the pathetic image of Schumann absentmindedly dropping his baton in the middle of rehearsals must have made a striking contrast to the robust image of the young Schumann of the 1830s leading the charge in his Leipzig journal against musical mediocrity. And, not surprisingly, Schumann's late music was viewed as providing ample documentation of his mental deterioration. Publication of some of the very late, stylistically discontinuous works was delayed; indeed, the Violin Concerto and the so-called "Geister" Variations (the piano variations inspired, Schumann claimed, by a theme sent to him by Mendelssohn and Schubert) did not appear until 1937 and 1939. In fact, not until recent decades have Schumann's late works such as the Mass and the choral ballades begun to receive the critical attention they deserve.[7]

Today we know Robert Schumann in several ways: as the composer who created, behind the masks of Florestan and Eusebius, visionary music during the German romantic efflorescence of the 1830s and 1840s; as the seasoned journalist who in the pages of the *Neue Zeitschrift für Musik* assaulted philistinism in the arts; as a cultured man of letters whose career was ultimately eclipsed at midcentury by the new music and philosophy of music of Richard Wagner and his circle; and as a genius who, having passed his mantle on to the young Brahms, succumbed to mental disease.

The present volume, occasioned by the 1994 Bard Music Festival devoted to Schumann and his contemporaries, seeks to examine several facets of this seminal nineteenth-century figure. In Part I, several scholars explore a wide range of approaches to the composer and his music. Leon Botstein and Michael Steinberg assess Schumann's efforts to place music at the center of German culture, in public and private sectors. Bernhard R. Appel offers a probing source study of one of Schumann's most personal works, the *Album für die Jugend*, while John Daverio considers the generic identity and early reception of *Das Paradies und die Peri*, and Jon W. Finson reexamines the first version of the Eichendorff *Liederkreis*. Gerd Nauhaus compares Schumann's treatments of the symphonic finale, and my own essay addresses the issue of quotations and allusions in Schumann's music.

Modern Schumann scholarship of the past few decades has been fortunate to have at its disposal a wealth of documentary sources, as evidenced, for example, by the publication of the composer's diaries and household accounts.[8] Still, new and little-known sources continue to shape our critical reappraisals of the composer. In Part II we present letters and memoirs, including the unpublished correspondence between Clara Schumann and Felix and Paul Mendelssohn Bartholdy, personal memoirs of Schumann by the critic Richard Pohl and assembled by Frederick Niecks, and Eduard Hanslick's essay on Schumann's correspondence from the asylum at Endenich. Finally, Part III assembles opposing critical views of Schumann. These include articles by Carl Koßmaly, one of the earliest to write a substantial review of Schumann's music; Franz Brendel, Schumann's successor as editor of the *Neue Zeitschrift für Musik*; Franz Liszt, who produced a lengthy, though still little-known article about Schumann in 1855, the year before his death; Adolf Schubring, who endeavored to define a school of composers centered around Schumann; and Felix Weingartner, the celebrated conductor who offered specific recommendations for improving Schumann's symphonies.

R.L.T.

April 1994

NOTES

1. "From My Diary. No. XXV," *Dwight's Journal of Music* 3 (1853): 36. On Thayer's contributions to *Dwight's Journal*, see Michael Ochs, "A. W. Thayer, the Diarist, and the Late Mr. Brown: A Bibliography of Writings in *Dwight's Journal of Music*," in *Beethoven Essays: Studies in Honor of Elliot Forbes*, ed. Lewis Lockwood and Phyllis Benjamin (Cambridge, Mass., 1984), pp. 78–95.

2. Ibid. Hawthorne's cabinet of a virtuoso: the reference is to Nathaniel Hawthorne's "A Virtuoso's Collection," which appears in the collection *Mosses from an Old Manse* (1846). In this tale the narrator visits a new museum filled with artifacts and rarities culled from history and literature, among them Nero's fiddle, Arthur's sword Excalibur, Daniel Boone's rifle, Coleridge's Albatross, and Cinderella's glass slipper. His tour guide, the Virtuoso, identified at the end of the tale as the Wandering Jew, has placed the most valuable rarities, including "the original fire which Prometheus stole from heaven," inside a closet.

3. See p. 308.

4. See Anthony Newcomb, "Schumann and the Marketplace: From Butterflies to *Hausmusik*," in *Nineteenth-Century Piano Music*, ed. R. Larry Todd (New York, 1990), pp. 258–315.

5. See Nicholas Marston, *Schumann: "Fantasie," Op. 17* (Cambridge, 1992), pp. 93ff.

6. Robert Schumann, "Neue Bahnen," *Neue Zeitschrift für Musik* 39 (1853): 185.

7. See, for instance, Reinhard Kapp, *Studien zum Spätwerk Robert Schumanns* (Tutzing, 1984).

8. Robert Schumann, *Tagebücher, Band I: 1827–1838*, ed. Georg Eismann (Leipzig, 1971), *Band II: 1836–1854*, ed. Gerd Nauhaus (Leipzig, 1987), and *Band III: Haushaltbücher, Teil I: 1837–1847* and *Teil II: 1847–1856*, ed. Gerd Nauhaus (Leipzig, 1982).

Acknowledgments

Several individuals and institutions have assisted in bringing this volume to press, and it is a pleasure to acknowledge them here. First of all, thanks are due to Leon Botstein and his colleagues at Bard College, Susan Gillespie, Mark Loftin, and Sarah Rothenberg, whose dedication and hard work have realized the Bard Music Festival, the intellectual and musical inspiration for this volume. At Princeton University Press, production of the volume was considerably expedited by Lauren Oppenheim. Several colleagues offered assistance in identifying several citations in the primary sources; among them I wish to thank George W. Williams and Diskin Clay of Duke University, Wm. A. Little of the University of Virginia, and Julie Prandi and John Michael Cooper of Illinois Wesleyan University (special thanks are owed John Michael Cooper for editorial assistance, including the preparation of the index). Additional advice was offered by Matthias Wendt and Bernhard R. Appel of the Robert-Schumann-Forschungsstelle in Düsseldorf and by Gerd Nauhaus of the Robert-Schumann-Haus in Zwickau. For further help I am indebted to Stephen Keyl and Carol Lynn Flanigan of the Library of Congress, Music Division. Finally, for permission to publish documents and illustrations, the following institutions are gratefully acknowledged: the Staatsbibliothek zu Berlin, Musikabteilung mit Mendelssohn-Archiv; the Boston University Library; the Robert-Schumann-Forschungsstelle, Düsseldorf; the Pierpont Morgan Library, New York; the Bodleian Library, Oxford; and the Robert-Schumann-Haus, Zwickau.

PART I

Essays

History, Rhetoric, and the Self: Robert Schumann and Music Making in German-Speaking Europe, 1800–1860

LEON BOTSTEIN

Introduction: Rescuing the Historical Schumann

"I often wonder whether my cultural ideal is a new one, i.e. contemporary, or whether it derives from Schumann's time." This thought, jotted down by Ludwig Wittgenstein in 1929, identifies how the work of Robert Schumann has come to be thought of as emblematic of a past discontinuous with our own.[1] Schumann's music is understood to represent a critique of the twentieth-century present. An idealized and vanished culture whose qualities we wish we retained reappears to us in the music.

Wittgenstein's observation was a species of early twentieth-century nostalgia for a preindustrial world of *Hausmusik* (obliterated by a late nineteenth century that Wittgenstein found uncongenial)—for a civilized *Biedermeier*, bourgeois, domestic life of culture readily associated with Schumann, particularly with his piano and vocal music. The interconnection between the literary and musical in much of Schumann's music, particularly the keyboard works, evoked a moment in the past when art and ideas mattered to the individual.

No composer in the European tradition, in fact, was so actively engaged in the public arena with literature and, indirectly, aesthetic philosophy.[2] Felix Mendelssohn, who worked to further Schumann's career as a composer and who stood as godfather to Schumann's offspring, never freed himself from the doubt—owing to Schumann's considerable reputation and achievement as a critic—that in some fundamental manner Schumann was, as a composer, a remarkable amateur.

Wittgenstein's implicit understanding of Schumann as somehow at odds with a twentieth-century cultural ideal mirrors a distinctly modernist enthusiasm for Schumann. Theodor Adorno identified Schumann rather than Richard Wagner as a forerunner of Alban Berg. In Adorno's view, Schumann's music was not manipulative. It did not employ a surface of lyricism or a clear pattern of tonal structure and resolution intended to lull the listener into a false sense of security. Schumann's music was not, therefore, an example of how music was consumed successfully to induce in the listener the arrogant inner sense of authentic aesthetic judgment. It resisted the use of the musical experience to falsify or camouflage the painful contradictions of existence.[3] The epigrammatic character of the early Schumann was therefore not the only point of comparison that Adorno had in mind. In 1941 Adorno orchestrated selections from the *Album für die Jugend*, Op. 68, in order to underscore the modernist essence beneath the surface of Schumann's most accessible music.[4]

The fascination with Schumann from the perspective of a critique of modernity is observed best, however, in Roland Barthes' view of Schumann. Barthes used Schumann to suggest a debasement in the evolution of our connection to music. The matter was not entirely left the prisoner of a musical text. When one played and listened to Schumann, one realized how faulty modern habits of listening had become.

Schumann, for Barthes, was "truly the musician of solitary intimacy, of the amorous and imprisoned soul that *speaks to itself* . . . ; loving Schumann, doing so in a certain fashion against the age . . . can only be a responsible way of loving."[5] Playing Schumann could reaffirm the sensual and spiritual sense of oneself; a respite from contemporary psychic alienation could be discovered.

Although it may be methodologically self-deceptive, one needs to set aside carefully this legacy of modernist and postmodern enthusiasm for Schumann and try to reconstruct the historical Schumann. In what sense was he typical of a culture? As early as December 1846, Eduard Hanslick, in one of his first published essays, sought to explain why Schumann would never be popular. He noted that his works were "too interior and strange . . . too deep, too simple, too sharp, and too dry . . . I believe Schumann is not for the majority but for individuals."[6]

Indeed, the most well-remembered aspect of Schumann's life was his strangeness. The story of his attempted suicide, mental illness, and hospitalization, not to speak of his carefully documented romantic life, has been the object of uninterrupted popular and scholarly fascination from the time of his death to the present.[7] Schumann's reputation as psychologically deviant has played into historical generalizations about the nineteenth century, particularly with respect to the image and role of art and the artist in society.

The idea that this manic-depressive and pathologically laconic musician can stand as a symbol of creativity per se continues to be argued.[8] In the later nineteenth century Schumann exemplified the ideal type of the genuine artist as necessarily abnormal (one thinks of Thomas Mann's views on this issue). In 1905 Wilhelm Dilthey, in an essay on Hölderlin, noted: "Feeling and fantasy proceed unregulated on their eccentric path. Who does not think immediately of Robert Schumann and Friedrich Nietzsche."[9] Great art and thought ("feeling and fantasy") needed to be "out of season."

Schumann and his music have become synonymous with the aesthetics of authenticity. Both the realization of self-critical individuality and the costs of that ambition can be found in the case of Schumann. His life story and his music vindicate the struggle to protect the intimate power of art against the brutal facts of modernity. Intimacy and autonomy seem to have been systematically suppressed and nearly obliterated by the world after 1848. Counted among the enemies of the aesthetic values realized in Schumann have been industrialization and the politics of the modern nation-state, capitalist commerce in the arts—the exploitation of sentimentality—and the musical aesthetics of Wagner and late romanticism.

In order to reconstruct the historical Schumann, one needs to respond to the challenge most recently put forward by Anthony Newcomb about whether there was *one* Schumann, so to speak, or several different incarnations of Schumann engineered by the composer himself. Newcomb alleges that the habitual reliance on Schumann's critical writings, which date from only one period of his life, as the key to the entire range of his music has resulted in a distorted view.[10]

Scholars frequently have noted apparent contradictions in Schumann's ideas and wide disparities in the quality of his music.[11] Some have argued that these were the result of his fleeting self-conscious imitations of Jean Paul's own *Doppelgänger* literary technique. Schumann's extreme mood shifts and outbursts of short-lived enthusiasm are used to explain inconsistencies. Newcomb suggests, however, that the shifts in Schumann's career are fundamental.

The claim that one must not consider the life and work of Schumann as a whole was first put forth by Richard Wagner. Wagner argued that there was an early Schumann marked by a distinct and promising originality and a late Schumann whose talent was trivialized and destroyed by the Jewish influence of Mendelssohn. Schumann's unexceptional but persistent anti-Semitism aside—evident in his not entirely admirable relationship to Mendelssohn[12]—the Wagnerian view has had a permanent echo in the conventional devaluation of the late music of Schumann.[13]

Recent scholarship, for example, has nearly unanimously indicated a preference for the first editions of the early piano music. The mature Schumann had severe doubts about his early piano compositions. Not unlike many other composers, he was critical of his early work. When the opportunity came to bring out new editions, he reheard his work and made changes. The rejection of these emendations has been implicitly tied to the judgment that the new music he was writing when he re-edited the early work is inferior.[14]

The claim of this essay is that there was indeed just "one" Schumann. His work presents the historian with a uniquely coherent subject. By implication, therefore, neither the late work nor the later editions deserve diminished respect. Furthermore, late Schumann is not inconsistent with the composer's earlier achievements and ideas. The phases in his career, his approach to the acts of music making—to playing, listening, and writing music—as well as his construction of the role of music in personal and social life were indelibly and coherently shaped by the intellectual and social foundations of his early years.

Perhaps Schumann was representative, in Wittgenstein's sense, of a cultural ideal precisely because he was, of all composers of his generation, the least professional. His career was even less the consequence of the heritage of guildlike patterns in musical training characteristic of the eighteenth and earlier centuries than Richard Wagner's. Schumann's approach to music was distinctly from the outside.[15]

In Schumann's childhood home the practice of music was a component in a conception of the cultivated individual characteristic of a segment of society ascendant in the early 1800s. In contrast to Bach, Mozart, Beethoven, and Brahms, Schumann's turn to music as a career was not the result of any family pattern. Unlike the case of Mendelssohn, it was not the result of stunning precocity. Schumann was perhaps the first in a line of great musicians whose prominent, affluent middle-class family, despite the prestige it placed on musical culture, fought the turn to music as a profession.

In Schumann the extramusical was transposed, self-consciously, into the musical. This did not prevent subsequent generations, particularly Hanslick, from recasting Schumann's music and aesthetics into an ideology of so-called absolute music. In contrast, the least sophisticated and nearly vulgar current in late nineteenth-century bourgeois culture remained, rather, closer to Schumann's ambitions. His vocal and keyboard music served as models for salon music during the later nineteenth century. The emotional relationship to music exploited by the mass-produced, sentimental piano works that made up the popular domestic repertoire around the turn of the century was an authentic extension of a compositional intent characteristic of Schumann's work. Salon music adopted his strategies in the reciprocal association between music, emotion, images, and ideas.[16]

Four dimensions of the composer's life and world merit reconsideration in the search for the historical Schumann: first, his relationship to the work of Jean Paul and Wolfgang Menzel and to early nineteenth-century constructs of reading and writing; second, the philosophical discourse that Schumann encountered as a young man regarding the place of aesthetics within systematic accounts of knowledge and experience; third, his relationship to his own historical age in terms of past and future; and fourth, his interest in art history and early nineteenth-century painting.

Jean Paul and Wolfgang Menzel

No fact is more often repeated in the literature on Robert Schumann than his profound admiration for Jean Paul Richter. Schumann asserted that he learned more from Jean Paul about counterpoint than from anyone else. Hermann Kretzschmar placed Jean Paul at the center of Schumann's aesthetics.[17] Newcomb has alleged, however, that by the 1840s Schumann had drifted away from Jean Paul. Public taste had already abandoned his novels. It was Jean Paul's posthumous fate that most of the more than sixty volumes of his collected works were ultimately forgotten, even though his reputation during his lifetime and for decades thereafter rivaled that of Goethe and Schiller.

Robert Schumann's diaries cast doubt on Newcomb's assertion. Throughout the late 1840s and 1850s Schumann noted his persistent rereading of Jean Paul. The last references are in the spring, summer, and fall of 1853, when Schumann reported that he (and Clara) read *Flegeljahre, Die unsichtbare Loge, Hesperus, Siebenkäs,* and *Titan.*[18]

What were the consequences of this lifelong fascination and admiration for Jean Paul? In one of the most famous prose passages in

Jean Paul's work, "Das Kampaner Tal," in the subsection called "Suffering without Consolation," Jean Paul writes:

> Human suffering is also substantively different from the suffering of animals. The animal feels wounds somewhat the way we do in our sleep. The animal, however, does not see those wounds, and its pain is a fleeting moment and not more. It is not enlarged threefold and made more intense by expectation, memory, and consciousness. And therefore tears appear in our eyes alone.[19]

Within the human soul lies the capacity to transform mundane existence into the spiritual confrontation with the ecstasy of sorrow and joy. In contrast to Goethe and Schiller, Jean Paul saw his task as a writer to evoke in readers a sense of the profound and the beautiful within the ordinary and frequently dismal surroundings of life. However, by comparison with the realism of the later nineteenth century, Jean Paul was not politically didactic. The intent of the systematic philosophy and theology of Jean Paul's father's generation—together with its idealization of universal categories such as humanity, truth, and beauty—remained.

The truth of those ideas had to be discovered in life by the individual. Jean Paul set aside the mid–eighteenth-century philosophic traditions about the proper forms and subjects of art. His turn to the ephemeral and modest facts of daily life reflected a closer affinity to Herder, and his experiments with forms of fiction vindicated Friedrich Schlegel's comparison of him to Friedrich Schleiermacher. For Jean Paul, the power of subjective imagination and feeling was stronger than the self-conscious act of abstract reasoning. If a synthesis of art and life was achieved in fiction to which the reader responded in the act of reading, the surface of the work need not necessarily conform to formalist conventions that had been validated by classical and neoclassical-classical aesthetic theory. This point was not lost on the young Schumann. Reading Jean Paul induced an inner transformation that the reader could transfer from the book to his own everyday surroundings. A synthesis of art and life emerged from the book that altered the reader's sense of his own capacities.

As Dilthey pointed out, what was unusual about Jean Paul was that in his prose there were no memorable descriptions, and there was a striking absence of the evidently artful poetic use of language.[20] One of the reasons later generations abandoned Jean Paul was that in the language and narrative there was little surface evidence of artistry and no text of representation sufficiently compelling to hold the attention of later nineteenth-century readers in search of an evidently literary aesthetic achievement.

Jean Paul's long-winded and rambling prose works were designed to render the act of reading the temporal equivalent of philosophical and emotional contemplation. The use of extended imagination by the reader was indispensable; characters and events were never fully realized. With respect to Jean Paul the conceit that the text is defined or becomes complete only in the act of reading, therefore, does not derive from the imposition of modern criticism. That idea was integral to authorial intention.

For Schumann, the reading of Jean Paul successfully induced what might be considered a sympathetic experience. The reader—in this case Schumann—felt parallels to what the protagonists in the novels felt as they responded to events; even to Jean Paul's philosophical interventions into the text. Schumann, as reader, sensed the experience of the act of writing. This was achieved by subordinating descriptions of events and objects, which remained opaque. The process of subjective reaction to the world was at the center. Schumann's *Papillons*, Op. 2—the work he himself linked most closely to Jean Paul—reveals fragmentary, descriptive, and evocative musical references to recognizable external experience, which are organized into a loose musical narrative that communicates the inner reaction of the composer. In the many transitions within each piece the player's own expressive response is given room.

At stake was a sympathetic vibration—in terms of the expressive reactions to life—with the characters and the author. The key to Jean Paul can be expressed in the German word *Ausdruck*, which, as Arnfried Edler has pointed out, played a central role in Schumann's musical aesthetics.[21] Jean Paul and Beethoven were frequently compared in the early nineteenth century. This seemed appropriate, particularly for Schumann, since Beethoven's ambitions regarding the playing and hearing of music paralleled Jean Paul's ideas about writing and reading. In his notations concerning the "Pastoral" Symphony, Beethoven distinguished between description and illustration, and the expressive realization through music of the impact of nature, people, and events—items of real experience.

Jean Paul helped to shape Schumann's views about the function of improvisation and the playing and hearing of worked-out musical texts. The use of the interrupted phrase, distorted repetition, self-quotation, sudden modulations and shifts in pulse, fragmentary echoes, and clearly undramatic endings in the early piano music speak to Schumann's ideal of how the author could best stimulate the creative fantasy of the player and listener. The musical text re-created the relationship of the reader and the book as constructed by Jean Paul.

In a letter to Friedrich Wieck, describing a performance of Schubert's four-hand Rondo in A major, D. 951, published in 1828, Schumann wrote:

> Schubert remains my "one and only" Schubert just as Jean Paul remains my "one and only." They share everything in common. When I play Schubert it is as if I were reading a novel of Jean Paul's turned into music. . . . Can you compare it to anything that has the same eerie, quiet, compact, and lyrical madness [*Wahnsinn*] and the same unified, profound, graceful, and ethereal melancholy that wafts over the absolutely true whole? I can visualize Schubert clearly: in his room, pacing back and forth, wringing his hands full of despair; how it resonates in music in his soul. . . . I remember having played this Rondo for the first time at a soiree at Probst's. At the end, players and listeners looked at each other for a long time and did not know what they sensed or what Schubert intended. As far as I know they never talked about it. . . . Apart from Schubert, there is no music that is so psychologically remarkable in the sequence of ideas, their interrelationships and in the seemingly logical transitions. How few, like Schubert, have been able to impress one single individuality onto such a diversity of tonal images. How few have written so much for themselves and their own heart. What the diary is to others, in which their momentary emotions and so forth are recorded, so to Schubert was music paper, to which he entrusted all his moods. His thoroughly musical soul wrote notes where others used words. This is my humble opinion.[22]

Dilthey, writing in the late nineteenth century, reversed the historical sequence and termed Jean Paul Richter a musical writer. Too often modern commentators have focused only on Jean Paul's overt celebration of the power of music—his aesthetic theories and the response of musicians to his embrace of the musical experience—and not enough on the fact that Jean Paul himself was inspired by his encounter with music.[23] He employed musical terms to delineate discrete sections of his prose. Jean Paul's use of words and formal structure inspired techniques that, owing largely to Schumann's influence, composers emulated in structuring rhythm, melody, and harmony within the musical time of a composition. Through Jean Paul, reading became the nineteenth-century model for the shift in musical culture from playing to listening.

Included in a popular book entitled *Original Musical Anecdotes and Miscellany for the Elevation of the Music-Loving Public as Well as for the Pleasurable Entertainment of Every Man*, edited by C. F. Müller and published in 1836, was Jean Paul's allegory about how the pagan gods gave humanity a "better language" by which to feel "unending desire . . . the language of the heart." That language, of course, was music. Jean Paul's father was an organist. Writing, for Jean Paul, aspired to the status of music.[24]

Jean Paul's metaphor of music as language stayed with Schumann to the very end of his career. The use of music in *Manfred* and Schumann's allegiance to the melodrama are explicable by the tripartite consequences of Jean Paul's idea. First, music can speak together with words, as in song and opera, at a level extending the meaning of words. But poetry has a power on its own, as does music in its instrumental form. Therefore, it was in third type, in the melodrama, that the reader-listener, the observer, was placed in the most elevated position. The audience was left to integrate the events and levels of meaning to create the unified aesthetic experience.

The key was Jean Paul's idea that "music was, in itself . . . a recollection of the beautiful, in what lived and died on earth."[25] In *Manfred*, the music evoked the past both for the characters of the drama and for the listeners. The poetry defined the present moment. Neither medium was subordinated; each was left to exert its unique power to fire the imagination of the individual.

The inner imagination and the intensity of feeling generated by poetry and music could create a bittersweet but redeeming reflection on the beauty contained in the ugly. In 1827 Schumann quoted in his diary Jean Paul's observation that when "life becomes darkened by great suffering" the individual can respond with the expectation of sunrise. Likewise, at sunrise one recognizes the inevitability of twilight and therefore of youth and death.[26]

The confrontation of how time reverses the contradictory experience of the moment demanded humor, irony, and an appreciation for the ugly and bizarre as opposed to a refined exclusive concentration on the harmonious, the symmetrical, the profound, and the beautiful. The reversals encountered in life mirrored Jean Paul's concentration on dualities in life. "The human being has a heavy double role on earth," he wrote.[27] The flight of fantasy and the emotional journey induced by reading and playing music required not only lyricism, resolution, and regularity but dissonance, harshness, accentuated asymmetry, and the reversal of expectation, because these qualities were analogous to the harsh contrasts in life. The work of art exploited these dualities in order to create a transcendent imaginative self.

In Jean Paul's novel *Die unsichtbare Loge* (which Schumann read), the young Gustav is described as never having heard music ("the poetry of the air"). After hearing a French horn ("the flute of desire"), Gustav (the name Schumann used in his notes for a novel entitled *Selene*) experiences his first tears of joy.[28] Art creates the interior emotional space of the individual by manipulating the consciousness of expectation and memory. The result of art, however, is a real experience in life—manifested by tears—of which the individual may not otherwise be capable.

In the short autobiographical fragment written at the end of his career, Jean Paul relates, with a typical tinge of irony, one of the most seminal experiences of his childhood:

> My soul (perhaps just like my father's) was entirely open to music
> . . . I devoted hours banging out my fantasies on an old out-of-
> tune piano whose tuner and regulator was the weather; these fan-
> tasies were no doubt freer and more daring than any other in all
> of Europe, just because I didn't know a single note or any hand
> position . . . [29]

This is reminiscent of Schumann's descriptions of his own passionate fantasizing at the piano, particularly early in his life. Even the un-trained but aspiring individual could sense the intensity of musical fantasy and creation. The keyboard was the musical mirror of ordi-nary language. The power of music, in Jean Paul's view, could be emancipated from the monopoly of systematic learning, theory, and professionalism. Schumann's later derision of virtuosity and mere technical proficiency and his lifelong effort to write for amateurs and children derived from his encounter with Jean Paul's construct of how accessible the transformative act of music making in one's private space could be.

For Jean Paul, twilight and sunrise were the decisive metaphors for the human being's relationship to nature. These changes in the day— the essence of nature's logic—were matched by the power of music to achieve, in the duration of time, the reconciliation between the pain-ful experience of temporality, and faith in God and immortality. Mu-sic was the language of the heart because it could parallel the sorrow (twilight) and desire (sunrise) that emerged in the conduct of every-day life.

Jean Paul and Schumann recognized that playing and hearing instrumental music paralleled the time-bound nature of events and the internal emotional reactions to those events. Tears came to the player and listener because conscious anticipation of desire carried with it the awareness and fear of loss, just as the suffering of loss reminded one of desire. Jean Paul's coherence of opposites was completed by the reader-player. The direct and fragmentary character—as well as the mix of sustained lyricism with displaced harsh interjections— evident in early Schumann parallels the comparable shifts Schumann experienced in reading Jean Paul's writings.

Among Jean Paul's most celebrated ideas was his focus on the jest (*Witz*) as a primary aesthetic form. The jest mirrored the event in time, replete with its emotional residue and reflection of the duality within nature and life. The jest revealed the irrationality of daily life and the individual's resentment of that irrationality. Disguised sim- ilarities were unmasked. The rational and unexceptional, therefore, masked the grotesque and bizarre. Likewise, the eccentric, the ironic, and the unusual overtly camouflaged the reasonable, the ordinary, and the decorous.[30]

Jean Paul's affection in his novels for contrasting twins and interre- lated dualities was part of his aesthetic translation of a systematic philosophical and theological effort at universally valid explanations and descriptions. Through the act of writing fiction as a profession, Jean Paul reshaped the systematic philosophical agenda of his father's generation. The ambitions of Leibnitz and Kant could be mediated by the encounter with the work of art. Jean Paul was central to the flow- ering of romantic writing out of the "self-satisfaction" and "self- absorption" of German philosophy.[31] As a locus for the recognition of philosophical truth, the jest was itself a provocative irony that commu- nicated the contingent limitations (body) and the infinite and free es- sence of human existence (soul).

The individual's capacity for aesthetic perception and fantasy and its translation into ideas required the assertion of the freedom of each human being's soul. The role of the aesthetic, whether in poetry or in music, was to inspire the reader, the observer (in the case of painting), the draftsman, the player, the listener, the writer—all these incarna- tions of the subjective self—to recognize the interior freedom of the individual. The psychic and emotionally plausible resolution of the terrifying truth about life's tenuous and finite dimensions could be found in the "anticipation of a better future." Remote and abstract claims regarding the immortality of the soul were replaced by the un- seen and nearly infinite possibilities conjured up by the imagination in its contact with art.[32]

Hegel gave Jean Paul's version of the specific power of the musical experience—particularly of instrumental music—a coherent philosophical form:[33]

> music . . . lies too near the essence of that formal freedom of the inner life to be denied the right of turning more or less above the content. . . . Recollection of the theme adopted is at the same time the artist's inner collection of himself, i.e. an inner conviction that he is the artist . . . and yet the free exercise of imagination in this way is expressly to be distinguished from a perfectly finished piece of music. . . . In the free exercise of imagination, liberation from restriction is an end in itself so that the artist can display . . . freedom to interweave familiar melodies and passages into what he is producing at present, to give them a new aspect, to transform them by nuances of various kinds.[34]

Jean Paul came out of a fundamentally theological intellectual milieu. The Protestant theology that framed his outlook took as a premise the essential depravity of the human being. Mortality was justified. By virtue of human consciousness, the pain associated with mortality was itself evidence of some residue of immortality and freedom from a predetermined death. The individual, therefore, was left to search for the underlying truth—the unity of spiritual immortality and inevitable finitude. These ideas help to explain Schumann's attraction to Byron's *Manfred*. Schumann's decision to leave long stretches of Byron's text free of a musical setting may have been in part because the long soliloquies by Manfred constitute an intense distillation of thoughts and sentiments with which the mature Schumann was intimately familiar through his encounter with Jean Paul.[35]

Jean Paul's ambitions as a writer masked a secularization of theology. Through reading and the engagement with art the willing individual could find access to the inner experience (however fleeting) of the power of divine grace. The achievement of philosophical conviction and theological belief in the systematic sense practiced by the academics of the mid–eighteenth century was a tortuous accomplishment of abstract reasoning. The aesthetic surrogate peddled by Jean Paul, as the evidence of the young Schumann's manic vacillations in mood when reading Jean Paul, was far less stable.

Jean Paul's aesthetic route to the recognition of inner freedom and the immortality of the individual soul demanded constant reaffirmation, because its source, as Jean Paul knew, was temporal and emotional. The transference to reflection demanded the constant engagement with reading and playing, the wholesale integration of the aesthetic experience into everyday life.

For Jean Paul the key element remained language, the instrument of abstract thought. Although ordinary language could connect exterior experience to interior experience, its limitations, vis-à-vis music, demanded testing. Philosophical language and stylized aesthetic formal procedures were too distant from life. The virtues of rational philosophic discourse—clear and distinct ideas and impeccable logic —could not suffice.

In his autobiographical fragment Jean Paul described how as a child he sought to construct a new language by creating a new alphabet. He wanted to become a "writer of secrets" and a "player of hide-and-seek with himself."[36] This playful creation of an individualistic language, comprehensible only to oneself, that generates exclusive secrets and games in the interior soul, described Jean Paul's sense of what the writer must do for himself and his readers.

This illuminates Robert Schumann's vision of the composer. The short musical text, like the jest, possesses carefully constructed secrets. The player-reader engages the hide-and-seek search for meaning. Aesthetic appreciation demands the capacity to decode the secret languages of others, to discover hidden treasures, and to appropriate the findings into one's own everyday existence. The reader becomes the young Jean Paul, improvising and creating, by interpretation, a new personal alphabet.

Pain and sorrow become ennobled and rendered tolerable, if not desirable. The confrontation with the sources of sorrow and suffering is welcome as the occasion for the self-affirming task and game of unraveling the hidden. Irony, satire, and humor are the most honest means by which the aesthetic transfiguration of pain can be accomplished, not only because they acknowledge contradiction but because they test the capacity for imagination and fantasy. The location of foreground and background material in Schumann's keyboard and vocal music can be seen as structural devices that organize (metaphorically speaking) the relationships among single events, the surroundings of the world, individual protagonists, and the writer, which the reader unravels in a unique fashion.

Not unlike many of his contemporaries, Jean Paul was a polymath. His belief in the ultimate reconcilability of contradiction, in the symbiosis between the bizarre and the refined, led him to an insatiable curiosity. Everything, including natural philosophy (science), religion, and art, was integral to a unified physical and spiritual universe.

Through art the individual could mirror in himself unity within diversity. That emotional and intellectual achievement reinforced the sense of the self. Like the stars, the individual was at once part of a system and yet distinct and self-contained. Surface originality revealed universality.

Dilthey was right: Jean Paul's prose appears episodic to the modern reader. Small units of narrative are punctuated by direct addresses to the reader. Characters speak to one another as the reader observes stories being told to someone else. Books appear within books, as do letters. Writing becomes its own character in the novel, and seemingly tangential texts appear. No doubt much of this was the result of Jean Paul's imitation of known eighteenth-century models, particularly Laurence Sterne. But the effect on Robert Schumann and his generation was profound. Books themselves became protagonists. The reader encountered readers within the book he was reading. The reading self became the metaphor for an underlying spiritual idealism.

Jean Paul's prose was a version of the *Bildungsroman*; the act of reading inspired, as it did in Schumann, the individual's own novel of self-creation.[37] The remembrance of emotional experience through the work of art helped to generate an internal sense of coherence. Music, therefore, had to be written in relationship to the capacity to recall it, even in fragments. Rereading—returning to the text—had its analogue in memory and rehearing.

Stendhal, another author with strong affinities to music, described in *The Red and the Black* the power of books during the first half of the nineteenth century to shape the course of life of an individual. Jean Paul flattered the self-confidence and sense of self-importance of the explosively growing number of civil servants, merchants, and professionals who, not unlike Schumann's father, made up the reading public at the end of the eighteenth century and beginning of the nineteenth. Like the romances of Walter Scott, Jean Paul's prose gave the reader the sense of his own creative powers of imagination and inner enthusiasm. The marriage of unpretentious and ordinary material with a never-ending stream of allusions to the whole encyclopedia of knowledge through a prose that did not draw attention to itself in a sequence of anecdotes and small stories and events, each of which was a mirror of the short form model—the jest—was a unique triumph of the age.

Jean Paul's stature was confirmed decisively for Schumann's generation by Wolfgang Menzel (1798–1873). In the summer of 1828 Schumann remarked in his diary, "Menzel has penetrated more deeply than anyone else into our character. . . ." A few days later he returned to his reading of Menzel.[38] The book in question, *Die deutsche Literatur*, had been published earlier that year and created a great sensation. A second edition came out in 1836. Menzel's tract earned a long and admiring view from Heinrich Heine.

Menzel took the contrast between Jean Paul and Goethe and made it the basis of a coherent analysis of the relationship between German literature and politics. *Die deutsche Literatur*, written in an almost Jean Paul–like style, was marked by irony, humor, and self-consciously outrageous claims, the most famous of which was that "Goethe was no genius, only a great talent."[39] Menzel divided the politics of the age into the "servile" and the liberal. Freedom, and therefore what in the 1820s was regarded as political liberalism, was the only legitimate foundation for art and culture.

Menzel used his analysis of Goethe's limitations to outline an aesthetics that could serve as a political symbol of a new generation. Jean Paul marked the emancipation of art from the politics of servility. Menzel spoke directly to his fellow German readers, including Schumann, about what it meant to make reading and aesthetics a central part of life without succumbing to fake sentimentality.

Art was conceived no longer as an abstract idea but rather as a social fact central to the possibilities of a new and vital political and communal life. Not the solitary reader but a nation of readers who embraced the transformative intervention of the aesthetic into everyday life became the focus. The first half of Menzel's tract outlined the social significance of the production of literary output, the reading public, book publishers, the influence of schools and school reform, and the university.[40]

Germany was at a crossroads. Either it gave way to foreign influence, commerce, outmoded traditions of schooling, and superficiality or it built carefully upon the achievement of the early romantic movement in German literature to create language and writing befitting the unique German character and its historical role. For Menzel there were dangers lurking on all sides. At one extreme was irrelevant aesthetic formalism; on the other, cheap and ephemeral but fashionable and destructive popular literature.[41]

Literary work had emerged as the decisive public medium for Menzel. He identified for the eighteen-year-old Schumann the extended community—a public—that was poised to play a significant role in history. The young Schumann recognized that community, for it described a world he had seen in his father's milieu in Zwickau.

Menzel, whose *en passant* observations on music corresponded closely to Schumann's, provided Schumann with an ideological framework. Bach was given a central place, as was the work of Schumann's teacher Anton Friedrich Justus Thibaut. The context, once again, was the cultural crisis, the need to generate a new German spirit and taste in music. Menzel deplored the dominance in writing about music of the "false spontaneity of the romantics, the excessive desire for conclusions and the high-minded rhetoric of the philosophers, and even the frivolity of humorists and masters of irony."[42]

Following Jean Paul's literary transformation of the tradition of systematic philosophy, Menzel filled his text with material from the widest range of subjects. In his attack on an older generation's conception of schooling, philosophy, literature, and art and its role in society, Menzel, like Jean Paul, turned to the jest as an essential aesthetic unit. As aspects of literature, humor and sarcasm were species of realism that undercut the high-minded, theoretical, abstract claims of neoclassical art and Kantian idealism.

Menzel's forte was not only satire; his prose communicated energy and enthusiasm. His directness, simplicity, and candor celebrated the vital power of youth and its response, through literature, to the distinct social and natural character of Germany. His description of the German university and the aristocratic sensibilities of the reading public of the past was devastating.

The language and strategy of Schumann's music criticism, particularly his attack on old-fashioned pedantry and contemporary philistinism—his explicit political ideal of a public emancipated from superficiality—were inspired by Menzel. The result was Jean Paul's prose strategy (the use of characters, e.g., Eusebius, Florestan, Raro, and the creation of an internal dialogue with differing points of view), filled with Menzel's tone and ideas. Schumann's use of the word *philistine* may have derived from Menzel's furious attack on popular poetry that created a veneer of formal beautification and therefore falsification. Menzel decried its popularity among readers.[43]

Menzel's satirical critique of the heritage of abstract academic philosophy was motivated by the realization that in order to create new cultural ideology, writing had to engage politics, religion, history, and science in a new manner. Given the explosion in the reading public, the danger, of course, was that in the rage for books and the expanding market the opportunity for corrupt influences to dominate was equally great. In a line typical of Menzel, the evil of censorship was characterized in terms not of the loss—what censorship suppressed—but of what it encouraged.[44]

Menzel's outspoken admiration for Jean Paul as a forerunner reinforced the idea that the new generation of readers and writers could be freed from seemingly transhistorical and transnational normative claims about beauty and the heavy hand of classical models. As Heine put it, Menzel dismissed the idea of art of the age of Goethe. New ideas for a new age heralding "nature and youth" were forcing back the "troops" of "art and antiquity." The memorable moment in Menzel's manifesto, the wholesale attack on Goethe (without question in 1828 the leading figure in German-speaking Europe), was too much for Heine, who, unlike Schumann, recognized that underneath Menzel's brilliance, insight, and wit lurked something uncivilized and disturbing.[45]

Indeed, Menzel's own advocacy of his generation's unique credo was short-lived. He went on to betray the radicals of 1830 during the reaction and was later pilloried by Ludwig Börne, Heine, and D. F. Strauss. Menzel's vision of the political potential of the new aesthetics later led him to embrace a rabid nationalism and to wage a moralistic campaign against his former allies. As early as 1828, unlike Heine and others in the "Young Germany" movement, Menzel professed a seemingly uncritical admiration for the pietistic movement in Protestantism, which, in part, anticipated a subsequent sharp turn in his views.[46]

What remained with Schumann (who, for example, was unsympathetic to the *Burschenschaften* movement that influenced the nationalism Menzel later endorsed) was Menzel's framing of the historical role of the artist in society in political and generational terms. Reading Menzel confirmed the social significance of a career as a creative artist. Menzel's cultural nationalism circa 1828 underwent little change in Schumann, whose nationalism, although pronounced, never evolved into the more aggressive and modern form he would encounter in Dresden in the 1840s. The narrow realm of aesthetics as politics (the creation of a like-minded public) remained Schumann's arena.

Menzel offered Schumann a way to bypass legitimately the strenuous effort of writing and studying systematic philosophy. Unlike Jean Paul, who wrote his own aesthetic tract, Menzel provided Schumann an example of the legitimacy of journalism, intellectually and politically. His book vindicated the idea that criticism could and would be taken seriously, even when it dealt with religion and philosophy. It elevated criticism as creative work. As Schumann wrote in his diary, "Censure elevates those with great character; the petty individual is undone. Praise has the opposite effect."[47]

As the legendary eccentric and impoverished vagabond of the previous generation who finally settled down to an idyllic domestic life, Jean Paul served as a personal model for the young Schumann. Menzel offered the professional example. The significance of the social station from which Schumann came becomes evident in his identification with Menzel, whose explicit assignment of a cultural role to Schumann's social class rang true. Menzel's observation—that there was perhaps too much silly talking about music and too little listening—may have functioned as a challenge.

Schumann's father, despite his success and relative fame as a bookseller and publisher (Heine mentioned him as the publisher of Walter Scott[48]), did not mask the fact that he did not complete formal university training. In terms of the social hierarchy of intellect of the mid–eighteenth century, the elder Schumann was an aspirant and a parvenu. The ethos of Schumann's household, apart from its love of books, was tinged with a sharp sense of practicality. Literacy clearly afforded avenues by which one might earn a decent living. The achievement of a proper standard of living and the domestic comfort necessary for the pursuit of culture were central to Schumann and never, in theory, in conflict with artistic integrity.

In terms of the late eighteenth-century debate on the quality and influence of books, the goal was to produce works that edified the public and were, like classical texts, worthy not only of initial reading but of rereading. The emulation in the world of music by critics and musicians of Schumann's generation of the widespread late eighteenth- and early nineteenth-century debate over the influence of ephemeral literature (to be read and then forgotten) as opposed to books of lasting value has been overlooked. Consider Schumann's active part in defining the right "classical" models for composers and the music public; his references to classicism in form; the use of quotation in his music; his crusade against ephemeral music; and his ambition to create new music that could function as classical texts did, as works to which the individual could return profitably over and over again.[49]

Schumann's father not only dealt in the commerce of publishing but wrote and edited others' work. Just as the activities of performing, composing, publishing, and commercial trade in instruments (e.g., Clementi, Diabelli, Kalkbrenner, and Pleyel) were inextricably linked in the careers of musicians in the early nineteenth century, so too were book publishing and selling, journalism, and the writing of fiction. Menzel's chapter "The Commerce of Literature" confirms the extent to which the generations of the early nineteenth century were aware of the social, economic, and political significance of the expanded reading public.[50]

In accounts of the early nineteenth century the term *Bildungsbürger-*

tum is often used without a specific context. Menzel calculated that between 1814 and 1835, one hundred thousand books were published in Germany.[51] That growth catapulted men like Schumann's father—those without academic careers—into a position of unanticipated success. One of the reasons Robert Schumann was always more at home in Leipzig as opposed to Düsseldorf or Dresden was that Leipzig, which had become the center of the printing industry, contained more citizens like the elder Schumann than any other city of comparable size. The allegation that the Leipzig public was more sophisticated than its counterparts elsewhere was not unfounded. Self-made men of business who established their careers in the wake of the growth of literacy at the end of the eighteenth century mixed freely with an older commercial elite and the academic community of Leipzig's university.[52]

Schumann easily could feel comfortable in Leipzig. Owing to the commercial opportunities that stemmed from expanded literacy, the city became a magnet for writers, journalists, and free-lance intellectuals of all kinds. It was not dominated by an aristocracy of birth. In his legendary *Konversations-Lexikon*, the great Viennese satirist Moritz Saphir (with whom the Schumanns became acquainted in Vienna and who then wrote a penetrating but unflattering critique of Clara Schumann's playing that earned their lifelong enmity)[53] printed the following description:

> Leipzig is made up of fifty thousand writers, among whom there are only a few inhabitants. The streets are to a large extent paved with square novellas. The sidewalks are made of very wide prose romances on which pedestrians walk comfortably. The trees in Leipzig sprout leaves of opinion. . . . The citizens of Leipzig wear waterproof pants in order to protect themselves from damp translations.[54]

The Leipzig of the 1830s and 1840s was the beneficiary of a marked social transformation in the access to schooling, which began during the second half of the eighteenth century. The association between the acquisition of culture and political liberalism heralded by Menzel was more than theoretical. The school reforms of the previous century gave individuals the means to construct notions of personal and political autonomy. By the early nineteenth century approximately 20 percent of all pupils in German municipal schools had completed pre-university schooling, the *Abitur*. Of that group, a third came from the lower middle class. For the very lowest strata, particularly in rural areas, schooling was severely limited. Ten percent of all *Abiturienten* came from petit-bourgeois families, 35 percent from artisans and tradespeople, and 25 percent from middle-level civil servants.[55]

The marked explosion in advanced schooling was felt by the German university system after 1815. In 1800 there were approximately six thousand university students in Germany; by 1830 there were sixteen thousand. In the 1820s approximately 0.5 percent of the urban population was studying at a university. Robert Schumann had good reason to think of himself as a member of a new generation determined to make its own way and imagine a role for himself. Among the tasks was the effort to free culture from the nearly exclusive domination by an aristocracy and by men of letters committed to an aesthetic ideology linked to absolutism, no matter how enlightened by eighteenth-century ideas.[56]

It is ironic that around 1830 the turn away from cultural currents of the late eighteenth century in part was the result of pedagogical reforms based on Enlightenment ideas regarding the humanism and power of reason as an instrument of progress. A philosophical psychology that was egalitarian with respect to an individual's susceptibility to the cultivation of reason through schooling spurred entirely new pedagogical strategies. Menzel devoted a considerable portion of his book to the consequences of the new pedagogy. Jean Paul, for example, was an advocate of pedagogical reforms along the lines of Rousseau and Pestalozzi (who, as Schumann knew, also placed great emphasis on the role of music in education). The notion of the reader implicit in Jean Paul's writings and the link between art and life led to an emphasis in schooling on freedom and the development of the individual. The burden in pre-university schooling was shifted from a theologically based scheme of indoctrination (*Erziehung*) to the cultivation of the self-directed intellectual faculties of each individual. This pedagogical theory fit neatly with the notion that each individual was capable of developing the capacity for creation and criticism. The cultivation of ambition and self-conscious individualism was the pedagogical ideology of Schumann's years in school.[57]

Napoleon was the single most powerful symbol in German-speaking Europe during Schumann's youth. His portrait hung in Schumann's student rooms, alongside those of his father and Jean Paul.[58] Schumann was born just four years after the seminal event in German history, Napoleon's defeat of Prussia at Jena in 1806. The attitude of Schumann's generation toward Napoleon was ambivalent. On the one hand Napoleon was a symbol of the emancipation of career and achievement from birth and aristocracy. But at the same time he was viewed in terms of Fichte's challenge to his countrymen in 1808 and the cultural patriotism of Friedrich Jähns's *Berlinische Gesellschaft für deutsche Sprache.*

In Schumann's generation the definition of national character and the concomitant rediscovery of a distinct cultural past and mission were at the center of literary, philosophical, and cultural debate. Schumann's and Menzel's cultural nationalism of the late 1820s was radical—in opposition to the post-1815 restoration. Napoleonic ambitions were internalized and directed through cultural achievement. The complementary coherence between an individual's ambition to gain public prominence as a musician and man of letters and a generational politics in which culture served as an instrument of national identity was central to Schumann's intellectual development. The achievement of greatness in the image of Jean Paul was therefore a distinctly German task. The challenge was to find a way to reach the new public in a manner that did not debase culture and lull the reader-player-listener—through his or her newfound skills—into political and cultural indifference. Friedrich Schlegel, in his lectures on the history of literature, given first in Vienna during the winter of 1812, articulated eloquently the larger context in which both Menzel and the young Robert Schumann explicitly defined their ambitions:

> In Germany, owing to the special character of the nation, the spirit of the age was mirrored not in bloody revolution but in the tangled conflicts of metaphysical philosophy. The rebirth of fantasy has become evident in many countries through the revival of past traditions and through romantic poetry. No nation in Europe, however, can compete with the extent and profundity with which Germans have developed the love of fantasy. These nations have had their moment in history. It is only fitting that we should now have our own.[59]

"The Very Image of Life . . . ": Schumann and the Rhetoric of Aesthetic Discourse

Few writers were so much at the center of turn-of-the-century aesthetic debates as Friedrich Schlegel.[60] Menzel, who was decidedly ambivalent about Schlegel, singled him out for "his enormous influence." The evidence of Schumann's direct relationship to Schlegel, however, is thin. Although Schumann was familiar with Schlegel's poetry, neither the diaries nor the letters indicate that he read Schlegel's philosophic and critical writings to any extent. Nothing approximating Schumann's relationship to Jean Paul or E.T.A. Hoffmann can be located. The importance of Schlegel in the discussion of Schumann, therefore, rests on the extent to which Schlegel's ideas shaped the rhetoric of aesthetics of the early nineteenth century.[61]

John Daverio ties Schlegel's prominence as the master of the philosophically loaded aphorism to a set of aphorisms Schumann published in the *Neue Zeitschrift für Musik* in 1834. Schumann made the following claim: "To be sure, it might not be without interest to sketch out the very image of life in art, just as Platner and Jacobi have similarly done in entire philosophical systems."[62]

The reference to Platner and Jacobi is most revealing. Platner (1744–1818) was a professor of medicine and philosophy in Leipzig whose *Philosophische Aphorismen*, published in various editions from 1776–1800, was widely read. He was the one academic who exerted a profound influence on Jean Paul. Platner's critique of Kant led him to a position of profound skepticism. Little else was left of philosophy but the "way of thinking of the individual," the perspective of the subject.[63]

Friedrich Heinrich Jacobi (1743–1819) was a contemporary of Goethe and Herder who also attempted a critique of Kant's epistemology. He generated a comprehensive philosophy based on Spinoza and the limits of rational atheism. Jacobi was convinced that Kant had not succeeded in dispensing with the need to assume a basic naive faith in the reality of external phenomena. Rationalism demanded a leap of faith, which in turn was based on feeling. Jacobi's synthesis of religious and aesthetic sensualism with empiricism gave his work a close affinity to Jean Paul.

Schumann referred to Jacobi admiringly and extensively during the 1820s. Jacobi went farther than Jean Paul in the critique of rational philosophy. Feeling was prior to reason and therefore the source of aesthetic recognition. The sentiments an individual felt in his "beautiful soul" took precedence. Despite the absence of a Kantian or Hegelian thoroughness, Jacobi's emotionalism resulted in a comprehensive outlook. The individual without a conventional religious faith (e.g., Schumann) could find truth and the divine—precisely through a transformative emotional contact with the real world. This became the task of art.[64]

Jacobi's example encouraged Schumann in the idea that by making and criticizing art a comprehensive, overarching approach, merging feeling and reason, could be developed. The task of the artist in creative work and journalism was the construction of "the very image

of life" in a manner directly understood as an alternative to the philosophical systems of an earlier generation. Aesthetics became the common ground between a rational empirical epistemology and emotion.
Jean Paul had taken the first step by linking art with real life. Jacobi
had substituted the experience of feeling and faith as the source of a
comprehensive *Weltanschauung*.

Schumann believed that the aesthetic experience through the non-
literary medium closest to the emotional experience—music—could
realize this project. In this sense Schumann's aesthetics confirm
Hegel's description of the role of music in romanticism. Music, by
being the "language of the heart," was the language of the consciousness of time and nature. Therefore it was capable of generating a true
image of life. Schumann took from Jacobi the idea that emotion possessed an ontological priority as the root of a unified approach to
ethics and knowledge. Schumann's perspective can be compared with
that of Schleiermacher's, in which the priority of feeling and the emphasis on the aesthetic led to a conception of individuality that implied the necessity to create a religious community of like-minded
individuals not dissimilar to Schumann's own organizing efforts in
this regard.[65]

Friedrich Schlegel's rhetoric and ideas most clearly illuminate the
path traveled by Schumann's generation, from Kant to Jacobi, and
from Jean Paul and Menzel to Hegel. The preponderance of fragments in Schlegel's work was the result of his desire to reclaim philosophy for the arena of poetics. Schlegel, like Schumann, sought to inno-
vate in formal terms. The fragment, like the jest, despite its outward
appearance, could encompass the comprehensive. The fragment and
aphorism were aesthetic alternatives to the philosophical argument.

In certain fragments Schlegel included diagrams describing the
unified scope of aesthetic expression. By visualizing the disparate
arenas of aesthetic activity, the individual's aesthetic experience could
be understood to encompass the spiritual geography of the whole
world. In a fragment written during the first decade of the nineteenth
century, Schlegel untangled the strands by which the individual
"grasped the divine." He pursued Jacobi's and Jean Paul's project.
Using the vocabulary and traditions he associated with Schelling,
Fichte, Schleiermacher, and Schiller, Schlegel divided the aesthetic
realm into four modes of apperception, which he placed visually in a
configuration comparable to a compass. On the northern point was
Anschauung—a visually based form of knowing that was the essence of
drama. Its opposite on the southern point was *Ahnung*—a suggestive

mix of foreboding and resentment that exemplified lyric poetry.[66] On the west was *Erklärung*—explanation (including representation and description) in language. This was the realm of the novel. On the east was *Erinnerung*, the realm of the epic.[67]

For Schlegel, language in drama was connected to the pictorial, and lyricism to the play element. The language of the epic was linked to song and therefore to music. The rhetoric of explanation of the novel was associated with myth and legend. Instrumental music emerged from the merger of language and music in the epic. In the *Athenaeum* fragment quoted on p. 28, Schlegel defended how the rhetoric of instrumental music displayed its historically contingent dependence on language. The relevance to Schumann's conception of musical form and its apperception lies in the idea that the logic and meaning of instrumental music were tied to the epic as the proper linguistic analogue.

Schlegel argued that an "infinitely progressive aesthetic" in the age of Christianity called for a return to the ancient combination of music and language: the merger of song and legend. Modernity demanded the integration of the epic and the novel. The modern forms were the romance, the *Novelle*, and the legend, all terms crucial to Schumann's musical compositions, including the notion from the manuscript of the Fantasy, Op. 17, *Erzählend in Legendenton*. These exemplify Schlegel's synthesis of song and legend.[68] In modern times, the epic's dependency on memory and its role in collective consciousness had to be expanded through the novel and the art of explanation. Music uniquely achieved that. It could express remembrance and ideas within a community.

Schumann's search for the "very image of life" paralleled Schlegel's effort to identify, for the poetic and the aesthetic, an explanatory, rational function within a social and historical framework. In all Schumann's music the conscious merger of three elements—narrative, emotional expressiveness, and the evocative (in the sense of memory, including the historical citation and imitation)—was accomplished with a keen ear to the response of players-listeners.

The function of music, therefore, becomes more than an emotional solitary experience. Its capacity for linguistic logic in the philosophical, epistemological sense permits music to assume a public function. Jean Paul observed that music possessed a kind of language of both apperception and recollection. That aspect renders music capable of assuming a public function akin to the kind advocated by Menzel for literature.

In 1823 Schlegel pursued this line of thought further and created another map of parallel opposites. Poetry and philosophy were linked, further underscoring the idea that aesthetics and epistemology were inextricable in the modern age. In these 1823 fragments Schlegel returned to the theme of music as a dimension of the epic. Painting was ultimately "theological" and lyric poetry symbolic, particularly in its use of "allegories" and "hieroglyphics." "Music in its magical impact and psychological character is most related to the epic," Schlegel wrote.[69] The epic functioned through the use of myth. A work of music was therefore a narrative suffused with a nearly irrational link to the imagined past, replete with a contemporary collective aura and significance.

The mark of the aesthetic in the contemporary age of the 1820s was, for Schlegel, the overriding presence of the phantasmagoric, which was a synthesis of reason and fantasy. The rational (the explanatory function) was contained in formal procedures—in the case of Schumann's music, in sonata form, variation form, and counterpoint. The phantasmagoric emerged from the free interplay of fantasy in harmony, melody, and asymmetrical rhythm, which worked in contrast to the expectations of form. As if to parallel the distinction between the unconscious and the conscious, the epic and therefore each piece of music—in the spirit of Jean Paul's twins—had two levels of compositional intentionality in the text.

Unlike Menzel, Schlegel identified both Goethe and Jean Paul as having contributed to the achievement of this modern sensibility. In his musings about aesthetics Schlegel anticipated Schumann's embrace of both classical and romantic ideas in his observation that Schiller and Fichte were admirable writers of reason, even though Jean Paul and Schleiermacher had created the "dynamic rhetoric" of the age. For Schlegel that rhetoric was "encyclopedic," connected to a theology of feeling and experience. In modern life, the experience of music in the single work of art held the possibility of offering a comprehensive synthesis of life and experience superceding other forms of discourse: "The poetic is the original condition of humanity and also its final state. All oriental philosophy is poetic. . . . Only through the poetic can a human being expand his existence into the existence of humanity. Only in the poetic do all means serve one end. The jest is the path of return to the poetic."[70]

Rhetoric of this sort not only defined Robert Schumann's journey from literature to law, then to virtuoso performer, and finally to critic and composer (with intermittent phases of thinking of his father's business). The university years and the encounter with philosophical discourse in Leipzig and Heidelberg also strengthened the conclusion that a career in the arts was a humanistic and philosophic endeavor with moral overtones. Schlegel's musing also hints at a coherent compositional agenda. The musical epigram from Schumann's early work shares the ambition of *Genoveva* and the symphony: the coherent reflection and penetration of life through the formal structure and content of the single work of art brought forward to the public.

This ethical and epistemological framework helps to explain the severity of Schumann's critical judgments and his obsession with the formation of a public community of like-minded individuals. A crucial dimension of the ambition to render the arts (in Schumann's case, criticism and composing) something greater than mere entertainment —into a rival of the conduct of philosophy in the German university —was based on faith in music as a language more precisely in terms of explanation, not merely as Jean Paul's "language of the heart." In a well-known fragment, Schlegel put the matter succinctly. The pursuit of music was part of a larger political and cultural project tied to ordinary language discourse:

> Many people find it strange and ridiculous when musicians talk about the ideas in their compositions; and it often happens that one perceives they have more ideas in their music than they do about it. But whoever has a feeling for the wonderful affinity of all the arts and sciences will at least not consider the matter from the dull viewpoint of a so-called naturalness that maintains music is supposed to be only the language of the senses. Rather, he will consider a certain tendency of pure instrumental music toward philosophy as something not impossible in itself. Doesn't pure instrumental music have to create its own text? And aren't the themes in it developed, reaffirmed, varied, and contrasted in the same way as the subject of meditation in a philosophical succession of ideas?[71]

The parallelism between music and "the philosophical succession of ideas" demanded formal procedures dependent on rational notions of argument. Schumann's attention to counterpoint and sonata form and to classical models from Bach to Beethoven reflects the consequences of these philosophical premises. The public had to be educated to respond to music not only in the sense of Jean Paul or Jacobi but in Schlegel's terms. The ability to interpret through hearing and playing meant the capacity to generate a complementary discourse of ideas. *Audsruck*, then, for Schumann was more than expression of an emotional response or the flight of fantasy inspired by sound. The power of music was located in its logical function as the expression of thought.

One of Schlegel's many influential contributions was his role in placing the question of history at the center. An intensely self-conscious historical anxiety characterized Schumann and his contemporaries. The shift from the epistemological to the aesthetic was framed as a part of a larger historical process. The character and political function of art changed in history, Schlegel argued, initially in the transition from paganism to Christianity, and then within the evolution of Christendom.

Hegel continued this line of argument, claiming that the aesthetic experience, with its emphasis on subjectivity, had become in contemporary culture a historical phenomenon whose meaning could be unraveled only by a dialectic not entirely divorced from Jean Paul's *Doppelgänger* strategy of reconciling contradiction into unity. Lecturing in the 1820s, Hegel observed that in the aesthetics of romanticism "the fundamental character of the romantic is the musical."[72]

Schlegel's assertion—that "the poetry and romanticism of the north was an *Aeolsharfe* through which the storm of reality streams as melodies that culminate in a frenzy of sounds"—confirmed Hegel's more systematic argument that the true subject matter of the romantic movement was absolute interiorness, a form of spiritual subjectivity that the musical generated best. Hegel's historical characterization helps to illuminate Schumann's intense concern that his generation discharge its noble historical and moral obligation by generalizing the capacity for spiritual subjectivity.

Hegel located the sense of autonomy and freedom generated by the engagement with romantic art, particularly music, in the capacity of the individual to abandon aesthetic formalism. The recognition of an impersonal aesthetic ideal in objects of art was replaced by subjectivity. Therefore overt appearances, even of ugliness and emptiness, were given scope. The creator and receptor played (as in a game) at aesthetic transformation and punctured the surface illusions of empirical observation. The real, then, could be understood in a new way. Romantic art, therefore, did more than create a new formalism. Music, for the historic moment, revealed a reality that was otherwise hidden.

Music was the quintessential contemporary aesthetic vehicle of the everyday supplanting literature. Schumann's shift from literature to music during his university years found resonance in these ideas of aesthetic evolution in history. Music demanded a reconsideration of realism. The self and the subjective experience through music stripped away the masks of language and image. Philistinism and superficiality were crimes because, for both the individual and the age, they were lies analogous to surface realism; corruptions of the free capacity of the individual to penetrate the surface of existence.

The nineteenth-century historian Karl Lamprecht used the Hegelian premise as the justification for describing the early nineteenth century as the age of subjectivity. An explicit democratization in the embrace of spiritual autonomy of the self had taken place. From the point of view of musical life, the most significant consequence of Hegel and Lamprecht's characterizations was the prestige granted all art, criticism, and the process of critical reflection by the educated individual.[73] Reading alone at home or aloud with friends, Jean Paul's fantasizing at the piano, learning to draw, looking at art, and the concert experience were converted into public icons of freedom and a sea of change in history.[74] Subjectivity became a social reality. The act of criticism, therefore, gained new status. The critic did what every reader needed to do. The critic was the teacher of the reader in that he was, in Schlegel's terms, the secondary author. Each reading added to the text and enlarged the public capacity of any work of art to fulfill its historical, philosophical, and moral function. The same could be true for music.[75]

It was not surprising that during the first decades of the nineteenth century the drive to acquire musical culture followed rapidly on the heels of the spread of literacy. The making of music in the sense of Jean Paul's and Schumann's hours of "reveries" at the piano (*Schwärmerei*) became a popular image of the autonomy of the self. The public acts of playing and active listening underscored the conceit of the individual that through one's own subjectivity one became part of a community and a historical moment.

Music's new philosophical underpinnings only underscored the social prestige of music. The generation of Schumann's parents and Schumann himself knew very well that in the eighteenth century, music had been largely the province of an aristocracy, the nobility, and an elite upper strata of civil servants and merchants. The musical achievements of Frederick the Great and Louis Ferdinand were not distant memories.[76] The philosophical rhetoric of romantic writers and philosophers only added to music's aura as a dimension of aristocratic manners.

The enormous role that the aristocracy and royalty continued to play in the patronage of music was not lost on Schumann's contemporaries. It created a natural and understandable ambivalence with regard to the contradictions inherent in the pursuit of a musical career that was, at best, in transition from one form of exclusive patronage to the nineteenth-century mixed system of expanding commerce and patronage.

In rewriting the role of Beethoven, Mozart, Bach, and Palestrina in the creation of the present state of art, Schumann, unlike Wagner, skirted the task of interpreting the consequence of the economic and political conditions under which these figures from the past worked. Schumann's ambivalence toward the audience of the nonaristocratic public in Düsseldorf, Dresden, and Leipzig and his embarrassing enthusiasm for Metternich were part of his contradictory relationship to the realities of daily musical life, past and present. He hoped that in his generation there would be a new wave of connoisseurs that could replace, in economic terms, the lost aristocracy from the past.

The spread of musical culture between the years 1813 and 1840 was remarkable because it reflected both an aesthetic ideology specific to a new middle class conscious of its historical and political moment and the desire to imitate habits of life associated with an elite noble culture. This is no better revealed than in the public announcement issued in 1836 to the subscribers of the Gewandhaus concerts. Mendelssohn's appointment was designed to elevate taste. The concert became a forum for both bourgeois *Bildung* and aristocratic *Erziehung*, particularly in terms of civility.[77]

The historical specter against which Schumann fought was the possibility that the spread of musical culture and the removal of aristocratic privilege would result in the opposite of a utopia of freedom and culture, that it might debase the power of music. It was incumbent on the composer and the critic to reconcile novelty and originality with an indisputable respect and admiration for historical models. And this forced Schumann as a composer to confront the issue of history and his generation's conception of the relationship of past, present, and future.

Cultural Politics and the Critique of the Present, 1815–1848

Schumann and his generation, despite the rhetoric of philosophers, were profoundly ambivalent about the moment in time in which they lived.[78] The enthusiasm for reveries at the keyboard, particularly at twilight, were internalized personal expressions of a widespread desire to escape the present moment. Once again Jean Paul helped to set the tone. "Memory and hope . . . childhood and the beyond fill his spirit," wrote Dilthey, obliterating the "knife point of the present."[79] general enthusiasm for art and culture.

The use of art to escape present pain—through the evocations (no matter how fantastic) of both remembrances and dreams—fit precisely Schumann's careful description of his life in letters and diaries, not only before he began to train with Friedrich Wieck but during the years of separation from Clara. His art responded to a malaise that coexisted with his generation's sense of its historical mission and the general enthusiasm for art and culture.

The popularity of the fairy tale, the dream, and the romance—all self-conscious distortions of reality that trigger hope and expectation—mirrored the mix of nostalgia and cultural criticism inherent in music and literature of the *Vormärz*. Schumann's engagement with music for children and the fairy tale was part of a cultural obsession with childhood as the moment of vanished hope and the source of memory. In the act of playing music for children, adults could idealize a childhood they had lost or never had, with all its inherent unrealized possibilities and suggestions of innocence. The most characteristic and successful example of Schumann's engagement with these tendencies was his selection of the German translation of Thomas Moore's poetry and its use in *Das Paradies und die Peri*. The amalgam of naive religiosity, orientalism, and fairy tale–like simplicity helped to make this not only one of Schumann's greatest works but also his most significant public triumph.

"If writing is a form of prophecy," Jean Paul wrote, "so romantic writing is the anticipation of a greater future."[80] The critique of contemporary existence in the decades before 1848 triggered two dominant ideologies, both of which influenced Schumann: utopianism and historicism. Utopianism, with which Schumann flirted actively only in a restricted sense (in the creation of the *Davidsbund*), exaggerated the failings of the day by distorting the capacities for change. It paralleled an aesthetic experience familiar to Schumann: the flight of the imagination into the infinite.

The lure of utopianism and the aura attached to shattered utopian dreams can be understood, in terms of Schumann, through the example of Nikolaus Lenau, with whom Schumann was often compared in the nineteenth century. A few years after Schumann's death, Eduard Bernsdorf wrote, "They both had the same heavily laden seriousness, and a natural bent toward hypercritical contemplativeness . . . , and a certain coldness and reserve of expression with at the same time much warmth and energy in feeling; . . . they were possessed by restless, truly artistic drive that sought to realize aims in ever higher and more idealistic spheres."[81]

Lenau was devastated by the political reaction after the Revolution of 1830. In 1832 he went to America—his generation's symbol of all future possibilities (with which Clara and Robert also flirted and to which one charter member of the *Davidsbund* emigrated)—only to experience disappointment once again. Lenau's expectations were not dissimilar to those embodied by the utopian colony of New Harmony on the Wabash, founded by German Protestants seeking to re-create the ideals of primitive Christianity. The Lenau poems that Schumann set in 1850 were written in the years immediately following the poet's return. Two of the poems, "Kommen und Scheiden" and "Der schwere Abend," exemplify Lenau's sensibilities.[82] Schumann understood the facts of Lenau's life and work. The sense of failure in terms of the individual's engagement in a political project of extreme expectations, when transposed into the language of love poetry, deepened the rhetoric of desire, pain, and loss.

The reverse side of utopianism was the search for a way out of the present by means of the past. On the eve of the Revolutions of 1848 Joseph Eichendorff put it this way: "Romanticism was no mere literary movement. It undertook, far more, an inner regeneration of collective life."[83] Eichendorff credited the romantic movement with a rediscovery and construction of a cultural past that could serve the future. The revival of J. S. Bach was part of this phenomenon. As Schumann explained to Clara in 1841, "And it really is very necessary for an artist to be able to give an account of the entire history of his art."[84] History was essential to art because in the recognition of the past within art of the present day, the "inner "source of Eichendorff's collective regeneration could be found. The historical imagery, so to speak, within an individual artist's craft was central to the aesthetic and political project of the present. Bach's achievement formed the centerpiece of the "account" of the past because of its public and collective power and significance. Schumann's advocacy of Palestrina fit into the same pattern.[85]

The premium on historical memory and the link to a program of regeneration influenced Schumann's approach to the longer musical forms with which he worked in the early 1840s. In the late 1830s the process of listening to larger-scale musical forces deployed over a longer time period—in the symphony, for example, or the extended melodrama, the opera, or oratorio—had become a plausible arena for cultural politics.

An expanding community of listeners and participants in the world of choral music could encounter music in the concert hall on a temporal scale sufficient to make listening analogous to engaging a sustained account of history. Unlike the smaller piano work or the song, the large forms of oratorio and symphony were similar to narratives of history—a collective past—in terms of scale and complexity. The music was also modeled on forms that derived from the great ages gone by, yet the realization was novel and defied traditional habits of expectation in the listener.

Originality was integrated into the historical. The use of thematic reminiscence and linkages between movements paralleled the notion of how the past must return in the continuous process of life to assert itself into the future. Desire, rendered musical, became historical in the symphony. It became the vehicle for Eichendorff's project. A corrupt and faded present can be brought alive as the spiritual essence of the past is cast into a new future form. The four symphonies can be viewed structurally as Schumann's emulation of the romantic project of reclaiming history on behalf of the future.[86]

It is in this context that Schumann's relationship to Beethoven can be understood. A mixture of envy and nostalgia shaped Schumann's approach to Beethoven, who was the equivalent of Napoleon in musical culture. The generation of 1810 realized they had just missed the great classical age in their art. That sense of loss was tempered by the realization that therefore the process of regeneration in music was more hopeful than in the other arts.

In no piece of music is this complex of ideas more evident than in the Fantasy, Op. 17. Written in the late 1830s, it was put into its final form, appropriately enough, for the dedication ceremony for the 1845 Bonn Beethoven monument (which the Schumanns did not attend). Schumann's desire to present this work at the Bonn ceremony fit perfectly, as he knew, into the composition's own history, which was spurred by the plans, announced in 1836, to erect the Beethoven monument.

The original title bore the three words "ruins, trophies, palms." The references are all about the present's conception of the past within its midst. The ruin is the surviving remnant of greatness as realized in architecture (e.g., Rome). The trophy is the symbol of the great deed in the past, a symbol that partook of a classical as well as pagan mythological character. The palm is nature's expression of warmth and the sun—the "other" place evocative for Germans of both the historical Italy and the fantastic, utopian, and natural New World.[87]

German Romantic Painting and
the Music of Robert Schumann

Robert Schumann's lifelong interest in painting and sculpture was not exceptional. As both Jean Paul and Schlegel made clear, the visual was an integral part of the aesthetic experience. Karl Wörner, in a nearly inadvertent manner, compared one Schumann work to the paintings of the Nazarene group.[88] Schumann came of age in an era dominated in the visual arts by German painters who had gone to Italy.[89]

What drove Johann Overbeck and other Nazarenes and their successor German-Roman painters to Italy was not merely the neoclassical sensibilities we associate with the work of the architect Karl Friedrich Schinkel. Rather, the admiration for the pagan classical model became intertwined with the desire to reclaim the essential spirit of Christianity. This quest for spiritual regeneration seemed realizable only in that mix of "palms" and "ruins" found in Italy. It was the land of memories and the historical landscape of faith and hope.

The fascination with Italy also had literary and musical roots. Goethe's Italian sojourn of the 1780s had become a model for the requisite pilgrimage to the South, which every aspiring German intellectual writer and artist undertook, including Schumann. Present musical taste in the late 1820s was dominated by Rossini, and the past had more than its share of Italian masters.

In 1829, in a diary entry on the difference between universal geniuses and ideal human beings, Schumann placed Mozart, Shakespeare, and Michelangelo in the former group and Schiller, Handel, and Raphael into the latter.[90] Schumann's engagement with Raphael would be lifelong. As if to deny his own psychic nature, Schumann's ambitions were more to emulate the "ideal human being." In the universal genius, art entirely overpowered mundane life, as in the case of Michelangelo, Shakespeare, and Mozart. Following Jean Paul, Schumann sought a more intimate integration of mundane life and art.

During Schumann's trip to Italy in 1829 he filled his diary with detailed descriptions of art and architecture. One of the most interesting and revealing entries was his painstaking copying of what must have been a leftover newspaper clipping from 1825, which was from the *Elegante Zeitung* and referred to a set of parallels made by "Carpani." Carpani created two lists, one of composers and one of painters,and placed them side by side according to the most exact parallels. The curious matter, of course, was the historical asymmetry. Eighteenth-century composers were deemed the equivalents of Renaissance masters. Haydn was paired with Tintoretto, Cimarosa was compared to

Paolo Veronese, Mozart to G. Romano, Gluck to Caravaggio, Piccini to Titian, Handel to Michelangelo, and Pergolesi to Raphael.[91]

During his trip to Vienna in 1838 Schumann evidently spent a fair amount of time in museums. In a diary entry from November 1838 he responded to looking at the originals by Raphael, Titian, Rubens, and others with these words: "I was overcome with happiness at the memories of the engravings at which I looked so often in my childhood."[92] For Schumann, the experience of seeing was comparable, in terms of *Bildung*, to that of reading and, more important, to that of hearing music. Nowhere was this more evident than in the diary entry of 16 October 1837. Schumann described the following sequence of events. First he noted his revision of his essay on piano variations, then he remarked with delight at the landscape painting of K. F. Lessing and at paintings depicting Cinderella, an Italian maiden, Friedrich Barbarossa, and a Roman figure bent in prayer. Immediately thereafter Schumann noted that he began to read *Siebenkäs* by Jean Paul.[93]

The icons of art history that carried the aura of a brilliant past continued to serve their double function as inspirations for the artwork of the future and as occasions for interior self-recognition. Schumann's museumgoing was at once an affirmation and a spur to his creative work. During the somewhat ill-fated trip to Russia in 1844 he once again described his many sojourns to look at art. For him the work of Benvenuto Cellini stood out along with the architecture of Moscow. Among the most memorable events was his visit to the Winter Palace, the Hermitage, in St. Petersburg.

Of all the many diary entries from the 1844 trip, it was Schumann's contempt for the artificial ruins—the fake modern reconstruction of the ravages of history—that he saw in Tsarskoe Selo that is most revealing. Neither slavish imitation of the past nor the even more philistine affectation to create an artificial item from the past deserved respect.[94] Regeneration was not accomplished by either neoclassicism or the affectation of a historical patina but rather by the evocation of the past in new forms.

Schumann's youthful education in art and his lifelong attachment to contemplating the great art of the past, particularly that from the Renaissance, led him to be interested in painters and sculptors of his own generation. In Copenhagen in the 1840s he visited the Thorvaldsen Museum. Unlike Mendelssohn, Schumann did not take to Thorwaldsen's neoclassic, restrained, and somewhat cold formalism. He marveled, however, at Peter Cornelius's frescoes in Schinkel's buildings in Berlin.[95]

Indeed, Schumann's search for a like-minded community led him to his own generation of German romantic and historical painters who lived and worked in Leipzig, Dresden, and, most of all, Düsseldorf. The painter Schumann seems most to have favored was Eduard Bendemann, with whom he was quite friendly and through whom he developed a new and strong admiration for the North German heritage, particularly the work of Albrecht Dürer.[96] Schumann's interest during the 1840s in a Germanic historical past, mostly medieval in character, was not merely the function of changes in the political culture of the mid- and late 1840s. Rather, Schumann's interests were influenced in part by his contact with contemporary painters who remained in the North. Alfred Rethel, Karl Friedrich Lessing, Julius Hübner, Ludwig Richter, J. W. Schirmer, and Karl Sohn are among the most significant painters with whom Schumann came into contact.

As with music, Schumann's evaluation of his contemporaries was persistently mediated by his references to and experiences with an idealized painterly past. In 1851 in Antwerp and Brussels, Schumann marveled at Rubens and van Dyk. At the same time he reacted with enthusiasm at the narrative canvases of Bendemann and Hübner.[97] In March 1852 Schumann made one of his last references on art by noting his visit to a collection of etchings by Raphael on display in Leipzig.[98] As with the novels of Jean Paul, Schumann returned repeatedly to the passions of his youth.

Robert Schumann had closer contact with two schools of German painters, the Düsseldorf School and the Dresden School. The most significant Düsseldorf painters with whom he was familiar included Bendemann, Hübner, Theodor Mintrop, Lessing, and Schirmer. In Dresden the most significant figures to Schumann were Richter, Johann Christian Dahl, and Ernst Rietschel. Bendemann bridged both schools, since during Schumann's lifetime he was in Dresden and subsequently in Düsseldorf. What is significant in Schumann's engagement with Lessing, Schirmer, Rietschel, and Rethel is these painters' enthusiasm for the large narrative and landscape canvas,[99] an enthusiasm that might bear on the development of Schumann's career. Schumann's attraction not only to the iconography and surface of the painting of his time but to the act of seeing and interacting with the large-scale canvas betrays an ambition that can help to provide a key to his development as a composer and to the consistency of his aesthetic concerns.

Scholars have sought explanations for Schumann's transition as a composer from the short piano form to the longer form and from the song finally to the symphony, oratorio, and opera. One key to Schumann's evolution is psychological and has to do with his growing confidence, given his unsystematic training and autodidactic route to composition. Another hypothesis is based on his relationship to Men-

delssohn, which vacillated between adulation and envy. There is also
the thesis that Schumann wanted greater public recognition, which
led him to compose music that would enhance his reputation. The
more simplified and accessible late style is said to reflect Schumann's
awareness of particular domestic markets of the midcentury. Biographical events also have been cited, such as the impact of Mendelssohn's death in 1847. Did Schumann seek to assume a role as
Mendelssohn's successor in writing music, under the banner of Mendelssohn's conception of aesthetic education, which called for a more
neoclassical and transparent music?[100]

A further possibility lies in the notion that Schumann followed a
very self-conscious dynamic strategy derived from Jean Paul. He in-
vented himself along lines he had discovered in Jean Paul's prose as an
adolescent. For example, Jean Paul's continuing dialectic between short
and long forms and between the joke and the novel was emulated
directly. Schumann's search later in life for a style that was narrative
but also self-referential in formal terms conformed as well to the pattern of Jean Paul's own career. Like Schumann, Jean Paul began with
an attraction to the grotesque and bizarre and ended his career in a
celebration of idyllic domestic bliss. Indeed, like Flaubert's Emma Bov-
ary or Stendhal's Julien Sorel, Schumann led his life in imitation of
what he read in books. The sustained courtship of Clara, the flirtation
with public romantic martyrdom, the diaries, the marriage diaries, and
the correspondence, as well as the sequence of aesthetic projects in his
career, can be tied to close models in Jean Paul's life and work.

But yet another key may lie in Schumann's interest in painting. Rethel, about whom Schumann had mixed views, was immensely impressive in the small form, the miniature. One thinks of the *Märchenerzählungen*, Op. 132, and the *Märchenbilder*, Op. 113, in relationship to
Rethel's *Monatsbilder*. Rethel's and Richter's historicism was more self-
consciously German, linked to Dürer where the refined line evoked a
quality used by Schumann with regularity as a sign of approbation:
volkstümlich. Richter's painting *Der Brautzug* is a case in point.[101]

The Düsseldorf School painters followed the direction described by
Eichendorff. Likewise, in the work of the Dresden painters spiritual
regeneration took the form of the rediscovery of an indigenous German past, ranging from landscape to myth and to historical memory.
Their narrative painting would reach a large audience. Bendemann's
and Lessing's work may have inspired Schumann to undertake the
musical equivalent of their richly colored, spacious, scenic and narrative depictions. The evocation of the residues of the past and expectations transmitted to the viewer located in the present that were visible

in the landscape canvases of romantic painting can be compared to Schumann's larger-scale works.

The works of the late 1840s and early 1850s—*Manfred* and *Der Rose Pilgerfahrt*—are cases in point. The Düsseldorf painter Theodor Mintrop designed the title page of *Der Rose Pilgerfahrt*. These works and the "Rhenish" Symphony have their analogues in Lessing's *Fels- und Waldlandschaft mit dem Mutter-Gottes Bild* or the other version of this painting, *Die tausendjährige Eiche*.[102] Orchestral colors have their equivalents in Lessing's use of light and dark and color.[103] *Das Paradies und die Peri* constitutes the first massive work by Schumann that can be compared with the paintings and frescoes of his immediate contemporaries.[104]

Schumann's response to paintings such as *Die trauernden Juden* by Bendemann might be compared to the interior intensity associated with the reactions he sought to evoke in music. In that canvas Bendemann made the inner journey of the viewer the subject. In this sense, the late songs might be linked to Bendemann's work. The character of Schumann's late Violin Sonata in D minor, Op. 121, and the last section of *Faust* are reminiscent of the scale, coloration, and sweep of the canvases of Schirmer, just as the later, more bizarre and fragmentary work of late Schumann can be related to the smaller Rethel etchings.

In subject matter and execution, the emphasis in these paintings on the interior concentration of the human subjects on the canvas and the enormous disparity of scale between the figures and the natural environment helped the viewer to respond to the psychic power of nature and its mediation through art. The iconography was a Jean Paul–like mix of surface realism and fantasy. The Düsseldorf School painters eschewed the monumentality of the Munich School of historical painters. Nevertheless, evident in the paintings with which Schumann was most familiar and that he most admired was a constant reference either to the past or to the flight from the moment—toward legend, myth, and, periodically, Christianity.

History and Performance Practice:
The Case of Schumann

Robert Schumann's vacillation between the spiritual and aesthetic predicament of the individual (Jean Paul) and the aesthetic education of the public (Menzel) was lifelong. The various forms it took in Schumann's music speak to an evolution in strategy and a desire to accommodate the changes in the historical moment that occurred between 1830 and 1850. The engagement with history and painting in Schumann's later years helps to illuminate the sources of the strikingly simple style and formal fastidiousness of much of the choral and piano music of the later years, including the children's music. One thinks first of the Op. 60 B A C H fugues from 1845, piano works such as Opp. 85, 124, and 126, and the last secular choral pieces.

This self-conscious identification with a national movement of cultural regeneration, however, grew directly out of Schumann's encounter with Menzel in 1828. The concern for the standard of public taste that Schumann exhibited as a critic in the late 1830s reemerged in his musical work a decade later as he sought to emulate the public role of Mendelssohn after the latter's death.

As a young man, Robert Schumann began to imagine himself and create his world through the act of reading. With remarkable discipline he lived out an approach to the world that was characteristic of the reigning ideas and influences of his generation. It is necessary for late twentieth-century observers to note that Schumann wrote music with the full expectation that it would function for the listener the way reading functioned. The shared literary and linguistic foundation behind Schumann's sense of musical time and form are fundamental.

What this suggests may be nothing short of radical, particularly for the modern interpreter. As Schumann's own revisions of his earlier music imply, the act of making music resembles rereading. Rereading is never a replica of a past event. What is perceived and recalled has as much to do with the life history and place of the reader as it does with the printed text. Playing involves the creation of new meanings and experiences.

If printed music is, then, like a poetic or prose text, the conceit of faithful representation of past practices—including the category of authorial intention—as understood by late twentieth-century performance practice may be irrelevant. Only if that conceit inspires one to tears can it serve as a surrogate for imaginative interpretive transformation.

The twentieth century's notions of authenticity and the musical text demand redefinition if Schumann is the subject. Perhaps playing Schumann according to performance practices of his day requires that the player take striking liberties including improvisation, alteration, amplification, and addition to create the intensity of memory, expectation, and consciousness in the audience. Or perhaps Schumann should be set aside in favor of a living composer inspired directly by him (e.g., Adorno's advocacy of Berg).

The speculative historical reconstruction of the cultural world around Schumann suggests than when scholars and performers consider the musical canon written after the death of Beethoven, the imposition of seemingly objective notions of textual reading and interpretation not only are ahistorical but may cut directly against the meaning and role that music making and listening possessed in the historical era in which the works were written. It is ironic that our obsession with the sophisticated, self-critical historical methods designed to rescue the music of the past allegedly obscured by falsifying subsequent traditions, in the case of Schumann and his contemporaries, might compel us to abandon the historical critical enterprise as we now know it. The making of "correct" editions, re-creating old instruments, utilizing forgotten techniques, and wiping out traces of older reinterpretations may be, historically speaking, a travesty. Schumann's additions to the texts of his beloved Bach, his close emulations of Bach, and his early and late appropriations of Paganini are the alternative models of what we might do to Schumann, all in the name of history.

Exploring Schumann as history, then, reminds us of how performance strategies need to be evaluated in terms illuminated by extramusical historical categories, including reading and the viewing of art. The consequences of this approach need to be considered if we wish to conjure up among our fellow citizens the spirit as well as the personal and public significance that history teaches us actually marked music making and listening in Schumann's world.

NOTES

1. Ludwig Wittgenstein, *Culture and Value*, trans. Peter Winch (Chicago, 1980), p. 2.

2. See, for example, the work of John Daverio; and Anthony Newcomb's article "Schumann and Late Eighteenth-Century Narrative Strategies," *19th-Century Music* 11 (1987): 164–74.

3. Theodor W. Adorno, "Berg: Der Meister des kleinsten Übergangs," in *Musikalische Monographien* (Frankfurt, 1986), p. 330; see also Max Paddison, *Adorno's Aesthetics of Music* (Cambridge, 1993), pp. 242–45.

4. See Theodor W. Adorno, *Kompositionen*, ed. Heinz-Klaus Metzger and Reiner Riehn (Munich, 1980), vol. 2, pp. 73–113.

5. Roland Barthes, "Loving Schumann" and "Rasch," in *The Responsibility of Forms*, trans. Richard Howard (Berkeley and Los Angeles, 1991), particularly pp. 293, 298. In his recent book, in an analysis of F. Khnopff's 1883 painting *En écoutant du Schumann*, Richard Leppert extends Barthes' analysis to probe how Schumann came to be heard and how that hearing was represented in art at the end of the nineteenth century. Leppert's brilliant excursus assumes that the hand of the player in the painting is male and that the process of music making and hearing has been disembodied, making it "anti-conversational." This analysis is relevant only insofar as to assert that Leppert's reading of the

painting and Schumann may be genuine twentieth-century impositions that bear little resemblance to the experience of hearing and listening that either Schumann or enthusiasts (even Khnopff) circa 1883 of his music had. See Richard Leppert, *The Sight of Sound: Music Representation and the History of the Body* (Berkeley and Los Angeles, 1994), pp. 230–33.

6. Eduard Hanslick, *Sämtliche Schriften*, vol. 1: *Aufsätze und Reszensionen, 1844–1848*, ed. Dietmar Strauss (Vienna, 1993), p. 106.

7. Two recent studies are Peter Ostwald, *The Inner Voices of a Musical Genius* (Boston, 1985); and Udo Rauchfleisch, *Robert Schumann: Leben und Werk* (Stuttgart, 1990).

8. Kay Jamison, *Touched with Fire: Manic-Depressive Illness and the Artistic Temperament* (New York, 1993), pp. 144–46, 201–7.

9. Wilhelm Dilthey, *Das Erlebnis und die Dichtung* (Göttingen, 1905; reprint, 1985), p. 315.

10. Anthony Newcomb, "Schumann and the Marketplace: From Butterflies to *Hausmusik*," in *Nineteenth-Century Piano Music*, ed. R. Larry Todd (New York, 1990), pp. 258–315, esp. p. 271.

11. Hans Gál, *Schumann's Orchestral Music* (London, 1979), p. 7.

12. English-language readers can find two choice examples of Schumann's anti-Semitism in his marriage diaries. Schumann writes disparagingly of Mendelssohn's indelible Jewish characteristics and of how the "Jewish physiognomy" of E. Marxsen (Brahms's teacher) disgusted Clara and Robert. In *The Marriage Diaries of Robert and Clara Schumann*, ed. Gerd Nauhaus, trans. Peter Ostwald (Boston, 1994), pp. 31, 132.

13. Richard Wagner, "Judaism in Music," in *Richard Wagner's Prose Works*, trans. W. A. Ellis (New York, 1966), vol. 3, p. 117. See the precise echo of this view in, of all places, the ideas of Richard Strauss's father, Franz. Cited in R. Larry Todd, "Strauss before Liszt and Wagner: Some Observations," in Bryan Gilliam, ed., *Richard Strauss: New Perspectives* (Durham, N.C., 1992), p. 33.

14. See Newcomb, "Schumann and the Marketplace"; and Linda Correll Roesner, "The Sources for Schumann's *Davidsbündlertänze*, Op. 6: Composition, Textual Problems, and the Role of the Composer as Editor," in *Mendelssohn and Schumann: Essays on Their Music and Its Context*, ed. R. Larry Todd and Jon W. Finson (Durham, N.C., 1984), pp. 53–70.

15. See Jörg-Peter Mittmann, "Musikerberuf und bürgerliches Bildungsideal," in *Bildungsbürgertum im 19. Jahrhundert*, vol. 2: *Bildungsgüter und Bildungswissen*, ed. Reinhart Koselleck (Stuttgart, 1990), pp. 237–58.

16. See Andreas Ballstädt and Tobias Willmaier, *Salonmusik: Zur Geschichte und Funktion einer bürgerlichen Musikpraxis* (Stuttgart, 1989), pp. 52–53, 88–94, 255–57, 315–50, 385; also Carl Dahlhaus, *Klassische und romantische Musikästhetik* (Laaber, 1988), p. 171.

17. Hermann Kretzschmar, "Robert Schumann als Aesthetiker" (1906), in *Gesammelte Aufsätze aus den Jahrbüchern der Musikbibliothek Peters* (Leipzig, 1911; reprint, 1973) p. 297.

18. Robert Schumann, *Tagebücher, Band III: Haushaltbücher*, ed. Gerd Nauhaus (Leipzig, 1982), pp. 629–38.

19. Gerhard Stenzel, ed. *Die deutschen Romantiker* (Salzburg, n.d.), vol. 2, p. 394.

20. Wilhelm Dilthey, "Klopstock, Schiller, Jean Paul," in *Von deutscher Dichung und Musik: Aus den Studien zur Geschichte des deutschen Geistes* (Leipzig and Berlin, 1933), pp. 436–37.

21. Arnfried Edler, *Robert Schumann und seine Zeit* (Laaber, 1982), pp. 90–101, 212–22.

22. Clara Schumann, *Jugendbriefe von Robert Schumann* (Leipzig, 1886), pp. 82–83.

23. This is true not only of Oliver Strunk's extract in his classic 1950 collection of readings but also of Kretzschmar's essay.

24. C. F. Müller, *Musikalische Original-Anekdoten* (Erfurt, 1836), pp. 365–66. An English version can be found in Thomas A. Brown, *The Aesthetics of Robert Schumann* (New York, 1968), p. 16.

25. Quoted in Kretzschmar, "Robert Schumann als Aesthetiker," p. 301.

26. Schumann, *Tagebücher, Band I: 1827–1838*, ed. Georg Eismann (Leipzig, 1971), p. 36.

27. Quoted in Dilthey, "Klopstock, Schiller, Jean Paul," p. 442.

28. *Jean Pauls Sämtliche Werke: Historisch-kritische Ausgabe*, ed. Eduard Berend (Weimar, 1927; reprint, 1975), vol. 2, p. 51.

29. *Jean Paul's Werke*, ed. Wolgang Hecht (Berlin, 1987), vol. 1, p. 26.

30. Jean Paul, *Die Vorschule der Aesthetik*, in *Jean Pauls Sämtliche Werke*, vol. 11, pp. 89–93, 153–61. The *Witz* figured as well in Schlegel and in secondary figures of Schumann's generation such as Arnold Ruge (who later would play an important role in German politics), whose *Neue Vorschule der Aesthetik* (Halle, 1837) was derivative of Jean Paul.

31. G. G. Gervinus, *Geschichte des neunzehnten Jahrhunderts*, vol. 8, part 1 (Leipzig, 1866), p. 75.

32. Ibid., p. 77.

33. The tie between Hegel and Jean Paul, and ultimately Schumann, is not speculative. Hegel knew Jean Paul and Thibaut and spent time at Heidelberg with both of them at Thibaut's soirees. See Adolf Nowak, *Hegels Musikaesthetik* (Regensburg, 1970), p. 20.

34. Hegel, *Aesthetics*, trans. T. M. Knox (Oxford, 1975), vol. 2, p. 897.

35. Robert Schumann, *Manfred: Dramatisches Gedicht*, Op. 115 (Leipzig, 1853), piano score, pp. 1, 3, 5, 6.

36. Jean Paul, "Selberlebenbeschreibung," in *Jean Paul's Werke*, vol. 1, p. 25.

37. Dilthey, "Klopstock, Schiller, Jean Paul," p. 450.

38. Schumann, *Tagebücher, Band I: 1827–1838*, pp. 109, 115–16.

39. Heinrich Heine, *Sämtliche Schriften* (Munich, 1976), vol. 1, pp. 444–56, esp. p. 454.

40. Wolfgang Menzel, *Die deutsche Literatur*, 2d ed. (Stuttgart, 1836), part 1, pp. 42–48.

41. Ibid., pp. 3–41.

42. Ibid., part 3, p. 174.

43. Ibid., part 4, pp. 5f.

44. Ibid., part 1, p. 103.

45. Heine, *Sämtliche Schriften*, vol. 1, p. 455.

46. Ibid., p. 451.

47. Schumann, *Tagebücher, Band I: 1827–1838*, p 101; on the role of criticism see Walter Benjamin's "Der Begriff der Kunstkritik in der deutschen Romantik," in *Gesammelte Schriften* (Frankfurt, 1980), vol. 1, part 1, pp. 62–72.

48. Heine, *Sämtliche Schriften*, vol. 2, p. 34.

49. See Martha Woodmansee, *The Author, Art, and the Market: Rereading the History of Aesthetics* (New York, 1994), pp. 22–33, 87; on Schumann's criticism see the classic book by Leon B. Plantinga, *Schumann as Critic* (New Haven, 1967).

50. Menzel, *Die deutsche Literatur*, part 1, pp. 24–32, 86–116.

51. Ibid., p. 32.

52. See Hans Joachim Köhler, *Robert Schumann: Sein Leben und Wirken in den Leipziger Jahren* (Leipzig, 1986), pp. 7–18.

53. Eva Weissweiler, *Clara Schumann: Eine Biographie* (Hamburg, 1990), pp. 93–95.

54. *M. G. Saphir's Konversations-Lexikon* (Berlin, n.d.), pp. 259–60.

55. Hans Erich Bödeker, "Die 'gebildeten Stände' im 18. und frühen 19. Jahrhundert: Zugehörigkeit und Abgrenzungen, Mentalitäten und Handlungspotentiale," in *Bildungsbürgertum im 19. Jahrhundert*, vol. 4: *Politischer Einfluss und gesellschaftliche Formation*, ed. Jürgen Kocka (Stuttgart, 1989), pp. 26–30.

56. See Wolfgang Hardtwig, "Auf dem Weg zum Bildungsbürgertum: die Lebensführungsart der jugendlichen Bildungsschicht, 1750–1819," in *Politischer Bildungsbürgertum im 19. Jahrhundert*, vol. 3: *Lebensführung und ständische Vergesellschaftung*, ed. M. Rainer Lepsius (Stuttgart, 1992), pp. 35–41.

57. Karl Lamprecht, *Deutsche Geschichte* (Freiburg im Breisgau, 1905), vol. 1, part 3, pp. 297–302.

58. K. H. Wörner, *Robert Schumann* (Munich, 1987), p. 13.

59. Friedrich Schlegel, *Kritische Schriften und Fragmente*, ed. Ernst Behler and Hans Eichner (Paderborn, 1988), vol. 4, pp. 233–34.

60. See Gerald N. Izenberg, *Impossible Individuality: Romanticism, Revolution, and the Origins of Modern Selfhood, 1787–1802* (Princeton, 1992), pp. 54–138.

61. See, for example, Dahlhaus's references to Schlegel in *Klassische und Romantische Musikästhetik*. See the discussion of the origin of the motto for the Fantasy, Op. 17, which comes from Schlegel's "Die Gebüsche," in Nicholas Marston, *Schumann: "Fantasie," Op. 17* (Cambridge, 1992), pp. 21–22.

62. John Daverio, *Nineteenth-Century Music and the German Romantic Ideology* (New York, 1993), pp. 11–14, 55.

63. Frederick C. Beiser, *The Fate of Reason: German Philosophy from Kant to Fichte* (Cambridge, Mass., 1987), pp. 214–17.

64. See Schumann, *Tagebücher, Band I: 1827–1838*, pp. 109–16, 200–202. See also the discussion complementary to this point, in Norbert Nagler's "Der konfliktuöse Kompromiss zwischen Gefühl und Vernunft im Frühwerk Schu-

manns," in *Robert Schumann: Text und Kritik*, ed. Klaus Metzger and R. Riehn (Munich, 1981), vol. 1, pp. 221–80.

65. W. H. Bruford, *The German Tradition of Self-Cultivation: "Bildung" from Humboldt to Thomas Mann* (Cambridge, 1975), pp. 82–87.

66. Schlegel's idea of *Ahnung* calls for careful examination in terms of Schumann's approach to musical settings of lyric poetry.

67. Schlegel, *Kritische Schriften und Fragmente*, vol. 6, p. 44.

68. The derivation of the title "Novelettes" from Clara Novello's name does not undermine the obvious double meaning: the reference to the short novel form. See Edler, *Robert Schumann und seine Zeit*, p. 133.

69. Schlegel, *Kritische Schriften und Fragmente*, vol. 6, p. 54.

70. Ibid., vol. 5, p. 256.

71. Friedrich Schlegel, *Philosophical Fragments*, trans. Peter Firchow (Minneapolis, 1991), p. 92.

72. Hegel, *Aesthetics*, vol. 2, pp. 888–98.

73. Lamprecht, *Deutsche Geschichte*, pp. 3–93.

74. One forgets that musical gatherings such as the Schubertiade had their literary counterparts in reading aloud. Consider, for example, the drawing by L. Pietsch entitled *An Evening with Ludwig Tieck*.

75. Benjamin, "Der Begriff der Kunstkritik," p. 68.

76. See Carl Dahlhaus, "Der deutsche Bildungsbürgertum und die Musik," in *Bildungsgüter und Bildungswissen*, ed. Reinhart Koselleck, pp. 220–36; and Bödeker, "Die 'gebildeten Staende,' " in *Politischer Einfluss und gesellschaftliche Formation*, ed. Jürgen Kocka, pp. 33–41.

77. Alfred Dörfel, *Die Geschichte der Gewandhauskonzerte zu Leipzig: 1781–1881* (Leipzig, 1884; reprint, 1980), pp. 87–88.

78. See Werner Busch, "Die fehlende Gegenwart," in *Bildungsgüter und Bildungswissen*, ed. Reinhart Koselleck, pp. 286–316.

79. Dilthey, "Klopstock, Schiller, Jean Paul," p. 446.

80. Jean Paul, *Jean Pauls Sämtliche Werke*, vol. 11, part 1, p. 77.

81. Eduard Bernsdorf et al., *Neues Universal-Lexikon der Tonkunst* (Dresden, 1856–61), vol. 3, p. 536.

82. These are part of Op. 90 and were taken from a set entitled *Liebesklänge* in *Nikolaus Lenaus Sämtliche Werke*, ed. E. Castle (Leipzig, n.d.), vol. 1, p. 177. See Josef Haslinger, "Nikolaus Lenau," in *Österreichische Porträts*, ed. Jochen Jung (Salzburg, 1985), vol. 1, pp. 207–31.

83. Quoted in *Die deutschen Romantiker*, p. 258.

84. *The Marriage Diaries of Robert and Clara Schumann*, p. 98.

85. See Dahlhaus, "Zur Entstehung der romantischen Bach Deutung," in *Klassische und romantische Musikaesthetik*, pp. 121–39.

86. See Peter Gülke, "Zur Rheinischen Sinfonie," in Metzger and Riehn, *Robert Schumann: Text und Kritik*, vol. 2, pp. 237–53.

87. Marston, *Schumann: "Fantasie," Op. 17*, pp. 1–10; and Daverio, *Nineteenth-Century Music and the German Romantic Ideology*, pp. 42–47. The reference to "palm" is, of course, intimately connected with the Christian sym-

bolism of Palm Sunday and Easter. The pagan celebration of nature and life in springtime merges with the Christian notion of redemption and resurrection. Schumann's use of the palm is therefore not only characteristic but ideally matched to the notion of the ruin and the trophy.

88. Schumann knew the last of the Nazarene painters, Wilhelm Schadow, who was director of the fine arts academy in Düsseldorf. See Schumann, *Tagebücher, Band III: Haushaltbücher*, pp. 578, 589.

89. Wörner, *Robert Schumann*, p. 135; see also Theodore Ziolkowski, *German Romanticism and Its Institutions* (Princeton, 1990), pp. 337–55.

90. Schumann, *Tagebücher, Band I: 1827–1838*, p. 230.

91. Ibid., p. 281.

92. Ibid., *Band II: 1836–1854*, ed. Gerd Nauhaus (Leipzig, 1987), p. 81.

93. Ibid., p. 39.

94. Ibid., pp. 262–370.

95. Ibid., pp. 223 and 417.

96. Ibid., p. 398.

97. Ibid., pp. 428–29.

98. Ibid., p. 432.

99. In the *Tagebücher, Band III: Haushaltbücher, Teil I: 1837–1847* and *Teil II: 1847–1856*, see the many references to Schumann's contact with these painters—for example, pp. 453–55, 473, 495, 509, 543, 545, 547, and 638.

100. It is ironic that despite Schumann's numerous expressions of admiration and his sorrow at Mendelssohn's death, at the end of his life Mendelssohn was quite bitter about their relationship. Writing to his friend Karl Klingemann a few months before his death, Mendelssohn confided that Schumann acted in quite a "two-faced" manner and had engaged in some "ugly" behavior, decidedly cooling his enthusiasm for further dealings. See the letter dated 31 January 1847 in *Felix Mendelssohns Briefwechsel mit Karl Klingemann* (Essen, 1909), p. 320; also Leon B. Plantinga, "Schumann's Critical Reaction to Mendelssohn," in *Mendelssohn and Schumann: Essays on Their Music and Its Context*, ed. R. Larry Todd and Jon W. Finson, pp. 11–20.

101. Too frequently only Richter's etching *Hausmusik* is discussed because of its direct relationship to Opp. 68 and 79. Ludwig Richter was responsible for the illustrations on the title page of the first edition of the *Album für die Jugend*, Op. 68. See pp. 184ff. in this volume.

102. For information on and reproductions of the painters and painters discussed here, see Anton Springer, *Handbuch der Kunstgeschichte*, ed. Max Osborn (Leipzig, 1912), vol. 5, pp. 35–61; Friedrich Haack, *Die Kunst des 19. Jahrhunderts* (Esslingen, 1913), pp. 146–70; and Christoph Heilmann, *Die Kunst der Deutsch-Römer* (Munich, 1987), pp. 317–23.

103. See Reinhard Kapp, "Das Orchester Schumanns," in Metzger and Riehn, *Robert Schumann: Text und Kritik*, vol. 2, pp. 191–236.

104. The painterly dimension of the "Rhenish" Symphony was not lost on contemporaries; see Ernst Lichtenhahn, "Sinfonie als Dichtung: Zum geschichtlichen Ort von Schumanns 'Rhenischer,' " in *Schumanns Werke: Text und Interpretation*, ed. Akio Mayeda and Klaus Wolfgang Niemöller (Mainz, 1987), especially pp. 18–21.

Schumann's Homelessness

MICHAEL P. STEINBERG

Musical Homes

Music without words speaks in "unsung voices." When are these voices first-person voices? What does it mean to recognize a first-person voice in music? A musical first-person voice may refer to its composer just as a narrative literary voice may refer to its author. But neither needs to. And in the experience of a complicated work, the attentive listener, like the attentive reader, is likely to do better in assuming that narrative and authorial voices are not the same. At the same time, the musical first-person voice liberated from simple identification with its creator can become an exploratory discourse about the very nature of the first person—the nature of self-reference in relation to the world. This essay is about the musical exploration of subjectivity at a specific cultural moment. In comparing Felix Mendelssohn and Robert Schumann, it turns to two closely associated and radically differentiated personalities whose musical first-person voices can help us to redefine and renegotiate what I will call Biedermeier culture: a specifically German instance of the cultural moment when all Europe was at work at the creation of modern subjectivity.[1]

The nineteenth century is the century of subjectivity. Subjectivity, as I will use the term in this essay, denotes a specific mode of achieving and representing modern selfhood that is distinct from subjectivism, on one side, and identity, on the other. In question here is not, as in the case of subjectivism, the combination of the emotionalism and individual self-assertion often associated with romanticism. Still more important is the difference between subjectivity and identity. Identity implies sameness, usually a sameness (an identity) between the individual and a collectivity. Identity also implies constancy in and through time. Even if we insist, as many do, on the possibility of a mobile or changing identity, we still must deal with the burden of sameness that is inherent in the term. Subjectivity, in this essay, engages precisely these two axes: the spatial axis between person and world, between the personal and the public, and the temporal one extending from the past into the present and future. In both cases, subjectivity inscribes the coordinates of these axes as moving points, in a dialogue of fluidity and mutual reformation.

In bringing together subjectivity and music, I want to inscribe as an important aspect of nineteenth-century cultural history the drive to take music seriously as a language of selfhood: a complicated discourse of reason and emotion to equally complicated subjectivities. In this vein, music should not be said simply to represent the self, the composer's or any other, but rather to *have* a self (or not to have one) and thereby to allegorize voice and subjectivity (or their lack). If the composer's voice does indeed speak in and through music, then we might assume that music serves as the necessary medium for the discovery of that voice, for the making of subjectivity. In this way "the composer's voice"—to use Edward T. Cone's seminal phrase—is a musical voice not only in a formal or stylistic sense but for its inscriptions of psychological, existential, and cultural attributes. For its contingency on time, music is a particularly rich medium for the representation of subjectivity. Like a voice, it is heard in time and undergoes change. Music allegorizes subjectivity. To Adorno's paradoxical claim that music narrates without narrative content ("daß Musik . . . ohne Erzähltes erzähle") one might propose that music inscribes a subjectivity contingent on temporality and therefore distinct from a subject or subject position: not only mobile but in motion.[2] The century of subjectivity is, not accidentally, also the century of music.

As subjectivity is formed and informed according to changing patterns of sociability, the cognitive and emotional contents and rhetorics of music are informed by social context. Nineteenth-century musical forms are highly sensitive to the social contexts of the bourgeois age, where the court and its institutions are supplanted by opera houses, concert halls, choral and chamber music societies, and semiprivate salons. If the symphony presents the public face of German burgherly culture, the Lied presents its private face—both socially and emotionally. And indeed where public institutions of music are open to all who can pay, the bourgeois salon becomes the one venue that requires a personal invitation.

Musical mediation between the home and the public sphere shows that these spheres are not discretely divided. Domesticity entails performance as well as protection. The home is a place of refuge and privacy but also of self-representation and performance. The drawing room is a box in the world theater, as Walter Benjamin wrote.[3] In this way, the domestic formation of subjectivity, musical and in general, takes place in a necessary dialectic between personal and public contexts. The drawing room's centerpiece is the piano, which becomes the mediating instrument between private and public music, between personal expression and public performance. This axis is not broken when the piano is moved to a public stage. The piano mediates persistently among the social contexts of music, as it does among the social contexts of subjectivity. This mediation also inhabits its music, as pianistic rhetoric controls—and knows that it controls—the spectrum from the most intimate to the most public. Literally, but also in a psychologically and rhetorically highly complicated manner, the piano represents home for nineteenth-century music. As the piano and its musical writing becomes the bridge between the domestic and the public, it can also become the site where the impossibility of such transition is inscribed: the musical site of domestic entrapment, of impediments to subjectivity, of the musical uncanny.

For literary as well as many cultural historians, the European world around 1800 is often called the romantic era, both in German and in other European contexts. Traditionally, romantic sensibility has been characterized by a stress on individuality, the discovery of emotion, and an emotional discovery of self and world. Romantic selfhood is traditionally discussed with reference to class, nation, and religion, all of which can appear overtly (Fichte's nationalism, Austen's understanding of class); in sublimated forms (Byron's nationalism, Coleridge's religiosity); or through displacement and substitution (nationalism and aestheticism for religion, bourgeois behavior for aristocratic privilege). More recently, the category of gender has been stressed, a category essential to my developing argument here.

In her recent book *Romanticism and Gender*, Anne K. Mellor has described the scholarship that has understood romanticism "as a commitment to imagination, vision, and transcendence" as "unwittingly gender-biased" in its understanding of what are, as Mellor argues, attributes of "masculine Romanticism."[4] This interpretive tradition (including the work of M. H. Abrams, Harold Bloom, and John Beer) has focused on the sextet of Wordsworth, Coleridge, Blake, Byron, Shelley, and Keats. (The leading German analogue would be Beethoven.) In turning to Jane Austen, Mary Shelley, and many other women, Mellor attempts to define a style of "feminine Romanticism," which she associates with a resistance to polarities (of ego and non-ego, thesis and antithesis, for example) in favor of a more negotiational discourse of "sympathy and likeness," "an ethic of care which insists on the primacy of the family or the community," and a determination to rational discourse that originates in but is not limited to the home.[5] Of course, the resistance to polarities necessarily informs Mellor's own argumentative structure, and she therefore does not insist that feminine romanticism must issue from women's voices alone: "Any writer, male or female, could occupy the 'masculine' or 'feminine' ideological or subject position."[6] But, one might add, not so easily. Such a choice must itself be seen against a variety of cultural and ideological contexts that at the very least inform and more often penalize this very claim to gender fluidity in the making of subjectivity. We shall see how this works in the context of Biedermeier music.

In Germany, the enormous effects of the French Revolution and the Napoleonic sweep are tempered by a strong element of social and cultural continuity. The formation of a civic-minded, self-educated merchant middle class, the *Bürgertum*, is an arduous and small-scaled process that begins with the general reconstruction after the Thirty Years' War and begins to solidify with signals of cooperation between commerce and culture. That confluence, including a strong impulse of religious toleration across Catholic, Protestant, and Jewish boundaries, provides the energy and logic of the German Enlightenment.

In 1815 the Napoleonic era collapsed in Germany as well as elsewhere, and a generation of restoration and reaction was ushered in. Historians have had cause to judge the period harshly. At the end of his life and in the shadow of the Second World War, the great Prussian historian Friedrich Meinecke suggested that modern German history might be understood according to three tragic turning points: 1933, for the most obvious reason of the Nazi accession; 1866, for Bismarck's arrogation of power and reliance on Prussian militarism; and 1819, for the failure of the Prussian constitutional movement, the end of the period of reform, the initiation of what Meinecke called power without culture, and the inauguration, with the firing of Wilhelm von Humboldt and Metternich's Carlsbad Decrees, of a repressive and censorious politics that defined the period until 1848.[7] In this context, there is, undoubtedly, safety in music.

With similar logic, the so-called Biedermeier period (1815 or 1819 to 1848) is normally characterized in terms of the shrinking of the public sphere and the withdrawal of bourgeois life from politics into spheres of domesticity, privacy, and the cultivation of emotion: culture without power. "Biedermeier" is itself a pejorative term, coined by the Munich satirical rag *Die fliegende Blätter* in the mid-1840s with the claim—more relieved than triumphant—that this period was passing. The period's overwhelming cultural hero has remained Johann Wolfgang Goethe, who is lionized not only as a literary giant or an intellectual Renaissance man or a civil servant but for his integration of these personas into a model of personality formation that transcends the passage from *Aufklärung* to *Biedermeier*.

The Goethe industry perpetuates the model of personality formation according to the ideology of *Bildung*, or aesthetic education. And the continued normative presence of *Bildung* shrinks Biedermeier culture unfairly to a culture of sensibility. Biedermeier cultural style, Biedermeier *Bürgerlichkeit*, has a real politics and retains a commitment to a public sphere: a politics and a commitment that exist independently of and, to a degree, in opposition to the dominant Metternichian and generally antiliberal politics of the time. This is a deliberate politics of a limited scale—not imperial or national but civic politics, and a politics of selfhood, citizenship, and cultural context. I am not referring here to the model of *Bildung*, because at stake is not an aesthetic education, although art and aesthetics certainly play a role. The context is largely North German, Protestant, urban culture, and I would propose to characterize it according to the anachronistic category of *civic humanism*.[8]

Social and political historians of eighteenth- and nineteenth-century Germany have recently analyzed this context in terms of the category *civil society* (*bürgerliche Gesellschaft*), a dimension of social and political life that contemporary scholars, unlike their predecessors, see as autonomous from the structure and authority of the state. I accept this formulation, but as a cultural historian I am interested in bringing to it an angle of subjectivity and the construction of meaning. For this reason I am proposing that the term *civic humanism* may give existential focus to the important category of civil society.

Civic life relates to the self-perceptions of cities, and German cities in the Biedermeier period have varying profiles. Politically, they range from the free cities, autonomous republics, of Frankfurt, Hamburg, Bremen, and Lübeck to the Habsburg cities, including Vienna, which lay completely under imperial authority. Prussian cities, most importantly Berlin, answered to the state according to Baron Stein's *Städteordnung* of 1808. The history of nineteenth-century Berlin can be written according to this tension between the civic and the imperial, with the cosmic taking the lead after 1871 as civic consciousness gives way to the architectural and political self-representation as imperial capital. In Saxony, we can see a symmetrical divide between the court city of Dresden and the commercial, industrial city of Leipzig—a duality somewhat evocative of that between Washington and New York. As a textile and publishing center, Leipzig controlled manufacture (its city center had numerous mills) and trade, which was focused around the house of textiles, the Gewandhaus. Leipzig's growing industrial base generated an expanding economic elite that bridged class boundaries. Leipzig's culture of Biedermeier civic humanism can be mapped according to a network of devotion, art, and commerce.

The cultural map does change after 1848, if more slowly and less perceptibly than a revolutionary upheaval might suggest. As the category of political debate becomes the national rather than the local or the civic, national identity becomes the model for personal identity. Personal ideology, as George Mosse has argued in his recent books, accrues the burdens of respectability, solidity, constancy, and—not to be underestimated—masculinity.[9] Where identity is the norm, subjectivity becomes, after 1848, a mode of self-formation in deliberate resistance to the dominant norms of collective, national identity.

The censorious aura of German politics before 1848 contributes to the censorious aura of German personality formation after 1848. Thus, domesticity can turn on itself rather than lead into the open, into the public sphere. Domesticity that turns on itself acquires the pathology of the unhomely, the *unheimlich*, the uncanny—a category that will shape my treatment of Robert Schumann as it will not need to shape my discussion of Mendelssohn. Gender and domestic ideology open the uncanny dimension of German bourgeois culture, the unhomely aspects of private and public spheres that undermine the growth of that kind of subjectivity, like Mendelssohn's, able to move fluidly between the domestic and the public, the personal and the political.

Felix Mendelssohn and Robert Schumann are the musical giants of Biedermeier Leipzig. They are in an important sense of the same generation, representing a North German musical aesthetic grounded in Bach and the city of Leipzig, with which both, like Bach, had a close association. Between 1835, the year Mendelssohn arrived in Leipzig as director of the Gewandhaus Concerts, until Mendelssohn's death in 1847, they were friends and colleagues. After Mendelssohn's death Schumann strove until the end of his functioning life in 1854 to guard Mendelssohn's memory and the Leipzig aesthetic against the opinions of Liszt and Wagner, among others. The late nineteenth-century German musical pantheon placed both Schumann and Mendelssohn in second rank, in an intermezzo between the heroic discourses of Beethoven and Wagner. In music as in politics, the civic has been hard-pressed to compete with the cosmic, as the republican has been to compete with the imperial.

The Gewandhaus instantiates the triangle of music, commerce, and religious and civic devotion. When the new textile guild hall was inaugurated in 1781, a wing was dedicated to a concert hall and to the continuing patronage of the orchestra that had been founded in 1743 with the backing of eight merchants and eight noblemen. (Each had subsidized one musician to make an ensemble of sixteen.) The spatial organization of the hall's interior reveals the visual and cultural symbolism of North German musical experience. The cultural prototype for the concert hall of the first Gewandhaus is not a theater but rather a church: specifically, a choir. The listeners sit facing each other exactly as in the choir of the Thomaskirche. While listening to music, their visual referent is the community, not the music or its performance aspect. Above the musicians, the Gewandhaus motto is carved into the balustrade: RES SEVERA VERUM GAUDIUM ("True joy is a serious matter"). Seneca's phrase appears on the frontispiece of a locally published hymnal in 1783, and it has served as the Gewandhaus motto ever since. Aesthetic pleasure, it holds, is legitimized through internalization, meditation, and hence compatibility with devotion. Art does not supplant religion; art follows religion's rules. Music's mediation between subjectivity and community was a paradigm central to the Mendelssohn household and to Felix's upbringing. From 1835 until his death in 1847, he felt at home in Leipzig, as he did not in Berlin, where he was appointed general music director to the court of Frederick William IV in 1842.

The juxtaposition of Mendelssohn and Schumann has been dictated, not without reason, by the commonsense assertion that they were entirely different personalities. But it is not as easy to make the assertion precise. The first danger is the repetition of discredited clichés: Mendelssohn was pampered, carefree, superficial. This die was cast by Richard Wagner in "Das Judentum in der Musik," published pseudonymously in 1850 in the *Neue Zeitschrift für Musik*, the journal that had previously belonged to Schumann. Recovery has been uneasy. Wagner's position has been echoed often, most interestingly perhaps by Ludwig Wittgenstein, who reveals in the notes collected as *Culture and Value* what must be called a Mendelssohn obsession. Like Wagner, he is afraid of his sympathy; unlike Wagner, he is honest about it: "Tragedy is something un-Jewish. Mendelssohn is, I suppose, the most untragic of composers. . . . Mendelssohn is like a man who is only jolly when the people he is with are all jolly anyway, or like one who is only good when he is surrounded by good men; he does

not have the integrity of a tree which stands firmly in its place whatever may be going on around it. I too am like that and am attracted to
being so."[10] The second danger concerns Schumann and can be
called a diagnostic fallacy: Schumann faced repeated depression and
succumbed to mental illness; despair must therefore explain the music. This Schumann paradigm remains dominant as the Mendelssohn
paradigm does not. Both approaches look to a creative corpus to reaffirm trite assumptions about a life.

Personality and musical personality are formed in culture. I argue
here that with remarkable difference from the case of Mendelssohn,
Schumann does not seem to develop a coherent subjective voice that is
allegorized in music. Specifically, intimacy and privacy are split off
from the public and rhetorical. This seems especially true for the
years of the mature, mutual productivity from 1840 to 1847. Mendelssohn's music allegorizes a subjectivity that moves coherently between the private and the public, the intimate and the rhetorical,
whereas Schumann's does not. My argument seeks to make three
points.

First, Biedermeier culture provides potentialities for the formation
and representation of subjectivity, of negotiation and fluidity between
selfhood and world; between private life and public life; between femininity (usually associated with the private and domestic) and masculinity (usually associated with the public): Mendelssohn. Such po-
tentiality can be undermined by a foretaste of bourgeois essentialism
and rigidity: Schumann. As bourgeois rigidity and retrenchment advance, postures of the bourgeois-as-hero delegitimate, prospectively
and retrospectively, this Mendelssohnian subjectivity: Wagner.

Second, music is a prime discourse in this process—constitutive of
the new subjectivity rather than merely reflective of it. The subjectivities of composers form only one aspect of the issue in its relation to
musical culture in general. The perceptions of listeners and audiences constitute an enormous field into which this line of questioning
might be extended. Musical subjectivity is of special eminence in the
Biedermeier period—the generation between Beethoven and Wagner, between a legacy of revolutionary heroic discourse and a future
of nationalist mythification.

And third, in the comparison and juxtaposition of Mendelssohn
and Schumann, we have two different sides of subjectivity in music:
coherent versus fragmented subjectivity, in the first case an ability to
build a fluid ego between the poles of private and public, Jewish and
Gentile, masculine and feminine; in the second case a cultural and

psychological defeat to the pressures of an emerging, essentializing ideology of identity.

Mendelssohn; or, Subjectivity

Mendelssohn's subjectivity emerges as a successful negotiation between the Biedermeier coordinates of domestic and public life. To this spectrum we must add two more: that between feminine and masculine roles within and outside the home, and that between Jewish and Gentile culture. These three axes share a common center in the question of gender.

The person, career, and music of Felix Mendelssohn carry central significance for the discussion of gender in the nineteenth century. The importance of gender lies in its dual meaning, its dual aspect, as it forms and informs cultural experience. First, and in an irreducible way, gender has to do with the social roles of men and women and with the restrictions on the lives, minds, and careers of women. The talents, shared educations, and divergent careers of Fanny and Felix Mendelssohn provide one of modern history's most cogent experiences of gendered cultural and social difference. In their world, talent is recognized in men and women alike, but only men's lives are public lives. This leads us to gender's second aspect: the symbolic coding of culture along a spectrum of femininity and masculinity. Here, femininity is associated with dialogue, delicateness, interiority, and nurturing; masculinity with assertion, achievement, exteriority, and creation.

Within his professional circles and his family, Felix was a fairly typical male, conquering the world for a good and enlightened cause, respecting the talent of women, that of his sister above all, but inheriting his father's mantle of restriction on the public manifestation of women's talent. Yet the musical culture he absorbed from his family was transmitted through the work and talent of important women, especially his great aunt, Sara Levy, as well as his older sister. In the Berlin of Felix's and Fanny's youth, the Mendelssohn family stood famously at the vanguard of cultural negotiation between Judaism and Lutheranism, between piety and secularization, and between commerce and art. In the lives of its patriarchs, this negotiation was conducted in philosophy and commerce. In the lives of its matriarchs, especially Sara Levy, it was conducted in music. Philosophy and commerce brought the family into the world; music invited the world into the household. Music in the family sphere meant the promise of cultural dialogue. Felix and Fanny were educated musically in and for the household; when Felix exercised his male priority to take his music into the public sphere—an option denied to Fanny—he translated a domestic and in a specific sense female discourse into a public and male one. The public sphere involved travel, and the voyage is a metaphor as well as a literal producer of self-discovery for both Felix and Fanny. Yet in his public and international persona, Felix reproduced musically his family's culture of negotiation and dialogue through music, eschewing a musical discourse of heroism and assertion in favor of one of enlightened conversation. This tendency could be read, and did indeed come to be read, as a feminine trait by a nineteenth-century culture increasingly worried about masculinity as the key to nation building (Wagner). Thus in the larger, and largely posthumous, world of musical culture, Mendelssohn has been lumped along with Schubert as an allegedly feminine musical voice: unheroic, unassertive, and hence derivative, compromising, and ultimately unoriginal. The so-called "Mendelssohn problem," as we know, originates with Wagner and stands at the source of a powerful trope in which Jewishness, femininity, and the inability to create become shared indicators of cultural weakness, danger, and pollution. Subjectively, there is no Mendelssohn problem, just as there is no Jewish problem.

The "Mendelssohn problem" in its phantasmagoric persistence cannot productively be diffused by a defense of the "greatness" of Felix's music. Greatness is a claim foreign to the music, as it is foreign to that of his role model, J. S. Bach. But profundity *is* in question, for Mendelssohn has been dismissed as superficial, an accusation unthinkable in the case of Bach. In this respect it can be argued that Mendelssohn's profundity, like Bach's, lies in the music's self-fashioning as a carrier of cultural formation. And the roots of that music are found in the Mendelssohn family's inhabitations of culture, gender, and music.

The modernity, difficulty, and subjective allegory in Mendelssohn's music are not easy to discover after a century of the Wagnerian aesthetic. The Wagnerian aesthetic has taught our ears to listen for absolutes—for mythical representation through music or for "absolute music" in the nonrepresentational sense. I would suggest that Mendelssohn wrote a different kind of music, a music in which his personal subjectivity, his subtle sense of cultural affiliation, and his sensitivity to the historical moment all play a role. This is a music of cultural negotiation, cultural dialogue. Not only Wagner but also the reigning formalist aesthetic in professional musicology asks us not to listen in this way. The grace that the post-Wagnerian ear hears in Mendelssohn is not a mark of ease but one of dialogical subtlety—a property not found in Schumann and systematically suppressed in Wagner.

In order to understand the development and the vocabulary of this Mendelssohnian aesthetic, we must look to its sources in Bach—specifically, in Mendelssohn's intricate and multifaceted reception of Bach as musical and cultural model. We know that J. S. Bach is fundamental to Mendelssohn's musical as well as spiritual development. I would suggest that their dialogue forms an aesthetic discourse in which modernity and subjectivity are produced. I would add here that these two categories are interrelated; for now, I will define modernity as a sense of life that holds that self and world are ever formed and re-formed in an ongoing, moving dialogue. My argument will proceed by highlighting several musical and biographical milestones in Mendelssohn's career, citing along the way recent work by scholars in music history, cultural history, and philosophical aesthetics.

.

The young Mendelssohn wrote home from Paris in April 1825: "You also write me that I should set myself up as an evangelist and instruct Onslow and Reicha . . . how to love Sebastian Bach. I'm already doing that, as far as it goes. But just think, dear child, that the people here take Sebastian Bach to be a powdered wig properly stuffed with learning."[11] As so often with Mendelssohn, a seemingly precious gesture carries analytical riches. The comment reveals at least three things: that the young composer had long integrated an important and unusual esteem for Bach; that he learned this taste from within his family; and, most significantly, that Bach was, for him, not a relic or an ancestor, but a modern composer.

What Arnold Schoenberg did for Brahms in his essay "Brahms the Progressive" we must do for Mendelssohn, and we can do it by recognizing what Mendelssohn did for Bach. In other words, each generation has recognized an element of hidden modernism in a preceding master whom contemporary taste wrongly considers old-fashioned. To put the issue another way, did Mendelssohn prefigure the view of Bach that Theodor Adorno would elaborate, a century later, in the celebrated essay "Bach Defended against His Devotees"? In this well-known essay of 1956, Adorno addresses a polemic against two ideolo-

gies of authenticity: musical antiquarianism, which he calls historicism; and existentialism, by which he means the ideology of cultural
authenticity he later attacked in his book on Heidegger. Musicology,
he argues, has transformed Bach from a dynamic explorer of musical
modernity to a neutralized cultural monument, a final survivor of the
static and secure middle ages. What is neutralized in the process is
Bach's own subjectivity, and this is the principle that connects musical
antiquarianism with existential ideology. The dismissal of subjectivity
transforms life into Being. In Adorno's formulation, "To sacrifice the
subject in such works, to hear in them nothing but the Order of Being
and not the nostalgic echo that the decline of such an order finds in
the mind, is to grasp only the *caput mortuum*. The phantasma of Bach's
ontology arises through an act of force mechanically performed by
the Philistines, whose sole desire is to neutralize art since they lack the
capacity to comprehend it."[12] Bach's modernity, for Adorno, is found
in the fugue, in counterpoint and polyphony, and in the "duality of
mind" revealed by basso continuo harmony. The art of the fugue is an
"art of dissection; one could almost say, of dissolving Being, posited as
the theme, and hence incompatible with the common belief that this
Being maintains itself static and unchanged throughout the fugue."[13]
But he goes farther, to an interpretation of the cultural meaning of
Bach's modernity, and that is to the interpretation of Bach's musical
voice as that of the emancipated subject, "for only it can conceive music as the emphatic promise of objective salvation."[14]

The musical ego as the emancipated subject is a trope fundamental
to nineteenth-century German musical aesthetics. It is the tradition
that Carl Dahlhaus, to a great extent in the shadow of Adorno, analyzed in his book *The Idea of Absolute Music*. But Adorno parts from
tradition in his use of the trope. Dahlhaus shows how the idea of absolute music became, in fact, an ideology of absolute music in which the
autonomous musical ego in fact came to signify the German national
spirit. For Adorno, the trope of the emancipated subject, musical or
otherwise, emerges from and strives to recuperate the subjectivity of
the Jewish *Bildungsbürgertum*. Bach defended against his devotees
means music and spirit defended from German nationalism. Adorno's
valuation of Arnold Schoenberg carries the same task.

When we look at Felix Mendelssohn's sensibility, we must alter significantly our own sense of historical context to a prenationalist period in which the Jewish *Bildungsbürgertum* was in its cultural prime.
For Mendelssohn, subjective autonomy and an ideal of community
were fully compatible in a way that became impossible after the mid–

nineteenth century. Mendelssohn heard in Bach the same spirit of subjective modernity that German musical aesthetics from Wagner through Pfitzner would fail to recognize and that Adorno recovered. At the same time, he combined that principle of subjective modernity with an ideal of community that would in turn connect the private and female family tradition that had nurtured his love and knowledge of Bach with an overall cultural ideal. Thus, in hearing in Bach a straightforward rhetoric of individual emancipation, Adorno over-modernizes Bach's music and intentions.

Mendelssohn's youthful musical aesthetic grew from a dual context of family life and community. His youthful initiation into the North German Bach tradition, as the historian John Toews has recently written, "was nurtured almost in cult-like fashion" at home and within the Singakademie led by his composition teacher, Carl Friedrich Zelter.[15] As a Christmas present in 1823 he received a score of the *St. Matthew Passion*—a rare collector's item at the time, as Toews points out—from his maternal grandmother, Babette Salomon, née Itzig. Babette and even more her sister Sara Levy, a patron of Bach's son Wilhelm Friedemann, were responsible for the transmission of the Bach tradition in the Mendelssohn family. (Through her collection of scores and her patronage of composers, Sara Levy was instrumental in the creation of musical taste in late eighteenth-century Berlin, and her library formed the initial archive of the Singakademie.[16]) Outside the home, Zelter's Singakademie provided not only a model for music making but a model for community building through the collective pursuit of music, specifically of choral singing. The chorale was the musical form that both symbolized and actually enacted the creation of a community through music.

But how was this community defined—as one of art, one of faith, or one of politics? In a recent article, John Toews has argued for the slow accumulation of all three characteristics in Felix's generation. The Mendelssohn circle included at its core Felix and Fanny, the singer and actor Eduard Devrient, the family's classical language tutor, Johann Gustav Droysen, and the music critic A. B. Marx. For them, J. S. Bach provided not a model of musical and formal complexity but rather a font of spirituality and emotional expression. When, in 1827, in this company, Mendelssohn began to rehearse portions of the *St. Matthew Passion*, he did so against the will of his teacher, Zelter, who had doubts about the music's performability. The Mendelssohn circle strove to unite the aesthetic and confessional legacies of Bach into a newly formed and newly potent ethical community. Formally, the chorale was the vehicle of this community making. As Toews writes:

> Bach's arrangements of the chorales were imagined as an emancipation of the salvational process from the specific confines of traditional confessional liturgies. The art work universalized the particular confessional form, transforming the church congregation into a more inclusive cultural community. Although the *St. Matthew Passion* was performed in a neo-classical temple of art by lay musicians at a benefit concert for a ticket-holding, paying audience, both Fanny and Felix thought that the music had transformed the attenders of a secular concert into participants in a sacred service.[17]

In a letter to Franz Hauser in 1830, Mendelssohn wrote of the 1829 *St. Matthew Passion*: "Sie sangen mit einer Andacht, also ob sie in der Kirche waren"("They sang with a devotion, as if they were in church"). The community of North German music and its pious context clearly posited a countermodel to the French-Italian tradition represented in the 1820s by Rossini.[18]

The sacred musical community, secularized in its indication of a cultural rather than a religious identity, is represented musically by the chorale. Certainly, the chorale is a form that Mendelssohn borrowed from Bach with deep recognition of its historical and communitarian symbolism. But where, then, is Adorno's Bach, the Bach of musical modernism? Or, to put the question differently: alongside the chorale, what are we to make of the fugue, as well as of other musical indications of movement and counterpoint? Is the fugue a musical metaphor for modernism, movement, and the recognition of temporality? In a more general sense, my question can be posed as follows. If we agree that Mendelssohn absorbed the German Bach tradition not so much as a way of returning to past traditions but as a way of defining a new cultural identity in music, then to what extent can we argue that this birth of cultural identity through the spirit of music was in fact a modern discourse: an inscription of a modern subjectivity that exists in movement and constant self-reformation?

For clues to this side of Mendelssohn and his Bach reception, we can turn to some recent scholarship on the 1829 performance of the *St. Matthew Passion*. In a recent essay, Bach scholar Michael Marissen has reconstructed and interpreted Mendelssohn's performance version of the *St. Matthew Passion*, speculating on both the meaning of Mendelssohn's choice of this work and the reasoning behind the substantial excisions he made in its performance. We might recall that the

year 1829 was the centennial of the work's premiere, but it was also
the centennial of the birth of Moses Mendelssohn.

Marissen begins with an obvious but neglected question: why the *St.
Matthew Passion?* He suggests that no aesthetic criterion presents itself
that would clearly distinguish this work from other great Bach choral
works but that religious and cultural criteria do become evident. The
St. Matthew Passion tells a story of a universal community and religion.
Rather than focus on the culpability of the Jews in the trial and cruci-
fixion of Christ, it focuses, in Marissen's words, "much more on Christ
as 'suffering servant,' one who is guiltless and whose death is brought
on by the guilt of *all.*"[19] The tone is set in the opening chorus, the
E-minor lament and procession toward death, which Marissen describes splendidly as a "musical equivalent of a *Trauerspiel.*" The inscription of a universal community is achieved through reference to
Zion, understood both as the Christian Church and as the people of
Israel.

Marissen also investigates Mendelssohn's performance version of
the *St. Matthew.* Why did he cut all the arias, except "Erbarme dich,"
as well as six chorales and some recitatives (in the arrest and trial
scene)? There is some evidence from Eduard Devrient, who reports
that the work had to be shortened and that it was unthinkable to perform the entire work, which "showed so many signs of the tastes of its
times." Marissen argues that Mendelssohn's reading of Schleiermacher is evident in the reshaping of the work, with its stress on the
congregation rather than the religious experience of the individual.
Through a thorough analysis of the cuts, which I will not rehearse
here, Marissen arrives at a view of Mendelssohn's *St. Matthew Passion*
as an aesthetic expression of open community. We can speculate further that the excision of arias favors the presentation of a collectivity,
and thus an implicit rejection of the theatricality of the so-called
French and Italian tradition.

By 1829 and the revival of the *St. Matthew Passion,* the Bach-
Mendelssohn dialogue has produced an ongoing dialectic of community and modern temporality in the young composer's music. A third
element is added to this constellation, and that is the mature Mendelssohn's sense of musical allegory. When Mendelssohn leaves choral
music and its communitarian symbolism, he turns to the orchestra
with a musical discourse of nonrepresentation, allegory, and the inscription of an open, time-bound subjectivity.

The nineteenth-century antipathy to Mendelssohn was set by Wagner, but it was initiated by Adolph Bernhard Marx, the theorist from
whom Mendelssohn developed early ideas of programmatic music,

friend turned foe, who finally described Mendelssohn as a talent but no genius.[20] In a friendlier time, Marx shared in the paternity of the overture to *A Midsummer Night's Dream*, composed in 1826, during the peak years of their friendship, which lasted until 1830. Why did Marx turn against Mendelssohn—or, rather, why did Mendelssohn turn away from Marx and his aesthetic of musical allegory?

The "Reformation" Symphony is the watershed work for this problem. It presents a programmatic allegory of Reformation—that is clear, but its paradoxical quality lies in its reminiscence, in Judith Ballan's analysis, "of the so-called 'Palestrina school,' that musicians of Mendelssohn's time commonly associated with Catholicism."[21] For example, A.F.J. Thibaut, in his widely read treatise *Über Reinheit der Tonkunst* (1825), urged Protestant composers to adopt the Catholic aesthetic of Palestrina and Lotti.[22] In following Marx's charge, Mendelssohn gives us a Catholic-style musical allegory of a Protestant event.

Thibaut was a professor of jurisprudence—Schumann's law professor, in fact—in Heidelberg. Purity in music, as his translator suggests, meant for Thibaut not technical but moral purity, with church music the moral model for musical expression.[23] A Lutheran, Thibaut mourned the loss of musical inspiration that the Lutheran church allowed, despite the fabled devotion to chorale singing of Martin Luther himself. Sectarianism, he argued, had caused the dissipation of Catholic musical integrity, and because Luther had himself argued for the retention of Catholic music, that music should now be recovered for the Lutheran church.[24] Thibaut's agenda was to rescue the oratorio style from the clutches of the operatic and to return it to the church style: these were his three categories. It was this authentic church music, he argued, that Mozart went to the Sistine Chapel during Holy Week "for the purpose of purloining." Music, he concluded, is a gift from God, and "the divinity of music is only revealed when it transports us into an ideal state of being."[25]

Thibaut deified Handel, but for his parity with Palestrina and hence with an appreciation of his music for its devotional rigidity. Such an aesthetic did not long please or serve Mendelssohn. In this context we can invoke another milestone of 1842. This is the initiation of Mendelssohn's association with the *Berliner Domchor* within the responsibility of his position as general music director to the court of Frederick William IV. The association proved unhappy, largely because of a controversy between Mendelssohn and the clergy over the difference between *geistliche Musik* and *kirchliche Musik*.[26] This distinction and the resulting conflict duplicates that between Mendelssohnian musical allegory and the Catholicizing allegory of A.B. Marx, and the line from Palestrina to Pfitzner.

.

How, then, do we characterize Mendelssohnian allegory? I would suggest that the "Scottish" Symphony, premiered in 1842, ten years after the premiere of the "Reformation" Symphony, reveals a transformation of the Mendelssohnian practice of musical allegory, toward a Jewish-Protestant allegory, away from Marx and toward Bach. What we have in the "Scottish" Symphony, a long way from the "Reformation" Symphony, delivers a complicated discourse of musical allegory, in which subjective specificity communicates with the world without controlling, delimiting, and closing its gestures of signification.

I would suggest an allegorical way of hearing the *Allegro maestoso* in the final movement of the "Scottish" Symphony. First, I need to spend a moment on one of the most celebrated of Mendelssohn's works, and celebrated not only by musicians. The *Hebrides* Overture of 1829–32, always popular, is the subject of a recent essay by the philosopher Jerrold Levinson called "Hope in the *Hebrides*."[27] Levinson argues against Hanslick and holds, first, that music can express emotions, and second, that the *Hebrides* Overture expresses hope. Though Levinson does not deny the music's implied program, he chooses to analyze it as "absolute music." To this end he quotes Hans Keller's observation that "all the sea-gulls and salt-fish in the Hebrides did not prevent Mendelssohn from designing a complex sonata structure such as many a fanatically 'absolute' musician would have been proud of; if the sea-gulls helped, so much the better."[28] Levinson concentrates on the overture's celebrated second theme, which Donald Tovey described as "quite the greatest melody Mendelssohn ever wrote." It is stated first in mm. 47–56 by the bassoons and cellos, repeated in mm. 57–66 by the violins. For Levinson, the passage's expression of hope is carried by its upward and forward movement, and hope accompanies aspiration and "a little touch of faith as well."[29] Finally, Levinson argues that this expression of hope is unique, for other examples of positive emotion in Mendelssohn do not express hope: the first movement of the Octet is "too febrile, too controlled, too contextless"; the opening theme of the "Italian" Symphony "contains no element of straining," and so forth.[30]

I should say that I am quite sympathetic to Levinson's hearing—to his hermeneutic—of the *Hebrides*, but that as a cultural historian and not a philosopher I am interested in specifics rather than universals, allegories rather than symbols. Does this work carry the representation of a personal, compositional voice, and does that living voice express a certain emotional quality that may in fact include hope? Is it the hope of a particular cultural moment and personal constitution? I am interested in the articulation of a musical discourse that is neither programmatic—that is, allegorical in the conventional sense—nor universal, either as musical structure or as expression of an emotion. Rather, it is allegorical in a modernist way. The *Hebrides* Overture is a conception of the summer of 1829. Although its occasion is certainly a Scottish journey, its mood carries Mendelssohn's emotional and discursive vibrancy in the direct aftermath of the *St. Matthew Passion* in Berlin. The same mood inhabits the "Scottish" Symphony. The metaphor of Scotland clearly spoke to the composer's inner depths, matching a complicated but resolute subjectivity to a decisive musical rhetoric.

I would guess that, rather than rocks and fish, Scotland signified Protestant culture and enlightenment. But, one may object, this is a *Hebrides* Overture, not an *Edinburgh* Overture. It speaks of the exotic and the liberating, not of the historical and the rational. But this is precisely the point. For Mendelssohn and his cultural sensibility, personal subjectivity and freedom are contingent on history and the moral as well as aesthetic accomplishments of the past. Felix's voyage to the Hebrides, both in fact and in music, is a product of the lives and work of J. S. Bach and Moses Mendelssohn. For Felix Mendelssohn as for others of his generation, the romantic exotic is grounded in history and speaks to the formation of personality. In this duality, romantic travel literature is the precursor of later nineteenth-century anthropology.

The music that bears reference to Scotland exudes a rhetoric of subjectivity and not identity, as it is a rhetoric of motion. The unique contours of the great melody, mm. 47–66, articulate motion, striving, and hope, but they most explicitly articulate openness. The melody does not resolve; nor does it lead at any point, including its final recapitulation, to resolution or closure. Here we have what is to my ear Mendelssohn's most modernist moment: a musical inscription of what Baudelaire would define in 1859 as the principle of modernity: "the transitory, the fleeting, and the contingent: one half of art, of which the other is the absolute and the immutable." That Mendelssohn inscribed this attitude just after his performance of the *St. Matthew Passion*, in the year 1829 with its double commemoration of Bach and Moses Mendelssohn, is, to my mind, highly significant.

What we have in the *Allegro maestoso* of the "Scottish" Symphony seems to me to combine the *Hebrides* with the communitarian aspects of the Bach legacy. I would suggest that this theme, which *does* lead directly to the symphony's resolution, combines striving and openness with resolution and closure, the closure of the community-building chorale. The symphony has taken us on an exotic journey represented in sound and rhythm. The exotic thrives in the momentary suspension of the ego, as new landscapes are discovered. In the finale, however, the ego reasserts itself, absorbing the exotic into the moral postures developed at home. The seagulls have no place here at all, except perhaps in memory, as the musical line transports composer and listener alike back to the Gewandhaus and the Thomaskirche.

.

The diatribe in Wagner's "Das Judentum in der Musik" is most obviously aimed at Mendelssohn (as well as Meyerbeer), but it is also dismissive of Bach. Mendelssohn, Wagner writes, was attracted to Bach because his music is formal, unlike Beethoven's, which is human. Against this view, we can argue that, together with Bach, Mendelssohn instantiated what a Wagnerian century was unable to hear, a view expressed by Adorno: "Justice is done [to] Bach not through musicological usurpation but solely through the most advanced composition which in turn converges with the level of Bach's continually unfolding work."[31] For Mendelssohn, this imperative meant a musical discourse of cultural dialogue, conducted across contemporaneous divides (Judaism and Protestantism) and across temporal divides, such as that between the *Bachzeit* and Mendelssohn's own period, historically conscious and culturally reponsible.

Schumann; or, Homelessness

Mendelssohn's life and music threaten the ideology of personhood that concretized and calcified in Germany after 1848 and even more so after 1871. Bourgeois identity and respectability, and masculine propriety and control were clearly concerns for Schumann in ways they do not seem to have been for Mendelssohn. Although these ideological burdens do not banish clinical considerations from Schumann's biography, they form a powerful example of how identity becomes self-stereotyping, drives out subjectivity, and crushes the ego. Identity is the ideology of the spiritually homeless.

Music was one side of the Mendelssohn family's passage from private to public sphere. In the case of Schumann, music had no place in the family home, and the decision to make music a profession was a rebuke to the family, specifically to Schumann's mother. Schumann's almost lifelong attachment to his mother carried perforce a subjection to a certain *Kleinbürgerlichkeit*, a petit-bourgeois attitude, paradoxically a generation ahead of its time as a culturally dominant mentality. It was certainly a measure of Schumann's anxiety. In choosing music, Schumann also chose solitude. *Bildung*, for Schumann, had little to do with a *Bürgertum*. It was, rather, an escape from it. Reading is solitary, and listening follows reading's lead. That solitude was transformed by Clara Wieck, a musical presence as fundamental to Schumann as Fanny was to Felix Mendelssohn. Paradoxically, although Schumann was insecure in his own masculinity in a way that Mendelssohn was not, and although Schumann showed sporadic signs of jealousy with regard to Clara that Felix did not with regard to Fanny, Robert and Clara Schumann engaged European music as partners and equals, an option neither Felix nor Fanny ever considered.

As late as 1838, Robert Schumann looked on Mendelssohn's musical precocity with some resentment as a perk of family luxury and the musical education it had bestowed.[32] As their friendship solidified from late 1835 on, the resentment disengaged from the person, and it never questioned the music. Like Berlioz, Schumann the music critic thought Mendelssohn a supreme compositional talent.

Schumann first chose law, not music, for a profession. He was a law student in Leipzig in 1828–29 and in Heidelberg in 1829–30. At Heidelberg he was taught by Thibaut, professor of law and the author, as we have seen, of *Über Reinheit der Tonkunst* (1825). In October 1830 Schumann gave himself up to music and returned to Leipzig to study and live with Friedrich Wieck.

On his 1829 arrival in Heidelberg, Schumann recorded a humorous remark that carries resonance for ongoing questions of music and cultural ideology: "My lodgings face the asylum on the right and the Catholic church on the left, so that I'm really in doubt whether one is supposed to go crazy or become Catholic."[33] Whether Thibaut and his views played an important role in this configuration is unclear, but Schumann reveals here an unmistakable sensitivity to the cultural ramifications of the Protestant- Catholic, north-south distinction that continued to inform nineteenth-century musical aesthetics and taste. The issue of Catholicism remains a consistent, overdetermined cultural category for its association with theatricality against the Protestant insistence on inwardness. This opposition later pitted Schumann as guardian of the North German Bach-Mendelssohn tradition against Liszt and Wagner and their theatrical styles.

This tendency is revealed in Schumann's programmatic article

"Fragmente aus Leipzig," published in 1837 in his *Neue Zeitschrift für Musik*. Here he opposed Meyerbeer's *Les Huguenots*, which made him "weary and faint with anger," to Mendelssohn's oratorio *St. Paul*.[34] This identification with the Leipzig-Mendelssohnian aesthetic intensified, especially after Mendelssohn's death in November 1847. At the end of his active career, his installation in Düsseldorf in 1850 left him highly conscious of his Protestant status in the Catholic Rhineland; in this context Schumann planned a gigantic oratorio on the life of Martin Luther, a project he mused over for two years but without result.[35]

The loyalty to Mendelssohn's legacy provoked a skirmish with Lizst and discomfort with Wagner. Liszt was the guest of honor at the Schumann home in Dresden in 1848. Wagner was among the guests. On hearing Schumann's piano quintet, Liszt irritated his host by calling it too "Leipzig-like," a veiled slur against Mendelssohn that also activated the cultural divide between the Catholic-theatrical and the North German introverted aesthetics. Later in the evening Liszt spoke highly of Meyerbeer at Mendelssohn's expense, upon which Schumann told him to shut up and then stormed out of the room.[36] (On such occasions, we might speculate, the young Wagner may have learned how and why to straddle the two aesthetics.)

Musical inwardness travels with the sonic language of the piano. The piano moves on ambiguous terrain between privacy, domesticity, and performance. On one extreme is Liszt. In the middle is the discourse of the piano concerto, where a soloist converses with a more public collectivity in an elaborate metaphor of passage between the private and the public. At its most socially withdrawn is the style of "esoteric" music, the term recently and aptly used by Gerhard Dietel to describe Schumann's music for solo piano.[37] Schumann's pianistic voice not only releases an esoteric language but invokes that realm of secrecy, security, and terror that is contained in the proto-psychoanalytic word *heimlich*, or "homely." Schumann's piano is the site of the private, the secret, the *heimlich*, and thereby also of the *unheimlich*, or uncanny and terrifying.

Schumann's separation from Clara in 1836 inspired the composition between 1836 and 1838 of the ambitious and psychologically complicated Fantasy in C major, Op. 17. The second context for the Fantasy is the project for a Beethoven monument in Bonn, inaugurated on what would have been his sixty-fifth birthday in December 1835. In April 1836 Schumann dedicated the front page of his *Neue Zeitschrift* to the public appeal of the *Bonner Verein für Beethovens Monument*. Is the Fantasy's passion directed at Beethoven or at Clara, at public or at private monuments? The answer, of course, is both.[38]

The work's epigraph cites Friedrich Schlegel's poem "Die Ge-büsche" ("The Bushes"):

> Durch alle Töne tönet
> Im bunten Erdentraum
> Ein leiser Ton gezogen
> Für den der heimlich lauschet.

> Through all sounds resounds
> In earth's many-colored dream
> A soft sound drawn out
> For the secret listener.

Schumann, lover of puzzles, invested Schlegel's stanza with his own secret. The Schumann interpretive canon, beginning with his first bi-ographer, Wilhelm Joseph von Wasielewski, has placed Schumann's secret reference in the words *ein leiser Ton*, "a soft sound," which they assume must refer to Clara. But I would suggest that Schumann was both cleverer and less in control with regard to his own secrets and that the secret of the motto lodges in the word "secret," *heimlich*. Its interpretation requires attention to literary tradition extending from Schlegel and E.T.A. Hoffmann to Freud.[39]

First, the final line's extra syllable sets it apart metrically from the preceding three and gives it a hushed, private quality, separating it from the declamatory, public tone of the first three lines. That is the onomatopoeic work of the word *lauschet*. More important for the epi-graph as a whole and for this internalizing effect in particular, we must parse the word *heimlich*—with its marking of an emotional space that is secret, intimate, homely—in the way readers since Freud have analyzed its partner and antagonist, *unheimlich*.

In his essay "The Uncanny" of 1919, Freud defines the uncanny as the opposite of the *heimlich*, "that class of the terrifying which leads back to something long known to us, once very familiar."[40] But the opposites converge: "What is *heimlich* thus comes to be *unheimlich*. . . . *Unheimlich* is in some way or other a sub-species of *heimlich*. . . . some-thing familiar and old-established in the mind that has been es-tranged only by the process of repression."[41] The homely is the site also of the unhomely, the uncanny: *heimlich* and *unheimlich* coincide, and that is the root of terror, especially in childhood. Freud locates the modern archetype for the uncanny in the literary corpus of E.T.A. Hoffmann, a figure of great importance to Schumann, and for similar reasons.

An entry in Schumann's diary from 1831 reads, "One can barely breathe when reading Hoffmann. . . . Reading Hoffmann uninterruptedly. New worlds."[42] In 1838 he wrote the *Kreisleriana*, eight piano fantasies inspired by Hoffmann, which portray a combination of Hoffmann's mad musician Kapellmeister Johannes Kreisler along with strong doses of Liszt, Paganini, and Robert and Clara themselves. For Freud, the locus classicus for the categories of *heimlich* and *unheimlich* is Hoffmann's story "The Sandman," written in 1815, which contains the portraits of Nathaniel, Professor Spalanzani, and his "daughter," the doll Olympia. Peering through the professor's window, Nathaniel falls in love with the doll, which disintegrates into its component parts, including bleeding eyes that have been procured by Dr. Coppelius. The same Dr. Coppelius had been present at the death of Nathaniel's father in an explosion, during a period of his childhood when he was especially vulnerable to the Sandman, the figure of German legend who steals the eyes of children who refuse to go to sleep at night. In Nathaniel's adult psychosis, Coppelius is the Sandman, who has provided Olympia with eyes stolen from children.

In the context of Schumann's reading of Hoffmann, the opening of "The Sandman" is truly uncanny, *unheimlich*. It takes the form of a letter from Nathaniel to his best friend, Lothario:

> You must all be very worried that I have not written for such a long time. I expect mother is angry, and Clara may think I am living here in a state of debauchery and altogether forgetting the dear angel whose image is imprinted so deeply into my heart and mind. . . . But, ah, how could I have written to you in the utter melancholy which has been disrupting all my mind?[43]

Nathaniel's engagement to Clara is undermined by his obsession with Olympia and the Sandman. Waking from delirium, he pushes the horrified Clara away, calling her "you lifeless accursed automaton."[44] Finally, in a harbinger of Hitchcock's *Vertigo*, he nearly throws her to her death from a tower.

Now, for Nathaniel, Spalanzani, and Olympia we might be prepared to read: Schumann, Wieck, and Clara. In "The Sandman," Nathaniel's horror peaks when he learns that Olympia's eyes are in fact his own, previously stolen by the Sandman. If Schumann was anxious about Clara as puppet of her father, can we also extend this speculation of "puppet anxiety" to the most familiar, or *heimlich*, sphere—himself? Did he worry about himself as a puppet of Wieck, and might this be a context in which to understand the well-known and disastrous fourth-finger contraption with which he attached his finger to a string suspended from the ceiling, allegedly intending to strengthen it but instead causing permanent muscle damage that ended his performing viability? If, finally, we take the aspect of sexual anxiety from Freud's analysis, we can extend Freud's equation of eye anxiety with castration complex to the pianistically appropriate fear for the fingers.

In March 1838 Schumann wrote to Clara, "I have completed a fantasy in three movements which I had sketched down to the last detail in June 1836. The first movement is probably the most passionate thing I have ever written—a deep lament for you—the others are weaker, but need not exactly feel ashamed of themselves." Passion may be proud so long as it is strong; the association of weakness and shame is notable. In January 1839, however, Schumann described the work to Clara as "excessively melancholy" (*übermelancholisch*).[45]

If we can assert that the Fantasy builds an elaborate musical discourse of desire, then we can suggest that it does so in all three of its expansive movements through a complex incorporation of Beethovenian tropes. For Schumann, Beethoven's voice suggests, first of all, masculinity, perhaps masculinization. The first movement—marked *Leidenschaftlich vorzutragen*—has a heroic energy, the heroism for which the dominant contemporary aesthetic lionized Beethoven. (For this reason the implied "program" of the symphony in general was the heroic journey, a model that listeners would attach to Schumann's own C-major Symphony, as we shall see.) This heroic voice is a first-person voice. The second movement offers an internal dialectic that comments on the initial first-person heroic voice from, as it were, two opposing perspectives. The first is external: the movement begins in an unmistakably third-person narrative posture, with the telling of the story of the hero. It is formal and declamatory without assuming the emotional stance of the first-person voice. But this narrative posture is quickly and repeatedly infiltrated by a second voice that evokes the "jazz" variation from the second movement of Beethoven's last piano sonata, Op. 111; the suggestion is of an inner, psychological destabilization of the conventional narrative. The final movement reins in these distinct voices and, perhaps with echoes of the triplet motion in the first movement of Beethoven's "Moonlight" Sonata (albeit now in the major mode), transforms desire into a projected state of shared intimacy while retaining the imprimatur of masculinity.

In March 1839 Schumann abandoned his intention to move to Vienna, where Clara was to join him, when the Bureau of Censors refused to grant him permission to publish his journal there. In *Faschingsschwank aus Wien*, he teased Metternich's censors by mixing a quotation from the *Marseillaise* into the opening Allegro. This also served as a greeting to Clara, who was in Paris at the time. Thus Metternich and Wieck converged as Schumann's impediments. Wieck explicitly engaged politics to insult Schumann; early in 1841 he called the First Symphony, still in progress, an "opposition symphony." In response, Schumann dedicated the work to King Friedrich August II of Saxony.[46]

This gesture is at least as interesting psychoanalytically as it is politically. When Schumann returned to Leipzig in 1830 to study with Wieck, he clearly looked to his teacher for the union of fatherhood and music that he had lacked. The souring of the relationship with Wieck, complicated by the presence of Clara and the hints of incestuousness in her attachment to Wieck as well as to Schumann, who had first filled the place in the household of an older brother, represents the betrayal of a substitute father. The king of Saxony would seem to be a ceremonially appropriate, emotionally uninvested, and rhetorically powerful figure to usurp Wieck's fatherly position. But no one could absorb the paternal authority of Beethoven, Schumann's Commendatore.

In early 1839 Schumann discovered the manuscript of Franz Schubert's C-major Symphony, D. 944. The following year, he wrote a celebrated essay extolling the work but also investing it with the fear that evolved from his association of Schubert with the feminine, and thus the counterpart to Beethoven. Susan McClary has cited Schumann's essay with comments that bear quoting:

> The essay carefully establishes a dichotomy between the masculine example of Beethoven and the more sensitive, romantic Schubert, and throughout the essay, Schumann shields himself from Schubert's influence by calling upon Beethoven's "virile power" at moments when he is about to be overwhelmed by Schubert's charm. At the end, after he has succumbed to a rhapsodic account of what it is like to listen to the Schubert symphony, he seeks to recover his masculine authority by abruptly informing the reader: "I once found on Beethoven's grave a steel pen, which ever since I have reverently preserved. I never use it save on festive occasions like this one; may inspiration have flowed from it."[47]

Beethoven thus provided Schumann with a personal "tonic." I apologize for the musical pun, but it seems apt. Beethoven's masculine voice was therapeutic, and it represented the desired home position for Schumann's own musical and emotional voice. Schumann's ego ideology can be described according to the principle of "masculinity as home."

Schumann relied heavily on this posture as he endeavored to become a public figure in Leipzig, Dresden, and Düsseldorf between 1840 and 1852. Here again the closest model was Mendelssohn, whose public and performing gifts Schumann could not match. 1840, the "year of the song," commenced with the lawsuit against Friedrich Wieck for the right to marry Clara still pending. The song literature offers a discourse of focused desire, for Clara, and also for subjective autonomy. Thereafter, the genres of choice were larger-scaled and public: the symphony first, the hybrid oratorio in second place. Clara Schumann's two favorites among her husband's works were *Das Paradies und die Peri* (1843) and the Symphony in C major of 1845–46. What did she project into these two works?

Das Paradies, a hybrid mixture of opera, oratorio, and cantata, was completed in July 1843 and premiered that December in the Gewandhaus, led by Schumann in his conducting debut. His music combined oddly with the orientalizing text of Thomas Moore's *Lalla Rookh*, at the same time altering its orientalist pitch. The Peri is a fallen angel campaigning for admission into an eclectic Eden where Allah reigns. She is told to bring to heaven the most precious gift; she fails with her first two offerings (the blood of a fallen hero and the sighs of pure love) but succeeds with her third, the tear of a sinner. Heavenly authority is represented by vocal quartets, occasionally reminiscent of the temple guardians from *The Magic Flute*, that mark a realm of order and propriety rather than one of mystery and grace. Instead of the standard orientalist fare of cultural othering, we have a narrative of androgynous subjective flux placed against the benign but persistent authority of bourgeois culture.

The *Peri*'s immediate international success points in general to contemporary appreciation for dramatic concert forms. Its high place in Robert's and Clara's affections is more immediately relevant here. First, the scale of the work was a cheering indication of the composer's stamina. On its completion in July 1843 Schumann wrote to the Dutch composer Johann Verhulst of his gratitude that his strength had endured, and in 1847 he wrote to the music critic Franz Brendel that the work had claimed his "heart's blood": "Es hängt Herzblut an dieser Arbeit."[48] Second, Schumann's success at the work's Leipzig premiere was as conductor as well as composer. If we take to heart the burgherly tones of the work's heavenly voices, then both text and performance context tell of the redemptive acceptance of Peri/Robert by cultural authority. But there is more on which to speculate.

Peri becomes a personification of the androgynous voice. The redemption of that voice may well have contained a therapeutic dimension for Schumann. It suggests an issue in his life that is difficult to ponder: how his sporadic but intense homoerotic friendships figure in the discussions of masculinity that we have been considering. Two kinds of bisexuality present themselves: that of hetero- as well as homosexual attraction, and that of a self-contained perfection, which involves in turn the suspension of attraction. It is in this latter guise, with discussion originating in the theological treatment of a bisexual deity from which life can be created and informing traditions such as hermeticism, alchemy, and pietism, that the androgyne is a familiar type in the romantic literature and theory, that of the early Friedrich Schlegel above all.[49]

Schlegel's Jena romantics, focused between 1798 and 1800 around the journal *Athenäum*, discovered the ideal of androgynous perfection in the writings of Jacob Böhme, whom they read in 1798 on Ludwig Tieck's recommendation. The androgyne as the *"Urbild* of totality" was resexualized by Schlegel into the image of perfect heterosexual union. This transition was achieved by replacing Böhme's mystical view of romantic union with Franz von Baader's decidedly sensual view. Schlegel's trajectory here is remarkably similar to Schumann's. A law student in Leipzig between 1791 and 1794, he abandoned law for the study of antiquity at the same time that he met Caroline Böhmer, his ideal (at least until she married his brother) of the creative androgyne: his Diotima, to whom Schegel compared her. Like Diotima from Plato's *Symposium*, Caroline represented the equation of "beautiful femininity" as "completed humanity." Schlegel summed up his androgynous goal with the motto "Only independent femininity, only gentle masculinity is good and beautiful."[50]

Friedrich Schlegel was, then, Schumann's source for the trope of secret listening and for the valorization of androgyny. In *Das Paradies und die Peri*, androgynous fantasy is released to public hearing. Conducting the premiere with success, Schumann displayed, quite literally, a momentary ability to project a fantasy of the domestic uncanny into the public sphere.

.

Schumann's C-major Symphony has not been a favorite of twentieth-century audiences and critics. This century's leading Schumann commentators, including W. H. Hadow, August Halm, Gerald Abraham, and Mosco Carner, have found the piece seriously flawed and in many interesting instances, including Gerald Abraham's 1980 article in the

New Grove Dictionary, not worth discussing.[51] In an important article, Anthony Newcomb has argued for the distinction of the work and for its recanonization, proposing that a nineteenth-century aesthetic of reception is necessary for its appreciation. That aesthetic proposed that symphonies be listened to for their musical embodiments of what Schumann and others called *Seelenzustände*, or psychological states. The leading models are the Beethoven symphonies. Comparisons to literary forms, especially to the novel, were common. Wilhelm Fink, as Newcomb recounts, "compared the *grosse Symphonie* to the 'dramatically constructed *Gefühlsnovelle*,' " and A. B. Marx called the symphony "a living image [*Lebensbild*] unfolding in a series of psychologically natural steps."[52] For Newcomb, the musical portrayal of a psychological state involves a journey in time and can therefore be understood in terms of a narrative. The narrative in the C-major Symphony is that of the journey from despair to healing and redemption. For the work's form and inferred story, it was compared by mid-nineteenth-century interpreters to Beethoven's Fifth and Ninth Symphonies.

The problem with a general model of narrative is the implication of a consistent subjectivity. The problem with this specific model of narrative—the journey to redemption—is its teleology. When the story is one of redemption, everything points to the end. Predictably, and sensibly, Newcomb directs his analysis to the final movement.

Although many twentieth-century critics of this symphony have found particular fault with the disjointed final movement, this is not the only place in the work where Schumann's form seems stretched, out of order, or possibly incoherent. One such problem is the unconventional placement of the Scherzo as the second movement, followed by the slow movement marked *Adagio espressivo*. Presumably, the redemption narrative would not dictate the placement of the two inner movements, so long as the narrative were able to transcend the melancholy of the *Adagio*. Aside from the opening, transitional phrase (which Brahms may have invoked to open the final movement of his Fourth Symphony), the final movement, beginning as it does with, in Newcomb's phrase, "a rough shout of affirmation," is completely unconnected in rhetoric and mood to the *Adagio*. But the *Adagio* is voiced in direct relation and response to the preceding Scherzo. I would suggest an allegorical reading of the *Adagio* in relation to the Scherzo and argue accordingly that the middle movements of the work enable a reading in terms of allegory that is more helpful than one conceived in terms of narrative.

The Scherzo is clearly and brilliantly a Mendelssohnian movement, and no less so for the layer of melancholy that underlies its jocularity. Newcomb speaks of the "inactive, somewhat melancholy character and crawling chromaticism [that] lie behind the vigorous athleticism of the scherzo theme, and help to give it the unstable, contradictory character remarked in many early reviews." He suggests that the "antic scherzo is in fact not quite what it pretends to be."[53]

The exquisite *Adagio espressivo* unfolds in a confessional, first-person mode. It is the music that says "I"; the investment in the musical first person of Robert Schumann is certain but not readily decipherable. The overall posture of the movement seems to impart the thought—part confession, part defense, part self-assertion—"I am not Mendelssohn." In a way the movement turns away from—unwrites—the work of the Scherzo. This internal unwriting of previous movements may be figured in the work's tendency to quote Beethoven, central as this rhetorical property is to the Ninth Symphony. The *Adagio*'s first-person utterance offers a consistent melancholic mood but does not progress in a unified voice; multivocality is made clear by varied orchestration and use of solo instruments, especially the oboe and bassoon, in sequences of short figures and phrases that appear and withdraw. Schumann himself wrote in a letter of his affection for "my melancholy bassoon."[54] The main theme reorganizes material from the two principal thematic groups of the preceding two movements.[55] It adds to these materials the central gesture of the falling diminished fourth, which Newcomb identifies in a fascinating way as "a figure from the *Figurenlehre* of the Baroque music in which Schumann had immersed himself for months before writing the C major symphony"[56]—another connection, perhaps, to Mendelssohn. If we hear this movement's rhetoric in a larger frame of reference, we might suggest that its inscription of melancholy works as well through invocations of Mozartian as well as Schubertian gestures, especially in solo wind lines, in the fragmentary quality of phrases passed from one wind instrument to the other, supported by syncopations. (I am thinking, for example, of the Larghetto of the Clarinet Quintet, K. 581.) The movement ends—again in Newcomb's felicitous description—"not in an atmosphere of triumph: rather, in an atmosphere of resignation and near stasis." Nothing is worked through.

The finale reclaims an extroverted, public voice. Yet it does so not by transcending the private, interior melancholy of the *Adagio* but rather by momentarily suppressing it. For this reason the reading of the symphony as a salvation narrative is unconvincing. If the final movement is itself structurally and emotionally unconvincing, this may have to do with the authenticity of the melancholic state it has somewhat glibly left behind.

·

The association of modernity and spiritual homelessness has become a cliché. In perhaps its best-known formulations, Georg Lukács describes modernity according to the principle of "transcendental homelessness," and Martin Heidegger's "Letter on Humanism" proposes that "homelessness is coming to be the destiny of the world."[57] But these remain romantic critiques of modernity in terms of a wanderer fantasy, where "home" resides in a measure of cultural authenticity as opposed to a self-conscious subjective modernity. Another side of romantic culture and trope is the domestic, which divides between the secure and those "secret recesses of domesticity" in which the uncanny lodges.[58] This trope can be understood materially in terms of the early bourgeois phenomenon of a new class, "not quite at home in its own home."[59] It conjures the paradox of the homely and the unhomely: the centrality of the uncanny to modern experience. Its suppression transforms the home into the *kleinbürgerlich* nightmare from which Schumann could never free himself.

Mendelssohn's subjectivity and modernity reside in his successful disaggregation of cultural homelessness, which he embraced, from a homelessness of the ego, which that very embrace paradoxically foreclosed. The embrace, on the other hand, of identity and cultural authenticity engenders, paradoxically, the collapse of the ego and allows the onslaught of various forms of cultural pathology, prejudice and scapegoating among them. With anti-Semitism as the leading representative of such pathology, we have the result, as of 1850 and "Das Judentum in der Musik," of German identity ideology. This Wagnerian world is way beyond Schumann, but in Schumann's psychic battles we have the domestic dimensions of its ideological antecedents. Mendelssohn and Schumann are the *heimlich/unheimlich* twin peaks of Biedermeier music; Schumann speaks from the other side of Mendelssohn, in modernity's uncanny voice.

NOTES

1. I take the phrase "unsung voices" from Carolyn Abbate and her book *Unsung Voices: Opera and Musical Narrative in the Nineteenth Century* (Princeton, 1991). By "voice," Abbate means "not literally vocal performance, but rather a

sense of certain isolated and rare gestures in music, whether vocal or nonvocal, that may be perceived as modes of subjects' enunciations" (p. ix). The voices Abbate analyzes are narrative ones, and not for the most part first-person voices. My discussion will travel, therefore, in a different direction but will benefit nonetheless from her arguments and vocabulary.

2. Theodor Adorno, *Mahler: eine musikalische Physiognomik* (Frankfurt, 1960), p. 106; quoted in Abbate, *Unsung Voices*, p. 27.

3. Walter Benjamin, "Paris, Capital of the Nineteenth Century," trans. E. Jephcott, in *Reflections* (New York, 1978), p. 154.

4. Anne K. Mellor, *Romanticism and Gender* (New York, 1993), p. 1.

5. Ibid., pp. 1–5.

6. Ibid., p. 4.

7. Friedrich Meinecke, *The German Catastrophe*, trans. Sidney Fay (New York, 1950), pp. 5–16.

8. This category was developed by the Berlin-born historian Hans Baron with reference to early fifteenth-century Florence in *The Crisis of the Early Italian Renaissance* (Princeton, 1960). To what extent he developed the model in an allegorical relation, conscious or unconscious, to North Germany is difficult to know and interesting to ponder.

9. See George L. Mosse, *Nationalism and Sexuality* (Madison, Wis., 1985); *Fallen Soldiers* (New York, 1990); and "Manliness and Decadence," in *Sexual Knowledge in 1900* (Cambridge, forthcoming).

10. Ludwig Wittgenstein, *Culture and Value*, trans. Peter Winch (Chicago, 1980), pp. 1–2.

11. Letter of Felix Mendelssohn, New York Public Library, quoted in R. Larry Todd, "*Me voilà perruqué*: Mendelssohn's Six Preludes and Fugues, Op. 35, Reconsidered," in *Mendelssohn Studies*, ed. R. Larry Todd (Cambridge, 1992), p. 162.

12. Theodor Adorno, "Bach Defended against His Devotees," in *Prisms*, trans. S. Weber (Cambridge, Mass., 1981), p. 137.

13. Ibid., p. 139.

14. Ibid., p. 138.

15. John Toews, "Memory and Gender in the Remaking of Fanny Mendelssohn's Musical Identity: The Chorale in *Das Jahr*," *Musical Quarterly* 77, no. 4 (1993): 727–48. In this issue of the *Musical Quarterly*, see in general the special section called "Culture, Gender, and Music: A Forum on the Mendelssohn Family," pp. 648–748.

16. See Peter Wollny, "Sara Levy and the Making of Musical Taste in Berlin," ibid., pp. 651–88.

17. Toews, "Memory and Gender," p. 736.

18. See Arno Forchert, "Von Bach zu Mendelssohn," in Gunther Wagner, *Bachtage Berlin* (Stuttgart, 1985), pp. 211–33.

19. Michael Marissen, "Religious Aims in Mendelssohn's 1829 Berlin Singakademie Performances of Bach's St. Matthew Passion," *Musical Quarterly* 77, no. 4 (1993): 720.

20. See Judith Silber Ballan, "Marxian Programmatic Music: A Stage in Mendelssohn's Musical Development," in Todd, *Mendelssohn Studies*, p. 149.

21. Ibid., p. 154. See also Ballan's "Mendelssohn and the Reformation Symphony: A Critical and Historical Study" (Ph.D. dissertation, Yale University, 1987).

22. See Judith Ballan, "Marxian Programmatic Music," p. 154n. Anton Friedrich Justus Thibaut, *Über Reinheit der Tonkunst* (Darmstadt, 1967); trans. as *On Purity in Musical Art* by W. H. Gladstone (London, 1877).

23. See W. H. Gladstone, preface to Thibaut, *On Purity in Musical Art*, p. xiii.

24. Ibid., pp. 23–25.

25. Ibid., pp. 55, 85, 102, 194.

26. See David Brodbeck, "Mendelssohn and the *Berliner Domchor*," in Todd, *Mendelssohn Studies*, p. 23.

27. Jerrold Levinson, "Hope in the *Hebrides*," in *Music, Art, and Metaphysics: Essays in Philosophical Aesthetics* (Ithaca, 1990), pp. 336–75.

28. Ibid., pp. 358–66; and Hans Keller, *Of German Music*, ed. H. H. Schönzeler (London, 1976), p. 207.

29. Levinson, "Hope in the *Hebrides*," p. 370.

30. Ibid., p. 372.

31. Adorno, "Bach Defended against His Devotees," p. 146.

32. The source is a letter to Clara of 1838. See R. Larry Todd, *Mendelssohn's Musical Education: A Study and Edition of His Exercises in Composition* (Cambridge, 1982), p. 3.

33. See Peter Ostwald, *Schumann: Music and Madness* (London, 1985), p. 51.

34. See Leon Plantinga, "Schumann's Critical Reaction to Mendelssohn," in Jon W. Finson and R. Larry Todd, *Mendelssohn and Schumann: Essays on Their Music and Its Context* (Durham, N.C., 1984), p. 15.

35. See pp. 237ff. in this volume. [Ed.]

36. See Ostwald, *Schumann: Music and Madness*, pp. 221–22.

37. Gerhard Dietel, *"Eine neue poetische Zeit": Musikanschauung und stilistische Tendenzen im Klavierwerk Robert Schumanns* (Kassel, 1989), pp. 296–390.

38. See the discussion of this and other interpretive issues in Nicholas Marston, *Schumann: "Fantasie," Op. 17* (Cambridge, 1992), pp. 2–3.

39. For a superb history of the category of the uncanny, see Anthony Vidler, *The Architectural Uncanny: Essays in the Modern Unhomely* (Cambridge, Mass., 1992), pp. 1–66.

40. Sigmund Freud, "The 'Uncanny,' " in *Collected Papers* (London, 1925), vol. 4, pp. 369–70.

41. Ibid., pp. 375, 377, 394.

42. See Ostwald, *Schumann: Music and Madness*, p. 77.

43. E.T.A. Hoffmann, "The Sandman," trans. R. J. Hollingdale, in *Tales of Hoffmann* (Harmondsworth, 1982), p. 85.

44. Ibid., p. 106.

45. See Nicholas Marston, *Schumann: "Fantasie," Op. 17*, pp. 6, 98.

46. See Ostwald, *Schumann: Music and Madness*, pp. 147, 169–70.

47. Susan McClary, *Feminine Endings* (Minneapolis, 1991), p. 18. The Schumann article appeared in the *Neue Zeitschrift für Musik* on 10 March 1840. It is

perhaps only pointing out the obvious to say that Schumann rediscovered the phallus in Beethoven's steel pen, but then Schumann's own sexual and gender position is again rendered unclear.

48. See Richard Münnich, ed., *Aus Robert Schumanns Briefen und Schriften* (Weimar, 1956), pp. 264, 277.

49. See Sara Friedrichsmeyer, *The Androgyne in Early German Romanticism: Friedrich Schlegel, Novalis, and the Metaphysics of Love* (Bern, 1983.)

50. Ibid., pp. 37, 55, 59, 123, 127.

51. See Anthony Newcomb, "Once More 'Between Absolute and Program Music': Schumann's Second Symphony," *19th-Century Music* 7 (1984): 239.

52. Ibid., p. 234. I have adjusted the translation of *Lebensbild*.

53. Ibid., p. 242.

54. See Ostwald, *Schumann: Music and Madness*, p. 205.

55. See Newcomb, "Once More 'Between Absolute and Program Music,' " p. 243.

56. Ibid., p. 243. See also the discussion of the diminished fourth on p. 99 of this volume. [Ed.]

57. Georg Lukács, *The Theory of the Novel*, trans. Anna Bostock (Cambridge, Mass., 1971), p. 41; Martin Heidegger, "Letter on Humanism," trans. Frank Capuzzi and J. Glenn Gray, in *Basic Writings*, ed. David Farrell Krell (New York, 1977), p. 219.

58. See Vidler, *The Architectural Uncanny*, p. xi.

59. Ibid., p. 4.

On Quotation

in Schumann's Music

R. LARRY TODD

For much of the twentieth century Robert Schumann's compositional web of quotations and allusions has ensnared scholars pondering the remarkably rich layers of meaning in his music. Inevitably, it seems, they have become entangled in inextricable æsthetic questions. Does a given reference in a composition impress as an unmistakable quotation, or is the reference partially veiled, so that it functions more like an allusion, clear enough to be perceived as a reference but not exact enough to be recognized as a quotation? Is the reference explicit—as in the first number of *Papillons*, Op. 2, revived by Schumann in *Carnaval*, Op. 9, in the middle of "Florestan," where its intrusion is actually labeled "Papillon?" ("Butterfly?") and where its transitory flight impresses as what Schumann termed a *Gedankenanflug* (flight of thought)?[1] Or is the reference implicit—as in the "innere Stimme" of the "Hastig" from the *Humoreske*, Op. 20, allotted its own staff in the printed score but, as a romantic species of *Augenmusik*, intended to be seen and not heard?[2] Is the reference a deliberate, planned gesture, as in the overt quotations of the *Marseillaise* in the *Faschingsschwank aus Wien*, Op. 26, *Die beiden Grenadiere*, Op. 49, no. 1, and the Overture to *Hermann und Dorothea*, Op. 136? Or could the reference be part of Schumann's musical unconscious—as a possible example, the opening of the Second Symphony, Op. 61, with its *apparent* allusion to Haydn's last symphony[3]—in which Schumann draws more or less freely on the wellspring of German musical traditions stretching back to the eighteenth century and beyond?

There is, too, the complicating factor that Schumann's music embraces a wealth of literary and other extramusical ideas, and thus spins another web of allusions and cross references, with a second series of carnivallike masks.[4] To return to *Carnaval*: is the reappearance of the *Papillons* motive in "Florestan" merely a musical self-quotation intended to underscore the extramusical similarities between the two works?[5] Or is Schumann suggesting here something about the creative process, that composition entails a fleeting succession of changing ideas that are somehow shaped into a coherent whole—that for a brief moment the distracting image of the butterfly candidly reflects the inner world of Schumann's musical-literary imagination? In the case of the *Faschingsschwank aus Wien* (yet another type of *Carnaval*), the reason for the quotation of the *Marseillaise* is not too difficult to discern: here Schumann is indulging in a bit of political humor, offering a pointed jab, as he unfurls the French tricolors, at the repressive regime of Metternich's Vienna. But the quotation is short-lived and again comprises nothing more than a *Gedankenanflug*: only the first phrase of the French anthem appears, and not in its original duple meter; rather, it is made to conform to the bumptious triple time of Schumann's Allegro (example 1a).

Example 1a. Schumann, *Faschingsschwank aus Wien*, Op. 26, no. 1

A few measures later, the composer moves on to a more judicious allusion, to the trio from the Minuet of Beethoven's Piano Sonata in E♭ major, Op. 31, no. 3, which he playfully elaborates for nearly two pages (examples 1b and 1c). This constant commingling of musical and nonmusical ideas adds ever new strands to the web, rendering considerably more difficult the challenge of explicating the meaning of the music.

Schumann's playful prodding of his audience with references (familiar and unfamiliar) no doubt was a source of delight for his friends and colleagues. There are, for example, his liberal borrowings from

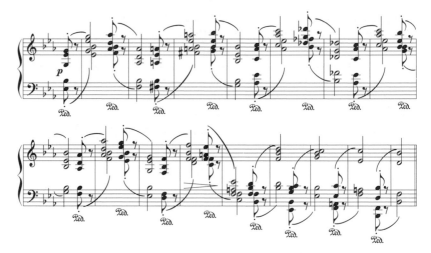

Example 1b. Schumann, *Faschingsschwank aus Wien*, Op. 26, no. 1

Example 1c. Beethoven, Piano Sonata in E♭, Op. 31, no. 3 (trio of the Minuet)

the piano works of his wife, and his charming homage to William Sterndale Bennett, the dedicatee of the Symphonic Etudes, Op. 13, in the finale of that piano cycle, wherein Schumann's English friend is likened to Richard the Lionhearted through a quotation from Marschner's *Der Templer und die Jüdin*. Schumann himself was subjected to similar treatment from that "young eagle" Johannes Brahms, whose Variations on a Theme by Robert Schumann, Op. 9 (1854), ostensibly based on the F♯-minor *Albumblatt* from Schumann's Op. 99 (1841; published in 1852), became the stage for a review of several works by Schumann. These include the B-minor *Albumblatt* from Op. 99 (variation 9), the theme of the Impromptus, Op. 5 (variation 10; this theme, of course, was borrowed by Robert from Clara, so that its reappearance in Brahms's Op. 9 completes a thematic triangle[6]), and the nocturnelike texture of "Chopin" from *Carnaval* (variation 14). Finally, Brahms concludes his set by extracting the bass of Schumann's theme, recalling a similar treatment in the Impromptus.

These references seem clear enough and have been discussed in the literature.[7] But another passage from Brahms's Op. 9 that plausibly contains a Schumann (and Schumannesque) allusion has escaped detection and reveals the thin lines separating quotations from allusions and mere thematic resemblances. In the tenth, D-major, variation Brahms appropriates the bass line of Schumann's theme, which now becomes a soprano melody set against its own mirror image in the bass (see examples 2a and 2b).

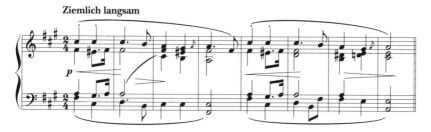

Example 2a. Brahms, Variations on a Theme by Robert Schumann, Op. 9 (theme)

This structural upending, by which the original bass now assumes a new thematic role in the soprano, is obvious enough, but what follows is not. In the ninth measure Brahms begins to repeat the opening (a repetition not in Schumann's original theme) but alters the texture. The soprano cantilena remains intact (imitated a bar later in the alto in mirror inversion), but the accompaniment now unfolds as a series of arpeggiated chords, and the bass line no longer mirrors the soprano in strict inversion. The contour of the soprano melody (falling fourth and half-step, F#–C#–D), the rolled, rising chords in the accompaniment (significantly punctuated by rests), the ascending, largely stepwise bass line, and the major modality (the initial F# of the melody functions as the third of D major) produce a passage that strikingly resembles the slow movement of Schumann's String Quartet Op. 41, no. 1 (example 2c). It is as if in designing the tenth variation Brahms stumbled upon a purely coincidental similarity—that the bass line of Schumann's theme resembles the melody of the quartet—and chose to transform that similarity into an allusion by invoking Schumann's quartet in more compelling terms. So, in a wonderfully romantic way (of which, presumably, Schumann would have approved), the implicit became explicit. The crucial question, however, remains: is the Brahms passage literal enough to function as a quotation? Perhaps not, though surely its expressive allure as an allusion is difficult to resist.

Example 2b. Brahms, Variations on a Theme by Robert Schumann, Op. 9
(variation 10)

If Brahms generated allusions to Schumann in musically creative ways, others sought early on to document in the press specific quotations by Schumann. Thus, in an 1844 review of the piano works, C. Koßmaly commented on the appearance of the seventeenth-century "Großvater-Tanz" ("Grandfather Dance") in *Papillons* and *Carnaval*, where as a bourgeois, philistine ("spießbürgerliche und philiströse") motive it makes a grotesque contrast and has a comic rococo effect.[8] Schumann's first biographer, Wilhelm Joseph von Wasielewski, occasionally took note of quotations, interpreting, for example, the clash between the March of the Davidites and the "Großvater-Tanz" in the finale of *Carnaval* as a "spiritual contest between youthful aims and the Philistines of art."[9] But none was more energetic in pur-

Example 2c. Schumann, String Quartet Op. 41, no. 1 (Adagio, opening measures)

suing quotations than Adolf Schubring, who devoted the second of his "Schumanniana," twelve articles serialized in the *Neue Zeitschrift für Musik* between 1860 and 1869, to exploring more thoroughly Schumann's use of the "Großvater-Tanz."[10]

Schubring begins by conjuring up an image of the grandfather in all his rococo finery, with embroidered vest, gilded jacket, and braided hair, dancing with the grandmother some fifteen years his junior. ("Und als der Großvater die Großmutter nahm, / Da war der Großvater ein Bräutigam" ["And when the grandfather took the grandmother, then the grandfather became a bridegroom"] is the couplet that was traditionally sung at wedding feasts to the first part of the dance.) Nineteenth-century Europeans, Schubring muses, are too world-weary and blasé to take up this outmoded dance. Still, it has a certain roguish appeal, and whoever has experienced it cannot easily break free from its influence. And so the "most romantic of the romantics," Robert Schumann, endeavored in his Op. 2 to link the "homely Papa Rococo" with a *papillon*, by which he meant not a butterfly but a little "psyche emerging from a cocoon." And, having introduced the grandfather into his music (example 3a), Schumann was committed to that symbol of obsolescent finery, for "the moment the topic of conversation [in Schumann's music] turns to olden times, to bridal processions and weddings, the grandfather immediately joins in with his say."

Example 3a. Schumann, *Papillons*, Op. 2, no. 12 (finale, opening measures)

Schubring is now off to the hunt. He culls more than a dozen examples from Schumann's works after *Papillons* as references to the "Großvater-Tanz." Of these, two are incontrovertible: the finale of *Carnaval* (already cited by Koßmaly and Wasielewski), and the second "Winterszeit" from the *Album für die Jugend*, Op. 68, in which two parts of the dance appear in the bass and treble registers, as if engaged in a musical conversation; here, according to Schubring, "Grandpapa and Grandmama sit by the warm fireplace and tell their grandchildren of bygone days" (example 3b).[11]

But Schubring's other examples, if ingeniously chosen, are not always thoroughly convincing. Generally his method is first to find passages with texted or extramusical references to weddings, bridal processions, or the opposition between the old and new, and then to discover the grandfather lurking behind motivic and rhythmic ideas reminiscent of the dance. These similarities usually involve upward leaps of a fourth or dotted rhythmic patterns—both, to be sure, characteristic of the dance but also present (indeed, omnipresent) in a vast quantity of nineteenth-century music. More often than not the trap is sprung on Schubring, and, like so many commentators who followed him, he becomes entangled in Schumann's web.

Thus in the Impromptus, Op. 5, which for Schubring represent Schumann's first musical effort to woo Clara Wieck (*Brautwerbung*; the Op. 5, of course, is based on a theme by her), the grandfather "appears" in two movements, first flattering Clara in no. 4 and then pressing her more urgently in the weighty fugal finale. But apart from a dotted rhythmic figure—itself surely insufficient to form a quotation or even an allusion—these two examples offer nothing that compel-

Example 3b. Schumann, *Album für die Jugend*, Op. 68, "Winterszeit II"

lingly suggests the dance. What is more, the Impromptus were composed in 1832, when Clara was thirteen (the second, revised edition appeared in 1850); Robert and Clara did not exchange their first kiss until November 1835.[12]

In the case of the Intermezzi, Op. 4, Schubring detects two *Anspielungen* of the dance, one dreamy, the other assertive and angry. Conveniently enough, they occur in adjacent intermezzi (nos. 4 and 5), and their juxtaposition evidently encouraged the critic to view them as a Eusebius-Florestan pair, in which the "Großvater-Tanz," in effect, is filtered through the opposite poles of Schumann's psyche. As attractive as this idea is, problems again surface in the musical comparison. The dreamy passage from the fourth intermezzo does begin with an ascending fourth and does display dotted rhythms (example 4a); but the superficial similarity to the dance simply does not warrant the label of a reference. Furthermore, as we now know, the fourth intermezzo is actually a piano transcription of "Hirtenknabe," a song Schumann wrote in 1828 albeit a source presumably unknown to Schubring;[13] in the Lied, we find no textual references that should

Example 4a. Schumann, Intermezzi, Op. 4, no. 4

stir the grandfather from his slumbers. On the other hand, the fifth intermezzo comes considerably closer to the mark (example 4b). Here (notwithstanding the minor mode), the rhythm, meter, and melodic profile do seem to allude to the dance.

To Schubring's ear, the sixth movement of *Kreisleriana* is suffused with the dance, though he offers no explanation of why it should appear here, and, again, the resemblance is at best tenuous. A more concerted attempt to trace the dance occurs in Schubring's discussion of the F♯-major interlude from the opening movement of the *Faschingsschwank aus Wien*:

Example 4b. Schumann, Intermezzi, Op. 4, no. 5

The rogue even dares to make trouble with the Viennese police. First the informers are reassured by the "Großvater-Tanz" and "Marlborough" (also the trio from the Scherzo of Schubert's symphony!); then, suddenly, in the middle of all this there sounds, as if it had to be, the *Marseillaise*. The informers sharpen their ears, already they want to—but wait; what they really heard was not that dangerous *sans-culotte*, for now comes Grandpapa again! And yet, you most wise gentleman, you are being led by the nose; for the jester knew well enough the difference between "Marlborough" and the *Marseillaise*. I denounce to you herewith *Die beiden Grenadiere, Hermann und Dorothea*, and "Der arme Peter" (Op. 53).[14]

So the process of quotation now takes on a certain element of intrigue. The new F♯-major theme (example 5a) conjures up for Schubring both "Marlborough" (known to German audiences as the melody Beethoven chose in *Wellington's Victory* for the entrance of the French army; see example 5b) and the trio from the Scherzo of Schubert's "Great" C-major Symphony (example 5c). Of course, the latter was discovered by Schumann during his Viennese sojourn in 1839, when he visited Schubert's brother Ferdinand.[15] The putative link between the symphony and the contemporaneous *Faschingsschwank* is an inge-

Example 5a. Schumann, *Faschingsschwank aus Wien*, Op. 26, no. 1

Example 5b. Beethoven, *Wellington's Victory* ("Marlborough")

Example 5c. Schubert, Symphony no. 9 in C major ("Great"), D. 944 (trio of the Scherzo)

nious idea, but whether Schumann's theme is close enough to qualify as an allusion to the Schubert is unclear, to say the least. And the supposed appearance of the "Großvater-Tanz," too, remains dubious. Schubring evidently means the figure in the alto voice (B–E–D♯), provided with note repetitions and dotted rhythms, not utterly unlike the dance (example 5d).

Example 5d. Schumann, *Faschingsschwank aus Wien*, Op. 26, no. 1

But that ascending leap of the fourth could also serve to prepare the ensuing (and unmistakable) entrance of the *Marseillaise* (cf. example 1a). Perhaps unwittingly, Schubring thus appears to join the others whom Schumann leads by the nose.

Schubring's other examples yield mixed results. In the fourth of the Hans Christian Andersen Lieder ("Der Spielmann," Op. 40), for example, a poor musician is forced to play at the wedding of his beloved, and Schubring takes it for granted that his material, characterized by a dotted rhythmic figure with a rising minor third, revives the "Großvater-Tanz." Similarly, the two settings of Eichendorff's "Im Walde" (the Lied Op. 39, no. 11, and the part-song Op. 75, no. 2), are made to respond to the image of the nocturnal bridal procession by invoking the "Großvater-Tanz"; of the two, the solo Lied comes closer to the dance. Schubring does not hesitate to have Siegfried in the third act of *Genoveva* and the Peri in the second part of *Das Paradies und die Peri* invest the old dance tune with new life, though in these cases the musical evidence seems contrived to meet the requirements of the critic's agenda.

If our reading of Schubring encourages caution in rummaging through Schumann's scores for musical quotations, what can we safely say about the composer's indulgence in references? Nicholas Marston has recently reminded us that allusions and quotations are a "means of bringing into a work material which exists independently of the work itself."[16] If quotations are intended to be easily recognizable (and therefore constitute more or less literal restatements of material), allusions embrace a considerably broader class of references, ranging from examples that impress as slightly revised or emended quotations to examples that allude to the external source in covert ways. Of course, it is this second subclass that poses special problems for the researcher: in a particular example, does the mask indeed conceal a reference; or does reexamination of the evidence suggest that the mask conceals nothing—that there is, in fact, no allusion?

In endeavoring to unmask allusions, we enter a realm of conjecture that can be as elusive and ephemeral as Schumann's butterflies. Yet the attempt must be made, even if we lose ourselves in the web: to explicate Schumann's music is inevitably to consider the possibility of external references, of the rich intertextuality between his music and external musical-literary ideas. The complexity of what is at stake is readily evident in that locus classicus of Schumann "quotations," the alleged reference to Beethoven's "An die ferne Geliebte" in the first movement of the Fantasy, Op. 17 (examples 6a and 6b).

Example 6a. Schumann, Fantasy, Op. 17 (first movement, conclusion)

Nimm sie— hin denn, die - se Lie - der,

Example 6b. Beethoven, "An die ferne Geliebte," Op. 98, no. 6

At first glance, the supporting evidence is impressive indeed. The Fantasy had its origins as a "Sonata for Beethoven," Schumann's response to the plan to raise a monument to the composer in Bonn. That Schumann would incorporate Beethoven references in his homage to that master should hardly be surprising. Second, the first movement was composed in June 1836, during Schumann's separation from Clara—thus, the reference to the "distant beloved" could reflect the composer's personal life. Third, the famous motto at the head of the Fantasy, the closing quatrain from Friedrich Schlegel's poem "Die Gebüsche," refers to a gentle tone intended for one who secretly listens. Surely that "leiser Ton" emerges at the end of the first movement in the Adagio, where the lyrical strains putatively associated with "An die ferne Geliebte" are heard several times (example 6a). The essential shape of the "quotation"—a rising third and falling fourth—has actually been subtly anticipated in various guises earlier in the movement.[17] Schumann's method thus apparently involves introducing a veiled allusion that is eventually clarified as a quotation—in short, the implicit, concealed reference is unmasked to become explicit.

But this marshaling of evidence does not remove all obstacles. Schumann's silence on the matter could be discounted; there is no pressing reason why we should expect him to remove the mask in his correspondence or diaries, to disclose for our benefit his quotation. But, as Anthony Newcomb and Nicholas Marston have demonstrated, the first published recognition of the "An die ferne Geliebte" quotation did not appear until 1910, in Hermann Abert's biography of Schumann.[18] How is it possible that the later nineteenth century remained silent about Schumann's quotation? In Newcomb's probing formulation, was the Beethoven reference "made by Schumann or created by a more recent critical tradition? . . . Might it be that for Schumann and for the musical culture of the nineteenth century, the quotation was not there—or at least . . . it was not for them part of the content and meaning of the piece, as we now consider it?"

Marston endeavors to reformulate the issue by identifying an "allusive network" that operates in the Fantasy. In labeling Op. 17 a fantasy, he argues, Schumann was effectively "alluding to a particular generic tradition against which we are invited to 'read' his composition. In this sense, the work alludes to all others bearing the same title."[19] Next, Marston seeks to establish a link between Schumann's Fantasy and Schubert's "Wanderer" Fantasy (1823). Analytical evidence of a subtle musical kind is presented (for example, Marston detects vestiges of the characteristic Schubert rhythm, long-short-short, in Schumann's opening and observes the turn to the mediant in both), and the speculation is developed along reasonable enough grounds. After all, as a young man Schumann revered Schubert's music, and in 1828 he wept at the news of the composer's death. Nevertheless, I find it difficult to hear, as Marston would have us do, the beginning of the last movement of Op. 17 as a muted echo of the stentorian beginning of the "Wanderer" Fantasy.

But Marston courageously casts the net farther, so that the allusive network can embrace genres other than the fantasy. Thus, the allusion to "An die ferne Geliebte" is expanded to include a reference to Schubert's Lied "An die Musik." Surely there is a musical resemblance here (the same diminished-seventh sonority and rising third, etc.; see example 6c), and surely Schober's ode to the power of music to enrapture could have lifted Schumann "out of the depths of despair to which he had recently sunk."[20]

Example 6c. Schubert, "An die Musik," D. 547

But, if this is the case, could the generic resonance of the "An die ferne Geliebte"/"An die Musik" references extend as well to encompass the opening of Haydn's Symphony no. 97, where we encounter the same diminished-seventh chord, the rising third and falling fourth, the same cadential progression (example 6d)? Or, casting the net farther yet, to the opening of Schubert's String Quintet, D. 956,

Example 6d. Haydn, Symphony no. 97 in C major (first movement, opening measures)

where the melodic gesture appears transposed a third above, on C, instead of the A (example 6e)? Are these generic resonances, covert allusions, or nothing more than coincidental resemblances?[21]

Example 6e. Schubert, String Quintet, D. 956 (first movement, opening measures)

There is, of course, no final answer to the question. In searching for these references, we may be satisfying our need to discover a meaning, to read, reread, and interpret Schumann's musical text, more than elucidating Schumann's need to indulge in allusions. We may be practicing a kind of fantasizing—an experience with which Schumann, who evidently designed the individual titles for the *Kinderszenen* only *after* their composition, would have been quite familiar.

It should now be clear that Schumann's musical quotations and allusions resist any ready-made classification according to a precise methodology. There may be some value, however, in arranging them loosely in three groups—references to earlier historical styles and composers, references to Schumann's contemporaries, and self-quotations. In closing, we shall consider a few examples of each group and examine the types of material to which Schumann referred and the musical contexts in which he placed references, thereby shedding, perhaps, some light on the way in which he spun his compositional web.

As a journalist Schumann shaped and refined his essential view of the historical progression of music; in his own music, he employed references to earlier periods and composers to corroborate that view, to establish a context in which to relate his own music to the historical tradition. Of course, in the 1830s, investigations into "early" music, especially into music before Bach, were at best rudimentary; a firm tradition of musical historiography was not yet established. Thus, as Leon Plantinga has observed, Schumann's musical memory (and that of his time) was relatively short; for Schumann, "Bach was the first of a series of great composers whose personal contributions comprised the locus of an inevitable line of progress leading to his own time."[22] From Bach the progression continued with Mozart (curiously, Schumann did not value Haydn highly), Beethoven, and Schubert, down to Schumann's own generation.[23]

Not surprisingly, Schumann paid homage to all these (and others) in a variety of references and allusions. Thus, Bach was memorialized in Schumann's penchant for learned counterpoint, culminating in that erudite fugal compendium for organ, the Six Fugues on B A C H, Op. 60 (1845); and Schumann may well have been thinking of Mozart and attempting to invoke a relatively lean, classical style in a series of orchestral works from the early 1840s, including the Second Symphony, the unfinished symphonic sketches in C minor (1841),[24] and the sinfoniettalike Overture, Scherzo, and Finale, Op. 52.[25] References to Beethoven are, to say the least, abundant.[26] Apart from the Fantasy, the early, unfinished G-minor Symphony (1832) has close ties to the *Eroica*; the *Etüden in Form freier Variationen über ein Beethovensches Thema* (1833) are based on the slow movement of the Seventh Symphony (but also display quotations from the first movement of the Seventh and from the *Pastoral* and Ninth Symphonies); the Impromptus (a variation set in which the bass line of the theme appears first, followed by the theme, variations, and culminating fugue) clearly allude to the finale of Beethoven's *Eroica*; and Beethoven's late string quartets and other works cast their long shadow over Schumann's String Quartets Op. 41.[27] As for Schubert, the *Papillons*, a chainlike series of dances, reflect Schubert's dance sets; moreover, the opening of *Carnaval* was originally conceived for the *Scènes musicales sur un thème connu de Fr. Schubert* (the *Sehnsuchtswalzer*, Op. 9, no. 2). Schumann's references occasionally extended to secondary figures, whom Schumann probably viewed as spurs off the main line of the "central tradition."[28] Thus, Carl Maria von Weber was invoked in the late *Konzert-Allegro mit Introduktion* in D minor for piano and orchestra, Op. 134 (1853). A virtuoso *Konzertstück* written for Brahms, Schumann's Allegro begins with a slow introduction whose opening gesture for the piano, with its characteristic descending diminished fourth, clearly alludes to Weber's celebrated *Konzertstück* of 1821 (examples 7a and 7b), the work that spawned an impressive progeny of nineteenth-century concertos, including those of Mendelssohn, Liszt, and Schumann himself.

R. Larry Todd

con duolo e ben tenuto la melodia

Example 7a. Weber, *Konzertstück*, Op. 79 (first movement, piano entrance)

sehr gehalten zu spielen
molto sostenuto
Solo

Example 7b. Schumann, *Konzert-Allegro mit Introduktion*, Op. 134 (mm. 4–7)

Though for Schumann (and certainly for many of his contemporaries) Bach was the *fons et origo* of the main German musical tradition, Schumann occasionally sought to evoke a prebaroque musical period by exploring the *stile antico*, a specific type of counterpoint associated with the sixteenth-century polyphony of Palestrina. Schumann's experiments here constitute a discrete class of examples that evidence the special power of historical allusions in his music. Whether he was encouraged in this endeavor through his studies of Bach—who in his later years had occasionally invoked the *stile antico* to respect the "purity and durability of the old style"[29]—remains unclear. In 1829, Schumann had met in Heidelberg Justus Thibaut, whose monograph, *Ueber Reinheit der Tonkunst* (1825), had reaffirmed for the romantic generation the viability of the Palestrinian ideal;[30] and it may be that Thibaut led Schumann to examine sixteenth-century polyphony. For Schumann the *stile antico* was distinguished by three stylistic features: 1) imitative writing, recalling the Palestrinian point of imitation; 2) careful control of dissonance, in keeping with the "pure" style of Palestrina, as exemplified in the celebrated *Pope Marcellus* Mass; and 3) rhythmic motion with the half note as the basic tactus, and experimentation with "antique" meters such as 2/2, 3/2, and 4/2.

These three features are evident in a variety of works from Schumann's mature and late periods; in each example, the allusion to the *stile antico* is prompted by textual or extramusical considerations. Thus, in the second Lied of the *Kerner Gedichte*, Op. 35, the essential poetic image of the Augsburg Cathedral explains the invocation of an "ancient" style: the Lied is written in 4/2 meter (notated as **¢¢**) and displays an imitative texture with carefully controlled dissonances (example 8).[31]

Example 8. Schumann, *Kerner Gedichte*, Op. 35, no. 2, "Stirb, Lieb und Freud!" (opening measures)

Similar in mood, and also in A♭ major, is the opening of the *Sanctus* from the Mass, Op. 147 (1852), again in 4/2 meter and with regulated dissonances. In the famous "Auf einer Burg" from the *Liederkreis* (Op. 39, no. 7), Eichendorff's antiquated knight, cloistered in his cell for several hundred years, is depicted in a sparse, imitative texture with falling fifths moving in half notes and modal inflections; the final cadence with the raised Picardy third, though not Palestrinian, creates a special aural effect temporally well removed from Schumann's time.

Perhaps the most extraordinary allusion to the *stile antico* occurs in the fourth movement of the "Rhenish" Symphony (1850). As is well known, this solemn music was inspired by the elevation of the archbishop of Cologne to the rank of cardinal; Schumann witnessed the proceedings at the Cathedral (at the time still under construction) and originally labeled the movement an "Accompaniment to a Solemn Ceremony."[32] The movement is in three parts, broadening in meter from c to 3/2 and 4/2, and contains imitative writing. But its severely chromatic style and use of fuguelike stretto and diminution also point to the richly affective music of Bach. Surely the head motive, a rising series in which two perfect fourths frame a diminished fourth (example 9a), has baroque antecedents (something like it may be found in the C♯-minor fugue from the first volume of Bach's *Well-Tempered Clavier*; see example 9b). Schumann later recalled this motive in the *Agnus Dei* of his Mass, where we find the same series of fourths, though in *descending* order (example 9c).

Example 9a. Schumann, Symphony no. 3 in E♭ ("Rhenish"), Op. 97 (fourth movement, beginning)

The effect of this ceremonial (*feierlich*) music is to revive the *stile antico* through the style of J. S. Bach, so that two historical allusions are conflated in the symphony in a uniquely Schumannesque, romantic way.

Example 9b. J. S. Bach, *Well-Tempered Clavier*, Fugue in C♯ minor, book 1 (opening)

Example 9c. Schumann, Mass, *Agnus Dei* (opening measures)

Much of Schumann's activity as the editor of the *Neue Zeitschrift für Musik* was devoted to reviewing sizeable quantities of new music. In alluding to his contemporaries in his own music, Schumann performed a complimentary critical role by singling out for musical treatment certain composers whom he especially respected—again, in keeping with the promulgated aim of the journal, to promote higher standards in music and to combat musical philistinism. To some extent Schumann's criticism informed the very style and contents of his own music. In effect, the sturdy League of Davidites assembled in Schumann's critical writings was revisited in his music through a series of references and allusions. Thus, Chopin appeared in the celebrated re-creation of a nocturnelike texture in *Carnaval*, and, moreover, Schumann began but never finished a set of variations on Chopin's Nocturne in G minor, Op. 15, no. 3.[33] Similarly, Mendelssohn, on whom the critic Schumann bestowed the sobriquet "Meritis," figured in Schumann's music in several allusions to the two genres especially associated with that contemporary, the *Lied ohne Worte* and the Scherzo (e.g., the String Quartets Op. 41, dedicated to "his friend Felix Mendelssohn Bartholdy," and the "Erinnerung" from the *Jugendalbum*, Op. 68, no. 28, written after Mendelssohn's death in November 1847).

In a special class by herself, of course, was Clara Wieck, whose piano music prompted numerous references in Schumann's works, most of them specific quotations that appeared in his piano music. Among the most striking is Schumann's introduction of the *Notturno*, Op. 6, no. 2 (1836), into the concluding number of the *Noveletten*, Op. 21, written in 1838 during the period of his separation from Clara (examples 10a and 10b).

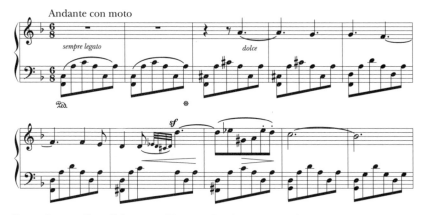

Example 10a. Clara Schumann, *Notturno*, Op. 6, no. 2 (opening measures)

Example 10b. Schumann, *Noveletten*, Op. 21, no. 8

Marked "Stimme aus der Ferne" ("Voice from afar"), the reference appears first in the "removed" key of D major (the *Notturno* is in F major), with the melody in augmented and largely unornamented values, and with the accompaniment altered so that its dotted rhythms accord with those of the preceding section in the *Noveletten* (trio II). In the following "Fortsetzung," Schumann elaborates the melodic sketch, now adding ornamental detail that brings its lyrical phrases closer to Clara's original. The concluding section of the cycle, marked "Fortsetzung und Schluß," begins with fresh material, and all traces of the *Notturno* are lost until the melody eventually returns in augmented values, now transposed to its proper pitch, as if to suggest a symbolic reunion with Clara.

The surprising extent and range of Schumann's references to his contemporaries may be gauged by one final reference, a striking, though so far overlooked, quotation. The Scherzo of the Fourth Symphony (first version, 1841) begins with a canonic head motive that almost certainly was borrowed from the Menuetto of Johann Wenzel Kalliwoda's Symphony no. 1, Op. 7 (1826; see examples 11a and 11b). In 1833 Schumann dedicated his Intermezzi, Op. 4, to this little-known Bohemian composer, who figures in several entries in the *Tage-*

Example 11a. Schumann, Symphony no. 4 in D minor, Op. 120 (Scherzo, opening measures)

Example 11b. J. W. Kalliwoda, Symphony no. 1, Op. 7 (Menuetto, opening measures)

bücher; indeed, at a concert in Zwickau on 28 April 1829, Schumann heard the particular Kalliwoda symphony in question.[34] Though the symphonies are in different keys (Kalliwoda's in F minor; Schumann's in D minor), the two movements begin with the same rising, triadically inspired figure that is imitated canonically two measures later at the octave below. Whereas Kalliwoda sustains the two-part canon for several measures (and introduces a fresh canon for the trio), Schumann soon breaks it off, so that the contrapuntal allusion is short-lived. But despite its brevity, the quotation assumes yet another significance: Kalliwoda's embrace of high counterpoint in his minuet reflects a long tradition in German instrumental music—witness, to mention a few examples, the canonic minuets of Haydn's Symphonies nos. 3, 23, and 44 and the String Quartet Op. 76, no. 2 ("Quinten"); the canonic minuets of Mozart's String Quintets K. 406 and 593; and the trio to the third movement of Beethoven's Fifth Symphony, with its mock fugato.[35] It may well be, then, that Schumann was not only paying homage to his friend but also endeavoring to relate his own music to an older historical tradition.

With the third and final class of references—self-quotations—Schumann turned his critical gaze inward, to contemplate the innermost strands of his compositional web. These examples are understandably the most mysterious and difficult to elucidate. We may propose that they involve critical rehearings or interpretations by the composer of his own music in unexpected contexts. In each case, the quoted material is clearly set off or articulated in the formal process. A cluster of examples centering around the final movement of *Kreisleriana* will serve to introduce the issues involved.

Kreisleriana (1838) has long remained one of Schumann's more enigmatic creations; its inspiration was no doubt the writings of E.T.A. Hoffmann, but whether Schumann had in mind Hoffmann's literary-musical cycle *Kreisleriana* (1814–15) or his novel *Kater Murr* (1820–21), with its intercalated, fragmentary biography of the madcap Kapellmeister Johannes Kreisler, is unclear.[36] The G-minor finale (no. 8) is usually remembered for its giguelike character (example 12a), and indeed its indebtedness to that dance form is not difficult to establish. In 1841 Schumann published his four *Klavierstücke*, Op. 32, the second of which is a gigue in G minor whose subject clearly recalls the opening of the *Kreisleriana* finale (example 12b).

Example 12a. Schumann, *Kreisleriana*, Op. 16, no. 8 (opening measures)

Example 12b. Schumann, *Klavierstück*, Op. 32, no. 2, "Gigue" (opening measures)

Comparing the two subjects, we see that in Op. 32 Schumann crafted a full-fledged fugal gigue that not only makes explicit the dance origins of the *Kreisleriana* finale but also realizes the contrapuntal potential of the subject. The latter feature bears critically on our understanding of the music, for in the *Kreisleriana* finale there are no signs of contrapuntal gamesmanship; rather, the dancelike subject is doubled throughout by an inner voice and accompanied by a slowly moving bass line. In Op. 32, the combination of fugue and gigue, of course, points to another allusion—to the dance suites of J. S. Bach, whose gigues are often coupled with elaborate fugal designs.[37] Thus the process of self-quotation in Op. 32 is allied with the deeper historical allusion to Bach. Schumann was especially intrigued by the gigue subject, for in 1841 he also used its opening measures in another finale, that of the First Symphony (example 12c).

Example 12c. Schumann, Symphony no. 1 in B♭, Op. 38 (finale, mm. 43–49)

Here the quotation appears as an interpolation within the first thematic group, where it is heard, with its dotted rhythms smoothed out and its 6/8 dance meter replaced, in G minor and D minor in the exposition and in C minor and G minor in the recapitulation. Its four capricious entries are thus connected through a chain of fifths (C–G–D), though in the context of the whole they impress as parenthetical interruptions, a series of *papillon*-like gestures that momentarily confound the expected order of events in the sonata-form finale in B♭ major. And, significantly, the giguelike origins of the subject are now well concealed.

In 1843 Schumann composed an Andante and Variations for the unusual combination of two pianos, horn, and two cellos. When the work was rehearsed in March 1843, Clara found that the tone quality

was not tender enough;[38] at Mendelssohn's suggestion Schumann revised the piece and rearranged it for two pianos,[39] and the work appeared later that year as Op. 46. In the original version, published by
Brahms in 1893,[40] Schumann designed the work to include a brief
introduction, the theme, eleven variations, and return of the theme.
The revised version, however, began with the theme and continued
with only nine variations before the return of the theme and the coda.
One of the deleted variations—the fifth and central variation of the
first version—contained an explicit quotation from the opening song
of *Frauenliebe und -leben*, Op. 42 (1840). As examples 13a and 13b
show, Schumann appropriated the first two bars of the song and
placed them in the cellos, in the same key and register. In the following measures, which are exchanged between the cellos and pianos, he
then departed from the Lied to descend harmonically by step to A♭
and G♭ major, in contrast to the original ascent to the supertonic C
minor.

Example 13a. Schumann, *Frauenliebe und -leben*, Op. 42, no. 1 (opening measures)

We do not know why Schumann chose to quote this particular Cha-
misso setting, but its critical position not only in the variations—it is
the central variation and is set off by fermatas on either side—but also
in the song cycle—the piano part of the opening song returns as a

Example 13b. Schumann, Andante and Variations, Op. 46 (first version, fifth variation)

piano postlude to conclude the eighth and final song of the cycle—
suggests that he had some special purpose. In her diaries Clara commented on the "innerliche gemütliche" quality of the variations and
of the "zartes, poetisches Spiel" necessary for their performance.[41]
The essential melodic gesture of the Lied—the neighbor-note motive
F–G–F—possibly inspired the original introduction to the variations
(example 13c) in which the same figure is featured prominently, and it
possibly affected as well the shape of the theme of Op. 46, which begins with an embellished version of the neighbor-note motive (example 13d).

Example 13c. Schumann, Andante and Variations, Op. 46 (opening measures)

Example 13d. Schumann, Andante and Variations, Op. 46 (theme)

Whatever Schumann's motivation, the removal of the central variation and the introduction also deleted the most important traces of
the song and the crucial evidence that the process of self-quotation
was once again integral to the compositional process of Op. 46.

By weaving into his music a diverse range of external musical references, Schumann considerably broadened the very meaning of his
music to embrace a historical progression of composers and styles
leading up to his own time. In its own way, Schumann's compositional
practice thus supported the formation of the traditional German musical canon, a process that was quickening during the 1830s and
1840s. Other composers, too, were involved with this process. For ex-

ample, Ludwig Spohr's "Historical" Symphony (no. 6; 1840), with its progression from Bach and Handel to Haydn and Mozart, Beethoven, and the "allerneueste Periode," betrays a similar kind of historicism, as do Mendelssohn's considerable efforts at the Gewandhaus concerts in Leipzig, where he designed and performed a series of historical concerts.[42] But none developed quotation as a compositional tool with the degree of sophistication, complexity, and subtlety that Schumann achieved. For him, the search for one's compositional roots, the perennial retracing (and rehearing) of one's compositional steps, was no mere slavish imitation of historical models, a charge often leveled against Mendelssohn. Rather, for Schumann, as he noted in his diary in 1831, "the future should be a higher echo of the past" ("Die Zukunft soll das höhere Echo der Vergangenheit sein").[43] Schumann's quotations and references are enriching echoes of the musical past—the musical past of Schumann's generation, and of Schumann himself.

NOTES

1. Schumann used the term in 1841, during the rapid composition of the Fourth Symphony. Robert Schumann, *Tagebücher, Band III: Haushaltbücher, Teil I: 1837–1847*, ed. Gerd Nauhaus (Leipzig, 1982), p. 184. Entry for 29 May 1841.

2. Embedded in the figuration of the treble staff is a rhythmically displaced doubling one octave above the unplayed inner voice, a suitably Schumann-esque masking of the material.

3. Fanfares of fifths and fourths are, of course, common in the symphonic literature, and it is difficult to determine whether Schumann intended the subdued opening of his Second Symphony to invoke the magisterial beginning of Haydn's Symphony no. 104 in D major. Nevertheless, Anthony Newcomb, labeling the opening an allusion, asserts that it "proclaims as effectively as a poetic preamble one quite specific program: Schumann's courageous and ambitious decision to measure for the first time his particular methods and abilities against the overwhelmingly, even terrifyingly prestigious tradition of the Viennese Classical symphony." See his "Once More 'Between Absolute and Program Music': Schumann's Second Symphony," *19th-Century Music* 7 (1984): 240.

4. Part of this web, of course, attracts the various bits of evidence that Schumann employed musical ciphers to convey verbal meanings, a thesis thoroughly explored during the 1960s by Eric Sams. See "Did Schumann Use Ciphers?" *Musical Times* 106 (1965): 584–91, and "The Schumann Ciphers," ibid., vol. 107 (1966): 392–400, 1050–51.

5. Both, of course, contain treatments of musical balls. Frederick Niecks

viewed the *Papillons* as a "young *Carnaval*" and the *Carnaval* as a "higher kind of *Papillons*." See *Programme Music in the Last Four Centuries* (Edinburgh, 1907; reprint, New York, 1969), pp. 193, 195.

6. In the seventh, concluding variation of Clara's own variations on Schumann's *Albumblatt*—written at the same time as Brahms's Op. 9 and published as her Op. 20 in 1854—Clara also cites her theme used by Robert in his Op. 5.

7. See Oliver Neighbour, "Brahms and Schumann: Two Opus Nines and Beyond," *19th-Century Music* 7 (1984): 266–70, which takes into account Constantin Floros, "Schumann und Brahms: Die Schumann-Variationen (Op. 9) von Brahms und die 'Davidsbündlertänze' von Schumann," in Floros's *Brahms und Bruckner: Studien zur musikalischen Exegetik* (Wiesbaden, 1980), pp. 115–43.

8. C. Koßmaly, "Ueber Robert Schumann's Claviercompositionen," *Allgemeine musikalische Zeitung* 46 (1844), col. 36. See also pp. 303–16 here.

9. Wilhelm Joseph von Wasielewski, *Life of Robert Schumann*, trans. A. L. Alger (Boston, 1871; reprint, Detroit, 1975), p. 94; Wasielewski's biography appeared in German in 1858, two years after the composer's death.

10. "Schumann und der Großvater," *Neue Zeitschrift für Musik* 53 (1860): 29–30. For a translation of the fourth in the series, "Die gegenwärtige Musikepoche und Robert Schumann's Stellung in der Musikgeschichte," see pp. 362–74 here. The eighth "Schumanniana," which treats Brahms as a Schumann disciple, has been examined by Walter Frisch in "Brahms and Schubring: Musical Criticism and Politics at Mid-Century," in *19th-Century Music* 7 (1984): 271–81. Adolf Schubring was the stepbrother of Julius Schubring, a pastor from Dessau who assisted Mendelssohn in preparing the libretti of the oratorios *St. Paul* (1836) and *Elijah* (1846).

11. On the position of *Winterszeit* in the *Jugendalbum*, see p. 186.

12. To be fair, Schubring is no doubt referring to the second edition of the Impromptus, which appeared in 1850, with a new fourth variation. Of course, in revising Op. 5, Schumann could have incorporated revisions retrospectively to strengthen the idea of a *Brautwerbung*, but the musical evidence still does not support Schubring's assertion.

13. It appeared in 1893 in series 14 of *Robert Schumann's Werke* (published by Breitkopf and Härtel), a supplementary volume edited by Brahms.

14. *Die beiden Grenadiere* and the overture to *Hermann und Dorothea* do quote the *Marseillaise*. Evidently for Schubring the opening of *Der arme Peter* (Op. 53, no. 3, to a text by Heine) resembled "Marlborough," though at the end of his article Schubring cites the same Lied for recalling the Grandfather Dance (presumably, he has in mind the passage "Der Hans und die Grete sind Bräut'gam und Braut" ["Hansel and Gretel are bridegroom and bride"]).

15. See Peter Krause, "Unbekannte Dokumente zur Uraufführung von Franz Schuberts großer C-Dur-Sinfonie durch Felix Mendelssohn Bartholdy," in *Beiträge zur Musikwissenschaft* 29 (1987): 240–50.

16. Nicholas Marston, *Schumann: "Fantasie," Op. 17* (Cambridge, 1992), p. 34.

17. See Anthony Newcomb, "Schumann and the Marketplace: From But-

terflies to *Hausmusik*," in *Nineteenth-Century Piano Music*, ed. R. Larry Todd (New York, 1990), pp. 295–96.

18. Hermann Abert, *Robert Schumann*, 2d ed. (Berlin, 1910), p. 64.

19. Marston, *Schumann: "Fantasie," Op. 17*, p. 40.

20. Ibid., p. 41.

21. Admittedly, no particular reason stands out why Schumann should allude to a Haydn symphony in his Fantasy for piano; the similarities among examples 6a, 6b, 6c, 6d, and 6e underscore again the elusive quality of quotations and allusions.

22. Leon Plantinga, *Schumann as Critic* (New Haven, 1967), p. 85.

23. As Bernhard Appel has shown, Schumann tested another historical progression by planning to include pieces by Bach, Handel, Gluck, Mozart, Haydn, Beethoven, Weber, and Mendelssohn in the *Jugendalbum* that he prepared for his daughter Marie in 1848. See p. 174.

24. See Gerd Nauhaus's essay in this volume, pp. 113–28.

25. Jon W. Finson sees Op. 52 as evidence of Schumann's attempt to achieve a "popular and marketable composition." See "Schumann, Popularity, and the *Ouvertüre, Scherzo, und Finale*, Opus 52," *Musical Quarterly* 69 (1983): 25.

26. For a speculative account, see J. Barrie Jones, "Beethoven and Schumann: Some Literary and Musical Allusions," *Music Review* 49 (1988): 114–25.

27. Thus the nontonic opening of the Third Quartet is modeled on the opening of Beethoven's Piano Sonata Op. 31, no. 3, and several references to Beethoven's String Quartet Op. 132 occur in Schumann's First Quartet.

28. Plantinga, *Schumann as Critic*, p. 98.

29. John Butt, *Bach: Mass in B Minor* (Cambridge, 1991), p. 2.

30. Two years before, in 1827, Mendelssohn had traveled to Heidelberg to see Thibaut; one result of the meeting was Mendelssohn's Palestrinian motet *Tu es Petrus*, Op. 111, for five-part chorus and orchestra.

31. We must pass over other unusual stylistic features: the use of the breve and *longa*, which gives the music an "ancient" look, the surprise nontonic ending, and the rhythmic stratification, with distinct layers of whole, half, and quarter notes, suggesting several temporal levels and, indeed, a certain timeless quality.

32. Wasielewski, *Life of Robert Schumann*, p. 173.

33. An edition by Joachim Draheim (Wiesbaden, 1992) is now available. As Draheim observes in his foreword, the Chopin variations were part of a series, tracing yet another historical progression, in which Schumann contemplated variation sets on themes by Beethoven, Prince Louis Ferdinand of Prussia, Weber, Schubert, and Paganini.

34. Robert Schumann, *Tagebücher, Band I: 1827–1838*, ed. Georg Eismann (Leipzig, 1971), p. 192.

35. On Haydn's canonic minuets, see Gretchen A. Wheelock, *Haydn's Ingenious Jesting with Art* (New York, 1992), pp. 43–45, 64–68.

36. For a fresh reevaluation of Hoffmann's *Kreisleriana*, see "E.T.A. Hoff-

mann's Musical Writings: Kreisleriana, the Poet, and the Composer," in E.T.A. Hoffmann, *Music Criticism*, ed. David Charlton, trans. Martyn Clarke (Cambridge, 1989), pp. 23–55.

37. A twentieth-century revival of this coupling may be found in the finale of Stravinsky's Septet (1954).

38. Robert Schumann, *Tagebücher, Band II: 1836–1854*, ed. Gerd Nauhaus (Leipzig, 1987), p. 260.

39. See Schumann's letter to Raimund Härtel of 7 March 1843, in F. Gustav Jansen, ed., *Robert Schumanns Briefe: Neue Folge* (Leipzig, 1904), p. 435 and p. 539, n. 530.

40. See n. 13.

41. Schumann, *Tagebücher, Band II: 1836–1854*, pp. 268, 337.

42. On Mendelssohn's performances of Mozart, for example, see R. Larry Todd, "Mozart According to Mendelssohn: A Contribution to *Rezeptionsgeschichte*," in *Perspectives on Mozart Performance*, ed. R. Larry Todd and Peter Williams (Cambridge, 1991), pp. 158–203.

43. *Tagebücher, Band I: 1827–1838*, p. 304.

Schumann's Symphonic Finales

GERD NAUHAUS

TRANSLATED BY SUSAN GILLESPIE

The tendency to let the final movement of a symphony become its most significant part, the goal and climax of all its developments, its summarizing apotheosis, evidently belongs more to the "second age of the symphony,"[1] the age of Brahms, Bruckner, and Mahler, than to the period after the deaths of Beethoven and Schubert, which was relatively dry in terms of symphonic production. Yet it appears beyond doubt that Schumann, following the familiar great models, Mozart's "Jupiter" and Beethoven's Fifth and Ninth Symphonies, and coincident with as unique and inimitable a work as Mendelssohn's *Lobgesang*,[2] made significant contributions toward solving the question of the finale, or at any rate attempted solutions, and in this way performed a historically indispensable transitional function. He did this, of course, in his own way; and only recent Schumann scholarship has really begun to assess this contribution in Schumann's own terms. I can do no more here than report some of the results as they pertain to this subject, paraphrase them, and perhaps set occasional accents of my own.

That in considering the finale of a symphony, or the ways and means involved in its creation, we always must consider the complete work—in a way not relevant to the slow movement, the Scherzo, or even the first movement—follows from what was stated above and is perhaps a truism in any case. Consequently, we must also reassess the question of the program, the content of Schumann's symphonies, as it has been posed repeatedly in recent decades with reference both to

This article first appeared in *Probleme der symphonischen Tradition im 19. Jahrhundert*, ed. Siegfried Kross and Marie Luise Maintz (Tutzing, 1990), pp. 307–20. The editor is grateful to Hans Schneider for permission to translate it here. [Ed.]

the symphonies as a whole and to the sequence of their parts. It may not be possible to establish a definitive and universally valid conclusion, but some basic facts can be considered secure.

Schumann begins his symphonic production—if one excludes the very early fragments, of interest only as way stations—in the year 1832 with the Symphony in G minor.[3] Already during its composition he felt "[mistrust] of his symphonic talent" while at the same time anticipating "without vanity, the greatest possible things for the future."[4] As is well known, the symphony has no presentable finale; but from the few rough sketches for a finale (one of which may be found in the archives of the Schumann-Haus in Zwickau[5]) it is possible to recognize Schumann's intention to incorporate in it a (final?) fugue on the cadential bass motive C–F–G–C, shown here transposed to G–C–D–G (example 1).

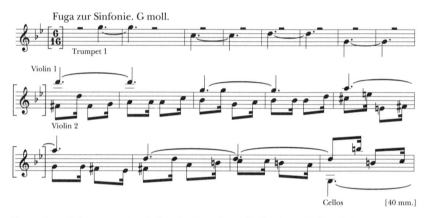

Example 1. Schumann, sketch for the Symphony in G minor (Robert-Schumann-Haus, Zwickau)

This motive turns up in Schumann's diary[6] around May–June 1832—in other words, months *before* he began the composition of the symphony—only, in the end, to be used in combination with Clara Wieck's romance melody as the basis for the Impromptus, Op. 5. In this way, Schumann transformed himself from a symphonic poet back into a composer for the piano. That his failure in the one genre was intimately connected with his reinvolvement in the other, and not separated by any period of reflection, is clear because the sketch in example 1 appears on the same page as a sketch for the finale of Op. 5. An intriguing question, suggested by Reinhard Kapp[7] and worthy of investigation, is whether the fiasco with the finale may have a connection to the attempt to integrate the Scherzo into the slow movement. In any case, the mere fact of this attempt at integration, as a characteristic symptom of the compromising of forms that would continue to haunt Schumann, deserves mention. One perhaps should not dismiss out of hand the supposition that the fugal opening of the G-minor finale finds a resonance in the extended fugatos of the finale of the Symphony in D minor. Indeed, in general, the entire complex of Schumann's symphonic music should be examined more fully for its subterranean relations and interconnections.

After the fragmentary performance of the G-minor Symphony in Leipzig in April 1833 produced no positive results—or, rather, produced the regressive ones described above—the symphonic composer did not reemerge until seven years later. (He worked on the piano concerto movement in D minor somewhat earlier than that, whereas the Allegro in C minor mentioned by Arnfried Edler[8] as an orchestral work was probably for piano solo.) Schumann composed the first of the symphonic fragments in C minor,[9] which is related in tendency, though not thematically, to the second sketch in four movements, written in September 1841. On the symphonic attempts of 13, 14, and 17 October 1840[10] he commented (already speculating on their futility) that he had "ventured into a territory where it is true that not every first step succeeds."[11] It is interesting to note that Edler's characterization[12] of the 1841 fragment, which was more fully developed and indeed probably already completed in his mind, as representing a kind of *symphonie classique* in the briefest terms and with the most limited orchestration, is also applicable to this first attempt. In it, the beginning of Haydn's last symphony is recalled with an abbreviation that can only be called rough and crude (examples 2a and 2b).

Example 2a. Haydn, Symphony no. 104

Example 2b. Schumann, symphonic fragment in C minor (1840)

The further development of the fragment is not of interest here, but it should be noted that the sketch also includes three measures entitled "Rondo" that were evidently intended for a finale and would recur to Schumann barely a year later, when he remembered his C-minor plans and utilized a slightly varied form of the sketch for the most extensive movement of the work, its concluding Rondo (example 3).

[cf. Finson, p. 408]

Example 3. Schumann, symphonic fragments in C minor (1840–41), Universitätsbibliothek, Bonn, autograph no. Schumann 19, pp. 13, 16, 27

That the composer would later be "unable to find his way back into this C-minor symphony"[13] probably has less to do with the difficulty of recalling compositional details from the period of its original creation than with the "classical" theme and conception, which no longer particularly interested Schumann after the composition of the Symphonies in B♭ major (the "Spring"), Op. 38, and D minor, Op. 120. As for the "small"-type symphony, which also seems to have been intended here, he had already come to terms with it with greater success and originality in his Overture, Scherzo, and Finale, Op. 52.

At this point I cannot resist mentioning a circumstance that is not strictly related to the present topic but that I feel remains (despite my own attempts)[14] in need of clarification. I refer to the origin of the undated "third" C-minor fragment, the draft score *Andante—Allegro agitato*, whose principal part has analogies with the first movement of the four-movement sketch of September 1841.[15] I would venture to suggest that this manuscript was created *before* the longer sketch, on 21/22 January 1841, in fact, which seems to be corroborated by a note in the *Haushaltbuch*: "Beginning [of] a symphony in C minor." Further evidence to support this suggestion is found in the inscription *b* (as a reference to the second place in the chronology), which Schumann added to the manuscript of the sketch.[16]

I would not have mentioned this ancillary question if it did not have an immediate bearing on the beginning of Schumann's work on the "Spring" Symphony on 23 January 1841. The abandonment of the one thematic idea—however constructed—and the adoption (and successful completion) of another can undoubtedly be attributed to the introduction of the poetic-programmatic stimulus, Adolf Böttger's poem, which would thus seem to take on an even greater significance for Schumann's creative process. Ludwig Finscher has reminded us in a stimulating essay[17] that we should take seriously the programmatic stimuli that were derived associatively from Böttger's poem and are manifested especially in the original titles of the movements. These stimuli lend the content of the "Spring" Symphony its characteristic color and give its form the otherwise inexplicable divergences from and tensions with the classical model. In the context of this essay, this means that in the first work Schumann composed during 1841, the "symphonic year," he began by completing preliminary studies for a future shift of emphasis to the symphonic finale. Among the notable characteristics of these preliminary studies, along with the expansion of the finale to a size comparable with the first movement, I would concur with Reinhard Kapp[18] in including the closer relationship of the two middle movements (which complement each other in the manner of "night" and "day" pieces);[19] the almost *attacca* beginning of the finale;[20] the greater importance the latter assumes because of its mottolike opening gesture, later fully integrated into the movement; and even a detail like the "transposition of the cadence for the programmatic instruments, the horn and flute—one could almost say: from the slow movement of Beethoven's "Pastoral" Symphony into the finale"[21] (that is, first, during the movement's opening, by presenting only the flute;[22] and then, when the reprise begins, both instruments together). Of particular interest is Arnfried Edler's[23] interpretation of the opening motto and, above all, its reformulation in the reprise (example 4).

Example 4. Schumann, Symphony no. 1 in B♭ major, Op. 38 ("Spring"), finale, reprise theme

Edler sees this rhythmically conceived central figure as a kind of general theme for the entire symphony, which, in keeping with the "novellalike character"[24] of all Schumann's symphonies, unfolds in a variety of metamorphoses and intensifications and finally appears—led by the poetic idea—near the conclusion of the cycle in its final formulation (full springtime, or spring's farewell), as summary and climax. Edler's inclusion of the "Spring" Symphony among the "finale symphonies" is equally convincing. Admittedly, one must consider that according to our listening habits the actual themes of the finale, which appear in their traditional places but no longer possess the specific gravity of actual thematic formulations, are not sufficiently weighty. This explains why the finale is generally not recognized for its sublimely new character but rather characterized as a "turbulent *Kehraus*[25] that does not attempt to fascinate us with deep meaning" and also why Schumann is accused of having reduced the sonata form to "no more than a formal shell."[26] This much is true: the development of new, freer formal ideas and with them the legitimate assignment of a new function to the finale was still some time off, even if the final jubilation of the "Spring" Symphony—whose last five measures correspond with those of the Symphony no. 2 in C major, Op. 61, which Schumann would write five years later—expressed, in part, the composer's justified feelings of joy at his successful, independent creation. Schumann could now apply his recent comments on Schubert's C-major Symphony,[27] D. 944, almost word-for-word to his own first-born symphony, which "has been received with an interest that I do not believe has greeted another recent symphony since Beethoven."[28]

The concept of the finale is already found—assuredly not by accident—in the title of the following symphonic composition of the year 1841.[29] The Overture, Scherzo, and Finale, which is characterized variously as "Sinfonietta," "Symphonette," "Suite," and once as "II. Sinfonie," represents, as noted above, the "small" symphony with a reduced number of movements, each of which was supposed to enjoy relative independence. (This license, however, is to be regarded more as an argument for increased sales of the work.) Here the integration is in fact looser than in the symphonies, but the finalelike character of the third movement is nevertheless clearly stressed, and the cyclical relationship is marked by a return to the introduction of the overture. The finale is given additional weight by the fugal treatment of the principal theme, a gesture Schumann did not repeat in later works. The hymnlike expansion of both themes in the coda should also be seen as an additional and significant intensification, which resonates through the diverse "breakthroughs" of subsequent compositions but probably could be used in such "naive" form only in a smaller work, such as Op. 52.

Jon W. Finson[30] has sought to show, with the help of Schumann's later revision of Op. 52 (which, however, was merely a reorchestration[31]), that the composer aimed to gain a particular popular success with the work. If we follow Finson's line of argument, the work's failure results primarily from its lack of a slow movement, without which apparently a symphonic work, whatever its size, simply cannot exist. And in fact a certain lack of contrast is perceptible in this little cycle of three lively movements, even if we look at it as only a suite; on the whole, this lack is more significant than the frequently criticized stereotypical rhythm of the Scherzo. Nevertheless, one knows how to appreciate the "light, friendly character"[32] of the whole and not demand too much of it in formal, cyclical terms.

In contrast, the Symphony in D minor, which was drafted in May–June 1841 and worked out in late summer, represents a radical step in this very regard:[33] it is the first attempt in the orchestral domain simultaneously to fulfill and to transcend the traditional symphonic sequence of movements by allowing the individual movements to merge into a single great sonata movement—in Clara Schumann's words,[34] "a symphony . . . that should consist of one movement and yet contain an Adagio [= Romanze] and Finale [i.e., Introduction, Allegro, and Scherzo]."[35] That this "one movement" was specifically to be in sonata form was not always recognized, and was in fact even denied until recently,[36] though this was most certainly Schumann's goal in a higher sense. In identifying the function of the various movements or parts, however, one must always think in terms of "as if," to avoid being puzzled at certain modifications that must also be considered under the rubric of the "poetical idea" or the "novellalike" progress of the action. In any case, an isolated consideration of the finale is neither possible nor sensible, though on the other hand the tendency toward the finale that this symphony betrays is powerfully intensified precisely as a result of the bold and original conception of the whole.

Within the overarching sonata form, the finale serves the function of a reprise, in this case a reprise of a theme emphasized in the development of the opening movement (where it appeared in D♭ and E major, framing the tonic key of D minor, as it were). Two additional themes are added in the finale—since it is not possible simply to repeat familiar material—of which the first is unique to this movement, whereas the second, which emerges during the development, tends to represent the secondary idea and is similar in character to the second theme of the opening movement (example 5).

The function of this reprise as the finale of the whole is strongly emphasized by the significant slow introduction and the doubly intensified coda, of which the "final Presto . . . has never yet failed to have its effect."[37] In the finale, as in the opening movement, the reprise itself is lacking, or is compressed into the first part of the coda and a few measures immediately preceding the conclusion. It is not possible here to give even a bare summary of the dense "net of correspon-

Example 5. Schumann, Symphony no. 4 in D minor, Op. 120, finale and first movement, secondary themes

dences—audible, not only visible on paper"[38]—that is woven through the entire symphony. This "net" guarantees the logical coherence and clarity of the symphony's content, which in its new 1851 version was given the tentative title *Symphonistische Phantasie*.[39] As Egon Voss correctly observes, it has "no program, not even an unspoken one," and yet it does not seem to leave the listener any unsolved riddles. Even more than with the "Spring" Symphony, one must emphasize the independence of Op. 120 from its great forebears, which led to a unique, unmistakable (and in a certain sense inimitable) solution to the problem of the form and the finale. Without repudiating or consciously engaging in the popular search for resemblances that Schumann himself rejected as "uncultivated,"[40] I would like to point out two small, hidden, and alienated reminiscences of Beethoven's *Fidelio* in the finale: the two long seventh chords preceding the final Presto, which reflect the conclusion, naturally much more abrupt and radical in the symphony, of the dungeon scene; and the double entry in the vocal continuation of the final theme (deleted by Schumann in 1851),[41] which recalls the passage in Florestan's aria "Meine Pflicht, ja meine Pflicht [hab ich getan]" (one may or may not take this to be significant). That *Fidelio*, and in particular Florestan's voice, should resonate here is not surprising in view of the much more clearly evident reminiscences from the opera in the A-minor Fantasy for piano and orchestra that Schumann composed immediately before the symphony.[42]

Even somewhat earlier, while composing the Overture, Scherzo, and Finale in April 1841, Schumann had conceived the plan of a *Sinfonia solemnis*[43] for the inauguration of Schwanthaker's Jean Paul monument in Bayreuth, an event that had been scheduled for the anniversary of the poet's birth on 14 November. The Symphony in C minor, which was sketched in September, might have come just in time for this event had Schumann been able to complete it. (It is, however, a nice coincidence that the "Spring" Symphony was intended to be performed on the day after the Leipzig Jean Paul celebration as part of a concert held there.[44]) But as noted above, the composer's second C-minor plan was inadvertently transformed into a classically styled copy in which the opening movement audibly resembled the *Sturm und Drang* symphonies by Haydn or, perhaps, the "little" G-minor Symphony of Mozart (K. 183).[45] Only the Scherzo— the sole movement of the symphony to be published, albeit in a piano reduction—turned out to be truly Schumannian.[46] Thus the draft did not become a *Sinfonia solemnis*, although solemn gestures can be heard in the Allegro of the score fragment (which, if our hypothesis is correct, was composed earlier); however, this material does not function thematically or as a motto (example 6).

Example 6. Schumann, symphonic fragment in C minor (score), Universitätsbibliothek, Bonn, autograph no. Schumann 19, pp. 4–6

The same gestures recur in the Symphony in C major of 1845–46, whose opening betrays a certain unmistakable, if mysteriously muted, solemnity. If any symphony represents the "finale symphony" par excellence in Schumann's oeuvre, it is this one. To nineteenth-century critics, it was a "finale symphony" in the well-known Beethovenian musical and narrative mold; they responded with great respect for Schumann's skill at combining themes, but without any real love for the work. Not until the turn of the century was there a rejection of this viewpoint from a more formal, analytical perspective, which has continued down to the recent past and focused primarily on the construction and function of the symphony's finale. Carl Dahlhaus considered Schumann's attempt to solve the "finale problem" here to be a failure or at best questionable and remarked about a "breaking apart of the form" that was conditioned by the composer's ambivalent approach to the "character and function of the finale" and the related

"exchange of themes" in the course of the movement's development.[47] In the context of the entire work, Dahlhaus spoke of a "lack
of tectonic solidity" that could be concealed, but not replaced, by the
"poetic element" of a wealth of "associative parentheses." One does
not wish to give complete credence to this point of view, although it is
accompanied by a number of keen observations (not, however, including the remark that the middle movements of Schumann's symphonies appear to be "episodes or intermezzi"). It seems to be based on
certain premises and expectations that Schumann—indeed a "genius
of form" for whom the notion of a work in sonata form containing
279 measures with no development and a coda of 309 measures
would have been sheer madness (naturally this is not attributable to
Dahlhaus)[48]—specifically considered not to be important. More appropriate to Schumann's intentions and their realization is the sympathetic commentary by Anthony Newcomb in an essay[49] that describes
the "novellalike" structure of the Symphony in C major with compelling arguments, the most important of which—the creation of "open"
characters in Jean Paul's sense[50]—also provides the justification for
the work's evolving structure, of substantive importance for Schumann's oeuvre as a whole. It would be superfluous to describe the
highly subtle, often imperceptible, development and transformation
of thematic forms to the point where they seem to disappear into the
final realization of the work's basic conceptual features—characteristics that are also noted, although not interpreted in the same way, by
Dahlhaus. I wish merely to emphasize the stringency of such interpretive models as the change in function of the finale from an apparent
lieto fine, or happy ending, to the culmination of the symphony, in
line with a calculation that can be seen from the outset in the harsh
formulation of the motto and main theme, which bear, as it were, the
seeds of their own negation within them. Corresponding to this
change is the radical reformulation of the themes toward a turning
point in their development and ultimately toward the emergence of
the continually prepared reprise theme (the character of which as a
quotation thus assumes secondary importance), which has the concomitant effect of strengthening the sonatalike, as opposed to the
rondolike, characteristics of the finale. The finale, in effect, under-
takes to summarize the entire symphony and consequently undergoes
a not inconsiderable but well-founded expansion.

As concerns the autobiographical aspects of the symphony, which
have been emphasized by many authors on the basis of Schumann's numerous candid statements, those based on musical references probably
have special significance. Here it is possible to contribute an additional

piece of evidence regarding the significant "strengthening" references to Bach (and B A C H), which Newcomb correctly identifies in the second trio of the Scherzo, characterized by its elevated cantabile tone, which recurs in the theme of the finale, and interwoven B A C H cipher. This new evidence leads directly back to the last B A C H fugue for organ, Op. 60, no. 6, which Schumann composed immediately before the symphony, and concerns the "symphonic" turn in the final section,[51] which now, in a new context, can be linked quite easily to a germ cell in the *sostenuto* introduction, positively reinterpreting its gesture of suffering and thus helping to lead the decisive dominant-seventh chord upward before the reprise. The "serene confidence"[52] that unfolds immediately afterward and is continually intensified until it gradually becomes a triumphal gesture takes on the character of something more and more impersonal, general, even public, which makes its emphatic description by Schumann's contemporary Ernst Gottschald as the work's "basic idea" understandable.[53] Gottschald characterizes this basic idea as the "victorious struggle of the particular individuality for the most profound unity with spiritual universality, in which all the egotistical barriers that separate the individual spirits from each other are destroyed, and they love each other as equals, for they live in the realm of freedom, equality, and fraternity." This takes our breath away, especially when we recall that Gottschald made this statement in 1850. And yet, do we not experience something similar when we listen to the "finale in the finale," which Dahlhaus says seems "like a summary of the symphony, as if Schumann were trying [to compose out] the aesthetic experience so that at the conclusion of a musical work all its parts come together again in imaginary simultaneity"?[54] Finscher's memorable comment tends toward the same direction when he says that in this symphony, in a "historically profound" way—blending the individual with the universal and personal creation with a musical-historical process—"the concept of the musical work itself becomes the theme."[55] The wealth and breadth of interpretive possibilities accentuates the work's greatness —even though its affirmative nature may be filled with tension,[56] or even forced—and does not contradict it. Schumann succeeded in this achievement only after many tries; the reader is reminded of the failed C-minor attempts as well as the long period of reflection, as odd as it is singular, between the first hint of the idea suggested in his letter to Mendelssohn ("There has been much drumming and trumpeting in me for the last few days . . . "[57]) and the actual start of the sketches. He treated the theme described by Finscher exhaustively in every sense, so that in his last symphony other paths lay open to him.

Schumann's Symphony in E♭ major, Op. 97, also had a relatively long incubation period between the time of the stimulus recorded by Wasielewski[58]—the sight of the Cologne cathedral on 29 September 1850—and the beginning of work on 2 November, after which, strangely, it was again postponed by a second sojourn in Cologne (with a tour of the cathedral on 6 November).[59] The composer subsequently had "difficulty spinning out the thread of the idea's development in a satisfactory way,"[60] leading to a "comprehensive structural revision" of the development of the opening movement.[61] The second stimulus, the newspaper report of the elevation of the archbishop von Geissel of Cologne to the position of cardinal, seems to have had a less ambivalent effect, because Schumann, when he heard the news, was still preoccupied with his other work and did not write down his vision of the "accompaniment for a solemn ceremony"[62] until two and a half weeks later. It should be noted that after he "brooded over the Adagio" on 1 December[63] the two final movements evidently came to him in a single rush, which confirms our impression of their indivisible unity. If in the finale of the C-major Symphony the reference to the Adagio (which immediately precedes it and constitutes the secondary theme of the exposition) seems considerably more "external" than the references to the Scherzo and the opening movement, the reference nevertheless achieves an antithetical union of the slow movement and finale, with generally stronger but less noticeable structural linkages. The slow movement and finale provide a counterweight to the Allegro-Scherzo pair, whereas the fifth, essentially interpolated, movement, the "Intermezzo,"[64] becomes the deciding factor that tips the scales. If we look upon the Adagio as the spiritual center of the symphony, the finale at first appears to be another *lieto fine* but nevertheless takes on qualities of summary and apotheosis even more convincingly than the Symphony in C major. These qualities begin with the emergence of the prominent new theme in B major that corresponds to the C♭-major fanfares in the Adagio, except that this time the new theme does not swallow up the opening theme but like a locomotive pushes it along in front at the beginning of the reprise. The reprise as the "last finale" is intensified until it becomes a "pushing and driving . . . that seems to toss out the entire thematic contents of the symphony and create new relationships within,"[65] before closing with a turbulent stretto.

If we take seriously Schumann's statement about the "[necessary] preponderance of popular elements"[66] in the symphony and seek them not in the supposedly "flat, almost popular stance" that Wasielewski attributed to the Scherzo and the finale, and that Clara

Schumann[67] attributed to the second and third movements, but rather in an overall conception of the work, then we may once more recall Gottschald's high-minded notion about the "idea" of the Symphony in C major. In the E♭-major Symphony, admittedly, the incorporation of the individual into the universal is completed before the first note sounds. The impression of the universality of community—regarding which the adjective *Rhenish*, thus far avoided, should be used but not overemphasized—of the mass of like-minded people inevitably comes to mind when one listens to Schumann's last symphony and determines its "historic place," as Ernst Lichtenhahn has pointed out.[68] (Peter Gülke's marginal notes to his important essay[69] are similar in tone.) This "historic place" is determined by, among other things, such indications as the lack of a dedication to a "high-ranking person," the more or less evident affinity with the *Marseillaise*,[70] and the like. The communal character of the symphony is present in the enthusiastic joy of the opening movement, the measured dance step of the Scherzo, the friendly nocturnal mood of the Intermezzo, the elevated celebratory tones of the Adagio, and the outpouring of song in the finale. It may be that at this particular time the communal character was illusory and could be achieved only through art. For this very reason one should note that Schumann succeeded in giving the work's "idea" a symphonic form that was as flexible as it was adequate[71] and thus created a model for the following decades and beyond, one that outlived the reign of symphonic composition and offered possibilities of identification and linkage for the "second era of the symphony." True—and this is Schumann's personal tragedy—the greatest public success of his "Rhenish years"[72] was achieved with the more abstract Symphony in D minor; and at the end of his creative existence there remained for him only the appeal to the "*secret* band of kindred spirits."[73]

NOTES

1. Cf. *Musik—zur Sprache gebracht. Musikästhetische Texte aus drei Jahrhunderten*, ed. Carl Dahlhaus and Michael Zimmermann (Munich and Kassel, 1984), p. 286.

2. Cf. Reinhard Kapp, "Lobgesang," in *Festschrift Rudolf Stephan zum 65. Geburtstag*, ed. Josef Kuckertz (Laaber, 1990), pp. 239–49. I am indebted to Dr. Kapp for allowing me access to his manuscript, from which I gained essential insights.

3. Published in 1972 in an edition by Marc Andreae (Frankfurt, C. F. Peters, no. 8157). See Egon Voss, "Robert Schumanns Sinfonie in g-Moll," *Neue Zeitschrift für Musik* 133 (1972): 312–19.

4. Robert Schumann, *Gesammelte Schriften über Musik und Musiker*, 5th ed., ed. Martin Kreisig (Leipzig, 1914), vol. 2, pp. 462, 463.

5. Archive no. 4644-A1.

6. Robert Schumann, *Tagebücher, Band I: 1827–1838*, ed. Georg Eismann (Leipzig, 1971), p. 302.

7. Kapp, "Lobgesang," p. 245.

8. Arnfried Edler, *Robert Schumann und seine Zeit* (Laaber, 1982), p. 146.

9. Autograph score in the Bonn Universitätsbibliothek, Ms. Schumann 19, pp. 13–16. I am grateful to the library's manuscript division for providing photocopies.

10. Robert Schumann, *Tagebücher, Band III: Haushaltbücher, Teil I: 1837–1847*, ed. Gerd Nauhaus (Leipzig, 1982), p. 164.

11. Robert Schumann, *Tagebücher, Band II: 1836–1854*, ed. Gerd Nauhaus (Leipzig, 1987), p. 112.

12. Edler, *Robert Schumann und seine Zeit*, p. 162.

13. See Wilhelm Josef von Wasielewski, *Robert Schumann*, 4th ed., ed. Waldemar von Wasielewski (Leipzig, 1906), p. 313.

14. Cf. Schumann, *Tagebücher, Band III: Haushaltbücher*, p. 705, n. 191, and p. 707, n. 210, and the revised citations in the edition from Stroemfeld/Roter Stern (Basel, 1988), p. 958.

15. Universitätsbibliothek Bonn, autograph score Schumann 19, pp. 1–9. See Jon W. Finson, "The Sketches for Schumann's C-Minor Symphony," *Journal of Musicology* 1 (1982): 395–418, with a transcription of the Andante introduction on pp. 415ff.

16. As further evidence one could cite the lack of other scores to which the previously mentioned entry in the *Haushaltbuch* could refer, the lack of verbal references to the date of the fragment's composition, the lack of an introduction in the larger sketch, and the different orchestration. Finson, on the other hand, assumes the composition of the fragment *after* the sketch of the whole work, which is logically understandable.

17. Ludwig Finscher, " 'Zwischen absoluter und Programmusik': Zur Interpretation der deutschen romantischen Symphonie," in *Über Symphonien: Beiträge zu einer musikalischen Gattung*, ed. Christoph-Hellmut Mahling (Tutzing, 1979), pp. 103–15. Finscher's title refers to a 1963 essay by Walter Wiora.

18. Kapp, "Lobgesang," p. 245.

19. Finscher, "Zwischen absoluter und Programmusik," p. 111.

20. See Norbert J. Schneider, *Robert Schumann, I. Symphonie B-Dur op. 38* (Munich, 1982), p. 45.

21. Kapp, "Lobgesang," p. 245.

22. In the first version of the score; cf. the recent recording by Otmar Suitner (Denon 33 CO-1516).

23. Edler, *Robert Schumann und seine Zeit*, pp. 151ff.

24. Cf. Schumann's essay "Die C-Dur Symphonie von Franz Schubert," in *Gesammelte Schriften über Musik und Musiker*, vol. 1, p. 464.

25. Last dance of a ball. [Trans.]

26. Schneider, *Robert Schumann, I. Symphonie B-Dur op. 38*, pp. 46, 47.

27. In "Die C-Dur Symphonie von Franz Schubert."

28. Letter of 5 September 1841 to Carl Koßmaly, in *Robert Schumanns Briefe: Neue Folge*, 2d ed., ed. F. Gustav Jansen (Leipzig, 1904), p. 205.

29. Kapp, "Lobgesang," p. 245.

30. Jon W. Finson, "Schumann, Popularity, and the *Ouvertüre, Scherzo, und Finale*, Opus 52," *Musical Quarterly* 69 (1983): 1–26.

31. This was Schumann's own characterization of his revision of the D-minor Symphony; cf. *Tagebücher, Band III: Haushaltbücher, Teil II: 1847–1856*, p. 579.

32. Letter of 5 November 1842 to F. Hofmeister, in *Robert Schumanns Briefe*, p. 434.

33. Reinhard Kapp calls it a "bold stroke aimed at fundamental issues" ("Lobgesang," p. 246).

34. *Tagebücher, Band II: 1836–1854*, p. 166.

35. Compare the program for the premiere of the revised version of 1851, a facsimile of which is in the Goldmann-Schott Pocket Score, with introduction and analysis by Egon Voss (Mainz, 1980), p. 154.

36. Ibid., p. 173.

37. Hermann Kretzschmar, *Führer durch den Concertsaal* (Leipzig, 1887), part 1: "Sinfonie und Suite," p. 164.

38. Reinhard Kapp, "Robert Schumann: Sinfonie No. 4 d-Moll op. 120," in *Neue Zeitschrift für Musik* 143 (1982): 56.

39. See the facsimile in the Goldmann-Schott Pocket Score, p. 140, and Kapp, "Robert Schumann: Sinfonie No. 4 d-Moll op. 120," p. 210.

40. *Gesammelte Schriften über Musik und Musiker*, vol. 1, p. 94.

41. According to Kapp this deletion was made because this "vocal element of contrast . . . referred all too obviously to the fugal finale of Mozart's 'Jupiter' Symphony." Kapp, "Robert Schumann: Sinfonie No. 4 d-Moll op. 120," p. 246.

42. See Edler, *Robert Schumann und seine Zeit*, pp. 158ff.

43. See *Tagebücher, Band II: 1836–1854*, p. 159.

44. Ibid., p. 192.

45. This was the only Mozart symphony Schumann conducted in Düsseldorf. See *Tagebücher, Band III: Haushaltbücher, Teil II: 1847–1856*, p. 585, and p. 796, n. 836. A performance of the "Jupiter" Symphony was intended for the music festival that was planned under Schumann's direction for October 1853 in the Palatine, but this did not take place (Stroemfeld/Roter Stern ed., p. 959, n. 899a).

46. As the "Bunte Blätter," Op. 99, no. 13 (1852).

47. Carl Dahlhaus, "Studien zu romantischen Symphonien—Das 'Final-problem' in Schumanns Zweiter Symphonie," in *Jahrbuch des Staatlichen Instituts für Musikforschung Preussischer Kulturbesitz*, ed. Dagmar Droysen (Berlin, 1973), pp. 110–15.

48. See the "formal summary" in the Peters edition, no. 552 (Leipzig, 1980), p. 198.

49. Anthony Newcomb, "Once More 'Between Absolute and Program Mu-

sic': Schumann's Second Symphony," *19th-Century Music* 7 (1984): 233–50; and Jon W. Finson, "The Sketches for the Fourth Movement of Schumann's Second Symphony, Op. 61," in *Journal of the American Musicological Society* 39 (1986): 142–68.

50. Newcomb, "Once More 'Between Absolute and Program Music,' " p. 240, n. 17.

51. Fugue no. 6, mm. 131–35; cf. mm. 344–51 in the finale of the C-major Symphony.

52. Newcomb, "Once More 'Between Absolute and Program Music,' " p. 247.

53. Ernst Gottschald, "Robert Schumann's zweite Symphonie," *Neue Zeitschrift für Musik* 32 (1850): 137ff. See also Newcomb, "Once More 'Between Absolute and Program Music,' " p. 236.

54. Dahlhaus, "Studien zu romantischen Symphonien," p. 113.

55. Finscher, "Zwischen absoluter und Programmusik," p. 112.

56. Reinhard Kapp speaks of the "tense 'greatness' of the symphony"; see the Goldmann-Schott Pocket Score of the Symphony in E♭ major, Op. 97 (Mainz, 1981), p. 172.

57. Letter of 20 September 1845, in *Robert Schumanns Briefe*, p. 249.

58. Wasielewski, *Robert Schumann*, p. 455.

59. *Tagebücher, Band III: Haushaltbücher, Teil II: 1847–1856*, p. 544.

60. Wasielewski, *Robert Schumann*, p. 456.

61. Linda Correll Roesner, preface to the Eulenburg edition of the Symphony in E♭ major, Op. 97 (Mainz, 1986), p. vi.

62. Title of the fourth movement in the autograph and in the program of the premiere: "In the character of the accompaniment of a solemn ceremony"; cf. the Goldmann-Schott Pocket Score, p. 169, and the facsimile on p. 180.

63. *Tagebücher, Band III: Haushaltbücher, Teil II: 1847–1856*, p. 546.

64. Kapp, "Lobgesang," p. 217.

65. Ibid., p. 248.

66. Wasielewski, *Robert Schumann*, p. 456.

67. Berthold Litzmann, *Clara Schumann*, 7th ed. (Leipzig, 1925), vol. 2, p. 259.

68. Ernst Lichtenhahn, "Sinfonie als Dichtung. Zum geschichtlichen Ort von Schumanns 'Rheinischer,' " in *Schumanns Werke—Text und Interpretation*, ed. A. Mayeda and K. W. Niemöller (Mainz, 1987), pp. 17–27.

69. Peter Gülke, "Zur Rheinischen Sinfonie," in *Musik-Konzepte: Robert Schumann II*, ed. H. K. Metzger and R. Riehn (Munich, 1982), pp. 251–53.

70. See Kapp, "Lobgesang," p. 226, n. 117.

71. Ibid., pp. 231ff.

72. Title of the exhibition of the Heinrich-Heine-Institut in Düsseldorf on the 125th anniversary of Schumann's death in 1981; catalog prepared by Paul Kast (Düsseldorf, 1981).

73. *Gesammelte Schriften über Musik und Musiker*, vol. 2, p. 302.

Schumann's "New Genre for the Concert Hall": *Das Paradies und die Peri* in the Eyes of a Contemporary

JOHN DAVERIO

The months of July and August 1843, Clara wrote in the Schumanns' marriage diary, "were less eventful than usual; of most interest were the visits of [mezzo-soprano Pauline] *Viardot* and *Doctor* [Eduard] *Krüger* from *Emden*, an ingenious man and an excellent musician, especially on the organ, which he learned to play in three years, or so he said in passing. Krüger spent quite a bit of time with us, and Robert and he developed a mutual affection for each other. On 13 [July] we accompanied him to *Halle*—afterward he traveled on to Berlin and then back home to resume his duties as a schoolteacher."[1]

On 16 June, less than a month before Krüger's arrival, Schumann had completed his most ambitious work to date, the secular oratorio *Das Paradies und die Peri*, thus bringing to a close a project that had occupied him at various points for over two years.[2] Although we cannot know for certain, the *Peri* probably figured in several conversations enjoyed by composer and schoolmaster in mid-July;[3] after all, Schumann had written to Krüger about his latest composition shortly before his journey to Leipzig ("Recently I've written 100,000 notes . . . by Ascension Day [25 May] I completed [the sketch for] a large work, the largest I've yet undertaken");[4] and just after Krüger's departure, Schumann subjected his score to a careful "inspection" (*Durchsicht*).[5] We can be certain, however, that the subject of opera—which less than a year before Schumann had referred to as his "morning and evening artist-prayer"[6]—loomed large in their discussions. Indeed, it is clear from subsequent correspondence that Schumann had broached the possibility of Krüger's providing the opera libretto he had so long sought.[7] And even though no commitment was forthcoming (the project, in any event, failed to materialize), the composer thought well enough of his guest to see him off with an interesting and valuable gift: a manuscript of Bach's *Kunst der Fuge*, copied out by Schumann himself and including his analytical markings.[8] Krüger, for his part, must have enjoyed the break from his pedagogical duties in provincial Emden. "It was a good thing I left Leipzig as soon as I did," he wrote to Schumann, "otherwise I might have been sucked in, headfirst, by the city's powerful torrents."[9]

Within two years of his visit to Leipzig, Krüger wrote a lengthy critique of Schumann's recently published *Das Paradies und die Peri*.[10] Signed 20 June 1845, Krüger's review appeared in four installments (20 and 27 August, 3 and 10 September) in the *Allgemeine musikalische Zeitung*.[11] This fascinating document—about which most commentaries on the early reception of Schumann's works have been curiously silent—is worth considering in detail for a number of reasons. Devoted as it is to a single composition, Krüger's account represents the most extended (and most thoughtful) effort of its type published during the composer's lifetime. It gives us an opportunity to reflect upon the manner in which a well-informed contemporary approached Schumann's music. Of course, there is no reason for us to accept uncritically what Krüger had to say. On the contrary, the real worth of his remarks may derive from their ability to serve as a springboard for revaluating a significant work that has received less than its fair share of scholarly and critical attention.[12]

It may surprise some devotees of Schumann's works on this side of the Atlantic that a critique as thorough as Krüger's was allotted not to a symphony, a song cycle, a chamber work, or a poetic cycle of keyboard miniatures but to an oratorio. Yet according to Carl Dahlhaus, it was precisely in genres such as the dramatic cantata, the choral ballad and ode, and the secular oratorio that "the nineteenth century recognized itself."[13] And even if these genres have not been so "completely forgotten" in our century as Dahlhaus claims, it is still undeniable that the institutional support for their cultivation has diminished. Schumann's *Peri* was the product of an age in which Handel's oratorios (and not just *Messiah*) were practically as popular as Beethoven's symphonies and in which the Gesangverein, the Singakademie, the Liedertafel, and the Männerchor were very much a part of musical culture. Given this context, Schumann understandably devoted much of his creative energy in the last dozen years of his career to choral music (Liszt was perhaps right in viewing the keyboard miniature and the secular oratorio as the central genres of Schumann's output),[14] and not surprisingly one of Leipzig's principal music jour-

nals commissioned a major essay on a choral-orchestral work by one
of the city's leading resident composers.

To be sure, the attention lavished on Schumann's *Peri* was closely
bound up with the quality of its first performances. By all reports, the
4 December 1843 premiere at the Leipzig Gewandhaus, with the composer conducting, created such a sensation (this even though at the
last minute soloist Heinrich Schmidt refused to go on, whereby the
Viennese tenor Johann Vesque von Püttlingen stepped in to sing at
sight the scene for the plague-stricken youth [nos. 14–15]) that a
second performance had to be arranged for the following week.[15]
One listener, the poetaster Hermann Stähnisch, felt compelled to pen
some (embarrassingly) sentimental verses in the composer's honor:
"Oh, how bleak it has become / Since the Peri was redeemed! / And
now the gates to heaven are closed [a reference to no. 26] / *Only she has
earned a place in Eden,* / And we are left behind, here on earth, / Gaz-
ing up at her happiness."[16] Within the next five years, the *Peri* was
given in most of the chief German musical centers, and it began
to make its way throughout Europe with performances in Utrecht
(1844/45), Amsterdam, Prague, Riga (1845/46), Zurich, and the
Hague (1846/47);[17] late in 1847, Schumann was surprised (and
amused) to learn that the American Musical Institute in New York was
planning a rendition for its 1848 season.[18] In short, the *Peri* was the
work that made Schumann into an international, as opposed to a
merely German, phenomenon.[19]

In many ways, Eduard Krüger was an appropriate choice to review
Schumann's first major composition for vocal and orchestral forces.[20]
An 1830 graduate of the University of Göttingen with a dissertation
on Greek music from the time of Pindar,[21] Krüger joined the faculty
of the Gymnasium at Emden in 1833, a post he held until 1851. His
duties there left him time enough to serve as conductor of the local
choral society, a position in which he gained firsthand knowledge of
the oratorios of Handel and Haydn. In the five years before reviewing
Schumann's *Peri*, Krüger contributed almost two dozen articles to the
Neue Zeitschrift für Musik on a broad range of topics, including Carl
Heinrich Graun's *Der Tod Jesu*, the current state of music conservato-
ries, the virtuoso concerto, contemporary opera, the music of Handel,
Hegel's philosophy of music, and J. S. Bach's Passions.[22] Schumann
apparently thought well enough of Krüger's critical skills to recommend that he be offered the post of editor for the *Allgemeine musikalische Zeitung*.[23] Although Krüger cannot be said to have enjoyed a
brilliant career, by the early 1840s he had nonetheless carved out a
respectable niche for himself in the musical and academic worlds.[24]

Krüger's review of Schumann's *Peri* falls into three parts (unevenly distributed over four issues of the *AmZ*). A longish introduction deals with questions of genre and textual content. The main body of the essay comprises a number-by-number analysis of the oratorio, touching on such issues as melodic style, overall layout, and text painting. Indeed, Krüger expressly states that his intention was to complement the "synthetic," philosophical observations in Franz Brendel's recently published "Robert Schumann mit Rücksicht auf Mendelssohn-Bartholdy und die Entwicklung der modernen Tonkunst überhaupt"[25] with a more thoroughly analytical account (col. 561). The concluding portion of the review is something of a catch-all, circling back to some earlier points (e.g., Schumann's handling of the relationship between voices and orchestra) and turning to other areas (namely, form) that had previously been accorded little attention. Krüger ties together the threads of his discussion by reiterating a central thesis—that Schumann is more adept as a composer of instrumental than of vocal music—linking this notion in turn with Brendel's view of Schumann as a "subjective" (as opposed to an "objective") artist.

Krüger begins with an assertion that had already become a commonplace: Schumann's *Peri*, he says, is the composer's "most richly conceived and best thought-out" work to date; it is the composition in which he definitively proves his absolute mastery of the largest musical forces.[26] But Krüger soon moves on to an issue that had likewise occupied several commentators, and continues to do so: the question of genre. Schumann provided little help on this point; the full score of the *Peri* bears the neutral designation "Dichtung aus Lalla Rookh von Th. Moore" (we shall see later that this rubric is not as neutral as it seems). And in a letter of 5 May 1843 to Carl Koßmaly, Schumann claimed, with untypical bravado, to have created nothing less than "a new genre for the concert hall."[27] The field was open, therefore, for critics to situate the work somewhere between oratorio (sacred and secular), opera, and cantata. But although most agreed that the *Peri* drew principally on oratorio and opera,[28] there was little consensus. The reviewer for the 23 December 1843 Dresden performance recognized the *Peri*'s singular status as a *Mischgattung* suspended between opera and oratorio; whereas he placed it closer to oratorio, the reviewer for the *Augsburger Allgemeine Zeitung* (no. 354, n.d.) decided in favor of opera without, however, providing a justification for his choice.[29] The critic who covered the first Leipzig performances despaired of hitting on an accurate genre designation, ultimately settling on such clumsy formulations as "epic-dramatic-secular oratorio" and "oriental-religious oratorio."[30]

Krüger takes a more reasoned stance. Given the blend of epic (i.e., narrative) and lyric (monologic) elements in Schumann's text, Krüger argues that the *Peri* belongs squarely within the oratorio tradition. But he wisely states his reluctance to become entangled in what had already become a tedious debate. (The notion of the *Mischgattung*, though valid for literary and musical artworks since the beginning of the nineteenth century, caused no end of headaches for neoclassically inclined critics.) Krüger is less interested in a normative, classificatory approach to Schumann's work than in the discovery of its essence—or so he claims. For here the discussion takes an odd turn:

> Certainly the decisive moment in the concept of the oratorio is that it should approach the dramatic form, albeit with more free, exotic, and fantastically vague digressions, whereby it even prepares for the opera, though without attaining that genre's lively and lifelike self-containment. This would also appear to represent the inner developmental course of R. Schumann himself, that he should strive, from his earlier Lieder through instrumental music and oratorio, toward opera as his true goal. (Cols. 561–62)

Krüger is justified in pointing to the teleology of Schumann's systematic conquest of the principal musical genres. Between 1840 and 1842 he concentrated alternately (and obsessively) on Lieder, symphonic works, and finally chamber music; in November 1843 (that is, at the end of the "oratorio year") Schumann noted in his diary: "An opera will be my next work, and I'm fired up to proceed."[31] But Krüger's privileging of the dramatic principle no doubt compromises the evenhandedness of his critique. The mixture of epic and lyric qualities characteristic of the oratorio as a genre—no less than Schumann's individual approach to this mixture—is devalued from the start. Later in the review Krüger takes issue with Schumann's simultaneous exposition of a reflective text (set to chorale-style music) and a discursive text (delivered rapidly by the basses) in the luminous chorus at the close of part 2 (no. 17): "Narration and feeling are so very different that one cannot understand this number at all without the libretto . . . [Furthermore, the basses] cannot declaim either distinctly or characteristically, and the music provides neither the occasion nor the freedom to do so" (col. 587). True enough, it *is* difficult to make out the basses' text; but at the same time, it is possible to explain Schumann's combination of epic ("narration") and lyric ("feeling"). The basses, after all, function as a kind of textural irritant to the placid chorale in the upper parts, thus preparing us for the unfortunate outcome that the sighs of the expiring maiden—the "gift" the Peri takes for her ticket to Paradise—will fail to appease the guardians of the heavenly gates. The tension between lyrical upper voices and epic basses creates a dissonance whose resolution is not achieved until the jubilant homophony of the "aria" and chorus closing part 3 (no. 26).

On the musical side, Krüger relates Schumann's approach to the genre to the oratorios of Handel, whose *Messiah, Joshua*, and *Samson* are frequently mentioned in the review (cols. 566, 567, 606). Yet Schumann arguably drew on a wide array of contemporary sources as well. Between 1840 and 1842 his thoughts turned increasingly to the oratorio (a genre he feared was languishing) in a series of reviews, for the *Neue Zeitschrift*, of new works by Marschner, Hiller, Sobolewski, and Loewe.[32] To judge from his comments, Schumann was much taken by the continuous flow from one movement to the next in Marschner's *Klänge aus Osten* (a feature he would adopt in the *Peri*) and by Loewe's attempt to mediate opera and sacred oratorio in his *Johann Huß*. Echoes of the Offertory from Berlioz's Requiem—which deeply impressed Schumann when he first heard it at a benefit concert, conducted by the composer on 23 February 1843[33]—take the form of prominent passages for ophicleide in nos. 6, 7, and 23 of the *Peri*. Earlier in the same month, Schumann attended the dress rehearsal and premiere of the final version of Mendelssohn's secular cantata on Goethe's ballad, *Die erste Walpurgisnacht*, Op. 60, a work whose expressive ariosi and colorful choruses likewise left their mark on the *Peri*.[34] Weber counts as another important influence. While Krüger notes that the chorus of Nile Genies (no. 11) recalls the chorus of elves (mermaids, nymphs, fairies, sylphs, and spirits of the air) from the act 2 finale of *Oberon* (col. 620), we might add that the Peri's triumphant "aria" with chorus, "Freud', ew'ge Freude, mein Werk ist gethan" (no. 26; finale of part 3) hearkens to the heroic tone of Weber's *Euryanthe* (specifically, to the heroine's aria with chorus, "Zu ihm! O weilet nicht" [no. 21]). Thus, the generic richness of Schumann's *Peri* derives, in part, from the multiplicity of genres upon which it draws: secular and sacred oratorio, secular cantata, requiem, fairy-tale opera, and grand opera.

On the literary side, Krüger takes his bearings from an Aristotelian conception of the drama. To state his position in the language of the *Poetics*: Krüger prizes *opsis* ("spectacle" or "visible action") over *dianoia* ("reasoned thought"). Mozart's *Don Giovanni*, he says, does not aim primarily to teach a lesson—"This is the reward for unchecked sensuality." On the contrary, its ends are rather spectacular and affective.

We are to "look on" (*schauen*) and "experience" (*erleben*), and thus re-live the self-destruction of a powerful personality (col. 562). Hence Krüger subscribes to an aesthetic of presence (in a footnote, he be-trays his distance from Lessing on this issue: "Actually, art concerns itself only with *that which is* . . . ; that which *becomes* lies beyond it" [col. 564]) that accords little with the lyrical, reflective tone of much of Schumann's *Peri*.

The point is driven home in a discussion of what Krüger considers to be the drawbacks of Moore's verse tale as a vehicle for music. And here it is obvious that he does not ground his (largely negative) con-clusions solely in the text as Schumann ultimately set it: Krüger is aware that the choruses of Nile Genies (no. 11), Houris (no. 18), and Peris (quartet of solo voices, no. 22) represent additions to the original poem, either by the composer or by an unacknowledged librettist (col. 564);[35] his references to the Great Chamberlain Fadladeen (who fig-ures in Moore's prose commentary on the poem) and to an 1829 translation of the *Lalla Rookh* by G. W. Bueren (cols. 563, 588) likewise attest to his familiarity with much of Moore's epic in verse.[36] It is worth mentioning too that the *Lalla Rookh* (literally, "Princess tulip-cheeks"), a group of four verse tales with connecting prose narrative, has not fared well with modern literary critics. As one writer puts it, reading Moore's work today "is a task, not a pleasure. It is long, drawn-out, florid, bathetic, and occasionally absurd."[37] For Krüger, the chief problem with Moore's poetry lay elsewhere. The *Peri* text, he claims, requires "more understanding [Kantian *Verstand*] and acumen [*Scharfsinn*, the cognitive faculty enabling us to differentiate between apparently similar entities] than are beneficial for or attainable through" a musical setting (col. 562). Furthermore, the poem is geared toward a didactic or dogmatic end, often resulting in a kind of "philosophical hocus-pocus," as Krüger calls it on one occasion (col. 588). The tale's implicit "moral question" is thus formulated as fol-lows: "What gift is dearest to heaven?" (col. 562). Each of the potential solutions to the riddle—the blood of a fearless warrior, the sighs of a maiden who dies in the arms of her plague-stricken beloved, the tears of a hardened criminal who softens at the sight of a young boy at prayer—in turn provides a focal point for the oratorio's three parts. But in Krüger's view, these central images are little more than "allego-ries" for affective qualities or states: the drop of blood for valor in the face of despotism, the sigh for true love, and the tear (through which, incidentally, the Peri ultimately gains admission to paradise) for redemption.

Krüger registers his distaste for the allegorical mode in discussing the Peri's arioso from no. 25 ("Es fällt ein Tropfen"), where Schumann's handling of the text comes in for sharp criticism:

[The verse "A drop falls to the ground from the moon" means] nothing in itself but rather serves as a cipher for the principal statement: "Läßt so, O Sünder . . . " ["O sinner, do not these tears of repentance speed your recovery?"] But a comparison of this sort, an allegory that occupies so much of the text, can only lead to an everlastingly laborious situation . . . in music. It is amazing enough that our Schumann nevertheless sets the first sentence [of the text] with such mystical beauty—the mysterious orchestral introduction and the tones of the Peri show, however, that he gives preference to this poetically weaker opening segment, the allegory, and thus understands it as the chief point; for afterward, the next statement ("Läßt so") dissolves quickly into recitative, as if it were a perfunctory narrative. Only the fervent but powerful close ("Ein Himmelstropfen") strikes the proper tone. (Cols. 607–8)

Schumann does indeed lavish special attention on the opening textual image, the drop of moonlight, by way of a plaintive fugato on an expressively chromatic subject. But the setting of "Läßt so, O Sünder" hardly "dissolves . . . into recitative." On the contrary, it recalls a lyrical phrase from the orchestral commentary on the baritone arioso at the close of no. 22, where the setting sun (a fitting complement to the radiant moon of no. 25) serves as a metaphor for the Peri's desolation. The musical-poetic cross reference thus ensures that "Läßt so, O Sünder" *is* perceived as the "chief point"; so too does the directional tonal scheme, moving from E minor, for the mysterious allegory of the drop of moonlight, to G major, for the more poetically transparent conclusion of the arioso.

In Krüger's view, the Peri's redemption through the delivery of the sinner's tear (an act whose visible presentation would create difficulties even in an opera) is "neither a fortunate nor a vivid" conceit (col. 563). The problem with Schumann's musical representations of such ideas is that they are not "comprehensible from the music alone. Therefore we must reach despairingly for the libretto, that evil crutch of civilized (that is, unhealthy) vocal music—an onus comparable to original sin, of which we knew nothing in the times when Don Juan was young" (col. 563). Not surprisingly, then, Krüger reserves special praise for those movements whose affective thrust is unequivocally encoded in purely musical gestures (such as the respectively joyous and reflective finales of parts 1 and 2 [cols. 564, 568]) and concludes this section of his critique with the assertion that it must have been "the vivid beauty of the details" in Moore's poem that fired Schumann's imagination (col. 563).

But Schumann may have seen more in the poem than an opportunity to contribute to the fad for orientalizing literature that had been sweeping Europe since the early days of the nineteenth century. After all, he noted in a diary entry for 21 November 1843 that "ideas of a very serious kind" were bound up with his oratorio;[38] these ideas were possibly related to the figure of the Peri herself. As Schumann well knew, the Peri of Persian folklore was a fairy whose exclusion from paradise came about through her descent from the union of a fallen angel and a mortal.[39] As an ethereal creature half-human and half-divine, the Peri is an emblem for the oratorio itself, at least as Schumann envisioned the genre. Although he emphasized, in a letter to Krüger of 3 June 1843, the secular character of his latest work— "The subject is *Das Paradies und die Peri* of Th. Moore, an oratorio, though not for the chapel [*Betsaal*] but rather for 'cheerful' [*heitre*] folk"[40]—Schumann's statement does not gainsay the presence of a distinctly religious element in his composition. It only suggests that the *Peri* was not conceived as a sacred work in the narrower sense. Similarly, the "concert hall" for which Schumann intended his "new genre"[41] was not an exclusively secular space. Drawing on a romantic topos that would likewise resonate in the writings of Liszt and Wagner, Schumann imagined it as an ideal, sanctified realm, a meeting ground for art and religion over which the composer officiates.[42] No less than the "new genre for the concert hall," the artist—a quasi-human, quasi-divine agent of redemption—finds a striking poetic counterpart in the figure of the Peri.

Because it would be tedious (and redundant) to follow Krüger's play-by-play march through the *Peri*, we shall consider the analytical portion of his critique topically, proceeding from larger to more circumscribed issues. Krüger counterbalances his negative reaction to the allegorical aspects of the oratorio's text with unqualified praise for the disposition and sequence of its scenes: "In the distribution of light and shadow, of preparation, development, transitions, and presentations, there appears a conscious yet unforced principle of order, so that these positive qualities almost completely conceal the [previously mentioned] deficiencies [in the text]" (col. 564). The logical order of the parts is furthermore enhanced, for Krüger, by the finely drawn contrasts between and among them: "The principal masses are clearly differentiated: the narrating tenor, the poetic pictures of warriors, lovers, fairies, and spirits, and finally the noble, human figure of the Peri, who is the soul and energetic center of the entire work. These three main entities are also differentiated musically after the manner of vividly comprehensible images, similar to freely appearing epic, lyric, and dramatic moments" (col. 565).

A closer look reveals that the "freely appearing . . . moments" are in fact regulated by the architecture of the whole. Each of the oratorio's three parts divides neatly into two scene-complexes: the first centered on the Peri's various exchanges at the heavenly gates, and the second on her search for an acceptable gift. And although the epic and lyric modes prevail throughout, it is eminently sensible that the dramatic principle—in the form of brief dialogues for the Indians and Conquerors (no. 6), Gazna and the young warrior (no. 7), and the maiden and her beloved (nos. 15–16)—surfaces as well in the portions directed to the Peri's quest.

Much of Krüger's analysis attempts to come to terms with Schumann's melodic style. Given his suspicion of Schumann's experimental fusion of narrative and lyrical modes (as in the closing half of no. 17), not surprisingly Krüger is most favorably disposed toward those movements in which an eloquent cantilena—untarnished by what he calls "Beethovenian trickery" (col. 609)—reigns supreme: examples include the Peri's "Ich kenne die Urnen" (from no. 4), her "Sei dies mein Geschenk" (from no. 9), "Das Blut für die Freiheit verspritzt" (also from no. 9), the maiden's "O laß mich von der Luft durchdringen" (no. 16), and the Peri's "Schlaf nun und ruh" (from no. 17) (col. 609). Like some other early critics of Schumann's *Peri* (such as Flodoard Geyer, a reviewer for the *Berliner Musikalische Zeitung*, and Ludwig Rellstab),[43] Krüger did have reservations about those settings where, in his judgment, the text was neither declaimed nor sung. He found the angel's exhortation in no. 3, for instance, "more declamatory than beautiful" (col. 567) and predictably blamed the "didactic" text for the "dullness" or "opacity" of the vocal writing.

Krüger's circumspection about this and other similarly wrought ariosi (e.g., the passage for the angel at the end of no. 19; see col. 588) betrays an insensitivity to the specific nature of the problem Schumann faced in the *Peri*: how could he best avoid a merely formulaic setting for the lengthy narrative stretches in the text? How, in other words, was he to treat the epic portions of the poem in a musically substantive manner? This is of course the same dilemma that Wagner would confront in composing the *Ring*.[44] But whereas Wagner's solution entailed the creation of a leitmotivic web (and a radical break with traditional musical syntax), Schumann emphasized a continuum of melodic styles, extending from simple recitative to unrestricted lyricism. From the start, Schumann thought in terms of a carefully graduated range of vocal idioms; his structural plan for the oratorio, superimposed on the manuscript copy of Flechsig's translation, labels the projected movements variously as "Rezitativ," "rezitativischer Gesang," "Gesang," "Lied," and "Arie."[45] In the published score, only the designation "Rezitativ" survives, all the other movements (the choruses, of course, excepted) being marked with the neutral "Solo." Still, the notion of the "rezitativischer Gesang"—a syntactically flexible vocal line supported by a motivically rich orchestral texture— aptly describes the writing in many of the oratorio's movements (e.g., sections of nos. 1, 3–5, 7, 9–12, 14, 16, 19, 20, and 25). Krüger's comments on "Im Waldesgrün" (no. 14), an arioso shared by the solo alto and tenor, are worth quoting in full: "The fragmented melodic snippets with which the narrating alto introduces the mortally ill youth are certainly expressive but hardly beautiful; even less can one justify the intention here by viewing the movement as a kind of Lied [two strophes for the alto, one for the youth] and relating it to the youth. To be sure, it is more suitable for him, as an expiring lover, and would have clearly been more effective without the preceding alto solo—nonetheless, this mixture of epic and lyric can only weaken the [overall] impression" (cols. 585–86). Later on he writes, "In such cases, wouldn't it be preferable to employ the simple but strict technique of older oratorios, in which the narrative portions [e.g., the alto strophes from no. 14] proceed in recitative, thus imparting individual life to this prosaic element by allowing the narrator to appear as the distinct embodiment of a typical figure, such as Bach's Evangelist?" (col. 620). Obviously then, issues of melodic style and genre interlock. But Krüger (and some of his contemporaries) failed to appreciate that Schumann set out to avoid "the simple but strict technique of older oratorios" for an excellent reason.[46] The mixture of epic and lyric qualities in the "rezitativische Gesänge" of his "new" genre served as a means of ensuring musical eloquence in precisely those spots (the narrative sections) that in earlier oratorios had often fallen into a stilted declamatory style.

As we have already seen, Krüger often frames his points in terms of binary oppositions: epic versus lyric, allegory versus genuine poetry, song versus declamation. This is no less true of the idea to which he frequently returns in the course of his review, that the essence of Schumann's compositional persona resided in instrumental as opposed to vocal styles. Krüger sought thereby to complement Brendel's recently published appraisal of the composer's output, in which Schumann's "subjectivity" (his "inwardness," his passion for individual, often eccentric forms) is contrasted with Mendelssohn's "objectivity" (his tendency toward "plastic representation" or formal clarity).[47] Krüger accepts the premise that Mendelssohn proceeds from already-existing ideals whereas in Schumann we sense "the discovery of new paths and the disclosure of an unknown world" (col. 565). But at the same time he feels that Brendel's critique requires amplification in certain areas: "Namely, his account of Schumann's vocal music is not complete or authoritative enough. The most important point, it seems to me at least, is that Mendelssohn takes his point of departure from vocal music, whereas Schumann, hearkening to Beethoven's spirit, originally displayed his powers best in the instrumental realm" (col. 565). Schumann thus shows his true character at those moments in the *Peri* where the orchestra "takes on the total content, illustrating and explaining the sung text" (col. 620). For Krüger, this is best exemplified in no. 6, the chorus of Indians and Conquerors (col. 620). But there are also times when Schumann's predilection for instrumental styles does not work to the advantage of his writing for the voice: "Very frequently the instrumental character [of Schumann's melodies] shows through and the vocal line winds like an arabesque through the orchestra; elsewhere the rhythm lacks clarity; at times a certain dullness or disjointedness is disturbing, the result being a profusion of melodies that fail to penetrate, to tug at the heartstrings" (col. 565). In no. 23, for example, the orchestra takes on "the principal role through dotted figures, skips, and modulations, while the Peri's melody (which continues with unusual intervals) portrays her anxiety only in general terms. Is the text also to blame here? Perhaps" (col. 607).

Hence Krüger's opposition of instrumental and vocal styles—a useful if overly generalized distinction—runs aground on the question of the text. Although the poetic content provides the justification for the predominance of the orchestra in no. 6, it is viewed as the motivating source for (what Krüger takes to be) the ungrateful vocal line in no. 23. The contradiction in the critic's argument is rooted in two potentially contradictory strands of the neoclassicizing aesthetic to which he owes more than he cares to admit: on the one hand, its allegiance to the word as the final arbiter in all matters concerning vocal music; and on the other, its consideration of the syntactically regular, singable melody as a norm for compositions of all types. But Schumann's *Peri* demonstrates that the demands of the "word" and those of the "melody" are not always in mutual agreement.

Krüger's neoclassical stance emerges in a binary opposition originally formulated by the early framers of romanticism: between the Characteristic (the striking but sometimes disruptive painterly detail) and the Beautiful (or statuesquely poised). But whereas the Schlegel brothers and their colleagues looked toward the Characteristic as the touchstone of the new and exciting in art, Krüger came down squarely on the side of the Beautiful.

As noted earlier, Krüger guessed that Schumann's attraction to the Peri tale had its basis in the colorful details, the "characteristic" elements of Moore's poetic text. Krüger himself homes in on Schumann's realization of many of these (the tortuous violin figuration in no. 15, for instance, suggests the fluttering of the maiden's garments [col. 586]) and therefore presents the composer as a master of musical portraiture. In doing so, Krüger gives special emphasis to an undervalued aspect of Schumann's art: his palette of orchestral colors. In no. 4 ("Ich kenne die Urnen"), for instance, the Peri's touchingly naive hopefulness is conveyed in part by the deftly handled orchestration: "The delicate repartee, the murmuring violas (engaged, as it were, in a quiet soliloquy), the gentle intermediary phrases in the winds, and finally, the regally resounding trumpets, as if in the distance, at the splendid climax, 'Und Lebenstropfen'—these are exquisite, wondrous poetic gems" (col. 567). But when Schumann moves from generalized mood painting (as in "Ich kenne die Urnen") to more specific depiction, Krüger does not always approve of the result. The orchestral interlude in no. 6, for example, is cast as a brief but "powerful battle portrait" (col. 567). Yet Schumann's colorful deployment of his instrumental forces (droning trombones, incisive violins, and janissary instruments) leads to "roughness of the most severe sort" (col. 568). (Krüger is probably alluding to the lean support, in the lower strings and brass, for the frantic rush of eighth notes in the violins). "Even the chorus," he goes on to say, "in duetting recitative, shares in this roughness; melodically, the choral writing is hardly beautiful and remains subordinate to the orchestra" (col. 568). In both cases, the orchestral "battle portrait" and the ensuing chorus, the laws of musical propriety are suspended; characterization has the upper hand over "beauty" (*Schönheit*).

Krüger's critical stance on the relationship between the Characteristic and the Beautiful thus turns on a paradox. In spite of his disdain for allegory, Krüger's own approach tends toward the allegorical insofar as the music is viewed as a discontinuous signifier for the text. Taken to its extremes, this approach can lead to a myopic concentration on insignificant minutiae, as when, for example, Krüger questions the use of a diminished-seventh chord on the definite article *das* in the choral fugue from no. 9 (col. 569). Furthermore, Krüger often fails to see that Schumann's "characteristic" touches can lend musical (and even dramatic) coherence to the score. Although he notes that the ophicleide contributes to the portrayal of the horrors of sinfulness in no. 23 (col. 607), Krüger might have added that the same instrument is associated with Gazna in nos. 6 and 7. The unrepentant sinner and the cruel tyrant are thus represented, musically, as variants of the same character type.

Although he does not call it by name, Krüger alludes to one last binary opposition. Like the dialectic of the Characteristic and the Beautiful, his implicit differentiation between *Naturpoesie* (naive, "artless" poetry) and *Kunstpoesie* (reflected, "artful" poetry) has its roots in the early romantic program. And Krüger again betrays his neoclassical orientation through his comments on the *Naturpoesie* of the scene for the dying lovers (nos. 15–17): "Passion is the hallmark of genius, whereas reflection is a sign of knowledge acquired through hard work; therefore both qualities (though in different ways) bear witness to the worth of an artist. . . . Thus I take great pleasure in the wonderfully sincere tones of the lovers' exchange, tones whose seriousness resides precisely in their artlessness" (cols. 586–87). Other writers had likewise detected in the *Peri* a moderation of the idiosyncratic manner that characterized much of Schumann's music from the 1830s. As Eduard Hanslick quipped, "Master Florestan is getting a little older."[48] It seemed to some that the tendency toward a more accessible style already evident in the earlier symphonic works—notably, the First Symphony and the Overture, Scherzo, and Finale, Op. 52, both from 1841—was finally coming into its own. According to one critic (probably J. C. Lobe), the *Peri* offered clear proof of Schumann's realization that "even the genuine artwork can and must be popular to a degree."[49]

On the whole, though, Krüger found more *Kunstpoesie* than *Naturpoesie* in Schumann's oratorio. Indeed, he feared that its technical and interpretive difficulties would mitigate against widespread performances beyond those larger musical centers capable of summoning the requisite instrumental and vocal forces: "I can hardly speak about us poor inhabitants of East Friesland; from the total population of 170,000 there are two, or in a pinch, three people who could negotiate the devilish violin passages [at the *Etwas bewegter* in no. 15] . . . To be sure, we can't command an artist: 'Compose in an easily understandable manner.' But still: 'Why do you always want to range so widely? See, the Good is near at hand'" (col. 621).

Certainly by the late 1830s Schumann was already working toward a fusion of "naive" and "artful" styles (we sense this in the *Kinderszenen*, Op. 15, the *Arabeske*, Op. 18, and the *Blumenstück*, Op. 19). At the same time, he questioned Mendelssohn's and Loewe's attempts, in *St. Paul* and *Johann Huß*, to cater to the tastes of the masses.[50] In the final analysis, Schumann remained faithful to the conviction that without recourse to an esoteric dimension, a work simply could not aspire to art.

Krüger closes by reaffirming the proximity of his views to Brendel's. On the surface, there are several points of contact between their respective positions on Schumann's output and the place of the *Peri* within it. For both critics, the oratorio marks a point of transition, though neither is certain of where it might lead. Likewise, both agree that the essence of Schumann's creativity lies in his cultivation of instrumental idioms. And finally, Krüger and Brendel are at one with many of their contemporaries in counting the *Peri* as a great work but a flawed one.

At the same time, the even more striking differences between them help us to place Krüger's outlook into sharper relief. If Brendel is a practitioner of "high," philosophical criticism, then Krüger's more analytical account may be fairly viewed as an example of "low," prosaic criticism. Brendel, ever the dialectician, looks forward to an ideal synthesis of "subjective" and "objective" qualities in Schumann's future works.[51] Krüger hopes only for "a freer employment of the human voice" and a "liberation from declamatory fetters" (col. 621). The earlier poetic cycles of piano pieces, in Brendel's view, are especially praiseworthy for their rhapsodic sweep, their "fantastic-humorous manner."[52] Krüger, on the other hand, singles out the *Fantasiestücke*, Op. 12, and the *Nachtstücke*, Op. 23, for their neatly rounded forms (col. 622). Brendel attributes the *Peri*'s occasional unevenness of style to Schumann's attempt to moderate his innately "subjective" manner with "objective" elements (first evident in the Lieder of 1840 and the symphonic works of 1841) that were essentially foreign to him.[53] For Krüger, however, the *Peri* is sometimes marred by obtrusive echoes of "Eusebius and the unruly Florestan" (col. 621). In short, Krüger remains suspicious of the "subjective" or fantastic quality that, in Brendel's critique, is identified as the nurturing source of Schumann's artistry.

We have focused thus far on the aspects of the *Peri* that Krüger found particularly noteworthy, but it is also instructive to consider some areas to which he gave short shrift. In a sense, Krüger was somewhat indifferent to precisely those features that stamp the work as a "new genre for the concert hall." We encountered one of these—the renunciation of formulaic recitative in favor of an expressive and eloquent "rezitativischer Gesang"—in our gloss on Krüger's discussion of Schumann's melodic style. Another equally important feature of the "new genre" can be intuited from Schumann's critical writings. In his 1840 review of Marschner's *Klänge aus Osten*, Schumann lauded his colleague for having made a beginning, a first attempt, "which others have only to develop further in order to enrich the concert hall with a new musical genre."[54] Specifically, the most notable aspect of Marschner's work was the disposition of its individual movements in a continuous, uninterrupted sequence; in a letter to Brendel written seven years later, Schumann would cite the same characteristic as one of the outstanding features of his *Peri*. The notion of a "new genre for the concert hall" was thus intimately tied to the question of musical continuity.

Like other composers before him (notably Weber, whose *Euryanthe* of 1823 may have provided a model for the *Peri*), Schumann employed both tonal and motivic means toward the end of ensuring musical coherence on the largest scale. Krüger has curiously little to say about the role of either in the *Peri*.[55] In fact, he looks askance at Schumann's fondness for the "evil mediant" (col. 610), regardless of whether it functions as a fleeting point of repose ("This usage," Krüger writes, "has become so common with recent Italian composers that one might want to ban it on patriotic grounds" [col. 609]) or a long-range modulatory goal (as in nos. 16, 23, and 26; col. 610). Yet third-related tonal pairs had figured prominently as unifying agents in the poetic cycles of the 1830s (especially the *Davidsbündlertänze*, Op. 6, *Fantasiestücke*, Op. 12, *Kreisleriana*, Op. 16, and *Humoreske*, Op. 20)[56] and would continue to do so in the larger works of the 1840s, the *Peri* among them. Almost the whole of the scene-complex at the close of part 3, for example, turns on the progression from E minor to its relative major, G:

No. 23	No. 24	No. 25	No. 26
Solos	Chorus	Solos and chorus	"Aria" with chorus
E minor → G → V of E minor	G	E minor → G	G

Similarly, Krüger is almost silent on Schumann's use of motivic recurrences both within and among the movements of the oratorio. He notes that the Peri's rejoinders to the Nile Genies in no. 11 "resound charmingly" (col. 585) but not that they recall her Lied, "Wie glücklich sie wandeln" (no. 2). The "new theme" introduced in the orchestral postlude to no. 20 (col. 589) turns out to be not so new after all; its graceful dip of a sixth and rise of a fourth relate to a portion of the opening gesture of no. 1. According to Krüger, the setting of the Peri's phrase "Süß Eden, wie finster sind gegen dich" in no. 26 "falls flat" (col. 608); he seems unimpressed that it brings back, almost exactly, the music of "Jetzt über Balbek's Thal" (no. 23). On one of the few occasions where Krüger does comment on a motivic cross reference (within the widely ranging no. 23), he questions its application on textual grounds:

> I especially hoped that Schumann would have been stricter in his handling of the genuinely Lied-like arias, and not only fashioned their motives carefully from out of the text but also conceived their outward forms more rigorously. This observation applies to those places where, for example, narrative and reflective sentences are alternately set to the same music. Hence the Lied-like recurrence of two melodies in no. 23 [see examples 1 and 2] is not justified by the textual content, for initially the Peri sings about Solomon's seal [first melody], then the narrating tenor introduces the boy and the old man [first and second melodies], whereupon the mezzo-soprano celebrates the eventide [second melody], and finally the tenor again comments on the man's feelings. (Cols. 619–20)

Example 1. *Das Paradies und die Peri*, no. 23, mm. 1–5

In addition to the two melodies to which Krüger alluded, the movement features two more (see examples 3 and 4). Taken together, these four phrases relate not only to one another but also (albeit obliquely) to the opening idea from the orchestral prelude to no. 1 (see examples 5 and 3).

Example 2. *Das Paradies und die Peri*, no. 23, mm. 64–72

Example 3. *Das Paradies und die Peri*, no. 23, mm. 57–64

Example 4. *Das Paradies und die Peri*, no. 23, mm. 84–88

Example 5. *Das Paradies und die Peri*, no. 1, mm. 1–4

They form, in other words, a loosely knit lyric family; and although it would be difficult to ascribe to any one of them a specific poetic referent, it is nonetheless clear that all are associated with the peripatetic nature of the oratorio's central figure. Schumann firms the point in no. 26, where the Peri's recall of two phrases from no. 23 (the settings of "Süß Eden, wie finster sind gegen dich" and "O was sind Blumen") signals a farewell to earthly existence in the moments before she is joyously welcomed to paradise.

It would be a mistake, however, to describe Schumann's recurrent materials as components of a leitmotivic network.[57] Even the opening gesture of no. 1 (which surfaces in a variety of guises in nos. 3, 20, and 23) hardly attains the relative associative fixity of a Wagnerian leitmotif. Nor should it. The more subdued reminiscences in the *Peri* are entirely appropriate for a work in which epic and lyric elements take precedence over dramatic action. The subtlety of Schumann's technique emerges with particular clarity in the finale of part 1 (no. 9). Toward the end of the movement, the optimism of the Peri's soaring line is darkened by an ominously outlined diminished-seventh harmony in the winds and strings (at "Pforten, willkommen"); as it turns out, the orchestral countermelody represents an augmented variant of the harp accompaniment to the Peri's sumptuous *cantilena*, "Sei dies, mein Geschenk," first heard near the beginning of the finale. The remarkable intersection of motivic and coloristic transformation at the close of the movement serves an important poetic purpose: it not only recalls the Peri's past confidence and yearning but also foreshadows the disappointments awaiting her.

Schumann's reactions to Krüger's critique are not known. Although he probably read it (an entry in the *Haushaltbücher* for 25 August 1845 reads, "Krüger's review of the Peri"),[58] the essay was not included in the six-volume collection of reviews and notices of his works.[59] We do know, however, that within a half-dozen years of its appearance, the cordial relations between composer and critic rapidly deteriorated. The two apparently fell out over Schumann's ill-fated opera *Genoveva*, which Krüger reviewed—unfavorably, to say the least—for a March 1851 issue of the *Neue Berliner Musikzeitung*.[60] Krüger attempted to soften the blow in a letter to Schumann of 18 March 1851: "We two won't come to a misunderstanding; after all, both of us are striving to promote the noble, genuine development of our beloved art."[61] Schumann saw things differently. Although only fragments of his reply (dated 5 April 1851) survive, they give indisputable testimony to his displeasure: "Don't make public pronouncements about something you don't properly understand. . . . As I've long suspected, you are very far from understanding me as an artist in the totality of my oeuvre."[62]

The second fragment from Schumann's rejoinder is perhaps overly harsh. Despite the occasionally provincial (even prudish) tone of Krüger's *Peri* review,[63] and despite its rootedness in a neoclassical critical stance that looks with circumspection on the composer's fondness for "characteristic" harmonies, melodies, and forms, the critique affords us real insights into the nature of Schumann's approach to genre and text depiction. Even Krüger's missteps and omissions point the way toward a more evenhanded appraisal. Thus, it might be fairer to say that his understanding of Schumann's work was less incorrect than imperfect.

Having the benefit of hindsight, we can recognize that the teleology of Schumann's career was directed not just toward opera—as Krüger suspected—but, even more significantly, toward a kind of *Literaturoper* or *Literaturmusik*. While proofreading the published full score of the *Peri* in the summer of 1844, Schumann jotted down "Faust beginnings" in the *Haushaltbücher*;[64] and indeed, the setting of the closing scene from Goethe's *Faust* did constitute his next major compositional effort after the *Peri*. The whole remarkable project—a setting of seven scenes from *Faust* with an orchestral overture—would occupy Schumann off and on for almost a decade. As other writers have commented, elements of the *Faust* music were already foreshadowed in the *Peri*. The notion of redemption, to take the most frequently cited example, is central to the thematic of both works.[65] Even more telling, in terms of Schumann's later cultivation of *Literaturmusik*, is the unusual but apt genre designation transmitted in the published score of the *Peri*; as we have observed, the work is called not an oratorio, a religious opera, or a secular cantata but rather a *Gedicht*—a poem. Yet Schumann's systematic exploration of the principal musical genres did not come to an end with the incipient *Literaturopern* of the Dresden and Düsseldorf years; the process arguably culminated in the liturgical works of 1852 and 1853, the Mass, Op. 147, and the Requiem, Op. 148. The *Peri*, therefore, is suspended between the fantastic, "profane" works of the 1830s and the darkly hued sacred works of the final years. It is, to trope on a category from the critical arsenal of one of our century's greatest thinkers, Walter Benjamin, a "dialectical sounding image"—perhaps the most significant such image from the composer's output. If Krüger helps us to come to this realization, he indeed accomplished more than many critics of Schumann's music.

NOTES

1. Robert Schumann, *Tagebücher, Band II: 1836–1854*, ed. Gerd Nauhaus (Leipzig, 1987), p. 267. A brief piece appeared on 20 July in the *Neue Zeitschrift für Musik* 19 (1843): 24, noting that Krüger had recently played the organs at the Thomas- and Nikolaikirche, demonstrating his considerable abilities with several of J. S. Bach's most difficult works.

2. Schumann's *Projektenbuch* for December 1840 lists three of the verse tales from Thomas Moore's *Lalla Rookh*—"Paradies und die Peri," "Der falsche Prophet," and "Das Rosenfest/Das Licht des Harams"—under the rubric "texts suitable for concert pieces"; the first two were further designated as "opera materials." (See Gerd Nauhaus, "Schumanns *Das Paradies und die Peri*: Quellen zur Entstehungs-, Aufführungs- und Rezeptionsgeschichte," in Akio Mayeda and Klaus Wolfgang Niemöller, eds., *Schumanns Werke: Text und Interpretation—16 Studien* [Mainz, 1987], pp. 134–35.) In early August 1841, at the height of the "symphonic year," Schumann's boyhood friend Emil Flechsig rekindled the composer's interest in the tale of the semidivine Peri's quest for a place in paradise. Drawing on Flechsig's translation of Moore's original (and also, in all likelihood, on Theodor Oelckers's 1839 translation of the poem), Schumann immediately set to work on a libretto, completed in its essential form by early January 1842; see Robert Schumann, *Tagebücher, Band III: Haushaltbücher, Teil I: 1837–1847* and *Teil II: 1847–1856*, ed. Gerd Nauhaus (Leipzig, 1982), pp. 189–92, 202–4. Although Schumann may have returned to the text in September 1842 (*Tagebücher, Band III: Haushaltbücher*, p. 225), the principal work on the musical sketches and orchestration was reserved for the four-month period from 23 February to 16 June 1843; see *Tagebücher, Band III: Haushaltbücher*, pp. 238–41, 248, 251–54, and *Tagebücher, Band II: 1836–1854*, pp. 260–63, 265–66. On 20 September 1843 Schumann reworked and expanded the last half of the closing chorus (no. 9) of part 1; see *Tagebücher, Band III: Haushaltbücher*, p. 353, and p. 741, n. 475.

3. See entries in the *Haushaltbücher* for 9, 10, and 12 July; pp. 255–56.

4. Letter of 3 June 1843 in F. Gustav Jansen, ed., *Robert Schumanns Briefe: Neue Folge* (Leipzig, 1904), p. 228.

5. See the entries for 18 and 22 July 1843 in *Tagebücher, Band III: Haushaltbücher*, p. 256.

6. Letter to Carl Koßmaly of 1 September 1842, *Robert Schumanns Briefe*, p. 220.

7. Krüger's letter of thanks for Schumann's hospitality (dated 5 August 1843) is quoted in Martin Uwe, "Ein unbekanntes Schumann-Autograph aus dem Nachlaß Eduard Krügers," *Die Musikforschung* 12 (1959): 413.

8. Ibid., pp. 405–9.

9. Ibid., p. 413.

10. The full score appeared in January 1845 from Breitkopf and Härtel; the piano-vocal score (largely prepared by Clara), together with the solo and choral parts, had been issued by September 1844.

11. *Allgemeine musikalische Zeitung* 47 (1845), cols. 561–70, 585–89, 606–11, 617–22. Subsequent references to the review will be made by column number in the text.

12. Both the main summary accounts of the *Peri* in English—Robert Chandler Godwin, "Schumann's Choral Works and the Romantic Movement" (D.M.A. dissertation, University of Iowa, 1967), pp. 125–43; and John Horton, "The Choral Works," in Gerald Abraham, ed., *Schumann: A Symposium* (London, 1952), pp. 283–87—are incomplete and badly out of date. German scholars have done better by Schumann's *Peri*; see Arnfried Edler, *Robert Schumann und seine Zeit* (Laaber, 1982), pp. 232–38; Gerd Nauhaus, "Schumanns *Das Paradies und die Peri*" (the same author's "Quellenuntersuchungen zu Schumanns 'Das Paradies und die Peri,' "*Robert-Schumann-Tage* [1985]: 68–75, is a shorter version of this study); Susanne Popp, "Untersuchungen zu Robert Schumanns Chorkompositionen" (Ph.D. dissertation, University of Bonn, 1971); and Gisela Probst, *Robert Schumanns Oratorien* (Wiesbaden, 1975). Brief but insightful observations may be found in Reinhard Kapp, *Studien zum Spätwerk Robert Schumanns* (Tutzing, 1984), pp. 113, 137, 264; and Akio Mayeda, *Robert Schumanns Weg zur Symphonie* (Zurich, 1992), pp. 557–58.

13. Carl Dahlhaus, "Zur Problematik der musikalischen Gattungen im 19. Jahrhundert" (1968), in *Gattungen der Musik in Einzeldarstellungen: Gedenkschrift Leo Schrade* (Bern and Munich, 1973), pp. 856–57.

14. Franz Liszt, "Robert Schumann" (1856), in *Gesammelte Schriften* (Leipzig, 1882), vol. 4, pp. 169–70.

15. For firsthand accounts of the December performances, see Clara's entry in the marriage diary for December 1843 (*Tagebücher, Band II: 1836–1854*, pp. 273–74); and Alfred Dörffel, *Geschichte der Gewandhausconcerte zu Leipzig vom 25. November 1781 bis 25. November 1881* (Leipzig, 1884), pp. 107–8. On the episode with von Püttlingen, see the review by O.L. (Oswald Lorenz) in *Allgemeine musikalische Zeitung* 45 (1843), col. 955; Dörffel, *Geschichte*, p. 216; and *Robert Schumanns Briefe*, p. 515, n. 293.

16. "Ach, so öde ist's geworden, Seit die Peri ausgesühnt! Und geschlossen sind die Pforten, *Eden nur hat sie verdient*, Und wir blieben hier zurücke, Schauten auf zu ihrem Glücke." The poem, entitled "Die Perle" and dated 4 December 1843, is reproduced in Wolfgang Boetticher, ed., *Briefe und Gedichte aus dem Album Robert und Clara Schumanns* (Leipzig, 1981), pp. 183–84.

17. Nauhaus, "Schumanns *Das Paradies und die Peri*," p. 133, n. 1.

18. See the entry for 30 December 1847 in *Tagebücher, Band III: Haus-*

haltbücher, p. 449; and Schumann's letter of 1 January 1848 to Ferdinand Hiller, in *Robert Schumanns Briefe*, p. 280.

19. With fifty-three performances (compared to the *Peri's* fifty), only the Symphony no. 1, Op. 38, was given more frequently during the composer's lifetime. See Nauhaus, "Schumanns *Das Paradies und die Peri*," p. 133.

20. In a letter to Raimund Härtel of 31 January 1845, Schumann suggested that the assignment go to E. F. Richter, whose review of the String Quartets, Op. 41, had just been published; see *Allgemeine musikalische Zeitung* 47 (1845), cols. 38–39. At various points in this brief piece, Richter's prose style approaches the fanciful manner of Schumann's own criticism from the *Davidsbündler* days.

21. *De musicis graecorum organis circa Pindari tempora florentibus*. Krüger's later books include *Grundriß der Metrik antiker und moderner Sprachen* (Emden, 1838), and *System der Tonkunst* (Leipzig, 1866).

22. "Ueber Graun's Tod Jesu," *Neue Zeitschrift für Musik* 10 (1839): 66–68, 71–72, 74–76, 79–80; "Ueber mus. Conservatorien," ibid., vol. 15 (1841): 169–71, 173–75, 177–79, 181–83, 185–87, 189–90; "Das Virtuosenconcert" (a dialogue between virtuoso and conductor), ibid., vol. 14 (1841): 159–61, 163–65, 167–69, 171–73; "Ueber die heutige Oper," ibid., vol. 12 (1840): 57–59, 61–62, 65–67, 73–75, 77–78, 85–87; "Accommodation älterer Kunstwerke für den Zeitgeschmack, mit besonderer Beziehung auf Händel," ibid., vol. 11 (1839): 73–75, 77–78, 81–83, 85–87; "Hegel's Philosophie der Musik," ibid., vol. 17 (1842): 25–28, 29–32, 35–37, 39–40, 43–45, 47–51, 53–56, 57–59, 63–64, 65–69; and "Die beiden Bach'schen Passionen," ibid., vol. 18 (1843): 57–59, 61–62, 65–67, 69–71, 73–74, 77–79, 85–88. Krüger continued as a regular contributor to the journal after Franz Brendel assumed the editorship in 1845.

23. See Schumann's letter to Krüger of 20 October 1843, *Robert Schumanns Briefe*, p. 232; and *Tagebücher, Band II: 1836–1854*, p. 270. Schumann himself was being courted for the position, which eventually went to J. C. Lobe.

24. In 1861 Krüger was appointed to a professorship at the University of Göttingen, where he served as director of musical studies and librarian.

25. *Neue Zeitschrift für Musik* 22 (1845). See pp. 317–37 here for a new translation by Jürgen Thym.

26. Cf. the very similar remarks in *Allgemeine musikalische Zeitung* 45 (1843), col. 953 (unsigned review of the December 1843 Leipzig performances); unsigned review, *Leipziger Zeitung* (7 December 1843), quoted in Nauhaus, "Schumanns *Das Paradies und die Peri*," p. 144; Dörffel, *Die Gewandhausconcerte*, pp. 107–8 (quotations from positive accounts by Moritz Hauptmann and Julius Becker); *Allgemeine musikalische Zeitung* 46 (1844), col. 28 (unsigned review of the 23 December 1843 Dresden performance); Brendel, "Robert Schumann," p. 121; and an unsigned review by J. C. Lobe in *Allgemeine musikalische Zeitung* 49 (1847), col. 144.

27. *Robert Schumanns Briefe*, pp. 226–27. Cf. also Schumann's diary entry for 28 June 1843: "Except for a few oratorios by [Karl] Loewe, I don't know of

anything similar [to the *Peri*] in the musical repertory"; *Tagebücher, Band II: 1836–1854*, p. 266.

28. Oswald Lorenz, however, questioned the appropriateness of classifying the work as an oratorio because of its departure from this genre in the areas of "subject matter, conception, style, and tendency." See *Allgemeine musikalische Zeitung* 45 (1843), col. 954. The reviewer for H. Hirschbach's *Musikalisch-kritisches Repertorium* (October 1844) counted the *Peri* as a cantata; see Nauhaus, "Schumanns *Das Paradies und die Peri*," p. 145.

29. Cf. *Allgemeine musikalische Zeitung* 46 (1844), col. 28; and Nauhaus, "Schumanns *Das Paradies und die Peri*," p. 144.

30. *Allgemeine musikalische Zeitung* 45 (1843), col. 952.

31. *Tagebücher, Band II: 1836–1854*, p. 270. In the same entry Schumann listed two possibilities for opera texts: "Der verschleierte Prophet v. Khorassan" (i.e., "The veiled prophet of Khorassan," the first of the verse tales from Moore's *Lalla Rookh*) and "Till Eulenspiegel." Anton von Zuccalmaglio was Schumann's librettist of choice for both projects, neither of which materialized.

32. See Schumann's reviews of Marschner's *Klänge aus Osten* (1840; *Gesammelte Schriften*, vol. 2, pp. 41–42); of Hiller's *Die Zerstörung Jerusalems* and Sobolewski's *Der Erlöser* (1841; ibid., pp. 3–10); and of Loewe's *Johann Huß* (1842; ibid., pp. 99–105).

33. See the entry in *Tagebücher, Band III: Haushaltbücher*, p. 238: "In the evening, Berlioz's beautiful Offertory." Berlioz claimed that "at the rehearsal [for the benefit concert], Schumann, breaking his habitual silence, exclaimed: 'That *Offertorium* beats everything' " (Hector Berlioz, *Memoirs*, trans. Rachel and Eleanor Holmes; annotated and rev. Ernest Newman [1932; reprint, New York, 1966], p. 285). For the period between 29 January and 1 March 1843, Schumann's diary and *Haushaltbücher* contain many references to Berlioz, whose German tour had brought him to Leipzig. In addition to the benefit performance of 23 February, Berlioz also presented a group of his works—the *King Lear* Overture, the *Symphonie fantastique*, and the song "Absence" (with Marie Récio)—at a concert of 4 February, which Schumann attended. Although he had some qualms about Berlioz's idiosyncratic compositional technique, Schumann was likewise impressed by "much that is extraordinarily ingenious and original" in his music (*Tagebücher, Band II: 1836–1854*, p. 256). Clara did not share her husband's enthusiasm for Berlioz, either as a person or as a musician (see *Tagebücher, Band II: 1836–1854*, pp. 258–59).

34. See the entries for 1–2 February 1843 in *Tagebücher, Band III: Haushaltbücher*, p. 236.

35. Other additions include no. 3 (recitative and arioso, "Der hehre Engel"/"Dir, Kind des Stamms"), no. 4 (the Peri's "Wo find ich sie?"), the opening of no. 10 (tenor arioso, "Die Peri tritt"), and no. 20 (the Peri's "Verstoßen!"). Strictly speaking, the chorus of Nile Genies is less an addition than an elaboration of a quatrain from Moore's poem; see Thomas Moore, *Poetical Works* (New York, 1846), p. 408: "Deep in these solitary woods / Where oft the Genii of the Floods . . . "

36. As suggested in n. 2, the genesis of Schumann's *Peri* text was a compli-

cated affair. Although Emil Flechsig is often credited with having introduced Schumann to Moore's *Peri* in translation (on the basis of entries in *Tagebücher, Band III: Haushaltbücher*, p. 189, for 4–5 August 1841), almost certainly the composer knew it in some form beforehand (see the comments on Schumann's *Projektenbuch* entries for December 1840 in n. 2; J. L. Witthaus's translation, published by the Verlag Gebrüder Schumann in 1822, would have been available to Schumann as a youth). The oratorio text in its final form probably resulted from a conflation of Flechsig's translation, Theodor Oelckers's translation (Leipzig, 1839), and Schumann's own ideas; nor can Adolf Böttger's participation be ruled out (see the entries in *Tagebücher, Band III: Haushaltbücher*, pp. 190–92, 202, for 10, 22, and 30 August 1841, and 21 December 1841). This scenario is supported by Flechsig's report to Wasielewski (7 May 1857), according to which Schumann "in part retained and in part shortened, improved, or altered" his friend's translation; see Wilhelm Joseph von Wasielewski, *Robert Schumann: Eine Biographie*, enlarged ed. (Leipzig, 1906), p. 327. For an excellent discussion of these and other text-related issues, see Nauhaus, "Schumanns *Das Paradies und die Peri*," pp. 134–39.

37. Miriam Allen de Ford, *Thomas Moore* (New York, 1967), p. 42. Howard Mumford Jones, the author of what was long considered the standard biography of the poet, was even more uncompromising: "[The *Lalla Rookh*] lies stranded in the Dead Sea of literature, and few there are who climb aboard and explore its faded interior"; see *The Harp that Once: A Chronicle of the Life of Thomas Moore* (New York, 1937), p. 171.

38. *Tagebücher, Band II: 1836–1854*, p. 270.

39. In his letter to Schumann of 8 August 1841, Flechsig paraphrased the entry on "Peris" from Herloßsohn's *Damen Conversations-Lexikon* (1837); see Boetticher, ed., *Briefe und Gedichte*, pp. 56–57. Further information on these "beautiful creatures of the air, who live upon . . . perfumes" and to whom a sumptuous garden "might make some amends for the Paradise they have lost," appears in the framing narrative to Moore's poem (see Moore, *Poetical Works*, p. 406), which Schumann probably read in translation.

40. *Robert Schumanns Briefe*, p. 228. The reference to *heitre Menschen* is to be understood in relation to a passage from Goethe's *Maximen und Reflexionen* that Schumann had copied into his *Mottosammlung*; Goethe differentiates between *heilig* (sacred) and *profan* (secular) music, the defining characteristic of the latter being *Heiterkeit* (cheerfulness). On this point, see Probst, *Robert Schumanns Oratorien*, pp. 15–16.

41. Letter to Koßmaly of 5 May 1843, *Robert Schumanns Briefe*, pp. 226–27.

42. The projected oratorio *Luther*, which occupied Schumann in the early 1850s, was to be "suitable for both the church and the concert hall"; see his letter to Richard Pohl of 14 February 1851, *Robert Schumanns Briefe*, p. 336; also pp. 237–39 here.

43. See the discussion in Nauhaus, "Schumanns *Das Paradies und die Peri*," p. 146.

44. Wagner too had toyed with the idea of setting Moore's poem to music.

He abandoned the project because, as he wrote to Schumann in a letter of 21 September 1843: "I couldn't find the proper form in which to render it [Moore's *Peri*], and congratulate you on having succeeded in doing so." Quoted from Richard Wagner, *Sämtliche Briefe*, ed. Gertrud Strobel and Werner Wolf (Leipzig, 1970), vol. 2, p. 326.

45. For a discussion of Schumann's structural plan, see Nauhaus, "Schumanns *Das Paradies und die Peri*," pp. 135–37, 146–48.

46. See Schumann's letter of 20 February 1847 to Brendel, in which he complains that one of the *Peri*'s "best qualities," its "lack of [simple] recitatives," had become the object of critical reproach; *Robert Schumanns Briefe*, p. 266.

47. *Neue Zeitschrift für Musik* 22 (1845): 114, 146–47.

48. From his *Davidsbündlerbrief*; quoted in Nauhaus, "Schumanns *Das Paradies und die Peri*," p. 145.

49. *Allgemeine musikalische Zeitung* 49 (1847): col. 144.

50. See Schumann's reviews of 1837 and 1842 in *Gesammelte Schriften*, vol. 1, p. 323, and vol. 2, p. 100. As he wrote of Loewe's oratorio, "There is a pedantry of simplicity that relates to genuine artistic naïveté like mannerism does to originality" (ibid., vol. 2, p. 100).

51. "Robert Schumann," p. 149. Brendel made the same point in his review of Schumann's Symphony no. 2, Op. 61, in *Neue Zeitschrift für Musik* 25 (1846): 181.

52. "Robert Schumann," p. 149.

53. Ibid., p. 145: "As splendid as the oratorio *Das Paradies und die Peri* must be judged, and in spite of its richness in content and its great advances from a musical point of view, still, an interpenetration of the subjective and objective elements . . . is not completely achieved. Indeed, it appears at times as if Schumann is untrue to his own nature at those moments when he feels compelled to step outside himself."

54. *Gesammelte Schriften*, vol. 2, p. 42.

55. Cf. ibid., pp. 41–42, and Schumann's letter of 20 February 1847, in *Robert Schumanns Briefe*, p. 267. Brendel did not fail to recognize the innovative structure of the *Peri*; in a review of Schumann's *Genoveva*, he called attention to the oratorio as a milestone on the way toward an ideal dramatic form: that in which "each act [of an opera] *proceeds with the uninterrupted flow of a finale*"; see *Neue Zeitschrift für Musik* 33 (1850): 3.

56. This point is treated in more detail in John Daverio, *Nineteenth-Century Music and the German Romantic Ideology* (New York, 1993), pp. 64–71.

57. Cf., for example, Godwin, "Schumann's Choral Works," pp. 126, 142–43; and Probst, *Robert Schumanns Oratorien*, pp. 60, 94, 109–11.

58. *Tagebücher, Band III: Haushaltbücher*, p. 398.

59. See Nauhaus's discussion of the *Peri* reviews in Schumann's *Zeitungsstimmen*; "Schumanns *Das Paradies und die Peri*," pp. 144–46.

60. As Jurgen Thym has suggested, Krüger was probably the author of an unsigned review of *Genoveva* for the 28 March and 4 April 1851 issues of the

Neue Zeitschrift; see "Schumann in Brendel's *Neue Zeitschrift für Musik* from 1845 to 1856," in Jon W. Finson and R. Larry Todd, eds., *Mendelssohn and Schumann: Essays on Their Music and Its Context* (Durham, N.C., 1984), pp. 29, 34. Thym is almost certainly correct. A number of points in the *Genoveva* review resonate with Krüger's earlier account of the *Peri*: the author's outlook on Schumann as an instrumentally oriented composer; the framing of the argument in terms of binary oppositions (the Beautiful versus the Characteristic, the allegorical versus the genuinely poetic, instrumental versus vocal styles); the general reliance on Brendel's essay of 1845 for the *Neue Zeitschrift*; and the references to the melodic peculiarities of the *Peri*. See *Neue Zeitschrift für Musik* 34 (1851): 129–31, 141–44.

61. Quoted in Martin, "Ein unbekanntes Schumann-Autograph," p. 414.

62. Ibid.

63. Consider, for instance, the commentary on the chorus of Houris (no. 18): "But we Germans would have preferred to do without the clattering and clanking of the bejeweled garments of the Muslim harem [as depicted] in the orchestra" (col. 587).

64. See the entry for 13 June 1844, *Tagebücher, Band III: Haushaltbücher*, p. 365.

65. In a letter of June 1848 to Friedrich Whistling, Schumann himself noted that both the musical and poetic content of the *Schlußszene* of *Faust* were prefigured in the corresponding scene from the *Peri*; *Robert Schumanns Briefe*, p. 454. Liszt was among the first writers to point out the relationships between the *Peri* and the later works involving chorus and orchestra (the *Faust* music; the *Manfred* music, Op. 115; the *Requiem for Mignon*, Op. 98b; and *Der Rose Pilgerfahrt*, Op. 112); see Liszt, "Robert Schumann," in *Gesammelte Schriften*, vol. 4, pp. 169–70. Cf. also Edler, *Schumann und seine Zeit*, p. 235; and Probst, *Robert Schumanns Oratorien*, pp. 33–34, 130.

The Intentional Tourist:

Romantic Irony in the Eichendorff

Liederkreis of Robert Schumann

JON W. FINSON

"The *Kreisleriana* have been heavily revised," Robert Schumann wrote to Friedrich Whistling in late 1849 and then confessed, "Unfortunately, I spoiled my pieces so often in earlier times, wantonly so. All that has now been eliminated."[1] The letter confirms in Schumann's own words what scholars of his piano music have drawn repeatedly to our attention—that is, his growing conservatism as he approached middle age. Most recently Anthony Newcomb has taken this change in character as his central theme in an overview of Schumann's compositions for the piano.[2] Schumann's retrenchment resulted in new editions of the Impromptus, Op. 5, the *Davidsbündlertänze*, Op. 6, the Symphonic Etudes, Op. 13, and the Third Sonata, Op. 14, as well as the *Kreisleriana*. In all these the composer softened clashing harmonies, regularized peculiar phrases, clarified cadences, and generally removed their more bizarre (some would say original and astonishing) features.

The idea that Schumann grew more conservative and more attuned to his prospective audience is hardly new. The notion stems from Schumann's earliest biographer, Wilhelm Joseph von Wasielewski, who used it as one of the central threads of his narrative, though he viewed it in the positive light of artistic maturation.[3] But whether we regard Schumann's revised editions as a sign of growth or of artistic retreat, one of the most striking instances has occasioned little more than passing mention. Schumann's self-critical comment to Whistling might just as well have been directed at the *Liederkreis*, Op. 39, which the composer referred to briefly in his letter of 1849 because the publisher was then engraving it in a second, altered edition. Here Schumann substituted a completely different song, "In der Fremde," for

"Der frohe Wandersmann," which had begun the first version published by Haslinger in 1842.[4]

This major revision of the Eichendorff cycle has not gone entirely unnoticed: Wasielewski mentions it in a footnote to his biography,[5] Leopold Hirschberg points it out again in an article from the late 1920s,[6] and the information appears sporadically in the liner notes for recordings of Op. 39 during the 1960s and 1970s and in the several volumes devoted to Schumann's songs during the past three decades. Yet for all this reiteration, the revision often startles knowledgeable musicologists and performers, simply because modern scholars have dismissed it briefly and rather lightly. For instance, Eric Sams writes laconically, "The first edition of Op. 39 began with the clearly inferior *Der frohe Wandersmann*."[7] Herwig Knaus supplies a more insightful but equally brief rationalization: "The poetically self-contained unity of the cycle was disturbed by this unrelated, dynamic opening, and this may have moved Schumann to eliminate the song from the second edition."[8] Stephen Walsh adds the question of tonal coherence to poetic incongruity: with the substitution of "In der Fremde" for "Der frohe Wandersmann," the cycle begins and ends on a tonic of F♯ (see table 1).[9]

Table 1
Contents of Op. 39 in the 1842 Edition

Title	Date in *Liederbücher*[a]	Key
"Der frohe Wandersmann"	22 June 1840	D major
"Intermezzo"	May 1840	A major
"Waldesgespräch"	1 May 1840	E major
"Die Stille"	4 May 1840	G major
"Mondnacht"	9 May 1840	E major
"Schöne Fremde"	16/17 May 1840	B major
"Auf einer Burg"	no date	A minor
"In der Fremde"	18 May 1840	A minor
"Wehmuth"	17/18 May 1840	E major
"Zwielicht"	19 May 1840	E minor
"Im Walde"	20 May 1840	A major
"Frühlingsnacht"	18 May 1840	F♯ major

[a] Schumann's initial manuscripts of his songs, Berlin, Deutsche Staatsbibliothek, Mus. ms. 16/2. See also Viktor Ernst Wolff, *Die Lieder Robert Schumanns in ersten und späteren Fassungen* (Berlin, 1913).

And Barbara Turchin's thoughtful analysis of the *Liederkreis* essentially repeats in more convincing fashion the points made by Knaus and Walsh: "Schumann must have realized [that] the tone and style of the poem and its setting run counter to those of the cycle as a whole."[10] Turchin adds that "Der frohe Wandersmann" occurred to the composer as an afterthought, over a month later than the rest of the songs in the cycle.

This notion of "Der frohe Wandersmann" as afterthought raises more questions, however, than it answers. For it reveals Schumann's decision to begin Op. 39 with the song as an act of reflection rather than momentary inspiration. We must ask, then, why Schumann selected "Der frohe Wandersmann" at all, given its apparent lack of suitability. Turchin's quick reply would be, as I read it, that Schumann included the text because of its contemporary popularity. But this explanation seems too facile in light of what we know about the composer's habits; he considered very carefully the psychological interaction between numbers in his cycles and could hardly remain indifferent to an opening song that affects the interpretation of the whole. If we wish to answer the question posed above, we must take "Der frohe Wandersmann" more seriously in itself, rather than pass over it lightly. And then we may see what it tells us about the tone and content of the song cycle that Schumann called "my most romantic."[11]

I

At first glance "Der frohe Wandersmann" is everything its detractors would have it be. Sams, who apparently thinks it too naive for Op. 39, dismisses it as exhibiting "ostensibly a brisk, rousing folk-song melody and accompaniment."[12] The combined themes of the song's simplicity and folkishness run through the other commentaries I have mentioned as well, and the characterization is entirely just. A rhythmically square and forthright march supports the cheerful melody in an uncomplicated way, never contradicting the vocal line, independent only long enough to sustain the mood between phrases and to provide a short postlude. We do not see the subtle interaction between piano and voice found in songs like "Mondnacht" or "Zwielicht," nor is the accompaniment nearly so intrusive as in many of the other selections from Op. 39, not to mention Schumann's remaining songs from 1840. The composer certainly invokes *Volkston* here, in the varied strophic form as well as in the usual symbols provided by a heavy-footed rhythm, occasional horn fifths, and the mostly diatonic palette. All these features reflect the heedless optimism of the text and comment on the ingenuous speaker:

> Wem Gott will rechte Gunst erweisen,
> den schickt er in die weite Welt,
> dem will er seine Wunder weisen
> in Berg und Wald und Strom und Feld.
>
> Die Trägen die zu Hause liegen,
> erquicket nicht das Morgenrot,
> sie wissen nur vom Kinderwiegen,
> von Sorgen, Last, und Not um Brot.
>
> Die Bächlein von den Bergen springen,
> die Lerchen schwirren hoch vor Lust,
> was sollt' ich nicht mit ihnen singen
> aus voller Kehl' und frischer Brust?
>
> Den lieben Gott nur lass' ich walten;
> der Bächlein, Lerchen, Wind und Feld,
> und Erd' und Himmel will erhalten,
> hat auch mein' Sach auf's best' bestellt.

> He whom God means to favor,
> He sends into the wide world
> And shows his wonders
> In mountain and forest, river and field.
>
> The sluggards who stay at home
> Are not thrilled by the dawn;
> They know only of cradles,
> Of worries, burdens, and the need for bread.
>
> Rivulets spring from the mountains,
> Larks soar high for joy;
> Why should I not join their singing,
> With full throat and lively heart?
>
> I let the good Lord do as he will;
> The brooks, larks, wind, and field,
> And earth and heaven are in his keeping,
> Who also knows what is best for me.

Our protagonist literally marches into the unknown without fear, expecting to encounter adventures in which he will be protected by divine providence. It is as if Schumann had in mind the episode of Eichendorff's *Ahnung und Gegenwart* wherein Leontin maintains that "nothing beats traveling, if one doesn't merely go from here to there but launches out into the wide world at God's pleasure."[13]

If both the lyrics and music of "Der frohe Wandersmann" strike a familiar chord, they may betray a kinship to the beginning of another famous cycle about a traveling protagonist, *Die schöne Müllerin*. Schumann does not quote "Das Wandern" (the first song in Schubert's cycle), but he intimates its folkish march just as Eichendorff's poem resembles Wilhelm Müller's, with its cheerful, heedless praise of travel as a salutary necessity for anybody with a bit of imagination. Schumann's early diaries indicate that he came to know Schubert's songs well during the 1830s,[14] and Schumann may have hoped to render Op. 39 immediately accessible to his audience by invoking Schubert's opening gesture. Moreover, "Der frohe Wandersmann" identifies the Eichendorff *Liederkreis* as belonging to the genre of "wanderer song cycles," in which, as Turchin observes, a youth typically leaves his home seeking his fortune and his beloved ("Intermezzo," the second song in Op. 39, confirms the goal of the quest).[15] We might think this obvious from the rest of the cycle, but in fact the theme connecting the various numbers in Op. 39 has eluded some writers. Sams, for instance, maintains that "this cycle may not be deliberately linked by any story or idea,"[16] and Walsh suggests that "although the songs are integrated in style and atmosphere there is no question of a circle or sequence of events."[17] Informed by "Der frohe Wandersmann," we know that the remaining songs represent the feelings, observations, and fantasies of our confident traveler as he wends his way through the world in search of his beloved. These are nothing less than the experiences with which God has favored his elect. In *Die schöne Müllerin*, however, a similar notion proves ironic: Schubert's protagonist finds the outcome of his journey so dismaying that he commits suicide. And Schumann's tourist in his turn also discovers that travel is less than an unalloyed delight.

The most obvious example of an unfortunate excursion appears in the first song Schumann composed for Op. 39, "Waldesgespräch." This miniature drama presents a situation familiar among the standard plots of German folklore (the beginning of Tieck's *Die schöne Melusine* comes to mind, for instance): while riding in the forest, a traveler happens upon a beautiful maiden whom he tries to seduce with a time-worn line, "It's late, it's cold, come home with me." Though lacking a narrator, "Waldesgespräch" is a ballad with the usual roster of players speaking their lines, and the composer casts it in a particularly dramatic fashion for this reason. The piano refrain plays an important part in establishing a folkish mood by means of distinct horn fifths and a dominant pedal at the opening—allusions to a male on the hunt, so to speak. The prelude is closely related to the opening of "Der frohe Wandersmann": the accompanimental figures in "Waldesgespräch" seem to constitute an embellished variation on the beginning of the earlier song (though to be chronologically correct, Schumann apparently had the prelude to "Waldesgespräch" in mind when he later composed the prelude to "Der frohe Wandersmann"). The implication of this allusion is clear: here we have another heedless tourist guilelessly pursuing one of traveling's pleasures. But in a peculiar twist, he finds something quite different from what he expected: no passive maiden but an infuriated and vengeful Lorelei (replete with "wave figure") who hates men. The hunter, it turns out, is really the prey. We find hints of this irony in the sorceress's reference to the hunt in her first strophe: "Wohl irrt das Waldhorn her und hin" ("The hunting horn strays to and fro"). But the full impact of the reversal does not reach us until she mocks the wanderer by throwing back his casual introductory line, "Es ist schon spät, es ist schon kalt," rhyming it with her pronouncement of his doom, "Kommst nimmermehr aus diesem Wald" ("You will never leave these woods"). Schumann concludes ironically with a citation of the prelude's horn fifths, as the female "victim" appropriates the music of her would-be seducer. The strains of the horn die away dreamily, the perfect postlude to one of those adventures with which God has favored his elect.

The other song in this cycle sporting an audible *Volkston*, "Im Walde," features a similar set of ironies. On a musical level, Schumann initially misleads us about the genre of this number by casting his accompaniment in "ballad style," a cliché involving a chordal drone (also used by Chopin, for instance, in the opening of his Ballade in F major, Op. 38). This pattern introduces what at first seems to be the beginning of a tale about a wedding party, but the ostensible story is interrupted by an unrelated event (a hunt). We never discover why these two occurrences are juxtaposed, but the coincidence of both exciting occasions produces unexpected misgivings in the narrator, who "shudders in the depths of [his] heart" as night falls and the two parties recede. The beginning holds the promise of a third-person narrative—a cheerful one at that—but the poet and composer suddenly usher us into the private, internalized world of the Lied. And thus the persistent folkish rhythms halt, replaced by the slow and solemn chords that accompany the peculiar closing lines. Like "Waldesgespräch," "Im Walde" brings us to a conclusion quite different from what the beginning intimates, in terms of both content and genre.

The combination of "Der frohe Wandersmann" and "Intermezzo" at the beginning of the first edition seems to imply a narrative; for this reason, songs in Op. 39 sometimes take an ironic tone through their juxtaposition as well as through their internal arrangement. In at least one case Schumann bolsters the inclination to see a succession of events by joining musically two adjacent songs, "Auf einer Burg" and "In der Fremde." The first of the pair begins as a portrait of a ruined castle on the Rhine, with its moldering statue and empty window frames. The faux-canonic accompaniment in half notes invokes the *stile antico* as part of the ancient ruin's solemn atmosphere (Schumann would call on much the same idiom for the fourth movement of the Third Symphony, which employs species counterpoint more strictly). From a vantage point within this ruin, the narrator then beholds a wedding procession in the valley below. Karen Hindenlang argues persuasively that the odd combination of stony knight and unhappy bride entails political symbolism.[18] But this understanding does not diminish the striking disjunction of musicians playing "merrily" while the bride weeps, especially when Schumann's setting emphasizes the word *munter* with a good deal of dissonance.

Schumann joins "Auf einer Burg" to "In der Fremde" by means both tonal (the first song ends on a half-cadence that serves as the dominant of the second song) and motivic (they share a common head motive combining a falling fifth with a scalar rise of a minor third).[19] The poems play against each other uneasily, however, with the second revisiting images from the first. "In der Fremde" also alludes to a castle from ancient times. But it now appears in a valley, viewed from outside and above. This scene holds a promise of happiness that turns out to be entirely ironic: at the very end the persona suddenly recalls that his beloved died long ago. Schumann responds to this last macabre reversal by using the motif of the melodic turn, which punctuates almost every phrase of his accompaniment, in an unusually low register to close his setting. We are left to ask why these two poems should be joined musically at all, inasmuch as they contain internal paradoxes and reversals and do not seem to portray a logical series of events. Does one precede the other chronologically? Have we viewed the beloved in "Auf einer Burg"; is the beloved dead or alive? The musical conjunction creates many problems that it does not solve.

The temptation to interpret one song in light of another pervades the whole cycle and almost always yields disquieting results. Most commentators agree that for reasons of tonality and content Op. 39 divides after "Schöne Fremde," and if we accept this view, then the largely optimistic mood of the first six songs ("Waldesgespräch" aside) is contradicted by the second half of the cycle. Could the cheerful journeyman of "Der frohe Wandersmann" really be the same person who speaks in "Wehmuth"?

> Ich kann wohl manchmal singen,
> Als ob ich fröhlich sei,
> Doch heimlich Tränen dringen,
> Da wird das Herz mir frei. . . .
>
> Da lauschen alle Herzen,
> Und alles ist erfreut,
> Doch keiner fühlt die Schmerzen,
> Im Lied das tiefe Leid.
>
> Truly I can sing at times
> As if I were happy.
> But secretly tears fall
> That relieve my heart. . . .
>
> Then all hearts listen,
> And all rejoice,
> But no one feels the pain,
> The deep grief in my song.

The ironic content of this piece seems even more so in light of the cheerful opening song. And by the time we reach the last lines of "Zwielicht," the reversal of the persona's character is complete:

> Hast du einen Freund hienieden,
> Trau ihm nicht zu dieser Stunde,
> Freundlich wohl mit Aug und Munde,
> Sinnt er Krieg im tück'schen Frieden.
>
> If you have a friend here below,
> Do not trust him at this hour,
> While his eyes and lips intimate friendliness,
> In false peace he thinks of war.

After "Im Walde," with its conjunction of a wedding and a hunt, we are prepared for the worst, only to discover the final irony: the persona succeeds in his quest and wins his beloved (thus frustrating expectations conditioned by the allusions to *Die schöne Müllerin*). Moreover, his success is accompanied by a piano part that seems positively maudlin in its insistent accompaniment. It is true that the *Liederkreis* does not present a coherent sequence of events, but it does portray a succession of quickly changing moods and situations juxtaposed to create irony.

II

In my brief discussion I have defined irony more broadly than the strict meanings given in most dictionaries, which usually refer to "a method of expression in which the intended meaning of the words used is directly opposite of their usual sense"[20] and trace the root back to the Greek *eiron*, "a dissembler in speech." Mocking by means of exaggerated praise was the usual use of *eironeia*, which generally carried humorous and derisive connotations. But in the late eighteenth century irony came to have a broader and more elevated meaning, especially in the writings of Friedrich Schlegel. "In true irony," he wrote, "not only striving for the *infinite* but possession of the *infinite* must be present, linked with micrological thoroughness to philosophy and poetry" ("Bei der wahren Ironie muß nicht bloß Streben nach *Unendlichkeit* sondern Besitz von *Unendlichkeit* mit mikrologischer Gründlichkeit in P[hilosophie] und P[oesie] verbunden, da sein"). "Irony is certainly no matter for jest" ("Mit der Ironie ist durchaus nicht zu scherzen"); "complete, absolute irony ceases to be irony and becomes serious" ("Die vollendete absolute Ironie hört auf Ironie zu seyn und wird ernsthaft"). As Lilian Furst puts it, "Irony is thus given a wholly new metaphysical status, and invested with an epistemological and ontological function."[21] Irony is the instrument by which an artist can transcend his creation and is therefore a means of self-conscious reflection. Schlegel regarded paradox as the essential condition of irony: "Irony is the form that paradox takes. Everything that is at once good and great is paradoxical" ("Ironie ist die Form des Paradoxons. Paradox ist alles, was zugleich gut und groß ist").[22] It was this elevated notion of irony, as well as the lower satirical notion, that informed the writings of authors like Jean Paul and Heinrich Heine, whom Schumann so adored.

The problem with irony, however, comes in its detection, for it often hides behind a mask. A knowledge of context can often provide a clue to the presence of irony. Jane Austen opens *Pride and Prejudice* with the observation that "it is a truth universally acknowledged, that a single man in possession of a good fortune, must be in want of a wife." As the story unfolds, we soon learn that Darcy and Bingley are not in want of wives, but that the Bennet and Lucas daughters' lack of a fortune places them in want of husbands.[23] Tone in speaking or writing also betrays irony: Austen indulges just a hint of overstatement in her phrase "truth universally acknowledged" that might lead us to believe that things are not what they appear.

In a composition combining words and music, the composer can supply the tone or context that aids in the detection of irony. The most celebrated instance in Schumann's works comes at the beginning of *Dichterliebe*. Taken at face value, "Im wunderschönen Monat Mai" is a simple love song:

> Im wunderschönen Monat Mai,
> Als alle Knospen sprangen
> Da hab' ich ihr gestanden
> Mein Sehnen und Verlangen.

> Im wunderschönen Monat Mai,
> Als alle Vögel sangen,
> Da ist in meinem Herzen,
> Die Liebe aufgegangen.

> In the wonderfully lovely month of May,
> When all the buds were bursting
> I confessed to her my longing and desire.

> In the wonderfully lovely month of May,
> When all the birds were singing,
> Love arose in my heart.

A listener who knows the source of the poetry, the "Lyrical Intermezzo" from Heine's *Liederbuch*, understands this text as ironic from the context of the intermezzo's prologue, about a poet who discovers that all love is mere fantasy. Schumann's title for the cycle, "Poet's Love," refers to this prologue, and eventually the truth about the mirage of love appears explicitly in "Aus alten Märchen winkt es." But for the uninitiated, Schumann signals the presence of this paradox at the beginning of *Dichterliebe* by setting "Im wunderschönen Monat Mai" in a way that is in itself ironic. The mechanism consists of a tonal conceit in which the piano prelude to each verse prepares phrases in minor mode, which always drop, however, into the relative major, an opposite result. Without reading Heine's prologue, we know that the surface meaning of this song cannot be taken quite literally (even if we do not yet know the nature of the paradox or where it might lead). The composer reads the poem in a tone of voice that allows us to detect the irony in this declaration of love.

Schumann's other Heine cycle from 1840, the *Liederkreis*, Op. 24, yields a rather different variety of ironic accompaniment, one that depends on external association rather than internal structure. The lyrics of "Anfangs wollt' ich fast verzagen" indulge in both paradox and injured overstatement:

> Anfangs wollt' ich fast verzagen,
> Und ich glaubt', ich trüg' es nie,
> Und ich hab' es doch getragen,
> Aber fragt mich nur nicht: wie?

> At first I almost wanted to despair,
> And believed I would never bear it;
> I have borne it nonetheless,
> But do not ask me how.

And Schumann's setting reinforces the effect by referring to an extremely well-known German chorale by Georg Neumark, "Wer nur den lieben Gott läßt walten" (compare examples 1 and 2).

Example 1. Georg Neumark's chorale "Wer nur den lieben Gott läßt walten," in a harmonization by J. S. Bach

An-fangs wollt' ich fast ver-za-gen, und ich glaubt', ich trüg' es nie,

Example 2. Schumann, *Liederkreis*, Op. 24, no. 8

Lest there be any doubt about the context, Schumann supports the tune with the block chords of a chorale texture. The use of the chorale may simply involve musical overstatement, but it may also call to mind the customary words of the hymn—not so much its first verse, which bids the pious trust in God, but the admonishing second verse:

> Was helfen uns die schweren Sorgen?
> Was hilft uns unser Weh und Ach?
> Was hilft es, daß wir alle Morgen
> Beseufzen unser Ungemach?
> Wir machen unser Kreuz und Leid
> Nur größer durch die Traurigkeit.

> What good is deep sorrow,
> What good are our doleful cries?
> What good does it do every morning
> To bemoan our troubles?
> We only make our cross and suffering
> Heavier by being melancholy.

The persona's lament in "Anfangs wollt' ich" runs exactly contrary to the text of Schumann's allusion. By closing "Anfangs wollt' ich" with a half-cadence leading to the next song, Schumann further intensifies the paradox. For after refusing to disclose how he has borne his tragedy, the persona gives a complete confession in the next number.

The use of "Der frohe Wandersmann" to open the first version of Op. 39 provides a context for the rest of the cycle and allies the Eichendorff *Liederkreis* closely to its cousins from around the same time. By alluding to *Die schöne Müllerin*, the song implies a conventional story that never materializes. Rather, the nonnarrative is full of false starts and missed connections, and it concludes "incorrectly," as well, in the context of Schubert's earlier cycle. At the same time, "Der frohe Wandersmann" provides a point of reference against which we can view other songs from Op. 39. Many take on a more ironic air in light of "Der frohe Wandersmann," for the disparity between its cheerful confidence and the unhappy confusion in other parts of the cycle is acute. Schumann's setting of the piece is also ironic in its strong accentuation of the folkloric, which indulges in overstatement, and in its choice of key, the "wrong" one to establish the tonic, if we take table 1 at face value. But then, Schumann dissembles even here, for if we listen to the second stanza, we hear that the song in fact cadences authentically on an F♯-minor chord, just where the text emphasizes the life of woe enjoyed uniquely by those who stay at home. "Der frohe Wandersmann" does "fit" Op. 39, but not in the more conventional way that "In der Fremde" does.

The replacement of "Der frohe Wandersmann" with "In der Fremde" ties Op. 39 to the piano pieces that Schumann chose to revise around the same time. Many of these compositions, especially the *Davidsbündlertänze* and *Kreisleriana*, also consist of short segments that shift ambience suddenly and incongruously. Recently Hans-Joachim Bracht has written that these sudden reversals lie at the very heart of "romantic irony" in Schumann's *Papillons* and in many similar pieces from the composer's output of the 1830s.[24] In adding extra repetitions of certain phrases and removing certain unorthodox cadences for later editions, Schumann sought to temper the abruptions that rendered these compositions ironic and perplexing. Eradicating the incongruity of "Der frohe Wandersmann" seems to have prompted the revision of Op. 39.

The case of the Eichendorff *Liederkreis* provides a particularly pointed instance of a dilemma sometimes known as "the author's final version" ("die Fassung letzter Hand"), after Georg von Dadelsen's 1961 article of the same title.[25] Are the composer's last revisions of a piece necessarily improvements? I have tried to show how "Der frohe Wandersmann" attaches poetically, melodically, and tonally to the remainder of Op. 39, where it stood in a privileged position for seven years during the composer's brief lifetime. Without this song at its beginning, many listeners have missed the subplot of the cycle and the ironic tone that pervades it.

Perhaps it is now plausible to return "Der frohe Wandersmann" to its original place in Schumann's Eichendorff *Liederkreis*. Performers might occasionally program the original version, and the modern recording industry could provide an even better solution. Compact discs of Op. 39 could begin with "Der frohe Wandersmann" and continue with its replacement, "In der Fremde." Those who wish to hear the first version of Op. 39 could then set their players to omit "In der Fremde," whereas those who prefer the second version could simply begin with "In der Fremde." Kenneth Slowik has provided just such an option in his recording of Bach's *St. John Passion*,[26] which includes an appendix of numbers from the 1725 version that the listener can insert according to instructions in the program notes. Many may feel that a restoration of Op. 39 to its original state entails a misbegotten historical piety. But alternate versions actually published by the composer cannot be dismissed lightly; if nothing else, they reveal the gulf between the older and younger Schumann.

NOTES

1. *Robert Schumann's Leben aus seinen Briefen geschildert*, ed. Hermann Erler (Berlin, 1887), vol. 2, p. 105; I have adapted this translation from Anthony Newcomb's "Schumann and the Marketplace: From Butterflies to *Hausmusik*," in *Nineteenth-Century Piano Music*, ed. R. Larry Todd (New York, 1990), p. 275.

2. Ibid., pp. 258–85.

3. See, for instance, Wasielewski's second, corrected edition of *Robert Schumann: Eine Biographie* (Dresden, 1869).

4. Kurt Hofmann reproduces the title pages and descriptions of both editions in *Die Erstdrucke der Werke von Robert Schumann* (Tutzing, 1979), pp. 90–93, but he mistakenly lists thirteen songs in the first edition. Recently I discussed these discrepancies with Reinhold Brinkmann, who kindly sent me a photocopy of the table of contents from the first edition.

5. Wasielewski, *Robert Schumann: Eine Biographie*, p. 173.

6. "Merkwürdiges aus einem Schumann-Erstdruck," *Die Musik* 21 (1929): 731–36.

7. Eric Sams, *The Songs of Robert Schumann* (New York, 1969), p. 93.

8. Herwig Knaus, *Musiksprache und Werkstruktur in Robert Schumanns "Liederkreis"* (Munich, 1974), p. 17.

9. Stephen Walsh, *The Lieder of Schumann* (Kassel and London, 1971), p. 35.

10. Barbara Turchin, "Schumann's Song Cycles: The Cycle within the Song," *19th-Century Music* 8 (1985): 238.

11. See Wolfgang Boetticher, *Robert Schumann in seinen Schriften und Briefen* (Berlin, 1942), p. 340.

12. Sams, *The Songs of Robert Schumann*, p. 106.

13. Joseph von Eichendorff, *Romane—Erzählungen*, vol. 2 in his *Werke* (Munich, 1970), p. 37.

14. Among the many entries about Schubert songs is one particularly revealing and amusing: "Mit Glock [an amateur singer] etliche zwanzig Hefte Schubert'scher Lieder abgeschrien!" In Robert Schumann, *Tagebücher, Band I: 1827–1838*, ed. Georg Eismann (Leipzig, 1971), p. 335.

15. Turchin, "Schumann's Song Cycles," 238.

16. Sams, *The Songs of Robert Schumann*, p. 92.

17. Walsh, *The Lieder of Schumann*, pp. 32–33.

18. Karen A. Hindenlang, "Eichendorff's 'Auf einer Burg' and Schumann's *Liederkreis*, Opus 39," *Journal of Musicology* 8 (1990): 569–87.

19. Turchin gives a good analysis of the interrelationship in "Schumann's Song Cycles," 242.

20. *Webster's New World Dictionary of the American Language*, college ed. (New York and Cleveland, 1966), p. 773.

21. *Fictions of Romantic Irony* (Cambridge, Mass., 1984), p. 26; my summary of Schlegel's views comes from Furst's account, and I use her translations.

22. Ibid., p. 27.

23. Ibid., p. 49.

24. "Schumann's 'Papillons' und die Ästhetik der Frühromantik," *Archiv für Musikwissenschaft* 50 (1993): 71–84.

25. "Die 'Fassung letzter Hand' in der Musik," *Acta Musicologica* 33 (1961): 1–14.

26. This recording is published by the Smithsonian Institution (1990) as ND 0381, 1–2.

"Actually, Taken Directly from Family Life": Robert Schumann's *Album für die Jugend*

BERNHARD R. APPEL

TRANSLATED BY JOHN MICHAEL COOPER

The popular reception of Schumann's celebrated *Album für die Jugend*, reflected in an uninterrupted history of editions, performances, and some fifty-odd related titles in the international secondary literature, stands in remarkable contrast to the few scholarly studies of the work's genesis and source situation. The following remarks address preliminary issues concerning the biographical origins of the individual pieces and summarize the current disposition of the sources, which are listed in the appendix. Though a review of already-established facts is unavoidable, sources that have turned up since 1991 may shed new light on what is known.[1] First of all, we may outline the compositional history of the *Album für die Jugend*, in order to document its relationship to the biographical circumstances surrounding its genesis.

I

On 31 August 1848 Schumann noted in his *Haushaltbuch*, "Idea for an album for the children—miniatures for Marie."[2] This entry was later supplemented by Clara Schumann's remark that "the pieces children usually study in piano lessons are so poor that it occurred to Robert to compose and publish a volume (a kind of album) consisting entirely of children's pieces. Already he has written a number of attractive miniatures."[3] On the day of Clara's entry, 1 September 1848, the eldest Schumann child, Marie, celebrated her seventh birthday. Among

Marie's gifts was a handwritten notebook of music bearing the title "*Stückchen für's Clavier* / Zu Marie'chens 7tem Geburtstag / den 1sten September 1848 / gemacht vom Papa" (see source *a* in the appendix).

Though 31 August 1848 is considered the "birthday" of the *Album für die Jugend*, the idea of a piece of music for and about children actually had been with the composer of the equally well known *Kinderszenen*, Op. 15, at least since 1841, when Marie was born. In that year, Schumann gave his wife and child a *Wiegenlied* (Cradle song) as a Christmas present, though of course the piece was not published until 1854, as the "Schlummerlied" ("Lullaby," Op. 124, no. 16).[4] The composer took great interest in Marie's first piano lesson with Clara and already in 1846 planned "a volume of 'children's melodies' for piano solo for Marie."[5] Finally, he contributed a piece to the piano lessons in 1847[6] and wrote out the child's first melodies and "compositions" with obvious pleasure and fatherly pride.[7] The creative roots of the *Album für die Jugend*, which Schumann began composing with almost childlike enthusiasm in the fall of 1848, thus extend back to 1841.[8]

Entries in the *Haushaltbuch*[9] and the dates on the individual pieces demonstrate that an additional series of piano compositions was written in close succession after Marie's birthday:

2 [September 1848]	Much composed for the children's album [including "Erinnerung," which is dated in *b*]
3	Many children's miniatures [*Kinderstückchen*]
4	Many children's miniatures [including "Fremder Mann," which is dated in *b*]
5	Many children's miniatures [including "Sylvesterlied" (no. 43), which is dated in *b* with the heading "Zum Schluß"]
8	"Mignon" [no. 35]
9	The album mostly finished
10	New miniatures
11	New children's miniatures [including "Schnitterliedchen," which is dated in *c*]
12	New miniatures
[13	"Rundgesang" (no. 22), dated in *b*]
17	The album for children
19	Four more children's miniatures
21	"Weinleselied" [no. 33]
22	"Winterszeit" [nos. 38 and 39]
24	Early: played the miniatures for

The piano piece originally entitled "Allererstes Clavierstückchen" and then renamed "Für ganz Kleine" ("For the very young"), though not included in Op. 68, was the first-composed piece represented in the extant sources for the *Album für die Jugend*. Schumann wrote it out in the *Erinnerungsbüchelchen* (source *k*) in note values half of those in the sketchbook and provided this annotation:

Five-year-old Marie now knows twenty-two piano exercises; on 8 June [1847], Papa's thirty-seventh birthday, she even played one of Papa's own pieces that went like this:[10]

If Marie's birthday album is considered the first compositional phase of the *Album für die Jugend* (30–31 August 1848), the second phase can be documented in a list of titles now held in the Boston University Library (source *d* in the appendix). According to the *Haushaltbuch*, this phase began on 2 September, and—if we take an entry in the *Tagebuch* ("the album mostly finished") to indicate a creative caesura—extended to 9 September.[11]

Source *d*, a single folio with writing on both sides, transmits on its verso nineteen *Musikalische Haus- und Lebensregeln*; Schumann later published thirteen of these in revised form. The folio also provides an ordered list of thirty-four pieces for the *Jugendalbum* (see figure 1 and the appendix):[12]

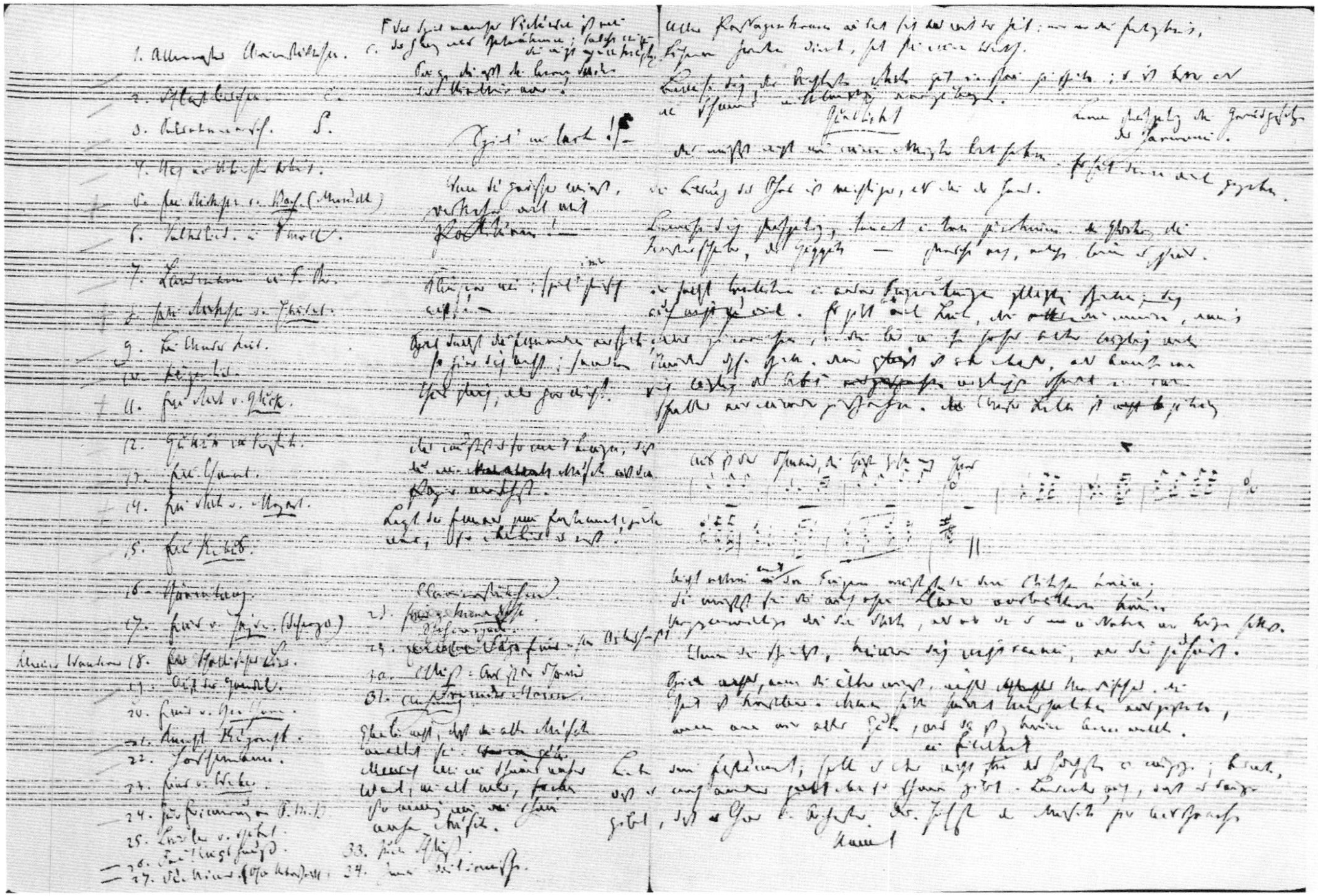

Figure 1. Sketch leaf for Schumann's *Album für die Jugend*, with drafts for the *Musikalische Haus- und Lebensregeln* (Paul C. Richards Special Collections, Boston University Libraries)

−   1. Allererstes Clavierstückchen [Very first piano miniature]. C. [No. 1]

−   2. Schlafliedchen [Little lullaby]. C. [No. 3]

−   3. Soldatenmarsch [Soldiers' march]. G. [No. 2]

−   4. Nach vollbrachter Arbeit [After work is finished; cf. *a*, p. 4].

+   5. Ein Stückchen v. *Bach.* (Menuett.) [Cf. *a*, pp. 9–10]

−   6. Volkslied. In D-moll. [No. 9]

−   7. Landmann. In F-dur. [No. 10]

+   8. Ein Stückchen v. *Händel.* [Cf. *a*, p. 11]

−   9. Bittendes Kind [Pleading child]. [No. 6?[13]]

− 10. Jägerlied [Hunter's song]. [No. 7]

+ 11. Ein Stück von *Gluck.*[14]

− 12. Gukuk im Versteck [Cuckoo in hiding]. [Sources *b*, p. 2; and *e*, p. 88]

− 13. Ein Choral. [No. 4]

+ 14. Ein Stück v. *Mozart.* [Source *a*, pp. 5, 12]

− 15. Ein *Rebus.* [Source *a*, p. 15]

− 16. Bärentanz [Bears' dance; source *a*, p. 6]

+ 17. Eines v. *Haydn.* (Scherzo)[15]

    18. <Ein schottisches Lied.> [Inserted before: Kleiner Wanderer]

− 19. Auf der Gondel [On the gondola; sources *a*, p. 11; and *e*, p. 36]

    20. Eins v. *Beethoven.* [Source *e*, p. 13]

− 21. Knecht Ruprecht [Bogeyman]. [No. 12]

− 22. Haschemann [Tag-man; sources *b*, p. 11; and *f*]

    23. Eins v. *Weber.* [Source *e*, p. 20]

− 24. Zur Erinnerung an F.M.B. [In remembrance of F(elix) M(endelssohn) B(artholdy); no. 28]

    25. Ländler v. Schubert. [Source *a*, p. 14]

− 26. Frühlingsgruß [Spring greeting; no. 15]

− 27. Duettino (ohne Überschrift) [Duettino (no heading); no. 30?]

    28. <Eins v. *Mendelssohn*>. [Inserted above: Clavierstückchen; = no. 21?]

    29. Eine kleine Fuge [no. 40]; F-dur ohne Überschrift [F major without heading; no. 26. Inserted above: "Sheherazade" (no. 32)]

    30. Schluß: Aus ist der Schmaus [Conclusion: the banquet is over; source *d*, recto]

31. Fremder Mann [The stranger; no. 29]
    [No number or title for no. 32]
33. Zum Schluß [In conclusion; no. 43]
34. Zwei Sicilianische [Two sicilianos; no. 11]

The inserted arrangements of works by other composers, proceeding chronologically from Bach, Handel, Gluck, Haydn, Mozart, Beethoven, and Weber to Schumann's contemporary Mendelssohn,[16] present a kind of representative tour through the historical progression of great composers.[17] No. 30 takes its title from a German saying.[18] The music for this piece was written on the same page, but Schumann omitted it from the published edition. We give as example 1 this naive canonic miniature, which, despite its high tessitura, might also have been conceived for voice.

Example 1. "Aus ist der Schmaus, die Gäste gehn nach Haus."

In the interest of completeness we also reproduce the *Musikalische Haus- und Lebensregeln* sketched in the second and third columns of source *d*—particularly because the manuscript, though barely legible, transmits variant readings for certain rules, documenting in exemplary fashion Schumann's "gradual completion of [his] ideas during writing."[19]

SECOND COLUMN:

"The playing of some virtuosos is like the walk of a drunkard; do not take these as your models." [Rule 4]

"Sing the notes of the open strings of the violin to yourself frequently! Play in tempo!" [Rule 4]

"When you grow older, spend much time with scores!" [Rule 33]

"Never 'strum': [inserted: always] start out *freshly*!" [Rule 7]

"<Playing>[:] If you are supposed to play for someone, do not play affectedly; do it straightforwardly, or not at all!"

"You have to get to the point where you understand what's on the paper as a 'page of notes' for *music*." [Rule 13]

"If someone gives you something to play at sight, look it over before starting!" [Rule 13]

"Do not believe that old music grows old[.] [Deleted: Just as a good person] Just as a good, true word never grows old, just so does good, true music."

THIRD COLUMN:

"All meaningless passagework changes [something deleted] with time; only when technical accomplishment serves a higher purpose is it valuable." [Rule 20]

"Make an effort to play the easiest pieces well and freely; this is better than a mediocre playing of a difficult one." [Rule 9]

"Study the basic rules of harmony early." [Rule 5]

"You do not have to revere only one master. There have been many of them."

"Developing the ear is more important than developing the hands."

"Make an effort early on to recognize notes and keys: bells, window-panes,[20] cuckoos—figure out what notes they are." [Rule 1]

"You should play scales and other finger exercises diligently; [deleted: but also not too often.] There are [inserted above the line: however] many people who [something deleted] believe that one should play such things many hours every day into advanced age in order to accomplish everything. But this [deleted: is the same] is just as if one tried to say the ABCs as quickly as possible every day, and ever more quickly. [Something deleted] Life is [deleted: not long] too short." [Rule 2]

"You must know your piece not only [originally: in; corrected to: with] your fingers; you must also be able to hum it without the piano."

"Make the pieces a part of your mind, as if you had the music for it [*recte*: them] [something deleted] before you." [Rule 11]

"When you are playing, do not worry about who is listening." [Rule 14]

"When you are older, play [deleted: nothing] nothing [deleted: bad] trendy. Time is valuable. One would need a hundred human lives if one were just to learn all the good things that are out there." [Rule 18]

"Love your instrument, but do not [inserted: vainly] consider it the one and only thing; remember that there are other, equally beautiful things. Remember, too, that singers exist so that the noblest in music will be pronounced in the chorus and orchestra." [Rule 32]

The third and final phase of the *Album*'s genesis began on 10 September—just one day after the end of the second phase—with the entry "New miniatures," and extended until 27 September. Schumann's entry in his *Kompositionsverzeichnis* suggests such a caesura, though there it is delayed somewhat, until 14 September.[21] This phase is documented by source *i*, a manuscript auctioned in London in 1991 and now housed in the Pierpont Morgan Library in New York, which establishes a sequence for the pieces very similar to that of the published edition. In this list the sequence of titles largely corresponds to that of the *Stichvorlage* (source *e* in the appendix). In the first column Schumann recorded numbers for the pieces; and in the right-hand column he indicated their planned distribution over the pages of the published edition (see figure 2).

[deleted: Choral]

1. 2. Melodie. Soldatenmarsch		1.
3. Trällerliedchen [Humming song].		2.
4. Choral. In F-dur.[22]		3.
5. Stückchen.		4.
6. Waise [Orphan].		5.
7. Jägerlied.		6.
8. [deleted: Schaukelpferd]		7.
Wilder Reiter [Wild rider]		
9. Volkslied.		8.
10. Landmann. Sicilianisch.[23]		9.
11. Knecht Ruprecht.		10.
		11.
12. Mai.		12.
		13.
13. Studie.		14.
		15.
14. Frühlingsgesang.		16.
		17.
15. Unglück [Misfortune].		18.
16. Morgenwanderer [Morning wanderer].		19.
17. Schnitterliedchen [Reaper's tune].		20.

Figure 2. List of titles for the *Album für die Jugend* (Pierpont Morgan Library, New York)

18. Romanze.   21.
19. Ländliches Lied [Rustic song].   22.
20. *⁑* in C-dur.[24]   23.
21. Rundgesang [Round].   24.
                                                    [deleted: 25]

[SECOND COLUMN]   [THIRD COLUMN]

22. Reiterstück. [Crossed out   26. 27.
    and then restored]
23. Erndteliedchen [Harvest song].   28[.] 29[.]
24. Theater.   u[nd] 30.
25. *⁑* in F.   31. [Deleted:
                                         Gesellschaftslied in A-dur]
26. Canon.   32. 33.
27. Erinnerung.   34.
28. [deleted: Fremder Mann]   35. 37. Fremder Mann.
29. [deleted: Sheherazade]   38. 39. Lied in F-dur.
30. [deleted: Kriegslied]   40. 41. (*⁑* in F-dur)
                                         Kriegslied [War song].
31. [deleted: Fuge]   42. 45. Sheherazade
32. Weinlesezeit [Grape-   46[.] 47.
    gathering time].
33. Thema.   48.
34. Mignon.   49.
35. Marinari.   50. 51.
36. 37. Matrosen.   52. 53.
38. 39. Winter.   54. [Originally 55;
                                         changed to 57]
40. F-dur.[25]   58. 59.
41. Beschluß [Conclusion].   60.

An additional summary on this page reveals that Schumann planned to release the pieces not only as a single album but also as four separate volumes (with the pagination running from 1 to 60); the contents were to be divided according to the seasons of the year:

Volume 1. [Pp.] 1–19. Spring.
Volume 2. [Pp.] 20–31. Summer.
Volume 3. [Pp.] 32–48. Fall.
Volume 4. [Pp.] 49–60. Winter.

Diagonal strokes in the list of titles—for example, between nos. 16, 25, and 34—delineated the intended divisions among the volumes.

Schumann's other notes in source *i* for the titles, which alternately precede or stand alongside the above list, demonstrate the gradual emergence of the final arrangement:

[BOTTOM OF SECOND COLUMN:]

Winter.
[Deleted: Thema. (Gruß an G)] ? Nordisches ? Lied.
Fuge. [Deleted: Nordisches Lied]
Figurierter Choral [Figured chorale].
[Deleted: Nordisches Lied]
[Deleted: Fuge.]
Zum Beschluß.

[BOTTOM OF THIRD COLUMN:]

Nordisches Lied.
(Gruß an G.)
Im Volkston.
(Gruß an G.)
Figurierter Choral.
(zur Neujahrzeit zu spielen[)]
Frühling. Schaukelpferd. Maiblümchen. Jägergemüth.[?] Soldaten.
Sommer. Schnitter. Erndte. Theater.
Herbst.
Winter.
[deleted: Fuge]
Nordisches Lied.
Fuge. [deleted: Fugirter (*sic*) Choral]
Nordisches Lied   Zum Beschluß.

Finally, there is the *Stichvorlage* (source *e*). Held today in the Robert-Schumann-Haus, Zwickau (archive no. 10955), this manuscript was prepared by Robert and Clara for the first edition of the *Album*. Its contents are summarized in column II of table 1, on pp. 193–96.

II

Schumann initially attempted to have the *Album* published by Breit-kopf and Härtel as a Christmas album entitled *Weihnachtsalbum für Kinder, die gern Clavier spielen* ("Christmas Album, for children who like to play the piano"), but this undertaking failed. With the assistance of Carl Reinecke, however, he successfully offered the work to the Hamburg publisher Julius Schuberth, though he was required to change the title from *Weihnachtsalbum* to *Jugendalbum*. His honorarium of 226 Thaler, 16 Groschen, was received in two installments in October and December 1848;[26] the unanticipated success of the volume later prompted the publisher to offer an additional payment.

On 4 October 1848 Schumann wrote to Carl Reinecke, "I wouldn't know if I have been in better musical spirits than when I wrote these pieces; they truly streamed down upon me."[27] Two days later he reported,

> I wrote the first pieces for the *Album* specifically for the birthday of our oldest child, and then more pieces came to me one after another; it was as if I were once again starting to compose from the very beginning. You will also detect something of my earlier humor [in them]. These pieces are completely different from the *Kinderszenen*. The latter are reminiscences written by an adult for adults, whereas the "Christmas album" contains more anticipation, presentiment, [and] forward-looking perspectives for youthful players.[28]

No other work of Schumann is so deeply and recognizably rooted in his biography as the *Album für die Jugend*. The composer's confession to Reinecke that these pieces "in particular had a special place in my heart and were taken directly from my family life"[29] refers not only to the occasion for the works' composition—Marie's seventh birthday—but also to certain programmatic elements in some of the pieces.[30] This was also confirmed by Clara Schumann to her children, whose piano lessons featured the *Album für die Jugend*:

> Your father translated everything he saw, read, and experienced into music. If he was lying on the sofa reading poems after dinner, they immediately became Lieder in his mind. If he saw you playing games, the games became little musical compositions. One day, while he was working on the *Humoreske*, some tightrope-dancers came down the street where we lived, and the music they played crept into that work. But the composer was completely *unconscious* of this; no one can ever suggest that it was intentional. Papa invented the titles to pieces only after they were completed. To be sure, they are very appropriate and may well aid in understanding the pieces—but they are not indispensable.[31]

Familial connections are indeed immediately evident in certain pieces. The "Trällerliedchen" bears the heading "Schlafliedchen für

Ludwig" ("Lullaby for Ludwig") in Marie's birthday album (source *a*) and thus was dedicated to the youngest member of the Schumann family in the fall of 1848.

Referring to 21 September 1847, Schumann recorded in the *Erinnerungsbüchelchen*: "Yesterday (Monday) was the big day when she (Marie), lap-desk under her arm, first wandered into the school for reading and writing."[32] This event, important in every child's life, was captured musically in the short march "Kleiner Morgenwanderer" (no. 17), in which the steps of the "little morning wanderer," happy with anticipation, first appear "fresh and sprightly" (*frisch und kräftig*) and then become "softer" (*schwächer*; m. 20) and disappear into the distance. Similarly, the early school experiences of Schumann's eldest daughter are recorded in no. 5 ("Stückchen"), which in Marie's birthday album is headed "to be played after schoolwork is finished."

During the winter of 1846–47 Marie and Elise were allowed to accompany their parents on a concert tour to Vienna. On their return trip the six-year-old Marie "visited the theater for the first time in Brünn, and did the same in Prague."[33] Thus, Marie would have associated quite specific memories with the title of no. 25, "Nachklänge aus dem Theater" ("Echoes from the theater")—which probably relates the expressive indication *etwas agitirt* (rather agitated) to the child's mood after her first theater experience.

As is well known, on 4 November 1847, the date given beneath no. 28 ("Erinnerung"), Mendelssohn died. This short musical homage, which so beautifully adapts the compositional inflections of Mendelssohn's *Lieder ohne Worte*, reflects the special relationships between Mendelssohn and Robert, Clara, and Marie. Schumann's remark of 28 January 1848 in the *Erinnerungsbüchelchen* reads like a commentary on the piano piece: "The world has suffered a great, irrecoverable loss at this time—one that you, too, little Marie, will appreciate someday years from now. Felix Mendelssohn died on 4 November. He was Marie's godfather, and you own a lovely silver goblet from him, bearing his name. Treasure it!"[34] And Schumann's *Erinnerungen an F. Mendelssohn vom Jahre 1835 bis zu s. Tode*,[35] written while Schumann was still grappling with the news of Mendelssohn's sudden death, represent, with their identical titles, a verbal counterpart to the composition.

That the *Album für die Jugend* was conceived in Dresden had definite consequences for the internal and external form of the entire work. The *Album* was intended as a "musical domestic album" that would ally music, illustrations, and texts in a penetrating document unified from various perspectives. The *Musikalische Haus- und Lebensregeln* first appeared in the *Album für die Jugend* as an appendix to the second edition (1850), after they had appeared as the supplement to no. 36 of the *Neue Zeitschrift für Musik* in May 1850.[36] That Schumann periodically planned to incorporate Lieder into the *Album* as well cannot be ruled out[37]—an undertaking that obviously was abandoned and realized separately as a vocal counterpart, the *Lieder-Album für die Jugend*, Op. 79 (1849). "At first," Schumann wrote to Carl Reinecke on 6 October 1848, "I intended to have a drawing in the margin (illustration) for *every* miniature—but . . . there was too little time for that before Christmas."[38] The plan to commission illustrations is clarified by Schumann's notes in source *b* for the title. The formulation he proposed to the publisher, "Zu Weihnachten / *für Kinder, / die gern Clavier spielen,*"[39] originally ran: "Musikalisches Weihnachtsalbum / [deleted: für kleine Kinder] / [für] clavierspielende kleine Kinder / im Alter v. 8–10 Jahren / mit Randzeichnungen / von Bendemann, Hübner, R. Reinick. / u. Richter" ("Musical Christmas album [deleted: for young children] for piano-playing young children, ages 8–10, with marginal illustrations by Bendemann, Hübner, R. Reinick, and Richter").

There was no lack of published models for such a conception. Schumann had set ten poems from his friend Robert Reinick's 1838 illustrated collection of poems, *Lieder eines Malers mit Randzeichnungen seiner Freunde.*[40] And the 1845 *ABC-Buch für kleine und große Kinder, gezeichnet von Dresdner Künstlern, mit Erzählungen und Liedern von R. Reinick und Singweisen von Ferdinand Hiller*, also edited by Reinick, was in a sense created before Schumann's very eyes. The composer was a friend of not only Reinick but also the composer Ferdinand Hiller (to whom Schumann dedicated his A-minor Piano Concerto, Op. 54) and some of the *ABC-Buch*'s illustrators—namely, Ludwig Richter, Eduard Bendemann, Julius Hübner, and Ernst Rietschel,[41] all of whom were active at the Dresden Academy. Reinick's *ABC-Buch*, which appeared three years before the *Album für die Jugend*, was probably the immediate model for the *Album*. It is hardly coincidental that for the final letter, *Z*, both Reinick's poem and Hübner's illustration cite the saying that Schumann intended to include in his *Album* as the "Aus ist der Schmaus, die Gäste geh'n nach Haus" canon.

Julius Hübner (1806–82) was the godfather of Ludwig Schumann, who was born in Dresden on 20 January 1848. Eduard Bendemann (1811–89) and his wife, Lida (1821–95), enjoyed an especially warm friendship with the Schumanns. The Bendemanns were the godparents of Emil Schumann, born on 8 February 1846. And in 1849, Lida Bendemann received the dedication of Schumann's *Bilder aus Osten*, Op. 66.

With the Dresden artists' circle, whose membership occasionally included Richard Wagner, Schumann partook in a lively exchange of ideas.[42] Thus, in a letter to Mendelssohn dated 18 December 1845 Schumann reported, "Now we all meet once a week every week— Bendemann, Rietschel, Hübner, Wagner, Hiller, and Reinick. So there are all kinds of things to relate or read to the others, and it really becomes quite stimulating."[43] The painters Bendemann, Hübner, and Gustav Metz were among the first to hear the *Album für die Jugend*, which Clara Schumann played for them from the *Stichvorlage* on 24 September 1848.[44] And incidentally, in July 1849 Hübner composed a poem as a poetic postscript to Schumann's homage to Mendelssohn, "Erinnerung."[45]

Although Schumann was forced to abandon his original plan for marginal illustrations (for reasons of time and money), he was still able to secure the services of the then well-known album illustrator Ludwig Richter for the title page of the *Album für die Jugend*.[46] In return for this favor, Schumann gave twenty-four hours of composition lessons to Ludwig Richter's son Heinrich between 16 November 1848 and 21 August 1849. According to Heinrich,

> [Ludwig] Richter grew closer to Robert Schumann. One day the
> . . . composer visited him [25 October 1848[47]] and asked him to
> prepare the title page to the piano miniatures in his *Album für die
> Jugend*. As Schumann wished, Richter returned so that the composer's wife could play for him the pieces Schumann wanted illustrated by vignettes. During the performance, the composer sat beside her with lowered head and half-closed eyes, whispering the title and some explanatory comments to her before she began each new piece.[48]

Christian Hahn prepared the lithograph for the publication after Richter's draft. In all, there were ten vignettes after the individual pieces in the *Album*. Beginning in the upper left-hand corner and moving downward, we find the following correspondences between the illustrations and the music (see figure 3):

> No. 15. "Frühlingsgesang"
> No. 22. "Rundgesang"
> No. 10. "Fröhlicher Landmann"
> No. 16. "Erster Verlust" ["First sorrow"]

Schumann's title for no. 16, possibly an allusion to Goethe's poem made familiar through Franz Schubert's setting (D. 226), obscures the definite biographical association of this short piano lament. Of

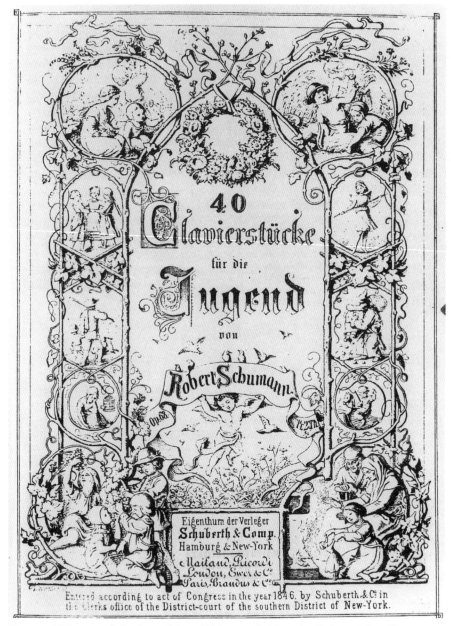

Figure 3. Title page of the first edition of Schumann's *Album für die Jugend*, Op. 68, containing Ludwig Richter's vignettes. Robert-Schumann-Forschungsstelle, Düsseldorf

course, what Schumann had in mind was not the general lover's plaint, as in Goethe and Schubert, but a specific children's sorrow (*Kinderunglück*; hence the original title in *b*) as represented in Richter's vignette. The illustration depicts a crying girl mourning for a little bird lying dead before an open cage. Eugenie, Schumann's youngest daughter, reported that her father once fed marrow-balls to the children's greenfinch. Though the bird enjoyed the treat, on 15 January 1848[49] it paid for it with its life.[50]

The following vignettes concern nos. 33 ("Weinlesezeit"), 24 ("Ernteliedchen"), and 35 ("Mignon"). In source *b* the draft for no. 35 was originally headed "Seiltänzermädchen" ("Tightrope girl"), but in the same draft this was changed to "Mignon (auf dem Seile tanzend)" ("Mignon, dancing on the rope"), thus clearly identifying the programmatic background, which is also depicted in the vignette. Richter's illustration and Schumann's piano piece draw upon Goethe's novel *Wilhelm Meisters Lehrjahre* (Berlin, 1795)—specifically, upon that crucial scene in which the title's hero first notices the curious child Mignon, who, along with a troupe of artists, performs acrobatic tricks:

> Wilhelm could not restrain his deep compassion when he saw the child, with whom he had felt an affinity from the first glance, performing the peculiar contortions with some difficulty. But soon the merry vaulters aroused a lively pleasure, first each alone, then one after the other, and then all together jumping over one another backward and forward into the air. Loud hand clapping and cheers rang out from the entire gathering. But now the attention was turned to a completely different object. One after another, the children had to walk the tightrope; first of all, the apprentices, in order to practice their performance and make obvious the difficulty of their art.[51]

The following vignettes illustrate "Knecht Ruprecht" (no. 12), "Wilder Reiter" (no. 8), and the paired movements "Winterzeit I" and "Winterzeit II" (nos. 38 and 39), which especially appealed to Ludwig Richter:

> Richter considered the composition entitled "Winterszeit" the most poetically pregnant of these tone poems [*Tongedichte*]; they clung to his imagination and resonated long and quietly. Schumann's explanation for the piece was something like this: "The forest and the ground are completely buried in snow all around; thick snow covers the city streets. Dusk. With soft flakes, it begins

to snow. Inside, in the cozy room, the grownups sit next to the brightly lit fireplace and observe the merry round-dances of the children and dolls."[52]

Schumann portrays the grownups pictured in Richter's illustration for no. 39 ("Winterszeit II") through quotations from the "Großvater-Tanz" ("Grandfather dance").[53] The "humor" he referred to in his letter of 6 October 1848 (see p. 182) is here expressed in exemplary fashion. In mm. 51–58 we find an allusion to the duple-meter *Nachtanz* of the "Großvater-Tanz," but not until mm. 59–62 does the triple-meter beginning (*Vortanz*) of the Lied begin to appear, and then only in an inner voice. The parts of the Lied are thus stood on their heads, and the Lied, widely known at the time, is ironically broken up: a mere allusion is transformed into a definite quotation (examples 2a and 2b).

Example 2. "Winterszeit II" and "Großvater-Tanz" (*Nachtanz* and *Vortanz*) from the *Album für die Jugend*, Op. 68

III

From the biographical sources and musical autographs we may divide the genesis of the *Album für die Jugend* into three phases that ultimately led to the published editions:

First, Schumann planned a volume of exercises for Marie's piano lessons. He did not grant it the status of a self-standing opus but wrote out the miniatures as if they were occasional pieces. There were as yet no plans for publication, and the miniatures were supplemented by arrangements of other composers' works, adapted for pedagogical purposes. Furthermore, the volume was left open for later additions and expansions.

In the second phase, Schumann's concept left the purely private realm and entered the public one. He now planned an anthology of thirty-four works by himself and other composers. The collection still had little pretension to standing as an opus, since Schumann's arrangements of works by Bach, Handel, Haydn, Mozart, Beethoven, Weber, and Mendelssohn were not original contributions but served merely as a pedagogical tour through musical history.

Third, the didactic ideas that accompanied the composition of the *Jugendalbum* were articulated on a more general level in Schumann's *Musikalische Haus- und Lebensregeln*. But with this verbal dimension (and the simple vocal canons, which obviously overlapped with the more poetic content of the collection), the original pedagogical idea collapsed. The collection of aphorisms and their associations with pictorial scenes (in any case already suggested in the poetic titles) led Schumann to the idea of an album in which music, pictures, and text could be joined together. For such an album we can trace not only the immediate conceptual models but also the would-be illustrators— well-experienced artists in Schumann's Dresden circle of acquaintances and friends.

But an album requires a convincing organization of its contents into parts. Schumann decided upon a division according to the seasons, as suggested by the titles of individual pieces. For this organization, the arrangements of works not by Schumann, which had been part of the *Album* from the beginning, had to be removed, for they were now extrinsic. Only the two chorale arrangements, which would be understood as a kind of nonindividual, collective, devotional music, were excepted. In addition, the new concept of the work necessitated that the private allusions in certain titles be replaced by more general headings: for example, the "Schlafliedchen für Ludwig" became the "Trällerliedchen."

On the one hand, Schumann's original designation "Christmas album," with its prosaic market appeal (something to be bought and given as a gift) and emotionally strong association with the "children's festival," underscored the particular character of the work: a poetic album that, unlike the usual piano instruction manuals, merited a place on the gift table. But on the other hand, the title limited the potential market of the work; for how would a Christmas album sell throughout the year? The Hamburg publisher Schuberth had good enough reason to request a change of title.

For financial reasons, and perhaps also because of the limited time Schumann allowed himself for editing his work, the idea of an album that would comprise the various arts was not realized and is only barely recognizable in the published edition. The division according to the seasons was replaced by a didactic division into two parts: eighteen pieces for "younger students" and twenty-five pieces for "more advanced" ones. In most recent editions, the layout of the two original editions is obscured almost beyond recognition, since neither the title page nor the *Musikalische Haus- und Lebensregeln* are typically included.

In two senses, then, Schumann's *Album für die Jugend* was "taken directly from his family life": it was conceived for a family occasion and developed for private use; but ultimately it grew out of family life and into the public sphere.

Appendix:
Sources of the *Album für die Jugend*

Source *a*. Birthday album for Marie Schumann (Beethoven-Haus, Bonn; H. C. Bodmer Collection, shelfmark ZMh 6). The volume of piano pieces for Marie Schumann that resurfaced in 1957 and today is housed in the Beethoven-Haus, Bonn, can be dated 30/31 August 1848 on the basis of Schumann's *Projektenbuch*.[54] Only six of its fourteen pieces (or fifteen; Schumann copied a piece by Mozart twice) were later used in the *Album für die Jugend*, some of them with different titles. Schumann's arrangements of other composers' works were omitted in the printed collection, as were two miniatures, "Bärentanz" and "Rebus" (see the inventory in column IV of table 1, on pp. 195–96).

"Rebus" is also transmitted in a second source (*j*), a manuscript contributed to the album of Schumann's friend Constanze Jacobi from Dresden.[55] Since 1991 this album has been in the possession of the Heinrich-Heine-Institut, Düsseldorf. The page for "Rebus" carries the dedication "Fräulein Constanze Jacobi / zur Erinnerung. / Robert Schumann" and is dated "Dresden, den 8ten Januar 1849"; thus, it was written out just after the publication of the *Album für die Jugend* in December 1848. In this piece, Schumann conveys in music a kind of puzzle popular during the Biedermeier period, the so-called *Dingrätsel* [literally, "thing-puzzle"]:[56] the letter *L*, written at the beginning, and the note names of the pitches of the melody, which is to be understood as a *soggetto cavato*,[57] produce the combination L–a–es [= E♭] d–a–es f–a–d–e f–a–es d–as [= A♭] a–e–c–h–d–e, which transliterates as "Laß das Fade, faß' das Aechde [= Echte]" ("Leave the trifling alone; seize the genuine").

Source *b*. Sketchbook (private collection in South Germany). The fair-copy pieces transmitted in the *Geburtstagsalbum für Marie* were preceded by drafts on 30 and 31 August 1848. These are found among numerous other sketches (some unfinished) in a sketchbook that, now in private possession, was reproduced in 1924 in a facsimile edition (see the inventory in column III of table 1, on pp. 193–96).

Source *c*. Travel sketchbook (Universitätsbibliothek, Bonn; shelfmark Schumann 23). Lacking in source *b* are sketches for nos. 7 ("Jäger-liedchen"), 12 ("Knecht Ruprecht"), 18 ("Schnitterliedchen"), 30 (∗∗∗; C, F major), 33 ("Weinlesezeit"), and 42 ("Figurierter Choral"). The so-called travel sketchbook (*Reiseskizzenbuch*), held since 1991 in the Bonn Universitätsbibliothek, fills half of these lacunae. It includes, along with nos. 18, 30, and 33, a sketch for no. 34 ("Thema") that is developed further than the draft in source *b* (see column III of table 1, on p. 195).

Schumann obviously used the travel sketchbook as a pocket note-book in which to jot down spontaneous ideas in pencil. Today barely legible in some places because of the faded pencil strokes, the note-book's twenty-two pages include fragments as well as drafts for *Bilder aus Osten*, Op. 66; *Genoveva*, Op. 81; and the *Spanische Liebes-Lieder*, Op. 138. A sketch on p. 19 for "Schnitterliedchen" (bearing the final title) is dated at the end "11 Sept. [18]48"; it records mm. 12–18 writ-ten on a single staff. The sketch on p. 22 for no. 30, which is identified by three asterisks in the published edition, bears no title. Unlike the F-major final version, this sketch, whose twenty measures differ sharply in their melodic contours from the final version, is in C major. Also untitled is the six-measure sketch for no. 33 ("Weinlesezeit— fröhliche Zeit"). This sketch corresponds to mm. 52–57 of the final version but provides the harmonies for only one cadence. On p. 11, mm. 1–8 appear, followed by five empty measures numbered 1–5 and then mm. 14–25, which are written out. On p. 10 are some ideas for mm. 26–43 that bear little resemblance to the final version: the sketch describes only the general contours, from which one can scarcely recognize the final shape of the piece. On p. 20 there is an untitled ten-measure sketch for no. 34 ("Thema") that breaks off in the third staff. Some of the pencil notes are written over in ink, and there are numerous cancellations.

Source *d*. Sketch leaf (Boston University Library, Special Collections): sketches for "Knecht Ruprecht," nineteen *Musikalische Haus- und Lebensregeln*, and an ordered list of thirty-four pieces for the *Jugend-album*. Source *d* formerly belonged to a sketchbook in South Germany (*b*), since on one side it transmits a draft for "Knecht Ruprecht," one of the pieces missing from sketchbook *b* and the travel sketchbook (*c*). If one considers sources *b*, *c*, and *d*, sketches are lacking for only the "Jägerliedchen" (no. 7, transmitted in fair copy in *a*) and the "Figurierter Choral" (no. 42, transmitted in the *Stichvorlage*). Source *d* is in oblong format, irregularly trimmed to 21.7–22.3 × 31.4–31.8 cm., and bearing no watermark; both sides contain fourteen staves that extend to the edge of the page. The leaf is written in brown ink and, occasionally, pencil and thus is consistent with the South German sketchbook. (I thank Margaret Goostray in the Special Collections Department of the Boston University Library for this information.) Unfortunately, Lothar Windsperger's commentary in the facsimile edition (Mainz, 1924) gives no information concerning the dimensions of the paper, the paper type, or the structure of the volume; so the original position of the Boston sketch leaf cannot be determined. The binding edge of the pages reproduced in facsimile, which measure approximately 22.0 × 31.5 cm., is probably slightly cut off in the reproduction (see, for example, p. 20). For another facsimile of the recto side of the Boston sketch leaf, see Walter Dahms, *Schumann* (Berlin and Leipzig, 1916), appendix, pp. 56–57.

Source *e*. *Stichvorlage* (Robert-Schumann-Haus, Zwickau; archive no. 10955): used in the preparation of the first edition. For unexplained reasons, nos. 20 ("Ländliches Lied," source *g*) and 24 ("Ernteliedchen," source *h*) were cut out of the original manuscript and later replaced with copies made by Schumann's grandson Ferdinand. In 1956 Georg Eismann released a facsimile of this manuscript,[58] which is in oblong format, with writing on forty-five pages.

Source *f*. Fair-copy manuscript of "Haschemann."[59] One folio, probably originally part of *a* (private collection in the United States).

Source *g*. Fair-copy manuscript of no. 20, "Ländliches Lied." One folio removed from *e* before 1870 (transmitted only in facsimile).

Source *h*. Fair-copy manuscript of no. 24, "Ernteliedchen." One single folio removed from *e*; now lost.

Source *i*. List of titles, formerly part of *e* (Pierpont Morgan Library, New York, Robert Owen Lehman Collection).

Source *j*. Album leaf with complete "Rebus" (Heinrich-Heine-Institut, Düsseldorf; album of Constanze Jacobi, accession no. 91.5001 TG).

Source *k*. "Allererstes Clavierstückchen," written in the *Erinnerungsbüchelchen für unsere Kinder* in 1847 (Robert-Schumann-Haus, Zwickau; archive no. 5978-A3).

Table 1
Musical Sketches for the Album für die Jugend

I. First Edition[a]	II. Stichvorlage[b]	III. Sketches[c]	IV. Album für Marie[d]
1. Melodie	<Für ganz Kleine> [p. 1] <Desgleichen> Melodie [p. 1]	<Allererstes Clavierstückchen> Für ganz Kleine [b, p. 11][e] —[b, p. 6]	
2. Soldatenmarsch	<Puppenschlafliedchen> [p. 2] Soldatenmarsch [p. 2]	Puppenschlafliedchen [b, p. 12][f] —[b, p. 1]	Nr. 2. Soldatenmarsch [pp. 2–3][g] Nr. 1. Schlafliedchen für Ludwig [p. 2][i]
3. Trällerliedchen	Trällerliedchen [p. 3][h]	—[b, p. 1]	Nr. 3. Ein Choral [p. 3–4][j] Nr. 4. Nach vollbrachter Schularbeit zu spielen [p. 4]
4. Ein Choral	Ein Choral [p. 5][h]	—[b, p. 34]	Nr. 7. Liedchen eines armen Kindes [pp. 6–7]
5. Stückchen	Stückchen [p. 7][h]	—[b, p. 1]	
6. Armes Waisenkind	Armes Waisenkind [p. 9][h] [Soldatenmarsch, deleted variant, p. 10][h]	Armes Bettlerkind [b, p. 34]	
7. Jägerliedchen	Jägerliedchen [p. 11]		Nr. 8. Jägerliedchen [pp. 7–8]
8. Wilder Reiter	<Schaukelpferdreiter> Wilder Reiter [p. 13]	Wilder Reiter [b, p. 22]	
9. Volksliedchen	Volksliedchen [p. 15]	Volkslied [b, p. 2; Volksliedchen p. 33]	
10. Fröhlicher Landmann, von der Arbeit zurückkehrend	Fröhlicher Landmann, von der Arbeit zurückkehrend [p. 17]	Fröhlicher Landmann, von der Arbeit zurückkehrend [b, p. 33]	

(continued)

Table 1 (*Continued*)

I. First Edition[a]	II. Stichvorlage[b]	III. Sketches[c]	IV. Album für Marie[d]
11. Sicilianisch	Sicilianisch [p. 19] <Ein Trinklied von C. M. v. Weber> [p. 20][l]	Zwei Sicilianische [b, pp. 16, 32][k]	
12. Knecht Ruprecht	Knecht Ruprecht [pp. 21–22]	Knecht Ruprecht [d, verso]	
13. Mai, lieber Mai,— Bald bist du wieder da!	Mai, <schöner> lieber Mai,—Bald bist du [inserted = wieder] da! [pp. 23–24]	Mai, schöner Mai, Bald bist du da! [b, pp. 4–5]	
14. Kleine Studie	Kleine Studie [p. 25]	—[b, p. 14]	
15. Frühlingsgesang	Frühlingsgesang [p. 27]	Frühlingsgesang [b, p. 28]	
16. Erster Verlust	<Erster Verlust> <Unglück> Erster Verlust [p. 29] <Andante, 3/4, E-dur> [p. 30][m]	Kinderunglück [b, p. 10]	
17. Kleiner Morgenwanderer	Kleiner Morgenwanderer [p. 31]	Kleiner Morgenwanderer [b, p. 4]	
18. Schnitterliedchen	Schnitterliedchen [pp. 33–34][n]	Schnitterliedchen [c, p. 19][o]	
19. Kleine Romanze	Kleine Romanze [p. 35] <Auf der Gondel> [p. 36]	—[b, p. 30] Auf der Gondel [b, p. 11][p]	
20. Ländliches Lied	Ländliches Lied [p. 37][q]	—[b, pp. 19, 21]	
21. **	** [C, C major] [pp. 39–40]	—[b, p. 24]	
22. Rundgesang	Rundgesang [p. 41]	Rundgesang [b, p. 32][r]	
23. Reiterstück	Reiterstück [pp. 43–45]	—[b, p. 27]	
24. Erndteliedchen	Erndteliedchen [p. 47][s]	Erndteliedchen [b, p. 30]	
25. Nachklänge aus dem Theater	Nachklänge aus dem Theater [p. 49]	Nachklänge a. d. Theater [b, p. 28]	
26. **	** [C, F major] [pp. 51–52]	—[b, p. 26]	
27. Canonisches Liedchen	Canonisches Liedchen [pp. 53–54]	Canon [b, pp. 9, 20]	
28. Erinnerung (4 November 1847)	<Zur Erinnerung an Felix Mendelssohn Bartholdy /	Erinnerung an F. Mendelssohn Bartholdy [b, p. 23][t]	

gestorben 4ten November 1847 im 38sten Jahr> Erinnerung / (4. November 1847) [p. 55]

29. Fremder Mann	Fremder Mann [pp. 57–59]	Fremder Mann [b, p. 17]^u	
30. **	** [C, F major] [pp. 61–62]^h	[c, p. 22]	
31. Kriegslied	Kriegslied [pp. 63–64]	[b, p. 9]	
32. Sheherazade	Sheherazade [pp. 65–66]	Sheherazade [b, p. 24]	
33. "Weinlesezeit—Fröhliche Zeit!"	"Weinlesezeit—Fröhliche Zeit!" [pp. 67–68]	—[c, pp. 8, 10–11]	Nr. 5. Ein Stückchen von Mozart [p. 5]^x
34. Thema	Thema [p. 69]	—[b, pp. 30, 32] and [c, pp. 20–21]	Nr. 6. Bärentanz [p. 6]^y
35. Mignon	Mignon <(auf dem Seile tanzend)> [pp. 71–72]	<Seiltänzermädchen> Mignon [b, p. 8]	
36. Lied italienischer Marinari	<Schifferlied> Lied italienischer Marinari [pp. 73–74]	<Italienisches Fischerlied> Schifferlied [b, p. 31]	
37. Matrosenlied	Matrosenlied <(Antwort auf das vorige)> [pp. 75–76]	Matrosenlied [b, p. 31]	
38. Winterszeit I	Winterszeit I [p. 77]	[b, p. 15]	
39. Winterszeit II	<Winterszeit> II [pp. 78–80]	Zur Winterszeit [b, p. 15]	
40. Kleine Fuge	Kleine Fuge [pp. 81–83]	Vorspiel [b, p. 18; Fuge, p. 29]	
41. Nordisches Lied (Gruß an G)	<Thema> Nordisches Lied (Gruß an G) [p. 85] [6/4, Es-dur] [p. 86]^v	—[b, p. 32]	
42. Figurierter Choral	Figurierter Choral [pp. 87–88] <Gukkuk im Versteck> [p. 88]	Guguk im Versteck [b, p. 2] Zum Schluß [b, p. 13]^w	
43. Sylvesterlied	Zum Beschluß [p. 89]	[b, p. 34]	

(continued)

Table 1 (*Continued*)

I. First Edition[a]	II. *Stichvorlage*[b]	III. Sketches[c]	IV. *Album für Marie*[d]
			[Nr. 9.] Ein Stückchen von J. S. Bach [pp. 9–10][z]
			[Nr. 10.] Ein Thema von G. F. Händel [p. 11][aa]
			[Nr. 11.] Ein Stückchen von Mozart [p. 12][bb]
			[Nr. 12.] Eine berühmte Melodie von L. van Beethoven [p. 13][cc]
			[Nr. 13.] Ein Ländler von Franz Schubert [p. 14][dd]
			[Nr. 15.] Rebus [p. 15][ee]
		Canon. Fest im Tact, im Tone rein [*b*, p. 2]	
		[Canon, 2/4, A major; *b*, pp. 5, 22]	
		Haschemann [*b*, p. 11][ff]	
		[Fragment, 2/4, C major, *b*, p. 12][gg]	
		Linke Hand, soll sich auch zeigen [*b*, p. 12][hh]	
		[C, A major, *b*, p. 21][ii]	
		[3/4, G major, *b*, p. 25][jj]	
		Lagune in Venedig [*b*, p. 27][kk]	
		Kleiner Canon [Fragment, *b*, p. 33]	
		[Fragment, 6/4, C minor(?); *b*, p. 34]	
		Aus ist der Schmaus, die Gäste gehn nach Haus [<*d*>, recto]	

a40 [recte: 43] Clavierstücke / für die / Jugend / von Robert Schumann. / Op. 68. / Schuberth & Comp. / Hamburg & New-York / Mailand, Ricordi / London, Ewer & Co. / Paris, Brandus & Co. [plate no. 1232] [December 1848].

bSource e: Robert-Schumann-Haus (archive no. 10955). References according to Georg Eismann, Jugend-Album Op. 68: Faksimile nach der im Besitz des Robert-Schumann-Museums Zwickau befindlichen Urschrift (Leipzig, 1956).

cSketches are transmitted in several manuscripts. Source references employ the sigla given here on pp. 190–92. A facsimile of source b is available in Robert Schumann: Skizzenbuch zu dem Album für die Jugend, Op. 68, ed. Lothar Windsperger and Martin Kreisig (Mainz, 1924).

dSource a (see p. 190). For a detailed description, see Dagmar Weise, "Ein bisher verschollenes Manuskript zu Schumanns 'Album für die Jugend,'" in Festschrift Joseph Schmidt-Görg zum 60. Geburtstag, ed. Dagmar Weise (Bonn, 1957), pp. 383–89.

eAlso transmitted in 2/4, with note values half those of the published edition, in the Erinnerungsbüchelchen für unsere Kinder (source k). First published in Eugenie Schumann, Erinnerungen (Stuttgart, 1925), p. 324. Six-year-old Marie played the piece for her father's thirty-seventh birthday on 8 June 1847.

fFirst published in Jack Werner, A New "Album for the Young": Nine Unpublished Pieces from Opus 68 (London, 1957). p. 4.

gResembles the Scherzo from Beethoven's Violin Sonata in F major, Op. 24. Unlike the published version, in 4/4, the "Soldatenmarsch" is here transmitted in 2/4.

hFair copy by Clara Schumann.

iBorn on 20 January 1848, Ludwig was the youngest family member when Op. 68 was composed.

jThe chorale "Freu dich sehr, O meine Seele," used in Lutheran Germany since around 1620, was adapted from the Calvinist hymn "Ainsi qu'on ouit le cerf bruire" (Psalm 42). See Werner Braun, "Romantische Klavierchoräle," in Geistliche Musik: Studien zu ihrer Geschichte und Funktion im 18. und 19. Jahrhundert, Hamburger Jahrbuch für Musikwissenschaft no. 8, ed. Constantin Floros, Hans Joachim Marx, and P. Petersen (Laaber, 1985), pp. 125–27.

kThe second "Sicilianisch" became the central part of a single piece in the published edition.

lCaspar's drinking song "Hier, im ird'schen Jammertal" (no. 4), from Der Freischütz. First published in Jörg Demus, Pezzi inediti dall' Album per la Gioventù," op. 68 (Milan, 1973), p. 4.

mIn Clara Schumann's hand, this is the theme from the third movement of Beethoven's Piano Sonata in E major, Op. 109.

nFinal measures in Clara Schumann's hand.

oDated at the end: "11. Sept. 48."

pFirst published in Werner, A New "Album," p. 8.

qIn the hand of Schumann's grandson Ferdinand. Removed from the Stichvorlage, the page was reportedly in the possession of C.F.L. Gürckhaus when it was reproduced in facsimile in the Leipzig Musikalisches Wochenblatt (1870): 649. For a reproduction of the facsimile, see Oswald Jonas, "Zu Schumanns Op. 68," Neue Zeitschrift für Musik 124 (1963): 225–26. The original page (source g) is lost.

rDated at the end: "d. 13ten Sept. 48."

sIn the hand of Schumann's grandson Ferdinand. The original page (source h) was removed from the manuscript and is lost.

tDated at the end: "d. 2 Sept. 1848."

uDated at the end: "d. 4ten Sept. 48."

vFirst published under the title "Fragment" in Demus, Pezzi inediti, p. 10.

wDated at the end: "d. 5ten Sept. 48."

(continued)

Table 1 (Continued)

ˣPiano arrangement of Zerlina's aria "Vedrai, carino" (no. 19), from *Don Giovanni*. Written out twice in *a*—here in Robert's hand, the second time in Clara's (see n. bb). First published in Demus, *Pezzi inediti*, pp. 20–21.

ʸReproduced in facsimile in Weise, "Ein bisher verschollenes Manuskript," Tafel xix after p. 392. First published in Demus, *Pezzi inediti*, p. 18. The title and several parts of the piece were later used in the "Bärentanz" (no. 2) of the *12 vierhändige Klavierstücke für kleine und große Kinder*, Op. 85 (1849).

ᶻFrom the Partita no. 5 in G major, BWV 829.

ᵃᵃThe theme of the so-called "Grobschmied Variations" in the fifth suite from part 1 of the *Suites de pièces pour le clavecin* (1720). In the hand of Clara Schumann, who included the Handel variations in her concert repertoire.

ᵇᵇIdentical to no. 5 (see n. x) but in Clara Schumann's hand.

ᶜᶜ"Freude schöner Götterfunke," from the finale of the Ninth Symphony, Op. 125. First published in Demus, *Pezzi inediti*, p. 19.

ᵈᵈNo. 14 of the German Dances, D. 783.

ᵉᵉFor a facsimile, see Weise, "Ein bisher verschollenes Manuskript," Tafel xix after p. 392. First published in Demus, *Pezzi inediti*, p. 18. "Rebus" is also transmitted as Schumann's *Albumblatt* dated Dresden, 8 January 1849, in the *Album der Constanze Jacobi* in the Heinrich-Heine-Institut, Düsseldorf (accession no. 91.5001 TG). The *Albumblatt* was reproduced in facsimile in the appendix to Wilhelm Joseph von Wasielewski, *Robert Schumann: Eine Biographie* (Dresden, 1858).

ᶠᶠFirst published in Windsperger, *Skizzenbuch*, p. xi. The piece shares only its title with Op. 15, no. 3. It is also transmitted in fair copy on a single folio (source *f*), now in a private collection, and may have belonged to Marie's birthday album (source *a*) or to the *Stichvorlage*. For a facsimile and discussion of source *f*, see Georg Kinsky, "Robert Schumanns 'Haschemann' Nr. 2," *Schweizerische Musikzeitung* 77 (1937): 410–12.

ᵍᵍThis unpublished fragment bears a faint resemblance to the *Puppenwiegenlied*, the third movement of the first *Clavier-Sonate für die Jugend*, Op. 118.

ʰʰFirst published in Werner, *A New "Album,"* p. 4.

ⁱⁱFirst published under the title "Preludio" in Demus, *Pezzi inediti*, pp. 16–17.

ʲʲFirst published under the title "A Little Waltz in Canonic Style" in Werner, *A New "Album,"* p. 10.

ᵏᵏFirst published in Windsperger, *Skizzenbuch*, p. x.

NOTES

1. Because of space constraints, the *Album für die Jugend*'s publication history (documented in the largely unpublished correspondence between Schumann and the Hamburg firm of Schuberth and the Leipzig office of Paez) will be discussed elsewhere.

2. Robert Schumann, *Tagebücher, Band III: Haushaltbücher, Teil II: 1847–1856*, ed. Gerd Nauhaus (Leipzig, 1988), p. 469.

3. Berthold Litzmann, *Clara Schumann: Ein Künstlerleben, nach Tagebüchern und Briefen*, vol. 2: *Ehejahre 1840–1856*, 7th ed. (Leipzig, 1925), p. 182.

4. In December 1841 Clara noted in the marriage diary, to which she and Robert contributed: "He gave me and my little Marie an attractive cradle song that he composed in the afternoon on Christmas day." *Tagebücher, Band II: 1836–1854*, ed. Gerd Nauhaus (Leipzig, 1988), p. 198.

5. Ibid., p. 399.

6. "Für ganz Kleine bzw. Allererstes Clavierstückchen" (source *k*); see p. 192, and col. III of table 1, on p. 193.

7. Transmitted in Schumann's *Notizbuch aus der Dresdner Zeit* (Heinrich-Heine-Institut, Düsseldorf, accession no. 51.4903).

8. Schumann's pleasure with the piece is documented, among other places, by the autograph entry in the *Erinnerungsbüchelchen für unsere Kinder*, first published in Eugenie Schumann, *Erinnerungen* (Stuttgart, 1925), p. 327: "For Marie's birthday Papa had given an entire volume of children's pieces with which he himself was most pleased." See also Schumann's letter to Carl Reinecke of 4 October 1848, cited here on p. 182.

9. *Tagebücher, Band III*, pp. 469–71.

10. Eugenie Schumann, *Erinnerungen*, p. 324. The variant readings in sketchbook *b* were first published in Jörg Demus, *Pezzi inediti dall' "Album per la gioventù," op. 68* (Milan, 1973), p. 1.

11. See n. 9. [Trans.]

12. Square-bracketed numbers refer to the ordering of the published edition or manuscript sources (identified by their respective sigla). Editorial additions appear in square brackets as well, and text passages that were crossed out but are still legible are given in angle brackets. The meaning of Schumann's slashes and the + and - signs that appear before the numbers cannot be conclusively determined. Schumann typically uses the + sign to indicate "finished" (*erledigt*).

13. This title, identical to that of Op. 15, no. 4, could be a variant of Op. 68, no. 6, which appears in *a* as the "Liedchen eines armen Kindes," in *b* as "Armes Bettlerkind" ("Poor beggar-child"), and in *e* and the published edition as "Armes Waisenkind" ("Poor orphan").

14. Source *b* (p. 23) gives only the indication "Gluck ( ) Iphigenie." Which part of *Iphigenie* had been copied was never clarified.

15. Source *b* (p. 23) transmits only the indication "Haydn (Thema) in F. (Symphonie)."

16. Source *b* (p. 23) reveals that at one point Schumann planned to use "Spohr (Jessonda)" for this position.

17. On Schumann's interests in the historical progression, see also pp. 95ff. [Trans.]

18. In the *Deutsches Sprichwörter-Lexikon*, ed. Karl Friedrich Wilhelm Wander (Leipzig, 1867), vol. 5, col. 1709, no. 11, the saying is defined as the "Beendigung einer Angelegenheit" (end of an occasion). I thank Heinz Rölleke for kindly providing this information.

19. Editorial additions and cross references are given in square brackets. Repeated references to the same numbers indicate that several sentences were condensed into a single rule in the published edition (Leipzig, 1850) [Appel]. For an English translation of the *Musikalische Haus- und Lebensregeln*, see Robert Schumann, *On Music and Musicians*, ed. Konrad Wolff, trans. Paul Rosenfeld (New York, 1946), pp. 30–38. [Trans.]

20. Matthias Wendt graciously pointed out that this rule was inspired by Mendelssohn. In his posthumously published notes for *Erinnerungen an Felix Mendelssohn Bartholdy*, ed. Georg Eismann (Zwickau, 1948), p. 47, Schumann wrote: "His criterion for developing the finest musical ear—that 'as a child one must learn to guess the pitch of the windowpane'—seemed to me valid for everyone."

21. See n. 54.

22. In the published edition, in G major. The "Figurierter Choral" (no. 42) is in F major.

23. In the published edition "Sicilianisch" was assigned its own number (no. 11).

24. Asked by her daughter Eugenie about the meaning of the asterisks, Clara Schumann could provide only a Sybil-like answer: "Perhaps your father wanted the stars to indicate parents' thoughts about their children." Eugenie Schumann, *Robert Schumann: Ein Lebensbild meines Vaters* (Leipzig, 1931), p. 11. See also Eugenie Schumann, *Erinnerungen*, p. 166.

25. The "Nordisches Lied" (no. 41).

26. *Tagebücher, Band III*, p. 674.

27. *Robert Schumanns Briefe: Neue Folge*, 2d ed., ed. F. Gustav Jansen (Leipzig, 1904), p. 290; see also *Robert Schumann's Leben aus seinen Briefen geschildert*, ed. Hermann Erler (Berlin, 1887), vol. 2, p. 60.

28. Erler, *Robert Schumann's Leben*, vol. 2, p. 61.

29. Ibid.

30. See Irmgard Knechtges-Obrecht, " . . . Auf daß das Aeußere einigermaßen dem innern Charakter entspreche: Robert Schumann und die Ausstattung seiner Notendrucke," in *Schumann und die Düsseldorfer Malerschule* (exhibition catalog, 1–19 June 1988, David-Hansemann-Haus, Düsseldorf), ed. Bernhard R. Appel and I. Knechtges-Obrecht (Düsseldorf, 1988), pp. 51–61.

31. Eugenie Schumann, *Erinnerungen*, pp. 165–66. Of course, the oft-repeated assertion that the titles were retroactively formulated is contradicted

by Schumann's title inventory at the very beginning of sketchbook *b*: "Soldier. Hunter. Shepherd. Smith. [Deleted: Dance.] Bears' Dance. Postillion. Children's Song. Shepherd Boy. Rider. Knight. Vesper Bells."

32. Eugenie Schumann, *Erinnerungen*, p. 325.

33. *Erinnerungsbüchelchen*, in ibid., p. 322. See also the diary entries for 21 January 1847 ("In the evening, to the theater for the first time with Marie"), 30 January 1847 ("In the evening *Don Giovanni*"), and 31 January 1847 ("*Zizka's Eiche* by Mazourek [opera, bad music]") in *Tagebücher, Band II*, pp. 412, 413.

34. Eugenie Schumann, *Erinnerungen*, p. 326.

35. Reproduced in facsimile and transcribed by Georg Eismann (Zwickau, 1947).

36. *Neue Zeitschrift für Musik* 32 (1850), supplement for issue of 3 May.

37. The two canonic pieces "Fest im Tact," published in *Robert Schumann: Album für die Jugend, Op. 68*, ed. Klaus Rönnau (Vienna, 1979), p. xv, and "Aus ist der Schmaus," as well as the remark "Quodlibet" (in *d*, recto), seem to corroborate this suggestion.

38. Erler, *Robert Schumann's Leben*, vol. 2, p. 62.

39. The same formulation is found in the *Kompositionsverzeichnis* in the *Projektenbuch*, p. 53.

40. Op. 33, no. 6 ("Frühlingsglocken"); Op. 34, no. 1 ("Liebesgarten"); Op. 36 ("Sonntags am Rhein," "Ständchen," "Nichts schöneres," "An den Sonnenschein," "Dichters Genesung," and "Liebesbotschaft"); Op. 43, no. 3 ("Schön Blümelein"); and Op. 91, no. 5 ("Der Bleicherin Nachtlied"). The lyricist, storyteller, and painter Robert Reinick (1805–52) was also employed by Schumann in various operatic projects; for example, at Schumann's request he drafted an outline for *Tristan und Isolde*. In 1847, he was supposed to write the libretto for *Genoveva*, but the collaboration failed because of Reinick's "fussiness" and differences regarding the setting of the subject.

41. Rietschel also made portraits of Robert and Clara.

42. See Bernhard R. Appel, "Robert Schumann und die Malerei," in *Schumann und die Düsseldorfer Malerschule*, pp. 9–12.

43. Jansen, *Robert Schumanns Briefe*, p. 255 (with the erroneous date of November).

44. *Tagebücher, Band III*, p. 471.

45. Published in *Briefe und Gedichte aus dem Album Robert und Clara Schumanns*, ed. Wolfgang Boetticher (Leipzig, 1979), p. 90.

46. The original sepia drawing is in the Robert-Schumann-Haus, Zwickau (archive no. 10 046-B2).

47. *Tagebücher, Band III*, p. 473: "Early morning with Prof. Richter."

48. Ludwig Richter, *Lebenserinnerungen eines deutschen Malers: Selbstbiographie nebst Tagebuchniederschriften und Briefen* (Leipzig, 1909), p. 399.

49. *Tagebücher, Band III*, p. 450.

50. Eugenie Schumann, *Robert Schumann: Ein Lebensbild*, p. 374.

51. Johann Wolfgang von Goethe, *Wilhelm Meisters Lehrjahre*, book 2, chap.

4, quoted from Goethe, *Sämtliche Werke*, ed. E. Beutler et al. (Zurich, 1977), vol. 7, p. 103.

52. Richter, *Lebenserinnerungen*, p. 399.

53. This piece, with a text by Langbein, was to be sung using an old dance melody. It was first printed in Becker's *Taschenbuch zum geselligen Vergnügen für 1813* (Leipzig, 1812), pp. 332–33. The "Großvater-Tanz" enjoyed great popularity and was often quoted by Schumann (for example, in *Papillons*, Op. 2, and *Carnaval*, Op. 9) probably ironically, because of the Biedermeier philistinism of its text. See Adolf Schubring, "Schumanniana Nr. 2: Schumann und der Großvater," *Neue Zeitschrift für Musik* 53 (1860): 29–30 [Appel]. Concerning the "Großvater-Tanz," see also pp. 84–91. [Trans.]

54. On p. 53 of a notebook of Robert Schumann that has been published only in excerpts (the original is in the Robert-Schumann-Haus, Zwickau, archive no. 4871/VII C, 8-A3): "From 30 August to 14 September: *Weihnachtsalbum für Kinder die gern Clavier spielen* (42 pieces).—Op. 68." Schumann entered the same dates on his personal copy of the printed edition (Robert-Schumann-Haus, Zwickau, archive no. 4501-A3/D1, Band 10).

55. See Bernhard R. Appel, "Musikbeiträge im Album der Constanze Erdmunde Jacobi," in *Heinrich-Heine-Institut: Das Stammbuch der Constanze Dawison geb. Jacobi*, Kulturstiftung der Länder-Patrimonia, no. 34 (Düsseldorf, 1991).

56. In 1953 the rebus was solved by the auction house that sold the manuscript. See J. A. Stargardt, *Catalogue No. 510* (Marburg, 17 November 1953), lot 150. Tafel III in the catalog contains a reduced facsimile of the "Bärentanz" and the "Lied eines armen Kindes."

57. *Soggetto cavato*: a musical phrase or subject derived from the pitch names present in a verbal text. (As originally employed by Renaissance composers, the musical text derived from the solmization syllables represented by the *vowels* of the verbal text.) [Trans.]

58. *Jugend-Album Op. 68. Faksimile nach der im Besitz des Robert-Schumann-Museums Zwickau befindlichen Urschrift* (Leipzig, 1956).

59. Not included in the published editions of the *Album für die Jugend*, "Haschemann" was later edited by Lothar Windsperger (Mainz, 1924) and reproduced, with five other pieces, in facsimile with notes by Georg Eismann (Leipzig, [1956]). [Trans.]

PART II

Letters and Memoirs

The Correspondence between Clara Wieck Schumann and Felix and Paul Mendelssohn

NANCY B. REICH

The previously unpublished correspondence between Clara Wieck Schumann and Felix and Paul Mendelssohn presented here provides a picture of musical life in Leipzig in the 1830s and 1840s and clarifies the position and interrelationships of three young musicians who lived and worked in that city during those years: Robert Schumann (1810–56), founder and editor of the *Neue Zeitschrift für Musik* and a relatively unknown composer; Clara Wieck (1819–96), Leipzig pianist and composer, who married Robert Schumann in 1840; and Felix Mendelssohn Bartholdy (1809–47), pianist, composer, and music director of the Leipzig Gewandhaus Orchestra.

Although the three were friends, their correspondence was, for the most part, concerned with music, programming, and performances. Felix Mendelssohn premiered a number of works by both Robert Schumann and Clara Wieck at the Gewandhaus and conducted twenty-one concerts at which Clara Wieck Schumann was the featured pianist.

After Felix Mendelssohn's sudden death at the age of thirty-eight, the friendship between the families continued. When Robert Schumann's attempted suicide and hospitalization in 1854 and subsequent death in 1856 shocked the musical world, Felix's younger brother Paul, who had gone into the family's banking business, helped Clara Schumann through the tragedy. Two of Paul's letters to her are included here. They show a rare understanding, sensitivity, and respect and were treasured by Clara Schumann and her family.

Thanks to John Michael Cooper, Gerda Lederer, and Herbert Weber for help with the transcriptions of these letters.

These twenty-two letters were selected from the collection of letters to Clara Schumann (*Briefe an Clara Schumann*) held in the Staatsbibliothek zu Berlin, Preussischer Kulturbesitz;[1] the letters to Felix Mendelssohn are from the so-called Green Books in the M. Deneke Mendelssohn Collection of the Bodleian Library, Oxford.[2]

When Felix Mendelssohn Bartholdy arrived in Leipzig in August 1835 to take over the leadership of the Gewandhaus orchestra, the twenty-six-year-old musician already had an established reputation as a conductor, performer, and composer. Born to wealth, Mendelssohn (and his siblings[3]) had been given all the advantages for which Schumann had to struggle: an excellent classical education from the best tutors, a thorough musical education from the leading musicians of Berlin, a "gentleman's tour" through Europe, and a cultivated home with family friends and visitors distinguished in the arts and sciences. Even his courtship and eventual marriage to Cécile Jeanrenaud went relatively smoothly, whereas Robert Schumann's marriage to Clara Wieck was vehemently opposed by her father and took place only after a bitter court battle. Schumann, one year younger, both admired and envied Mendelssohn. Although some ambivalence is evident in several anti-Jewish remarks in his letters and marriage diary, Schumann took pride in his musical and personal friendship with the Gewandhaus conductor and sang Mendelssohn's praises as a man and musician in his letters, diary entries, essays, and reviews, and through his music: the three String Quartets, Op. 41, were dedicated to Mendelssohn.

The relationship between Mendelssohn and Clara Wieck Schumann was simpler. Like Mendelssohn, Clara had been a child prodigy and had achieved fame and honors by the time she was eighteen. Felix Mendelssohn had high regard for her playing and respected her musical judgment. They played together publicly and privately, and the mutual admiration was genuine. His Op. 62, *Sechs Lieder ohne Worte*, was dedicated to her. She, in turn, considered him beyond compare as a performer, conductor, and composer. At least one Mendelssohn work appeared on almost every recital she gave throughout her sixty-year reign on the concert stage.

Mendelssohn may not always have been sympathetic to Robert Schumann's work as critic and even as composer, but he was a generous friend and as the conductor of a prestigious orchestra was able to help him in innumerable ways; these letters offer details of the first performances of Schumann's First and Second Symphonies, and the Leipzig premiere of the Piano Concerto.

Schumannians have often wondered why there is scarcely a mention of Robert Schumann in the published Mendelssohn correspondence and early biographies edited by Paul Mendelssohn and other family members after his death. This is not the place for speculation about their decisions, intriguing as they may be. It is known that during Mendelssohn's Leipzig years, the two men saw each other almost daily and thus had little need to correspond. But when Mendelssohn was in Berlin, and after the Schumanns settled in Dresden (1844), there was a lively and friendly exchange of letters between the Schumanns and Mendelssohn, as evidenced here.

The correspondence also sheds some light on the Schumann marriage, which has been described in many ways—from ideal to disastrous. It is clear that Clara's career played a leading role in their lives and opened doors for Robert. This untraditional nineteenth-century marriage was not without advantage to Robert, but it was also a potentially galling situation for him as Clara's husband. Almost every one of Robert Schumann's orchestral works was premiered at a concert for which his wife was the primary soloist. Fees from her concert tours helped pay the household expenses of a large family: eight children were born to Clara and Robert Schumann. Clara performed his works, established contacts with conductors, made piano arrangements of his symphonic and vocal scores, and took on the roles of wife, mother, secretary, and musical colleague as well.

These letters reveal many aspects of the character and personality of both Felix Mendelssohn and Clara Wieck Schumann. Clara is seen here as a professional musician, a decisive and energetic woman, devoted equally to her husband and to her career. And despite his success, fame, and wealth, Mendelssohn is remarkably modest and considerate. All three musicians worked incessantly; their output as composers and performers was prodigious.

The correspondence elucidates many details of concert life in Leipzig. The speed with which decisions about concerts were made, soloists engaged, and repertoire chosen, for example, is striking. Equally surprising is how quickly mail (and people) traveled. Fanny Hensel could write from Berlin on Tuesday with the certainty that her brother would receive her letter in Leipzig on Wednesday. Once the railroad from Leipzig to Dresden opened (in 1839), musicians could travel between these two centers in three to four hours, making it possible to give concerts in both cities within one week.

·

The first three letters here were written in the autumn of 1838. Clara Wieck had returned from her triumphant concert tour to Vienna

(October 1837 to May 1838) with the title of *Königliche-Kaiserliche Kam-
mervirtuosin* (Royal and Imperial Chamber Virtuoso) and was now
preparing for a brief concert trip to Dresden. She was back in Leipzig
by 1 December and played in the Gewandhaus on 6 December. She
was to leave home a few weeks later and begin her journey across
Europe to Paris. Robert Schumann, to whom she was secretly engaged, had left for Vienna in September. They did not see each other
again until August 1839.

GB VII, 101

Leipzig, 2 November 1838

Esteemed Herr Doctor,[4]

First of all, permit me to express my thanks for yesterday's delightful treat; it will be so difficult for me to leave and miss so many beautiful things here.

But now, I must get to the main reason I am writing. Yesterday I
heard that you are not playing in the Gewandhaus now for want of an
instrument; unless you wish to wait for your own, I am placing my
Graf[5] at your disposal with the greatest pleasure and expect just a
brief answer, so that in the event you are inclined to do me the honor
and give me the happiness of playing on it, I will leave the key here. I
would trust nobody with it, except you.

I would be very sorry if I could not be there when you play, but I
hope that when I return, you will not let me wait in vain to make up
for it.

Please convey my kind wishes to your wife.[6] I remain, with sincere
respect,

Yours most faithfully,
Clara Wieck

Leipzig, 3 November 1838

Highly esteemed Fräulein,

Many thanks for your kind note and all the kind words you wrote. I
would certainly not have neglected to tell you this personally, but I
simply could not get to do this today, and I am afraid you are leaving
early tomorrow.

If I had been prevented from playing until now for lack of an instrument, I would have accepted your friendly offer with great pleas-

ure; perhaps I may do this later. What has kept me from playing up to now are my continuing eye troubles and other pains, which become worse with any exertion. And that is why I must abstain from playing for the time being. However, whether my instrument is here or not, I would like to play on yours sometime in the course of the winter, if you will permit me to, mainly so that *I* would have the honor and pleasure of doing so. Will you promise me that?

I wish you all the best and much luck on your trip, as always. We look forward to your speedy return.

> Ever yours faithfully,
> Felix Mendelssohn Bartholdy

·

> Leipzig, 1 December 1838

Highly esteemed Fräulein,

I have learned from Herr Kistner[7] that you want to give us the pleasure of playing in one of the forthcoming subscription concerts. While I thank you most heartily in my name and for all the others as well, please let me know if you will play *once* or *twice*. (You know which we would like better, but it must absolutely be what you would rather do.) If possible, also let us know *what* you will play. As soon as I receive your answer, I will arrange the program, and therefore ask that you send me a few lines with the bearer.[8]

Will I have the pleasure of seeing you at my place early tomorrow morning and perhaps hearing you play as well? I know you have barely returned, and here you are being tortured again. Please forgive me,

> Your faithful,
> Felix Mendelssohn Bartholdy

·

The following letters concern professional as well as personal matters. Conductor and performer were preparing an "extra" Gewandhaus concert for the benefit of the orchestra's pension fund on 31 March 1841. Robert Schumann's First Symphony, the "Spring," had its first performance on this occasion. Clara Schumann was the featured piano soloist, and a song by her was also to be performed.

The concert on 31 March was Clara Schumann's first solo appearance in Leipzig since her marriage, and she was greeted with enormous enthusiasm. The premiere of her husband's symphony was almost obscured by her reception and all the other numbers on the

Letter of Felix Mendelssohn to Clara Wieck, dated 1 December 1838. Staatsbibliothek zu Berlin, Musikabteilung mit Mendelssohn-Archiv program. As these letters reveal, this flurry of arrangements took place just a few days before the concert.

About six months after this event, the Schumanns' first child was born, and Robert Schumann's letter of 25 September 1841 refers to the baptism. Mendelssohn was invited to be a godfather.

GB XIII, 145

26 [?] March 1841

Again, most honored Sir, I am coming to rob you of some precious minutes. I have three questions to which I beg the favor of a reply. Do you approve if we have your chorus, *Verleih' uns Frieden*,[9] sung at the beginning of my concert?[10] And are all the parts for it here? Second, Grenser[11] has proposed a rehearsal of the symphony for tomorrow morning at ten, and would you be satisfied with that? And now, may I put the Duo on the poster, and what shall I call it?

My husband would have written to you himself, but he is sitting in the midst of the orchestral parts,[12] which could give anyone (not to speak of a wife) grief and anxiety. He sends you a morning greeting; permit me to add my own to it.

Yours,
Schumanns

Leipzig, 26 March 1841

Esteemed Madame,

Many thanks for your kind note, which I will answer point by point. Complete parts are available for my *Verleih' uns Frieden*, and this, or any work you choose, will be perfectly fine with me. 2) I will be present at the rehearsal tomorrow at ten with much pleasure. 3) I am copying the Duo so beautifully that my head is aching; actually I would prefer it if we could play it through once before it appears on the poster, and until then you could just call the piece "Duet" without giving the name of the composer—since otherwise we would *have* to play it. But do whatever you want and feel is best. I simply cannot think of a proper title yet.[13]

Best regards to Schumann—has he used the red pencil yet?[14] That is always such great fun. I remain, as always, your sincerely devoted
Felix Mendelssohn Bartholdy

Concert program from the Leipzig Gewandhaus concert given on 31 March 1841 to benefit the musicians' pension fund. Robert-Schumann-Haus, Zwickau

Nancy B. Reich

Letter of Felix Mendelssohn to Clara Schumann, dated 26 March 1841. Staatsbibliothek zu Berlin, Musikabteilung mit Mendelssohn-Archiv

GB XIV, 99

Leipzig, 25 September 1841

Forgive me, dear Herr Doctor, for writing instead of my husband, but it will only be a few words—Robert will write you at length soon.

The baptism,[15] about which you wanted to hear, went very well. Herr Raymund Härtel was kind enough to take your place.[16] Incidentally, they were right to make me feel uneasy about that day, when so many things were happening at once. What is more, that day was also my birthday, which did not pass without many happy surprises.[17] We were very sorry that you couldn't be with us; it would have made our celebration even happier, and who knows if you might not have surprised me with a cradle song composed during the baptism?

I would really like to know if we hit upon your favorite name. Could it possibly be—Marie?[18] The little one was born on the 1st of September at eleven o'clock in the morning, in the midst of thunder and lightning. She is making us very happy; my husband even cried. She screamed very loudly.

Aren't you going to open our concert season? We are all hoping to welcome you very soon in our city again; and then, most honored Herr Godfather, you will not escape our grateful thanks.[19]

Please give your wife our kindest regards, and be assured of my greatest respect and sincerest esteem.
P.S. My husband charges me to send you his best regards,

[In Robert Schumann's hand:] After a long time, I have plunged into making music to such an extent that everything else has been forgotten.[20] Forgive me, dear Mendelssohn—the phrase with "Herr Godfather" that my wife wrote is quite nice. However, instead of "not" [escape] we should put "in no way." I agree with all the rest.

May we soon meet again,

Your faithful,
R. Sch.

GB XV, 3

Leipzig, 3 January 1842

Honored Herr Doctor,

I am turning to you today with a request and think it best that I come straight to the point.

Graf Baudissin[21] has been entreating me for several months now to get the Bach C-minor Concerto[22] that we played together last winter

Daguerreotype of Clara Schumann with Marie, circa 1845. Used with the kind permission of the Robert-Schumann-Haus, Zwickau

for him, and I promised him, since he did not have the courage to ask you for it himself, that I would put in a little word for him to you. Would you be favorably inclined to send me a copy of the concerto?

I believe I can assure you that Baudissin will make no use of it other than to play it with his wife. Please, dear Herr Doctor, write me a candid yes or no.[23]

Aren't we going to see you here again soon? And when? In the end, we will unfortunately not be able to attend any of the beautiful artistic treats that you always have ready for the Leipzig public. We are thinking of traveling to Hamburg in mid-February in response to an invitation. They want to perform my husband's symphony[24] in one of the Philharmonic concerts and rehearse it while he is there, and I am supposed to play in the same concert.[25]

I was very sorry that you were not here for the New Year's concert.[26] I believe you would have enjoyed hearing your G-minor Concerto. It went very well. I was very animated and would certainly have delighted in a friendly nod from you.

I hope you will write me a few lines very soon and let me know, at the same time, how your dear family is.

Please accept our most cordial greetings and also those from the little goddaughter who is growing in mind and body, a "Patschhändchen," as they say in Leipzig.

With the greatest respect,

Yours,
Clara Schumann

.

Leipzig, 30 January 1843

Honored Madame,

May I ask what you have decided about the next concert[27] and if you wish to and can grant the requests I made of you yesterday? You know how much all of us—but I *especially*—would like it if your name were on the program. You know how that gives the concert quite another spirit, but, on the other hand, we must not be presumptuous and take your kindness for granted. That is why I am simply asking; the rest is understood. Indeed, the more often you play, the better I like it, as a musician and as a program planner.[28] Do you have something of Schumann?—That would please me most. Or the Choral Fantasy[29] *and* something by Schumann.[30] Or if you don't want the latter—perhaps the Fantasy and something by Chopin. Or just whatever you think. I ask only for your answer and apologize for all the trouble I am causing. And please give my best regards to your dear husband.

Your always faithful godfather,
Felix Mendelssohn Bartholdy

.

Leipzig, 31 January 1843

Honored Madame,

My heartfelt thanks for today's letter and its contents. I just sent the program as it stands to the printer; but if it were possible for you to choose another song instead of the one by me, you would do me a favor. Don't misunderstand me! You know what a joy and honor it is for me every time you want to play something of mine; but in a concert in which the whole second part consists of my works, I would rather not have my name mentioned in the first part.[31] If it is all the same to you, and if you can think of another piece, I would be grateful for the renewed token of your kindness and make the changes in the program in the proofs. You will have to invite me for a visit to Inselstraße[32] to make up for what I will be missing in the Gewandhaus. In any event, you have my gratitude and everybody's thanks for all your kindness; and forgive me for this everlasting tiresomeness.

Yours most respectfully and faithfully,
Felix Mendelssohn Bartholdy

.

GB XVIII, 231

Leipzig, 9 December 1843

Honored Herr Doctor,

I have accepted happily my husband's charge to write to you about [your] coming to Leipzig next Monday when a repeat performance of the *Peri* is to take place.[33] My husband cherishes the hope that you will do it, since we have heard that you don't have a concert in Berlin next week.[34] It would be very nice of you if you could give my husband this great joy, which we had hoped to have the first time. The first performance went very well, and we are only hoping that the second will turn out as well. Unfortunately, Fräulein Sachse[35] has left Leipzig, so that another music student had to take her part, and we were anxious about it. Frau Dr. Frege[36] enchanted us and the whole audience with her delightful singing; you certainly would enjoy it enormously if you could come.

I have heard a great deal about how well you and your wife are and also many nice things about the magnificent concerts you have conducted. The Berliners are saying that they have *never* heard symphonies like that—and I can well believe it!

My husband is speaking seriously now about our trip,[37] for which I am very happy. However, I know well whom I have to thank for this. I feel ashamed when I think of the morning I came to you in such despair and think how childish I must have seemed to you, but I will never forget how kindly and patiently you listened to me and how you met all my wishes with such sympathy and consideration. Please accept once more my deepest thanks, which I was unable to express properly at the time.

My husband sends his most friendly regards and joins me in giving my regards most warmly to your wife.

Please accept my greetings, dear Herr Doctor, which I send with the most sincere respect,

Yours faithfully,
Clara Schumann

The final months of 1845 and the first months of 1846 were especially busy for both Clara and Robert Schumann. Despite the birth of Julie, their third child, in March 1845, and the birth of Emil in February 1846, Clara Schumann did not cease composing or performing. During the autumn months of 1845 Robert Schumann was suffering from many nervous complaints, and though he participated in planning the concert of 5 October,[38] he was unable to go to Leipzig for the performance. He did, however, continue to work on his Piano Concerto and the C-major Symphony. He was also an active member of the organizing committee for a Dresden orchestral subscription series. And it was in Dresden that the first performance of the Piano Concerto was given, conducted by Ferdinand Hiller (1811–85), pianist, composer, and a friend of Mendelssohn and Schumann. Clara Schumann was the soloist. The Piano Concerto was performed in Leipzig a few weeks later, with Mendelssohn conducting.

The following seven letters concern the planning and scheduling of the concerts of 5 October 1845 in Leipzig and 11 November and 4 December in Dresden; the New Year's Day concert of 1846 in Leipzig; and the two events in February 1846 at which Mendelssohn conducted the Gewandhaus Orchestra in Schumann's C-major Symphony. Mendelssohn's letter of 4 January 1846 to Clara, an invitation for an evening of playing chamber music at his home, is a charming postscript to the public performances of the previous months.

.

GB XXII, 124

Dresden, after 29 September 1845

Most honored Herr Doctor,

Once more today about the program! I beg you to put a second *Lied ohne Worte* instead of the Chopin Nocturne. Would you also please add: two *Lieder ohne Worte* (from book 6 of F.M.); and a fugue by R.S.[39]

My husband joins me in sending best regards.

Yours most faithfully,
Clara Schumann
Monday *in haste*

.

GB XXII, 226

Dresden, 18 November 1845

Highly esteemed Herr Doctor,

You know I always have something on my mind relating to you, and so I will come right out with my request. It concerns the Duo in A major[40] that we played together some time ago; won't you repeat it at my concert in Leipzig?[41] Won't you do me the honor of playing it with me again? And *when* will you be in Leipzig? We don't want to be there during your absence. My husband is already looking forward to chatting with you for a few hours, and I have all kinds of secret hopes, as, for example, to hear you play your new trio and the new concerto[42] and many other things besides. Please, let us know your plans a bit more precisely. For the time being, we have postponed the concerto[43] until the first week in December; hopefully there will be no obstacles then.

Now to my second request: I would also very much like to play your Duo at my concert I am giving here on 2 December, and to play it with Hiller.[44] Would you have the kindness to send it to me for this purpose? I need hardly assure you it will not leave my hands. You have already been so considerate of so many of my bold requests; please grant this one as well. And if you do not want to do this, just say— "no" frankly.

We assume you are not in Leipzig yet[45] and so have probably not yet received the last letter from Robert.* He sends you his kindest regards and is looking forward to seeing you soon again. His health is only fair, and he is not permitted to work too much.

You have probably already heard about the first subscription concert[46] here! The whole audience was very satisfied with it, and your *Meeresstille* aroused great enthusiasm. It was also, I understand, played very well, which was even more astonishing, since the orchestra was put together by musicians from many quarters. Unfortunately, I could not attend the concert, but Robert reveled in your wonderful works once again.

Please send my most cordial greetings to your wife, who is, I hope, in good health, and I am looking forward to seeing her again quite soon—and not just for a moment.

To you, dear Doctor Mendelssohn, once more an apology for my requests for which I thank you beforehand and hope you forgive me,

Most faithfully yours,
Clara Schumann

*My father gave it to Herr David.

.

Berlin, 24 November 1845

Dear Madame,

A thousand thanks for your friendly lines, which I must answer hastily here from Berlin between rehearsals and running about and every sort of worrisome business. The question of whether I would like to play something with you, however, does not have to be answered first, because you know that I am *always* ready to do that at any time, and am *always* thankful to you when you give me the pleasure of playing with me. If nothing better than the Duo in A major can be found, then that, naturally, still remains *at your service*. But the "when" is harder to answer; I had hoped to be in Leipzig again during the first week of December, but everything here is so uncertain that it might be another week to ten days. Because in no event do I want to be here on the 1st [of December], I have to stick it out this time until the performances that have begun are over. If I were to come in the middle of December, however, it would probably be too late for a concert (because of Christmas), and yet unfortunately I cannot, as I have said, give you any more definite word. If your concert remains set for the beginning of December, I must request that you do *not* put the Duo on the program because I am harboring the silent hope that in the event I am really able to get there, I would play it with you. However, if you do change the concert date to some time later this winter, then it is understood that I am at your disposal in any way you wish. As soon as I return, I will look for the Duo in A and send it to you in Dresden. I cannot do it from here, unfortunately, because I don't remember where it is, and what's more, I locked everything up when I left. Schumann's letter was probably also left behind in Leipzig; I did not receive it. Oh, please forgive these hasty and rushed lines and give your husband and children a thousand greetings from

Your most faithful,

Felix Mendelssohn Bartholdy

who just recently saw your mother in very good health.

.

GB XXII, 243

Dresden, 26 November 1845

Most honored Doctor,

No sooner do I receive your friendly letter than I hurry once more to bother you. However, it regards the fulfillment of a great wish of mine, and you must not be angry about it. Is it possible for you to let me have the Duo sooner? Can't your dear wife find it? I remember quite precisely that it was very easy to recognize. I am giving my concert here on 3 December[47] and was so looking forward to this Duo! Oh, dear Herr Doctor, please make it possible! I would have to have the music prepared by Monday, the 1st! Robert says, "He must do it!"

When all is said and done, there probably will be no concert in Leipzig this winter. We had thought of 15 December, but you won't be there! And after Christmas it just won't do![48]

I won't bother you for long, and just ask that you write me one word—yes or no—right away. I don't want a letter, just a yes—that would be nice of you!

My best regards to your dear wife and also from Robert, who sends his best to you. As for me, I beg you to forgive me, dear Doctor!

Your sincerely devoted,

Clara Schumann

.

GB XXII, 302

Dresden, 27 December 1845

Most honored Doctor,

These lines are just to inform you that we are thinking of coming to Leipzig on Monday and look forward to seeing you, but also to hearing you—you know all that already!

Is the rehearsal for the concert[49] on Wednesday? If you should hold it on Tuesday, however, I would like very much to rehearse the concerto then because there is never enough time in the dress rehearsal for a single piece. The concerto is rather difficult, so that we easily need over an hour for it. Please have the kindness to consider this in arranging the rehearsal! As far as the solos are concerned, they will remain as we had decided earlier![50]

My husband has been very diligent recently and delighted and surprised me at Christmas with the sketches for a new symphony;[51] he is all musician now, so that one can do nothing with him—but I like him best that way!

Verhulst[52] wants to go to Leipzig with us—he is very happy about the performance of his quartet.

I am looking forward to seeing your dear wife again! In the meantime, please send her my kindest regards. Robert charges me to send his best wishes to you, and I remain, with great respect,

Yours,
Clara Schumann

Leipzig, 4 January 1846

Dear Frau Doctor!

A few days ago, Schumann promised me that you would play his quartet[53] for me sometime. Since we are getting a trio together tonight, I have to let just two other musicians know, so that if you are not otherwise engaged the quartet could be played right away; or would you perhaps prefer the quintet?[54] Then Gade[55] will have to play viola—or shall I?[56] I would like it very much if you wanted to do one of the two pieces, because in addition to the enjoyment I would have from it, it would give my sister, who arrived here yesterday quite unexpectedly, the greatest pleasure. Otherwise you will find no other listeners!

I remain, as always, yours most faithfully,

Felix Mendelssohn Bartholdy

GB XXIII, 78

Dresden, 6 Feb. 1846[57]

Most honored Herr Doctor,

I am taking the liberty of writing you for my husband, who is not feeling well today. Your concertmaster, David, promised my husband to perform his Overture, Scherzo, and Finale in the musicians' concert[58] and at the same time gave him the hope that you would conduct it, which naturally doubled my husband's happiness. And he hopes that it was not a presumptuous request to have made, since you have already been so kind and have taken so many pains with the symphony.[59] In the event, however, that you are conducting the concert and also want to accept my husband's piece, he is sending you the score. Kistner has already got the quartet parts[60] so far along that they can be played.

We heard about the Liedertafel that you organized with great interest and would very much like to be there to hear it. You have provided music lovers with a great artistic pleasure with the performance of the Ninth Symphony.[61] I can well imagine that it was played magnificently.

I hope your dear wife is well; please convey my kindest regards to her.

Robert sends his best wishes to you, and I, dear Dr. Mendelssohn, beg to be forgiven for my terrible handwriting—but my speech is also rather horrible.

Please accept the assurance of my deep respect,

Most faithfully yours,
Clara Schumann

·

The final group of Clara Schumann–Felix Mendelssohn letters concerns concerts given in Dresden and Leipzig in October, November, and December 1846. Schumann's C-major Symphony, Op. 61, was premiered at the concert of 5 November 1846, but the program was long and the outcome was not altogether satisfactory. With some revisions, it was performed again, with greater success, at an *Extra concert* given on 16 November 1846 by the Gewandhaus Orchestra, conducted by Mendelssohn. This concert also included works by both Mendelssohn and his sister Fanny Hensel, and Clara Schumann's Scherzo, Op. 14. It was the last time that Clara Schumann and Mendelssohn worked together. Felix Mendelssohn died almost exactly one year later.

·

GB XXIV, 93

Dresden, 17 October 1846

Dear Herr Doctor,

I am happy to have the opportunity again to send our cordial greetings myself and let you know—according to Dr. Härtel's wish—the pieces I am thinking of playing on Thursday.[62] Again, it was hard to find a second piece, and if you were here, I would at least have asked you. Now, I can do nothing about it if you are not satisfied.—For my first piece, I want to play the Beethoven G-major Concerto, and for the second group—Nocturne by Chopin, a canon by my husband, and the Scherzo in B minor by Chopin. Unfortunately, there is so little that is new that one must always search through the old. Now, however, I have another request, this one about the instrument. Would you please ask Hofrath Seil whether he will lend me his piano? It is supposed to have a very easy action, which would be doubly dear to me right now since I don't have much strength.

I am arriving Tuesday evening and would really appreciate it if I could practice on the piano at that time, but only if Hofrath Seil gives instructions for me to have it when I arrive. In that case, let me know right away, so that if he says no, there will be enough time for me to get something I have played on before. I will most likely come alone, but as agreed upon, Robert will surprise me on Thursday.

Please give your dear wife my kind regards, and tell her I am looking forward to seeing her very much.

Robert sends most cordial greetings! He is working rather busily now. His health is quite tolerable.

I remain, dear Herr Doctor, with respectful regards,

Yours most faithfully,
Clara Schumann

GB XXIV, 114

Dresden, 31 October 1846

Dear Herr Doctor,

I am writing in my husband's name (he is still very occupied with the parts of the symphony),[63] to tell you that it takes a good half-hour, which you may like to know in arranging the program. Further, my husband does not need doubled horns but does need trombones. We are arriving Monday evening, and Robert will see you immediately. We are looking forward to coming to Leipzig again and I hope to be able to see your dear wife (to whom I would like to send my kind regards), longer than we were able to on our previous brief visit. Robert joins me in sending you both warm greetings.

Your very devoted,
Clara Schumann

GB XXIV, 117

Dresden, 1 November 1846

Dear Herr Doctor,

I am hurrying to request, for my husband, that you *not* arrange a rehearsal for early Tuesday. Since we were not able to bring the parts today, we decided to leave *early Tuesday*. Because of that my husband also asks that the extra rehearsal be set up for either Tuesday *afternoon* or Thursday. He is very sorry to give you so much trouble, but it is not his fault: they were not to be had.

We will stay either at the Blumenberg[64] or the Hôtel de Saxe. In the event that you have to communicate with my husband, please be so kind as to send it there, where we will be from eleven o'clock on. However, my husband will come to your place before noon.

Kindest regards, most esteemed Herr Doctor, from

Your most devoted,
Clara Schumann

On 27 February 1854, Robert Schumann attempted suicide by jumping into the Rhine. A few days later, he was hospitalized in Endenich (now part of Bonn), a short railway ride from Düsseldorf, and remained there until his death in July 1856. The news of his illness spread rapidly throughout the musical world, and Clara Schumann received letters from friends and musicians offering financial and other help. She was pregnant with their eighth child when the suicide attempt took place but began giving concerts again as soon as she could after the child was born. Leaving her children and the new baby (named Felix, after Mendelssohn) in the care of servants and a new young friend, Johannes Brahms, she began touring. She took great pride in the fact that she could earn the money to pay the medical bills and support the family herself and refused all offers of aid from others, except for the one here, from Paul Mendelssohn Bartholdy. She wrote in her diary that his letter was phrased so discreetly and tactfully, and the offer made so generously, that she agreed to accept his assistance. The last letter in this series was written by Paul Mendelssohn after Robert Schumann died.

Berlin, 16 March 1854

Esteemed Madame!

When my wife and I received the news of the indescribable misfortune that fate has inflicted upon you, our first thought and wish was to be able to be helpful and useful to you in some way; and if I express this wish through words at this time, I hope you will forgive me and not consider me intrusive. I hope you think of me as the representative of my departed brother,[65] who would certainly not have acted any differently. Permit me then to tell you that if you would offer me the opportunity—whether now or later—to be able to serve you in any way that would be of value to you, I would appreciate it with sincere thanks. I repeat that it is *I* who would have to thank *you*—not *you* who have to thank me—because to be helpful in *such* a situation is indeed the most urgent desire of any person who has even a spark of feeling!

It has occurred to me that peace and quiet will be a necessity for your physical and spiritual condition for a considerable time and that such an interruption of your professional activities may be detrimental to your household situation. In this case, just let me know with a word *what you would like*, and I am ready and willing to do whatever I can for you. And if my assumption is incorrect, I beg you again, if there is any opportunity for me to be useful in any other ways, treat me as you would have treated my brother, in whose spirit I turn to you!

About the misfortune itself, I will say nothing more. That I have ventured to write this letter to you may indicate to you how I feel about it. May God be with you in your difficult life's task.

With sincere respect
Your faithful,
Paul Mendelssohn Bartholdy

P.S. It occurs to me that the whole thing can be simpler and easier. I am taking the liberty of enclosing a letter of credit for 400 Thaler in case the occasion arises for you, now or later, when you can make use of it for one or another purpose. Portions of it can also be used at times when it is most convenient for you, and so you can just allow it to remain in your desk until it may be of good use. If you don't want this, just destroy it.[66] I am at your disposal in any way that can serve you.

P.M.

Berlin, 5 October 1856

Honored Madame!

I found your letter yesterday when I returned from a trip to Hamburg, and hastened to send you the enclosed documents and monies from the office. I am permitting myself a few words to follow the business letter.

We were in Carlsbad, where we had gone last summer, when we

learned with the deepest sorrow of the tragic conclusion of the tragic catastrophe. As with its commencement, so with its end; there is little that can be said.

There is much to do—to act—. The living must give proof of this. There is a designated path that you—and your friends in relation to you—must follow. *You* will know how to walk that path; the indomitable and faithful spirit you have already shown vouches for that. As for your friends, let me say for myself, at least, that you will always find me ready to walk the path of true helpfulness. That this is little comfort is certainly true; but perhaps it can offer some small peace of mind, and so I have expressed it, although I don't ordinarily like such words but prefer actions!

My wife greets you warmly, and we are happy to hear that you intend to visit us soon.

> Your sincerely faithful,
> Paul Mendelssohn Bartholdy

NOTES

1. Used with the kind permission of the Musikabteilung, Staatsbibliothek zu Berlin, Preussischer Kulturbesitz.

2. Used with the kind permission of the Bodleian Library, Oxford. The Green Book number is indicated on each letter.

3. Felix Mendelssohn was the second of four children. His siblings, Fanny, Paul, and Rebecka, had educational backgrounds similar to his. His older sister, Fanny, was equally gifted but was not afforded the opportunity to work as a professional musician. Paul, the youngest, went into the family's banking business. Although the two brothers used the name Mendelssohn Bartholdy, I shall refer to them here as Mendelssohn.

4. In 1836, Mendelssohn was granted an honorary doctorate by the University of Leipzig. Clara Schumann always addressed him by that title.

5. Conrad Graf (1783–1851) was a leading Viennese piano maker. Clara played a Graf (though she and her father spelled it Graff) at her first solo concert in November 1830. The Graf piano to which she is referring here was probably one she had received at Easter 1838 after she popularized the Graf pianos on her Viennese tour.

6. Felix Mendelssohn married Cécile Jeanrenaud on 28 March 1837.

7. Friedrich Kistner (1797–1844), a leading music publisher in Leipzig, was also a member of the Directorium of the Gewandhaus and one of the founders of the Leipzig Conservatory.

8. Clara Wieck played at the Gewandhaus subscription concert on 6 December. The program began with Weber's *Jubel* Overture and continued with Rossini arias. Between the vocal works, she played the Adagio and Finale

from Chopin's Concerto in E minor and—her second piece—the Caprice, Op. 15, by Thalberg. The second half of the program consisted entirely of the *Eroica* Symphony by Beethoven, conducted by Mendelssohn.

9. *Verleih' uns Frieden* (*Dona nobis pacem*), a work for mixed chorus and orchestra, was a prayer for peace. In a review of an earlier performance of the work, Robert Schumann wrote that *Verleih' uns Frieden* "deserved world fame."

10. In addition to the Schumann "Spring" Symphony, Clara Schumann and Mendelssohn played the Duo (written for this concert and later named *Allegro brillant*, Op. 92); as a soloist she performed the Adagio and Rondo from Chopin's Concerto in F minor, Robert Schumann's Allegro, Op. 8, a *Lied ohne Worte* by the conductor, a Scarlatti work, and the *Mosesphantasie* by Thalberg. The program included two songs by Robert Schumann and a new song by Clara Schumann, "Am Strand." Also performed at this gala event was a work by Haydn, an aria by Gluck, and a *Duo concertante* for melophone and violoncello! *Verleih' uns Frieden* was not given.

11. Carl Augustin Grenser (1794–1864), flutist in the Gewandhaus orchestra and secretary of the orchestra pension fund. He was also historian and archivist of the orchestra.

12. Schumann was working furiously on the proofs of his symphony up to the day before the premiere. In his *Haushaltbuch*, he referred to 30 March as an "ungeheurer Correcturtag" (monstrous day of correcting proofs).

13. See n. 10.

14. See n. 12.

15. Marie, the first Schumann child, was baptized on 13 September, Clara's twenty-second birthday. The day before the event, 12 September, was also their first wedding anniversary.

16. Mendelssohn had considered traveling to Leipzig on 10 September on the railroad line from Berlin that opened that day. But he was unable to come, and his place at the ceremony was taken by Dr. Härtel, the music publisher. The other godparents were Marianne Bargiel, Clara's mother; Madame Johanne Devrient, Robert Schumann's former landlady; and Robert's brother, Carl, whose deputy was Johann Ambrosius Barth, Leipzig bookseller and publisher.

17. Among the gifts she received were the newly published orchestral parts of Schumann's First Symphony, the manuscript of a new symphony, that in D minor, later known as the Symphony no. 4, and the published score of *Liebesfrühling*, the Rückert songs that included three songs she had composed. She also received a score of Mozart's *Don Giovanni*, as well as more personal gifts.

18. Cécile and Felix Mendelssohn also had a daughter named Marie, born in October 1839.

19. Mendelssohn had been called to Berlin by the Prussian king Wilhelm Friedrich IV and was named Royal Prussian Kapellmeister in October 1841. He did not resign his Gewandhaus position, however, and eventually returned to Leipzig as conductor. He finally saw his goddaughter in November 1841.

20. Robert Schumann had been working on many projects, among them the Symphony in D minor (no. 4), the proofs of his First Symphony in B♭, and a symphony in C minor (never completed).

21. Graf Wolf von Baudissin (1789–1878), Dresden diplomat, writer, and translator. Friendly with the Schumanns as well as with Mendelssohn, he shared a great enthusiasm for the music of Johann Sebastian Bach; husband of Sophie von Baudissin *née* Kaskel (1817–94), pianist and girlhood friend of Clara's.

22. Concerto in C minor, probably BWV 1060. Clara and Mendelssohn had played it together at the Schumann home in Leipzig in March 1841. The Baudissins were in Leipzig and may have heard it at that time.

23. Mendelssohn answered in the affirmative. An excerpt from his 14 January response to Clara Schumann, as given by Susanna Grossmann-Vendrey, *Felix Mendelssohn Bartholdy und die Musik der Vergangenheit* (Regensburg, 1969), p. 198, is indicative of his feelings about the Baudissins and his interest in Bach:

Verehrte Frau, anbei erfolgt die Partitur des verlangten Bachschen Concerts. Ich habe sie für Sie abschreiben lassen und bitte Sie als ein Andenken an den Abend, wo wir das Concert zusammen spielten zu behalten. Es versteht sich, daß es mir nur lieb sein kann, wenn Sie für Graf Baudissin und für jeden der sich dafür interessirt eine Copie davon nehmen lassen, je mehr die Sachen verbreit werden, desto besser. Bitte empfehlen Sie mich Grafen Baudissin wenn Sie ihm schreiben und sagen Sie ihm, daß ihm alles was ich von Bachschen Manuscripten besitze jederzeit mit Vergnügen zu Dienste steht.

[Honored Madame, the score of the Bach concerto you wished to have is enclosed. I had it copied for you and beg you to keep it as a remembrance of the evening on which we played it together. Understandably, I can only be pleased for you to have a copy made for Graf Baudissin and for anyone else who is interested. Indeed, the more these things are disseminated, the better. Please remember me to Graf Baudissin when you write to him, and tell him that I will gladly place each and every one of my Bach manuscripts at his service at any time.]

24. The Symphony no. 1 in B♭, Op. 38.

25. Robert and Clara Schumann left Leipzig on 18 February for a concert tour to Bremen, Oldenburg, and Hamburg. He returned on 12 March, but she continued on to Copenhagen for a series of concerts, returning to Leipzig and to her husband and child on 26 April.

26. Clara Schumann was the featured soloist in the twelfth subscription Gewandhaus concert on New Year's Day, 1842. She played Mendelssohn's G-minor Piano Concerto, Op. 25 (learning it on two weeks' notice), the *Moses-phantasie* by Thalberg, and Liszt's *Phantasie aus Donizetti's "Lucia di Lammermoor."* Ferdinand David conducted.

27. The subscription concert of 2 February 1843.

28. Mendelssohn writes "Concertprogrammenfabrikant"—literally, a manufacturer of concert programs.

29. Beethoven's Choral Fantasy, Op. 80, which she had played several times in the Gewandhaus.

30. Clara Schumann chose the Beethoven Choral Fantasy and also played a work by Henselt. She did not play any of Robert Schumann's works at this performance.

31. Mendelssohn conducted the first performance of his revised secular cantata *Die erste Walpurgisnacht*, Op. 60, at this concert.

32. The Schumanns lived in an apartment on Inselstraße.

33. *Das Paradies und die Peri*, Op. 50, was premiered in Leipzig on 4 December 1843 as a benefit for the Leipzig Conservatory, founded by Felix Mendelssohn that year. Robert Schumann conducted. The performance was repeated on 11 December.

34. Felix Mendelssohn had reluctantly left Leipzig in late November to take up his duties in Berlin and did not attend either performance of *Peri*.

35. Marie Sachse (Sachs) was a Leipzig singer who appeared at the Gewandhaus several times.

36. Livia Frege, *née* Gerhardt (1818–91), Leipzig singer who gave up most stage appearances when she married the wealthy Dr. Woldemar Frege in 1836. A girlhood intimate of Clara Schumann and a close friend of both the Schumanns and Felix Mendelssohn, Livia Frege occasionally sang for special performances of works by her composer friends. The Freges gave many private musicales in their imposing Leipzig residence, which still stands today.

37. Robert and Clara Schumann left Leipzig on a concert trip to Russia and were away from 25 January to 31 May 1844. Robert Schumann had many doubts about making the trip and vacillated for several months before he finally agreed to do so. Clara Schumann had gone to see Felix Mendelssohn to enlist his aid in persuading her husband to go.

38. See his letters to Mendelssohn in F. Gustav Jansen, ed., *Robert Schumanns Briefe: Neue Folge*, 2d ed. (Leipzig, 1904), pp. 249–56.

39. Clara Schumann was referring to the program of the forthcoming Gewandhaus concert of 5 October 1845. She played a newly composed concerto by Adolf Henselt (from the manuscript), a Schumann fugue (probably one of several composed in March 1845), and nos. 3 and 4 (the "Spinning Song") from vol. 6 of Mendelssohn's *Lieder ohne Worte* (Op. 67).

40. See p. 211.

41. A Leipzig concert had been planned for November, but a final date had not yet been arranged. Clara Schumann did not play again in that city until 1 January 1846.

42. She was probably referring to Mendelssohn's Piano Trio no. 2, Op. 66, and the Violin Concerto, Op. 64.

43. Robert Schumann's Piano Concerto in A minor, Op. 54, which was premiered in Dresden on 4 December 1845.

44. The second subscription concert of the Dresden season was given on 4

December (not 2 December). In addition to the premiere of Robert Schumann's Piano Concerto, Clara Schumann played the Duo in A major with Hiller. Other solos were the Ballade in A♭ major, Op. 47, of Chopin, a *Wiegenlied* by Henselt, a Bach fugue, and a *Lied ohne Worte* by Felix Mendelssohn. The program also included a revised version of Schumann's Overture, Scherzo, and Finale, Op. 52, as well as several Schumann songs and an overture by Hiller.

45. Mendelssohn had been in Berlin and returned to Leipzig in early December.

46. Clara Schumann was scheduled to be the soloist for the first concert on 11 November but was indisposed. Robert Schumann sent his father-in-law, Friedrich Wieck, to Leipzig with a letter to Mendelssohn requesting his assistance in getting the twelve-year-old violinist Joseph Joachim to Dresden to play in her place. Joachim was a student of Ferdinand David (1810–73), the concertmaster of the Gewandhaus orchestra. On one day's notice, Joachim played Mendelssohn's Violin Concerto with the Dresden orchestra. Also on the program were Mendelssohn's overture *Meeresstille und glückliche Fahrt*, Op. 27, several arias, a violin composition by David, and Beethoven's Fifth Symphony.

47. This concert actually took place on 4 December.

48. Ultimately, Clara Schumann did play in Leipzig on New Year's Day, 1846. Mendelssohn conducted.

49. The Leipzig premiere of Robert Schumann's Piano Concerto took place at the New Year's Day concert.

50. Schumann had written to Mendelssohn on 18 December regarding the concert and had designated the solos: an Impromptu by Hiller and two *Lieder ohne Worte*, nos. 4 and 6 from vol. 6 (Op. 67), by Mendelssohn.

51. The Symphony no. 2 in C major, Op. 61, which Mendelssohn was to premiere in November 1846. See pp. 223–25.

52. Johann Joseph Verhulst (1816–91), Dutch composer and conductor, student of Mendelssohn, and good friend of the Schumanns. Schumann's Overture, Scherzo, and Finale was dedicated to him.

53. Robert Schumann's Piano Quartet in E♭, Op. 47.

54. Schumann's Piano Quintet, Op. 44.

55. Niels Gade (1817–90), Danish violinist, conductor, and composer, studied in Leipzig and was Mendelssohn's successor as Gewandhaus conductor.

56. Mendelssohn was not only a brilliant pianist and organist but also an accomplished string player as well. In a January 1836 entry in her unpublished diary, the sixteen-year-old Clara described an afternoon in her home in which she played a Beethoven violin sonata with Mendelssohn as violinist, adding, "He is supposed to be absolutely wonderful on the viola. One can hardly understand how such a young man could have learned so much already."

57. Clara and Robert Schumann's fourth child, Emil, was born two days after this letter was written.

58. There had been uncertainty for several months about who would con-

duct. In the end, Mendelssohn conducted a concert for the benefit of the musicians' pension fund on 12 February 1846. A revised version of Schumann's Overture, Scherzo, and Finale was played from manuscript.

59. Mendelssohn had conducted Robert Schumann's First Symphony in Leipzig in October 1845 and several other times since the premiere in March 1841. See pp. 209–11.

60. The Overture, Scherzo, and Finale was published by Kistner in 1846. Clara Schumann is referring to the string parts, which evidently were already printed.

61. Felix Mendelssohn conducted a performance of Beethoven's Ninth Symphony in Leipzig on 5 February 1846.

62. Clara Schumann was the soloist for the Gewandhaus subscription concert on 22 October 1846. The program eventually included the works discussed in this letter, plus a Haydn symphony, several arias, and overtures by Hiller and Lachner.

63. The C-major Symphony, which was premiered at the concert of 5 November 1846.

64. A hotel, Zum großen Blumenberg, in Leipzig.

65. Felix Mendelssohn died on 4 November 1847. His younger brother, Paul, took over all the family business and financial affairs. After the death of Felix's wife, Cécile, on 25 September 1853, Paul became the legal guardian of Felix's sons.

66. Some or all of the money was used by Clara Schumann, but by the end of 1854 she had earned enough from her concert tours to repay the entire amount to Paul Mendelssohn.

Reminiscences of
Robert Schumann (1878)

RICHARD POHL

TRANSLATED BY JOHN MICHAEL COOPER

The music critic Richard Pohl (1826–96) began his career as an admirer of Schumann's music but, during the 1850s, changed allegiance to Liszt's and Wagner's "music of the future" (*Zukunftsmusik*). Pohl's memoirs of Schumann, published in 1878, not only shed considerable light on the composer's Düsseldorf years (1850–54) but also reveal the changing dynamics of German music criticism at midcentury. Introduced to Schumann in 1850 through the pianist Ernst Ferdinand Wenzel, Pohl worked as Schumann's librettist on a variety of compositions, including an opera libretto for Schiller's *Die Braut von Messina*, which inspired the concert overture Op. 100 (1850); the text for the oratorio *Luther*, planned as a trilogy to be performed on three consecutive evenings but ultimately rejected by Schumann; and a rendition of Ludwig Uhland's ballade *Des Sängers Fluch*, completed in a setting for soloists, chorus, and orchestra as Op. 139 (1852).

In 1852 Pohl began to contribute articles to the *Neue Zeitschrift für Musik*. The editor, Franz Brendel, had taken over the journal in 1845, after Schumann had retired as editor; under Brendel's direction, the journal was reoriented into an organ espousing the ideals of *Zukunftsmusik* (see pp. 317–37). In October 1853 Schumann published in the journal his celebrated article "Neue Bahnen" ("New avenues"); here Johannes Brahms, greeted as a new musical messiah, was set in opposition to the Liszt-Wagner camp. Rather than respond to Schumann directly, Brendel invited Pohl to contribute the lead article for the New Year's Day issue of 1854 ("Zur Eröffnung des zwanzigsten Jahrganges der Neuen Zeitschrift für Musik," vol. 40, pp. 1–3). Writing under the pen name of Hoplit, Pohl reviewed the twenty years of the journal's existence (Schumann had founded it in Leipzig in 1834) and pronounced that it was still pursuing the original goals: to elevate the beautiful and fight mediocrity in the arts. Of the journal's founders, Pohl observed, some had died or abandoned journalism, whereas others were essentially "dead for the journal" because they would no longer support the vital course of progress in German music. Thus the stage was set for a polemic in German musical criticism that would rage for decades.

According to Pohl's memoirs, the last letter he received from Schumann was dated 18 March 1853, several months before the "Neue Bahnen" and New Year's Day articles (see p. 258). But this was not the case: an unpublished letter from Schumann to Pohl dated 6 February 1854 survives in the Pierpont Morgan Library in New York. Having discovered the identity of "Hoplit," Schumann took the occasion to answer Pohl's recent writings, including the New Year's Day address. We present Schumann's eloquent, lucid rejoinder both in translation and in the original German in the appendix on pp. 259–63. Three weeks after writing the letter, the composer attempted suicide by jumping into the Rhine River. [Ed.]

[Source: Richard Pohl, "Erinnerungen an Robert Schumann, nebst ungedruckten Briefen," *Deutsche Revue* 2 (1878): 169ff., 306ff.]

.

The year 1850 marked an important turning point for Robert Schumann. With it, he entered the last phase of his life and creativity. Of course, he had no more presentiment of this than did his numerous friends and admirers when he left Dresden in the fall of 1850 to assume the position of municipal music director in Düsseldorf on 24 October. On the contrary, this move, occasioned by artistic activities, gave him renewed hope. He was just forty-one years old and had every reason to look forward to a long creative life. The fresh, pleasant life-style of the Rhenish city of art stimulated him; and he undertook the move with a host of plans, reaching an almost frenetic level of productivity and sustaining an inexhaustible intellectual activity— almost as if he had to hurry in order to say all that was still on his mind.

That same year his homeland, Saxony, had dealt him two bitter disappointments that made his departure easy. First, his prospect for becoming vice-Kapellmeister at the Royal Theater in Dresden had been dashed: Carl Krebs[1] was awarded the position that Schumann's influential friends had desired to secure for him; their efforts, made only after Düsseldorf had extended its invitation, were only a futile, belated attempt to keep the celebrated master in his immediate fatherland. Schumann could console himself all the more easily because the Düsseldorf position was more comfortable and independent.

The second disappointment was more difficult, for it was purely artistic: the meager success—less than anyone had expected— accorded the three performances of his first and only opera, *Genoveva*, on the Leipzig stage (25, 28, and 30 June 1850). The work had been eagerly anticipated, and its fate was decisive for Schumann's subsequent artistic efforts. Had *Genoveva* been given even a warmly encouraging reception, the composer certainly would have written a second opera. But its fate recalled that of Beethoven's *Fidelio*.[2] Even the efforts of Schumann's most zealous admirers were unable to salvage public opinion of the work, and in the musical press a most unseemly polemic unfolded that must have deeply wounded the already hypersensitive master; it was even said that Schumann utterly lacked dramatic gifts. This was a turning point for Schumann. However much he may have felt above the criticisms of the daily press, he nevertheless lost the happiness and security needed for composition.

Among the listeners at that problem-ridden premiere of *Genoveva* was a philosophy student who, since the dawning of his musical consciousness, had been an enthusiastic admirer of Schumann and was deeply indignant about (what he regarded as) the unjust reception given the opera of the master he so deeply respected: the author of these memoirs.

Schumann did not know me. I was uncomfortable with the idea of young enthusiasts pressing themselves upon famous artists, and I had no ties that might bring me any closer to Schumann. Not yet in the public eye, I had to watch the debate over *Genoveva* in silence—but later I resolved to remain silent no longer.

The question of the true musical-dramatic style—which I considered definitively solved when I later came to know Richard Wagner's works—already preoccupied me most intensely. I recognized that Schumann had come much closer to the conceptual and formal solution to this dilemma than had his predecessors; but I also knew that the last word had not yet been spoken, that the proper style had not yet been found. The reason for this became clear to me only the next year, when I read Wagner's *Opera and Drama*.[3] For the time being, I believed that the main reason for the failure of Schumann's opera had to lie in its *libretto*—and this viewpoint was indeed justified, even if not to the extent I thought at the time. Therefore, I devoted my most serious efforts to finding a *libretto* for Schumann, an artistically viable drama, a subject of high tragedy in flawless poetic form, something far removed from the enfeebled mainstream of the operatic style of the day. Given the proper poetic framework, I believed, a musically perfect work would issue from Schumann's hand.

That dramatic work was soon found: Schiller's *Die Braut von Messina*. Today, just as twenty-eight years ago, I still believe that *Die Braut von Messina* remains an artistic torso unless *music* is added as a redemptive force. One need only read the foreword Schiller published with this work, in which he came so remarkably close to embracing the art of the Greeks.[4] Even the immortal poet was evidently uncertain to what extent he wished to permit the introduction and development of music in his drama. This was not his task, however, but that of the creative musician—who is still undiscovered. Should just the choruses —certainly at least these—be set to music? And in what style? Or should melodrama be introduced to provide continuity? These were fundamental questions, and their answers challenge us even today; for *Die Braut von Messina* is actually Schiller's drama of the future.[5]

Having made up his mind, the young student went straight to work—and made an opera libretto. Everything would be sung in a declamatory fashion (Schumann would have to find the proper style), but the choruses would provide the formally incorporated points of repose in the work. Naturally Schiller's drama had to be shortened for this purpose; but does not every director also make cuts? Would we have ever seen *Don Carlos*, *William Tell*, *Wallenstein*,[6] or other works without cuts? So here there was no problem. Only Isabella's long narrative in the first act, which provides the entire background for the drama, seemed to present insurmountable difficulties. I sought to solve these by presenting the material narrated by Schiller in the past as a prelude in the present, an independent introduction to Schiller's drama.

Brimming with these ideas, I shared the plan with my teacher and friend, E. F. Wenzel (who still teaches at the Leipzig Conservatory of Music);[7] and he, a longtime friend of Schumann, encouraged me to submit my sketch to the musician himself. I wrote a long letter in which I presented my ideas in detail, and sent it, along with a letter of recommendation from Wenzel, to Schumann in Düsseldorf on 18 October 1850.

Three months passed without an answer. But finally the long-awaited letter from the master made its way into my hands through Whistling's music shop.[8] Here is the unabbreviated original text:

Düsseldorf, 19 January 1851

Honored sir,

I have certainly earned the most serious reproach for not answering you and your dear letter. I have been constantly vacillating between accepting and refusing this indisputably interesting subject. Finally, though, I believe I have to choose the latter, for such well-known subjects are always treacherous, as you yourself say. Indeed, I would accept this one in an instant if there were no such piece by Schiller.

Please accept my best thanks for everything else you wrote to me. I would so very much like to write an oratorio; would you perhaps offer to lend a hand with one? I have thought of Luther and of Ziska,[9] but a biblical subject would also be fine with me. And after this and something similar, probably also a cheerful opera. Perhaps this will stimulate you to further ideas.

Your first letter has already born fruit. After I read the tragedy again to reacquaint myself with it, ideas came to me for an overture, which I then completed.[10] May this, then, be an encouraging sign that artistic blessings will likewise not be denied to further undertakings!

Please send soon some good news to

Your servant
Robert Schumann

My best greetings to Herr Wenzel; may he forgive me for not yet having written to him.

·

Understandably, this letter made me unspeakably happy. Yes, my project had been discarded, but nonetheless it had provided the stimulus for a new, estimable creation by the master. And he had been sufficiently impressed to consider further collaborations. Obviously, he was willing to take a chance on me. Immediately I set furiously to work. Deciding without hesitation on Luther, I first undertook some historical studies, which made the power of the subject sufficiently clear so that I could present to Schumann a sketch showing the outlines of the whole in just a few weeks. I was fully aware that the plan was too broad, but I wanted to leave its compression to the master.

In a short time I received this answer:

Düsseldorf, 14 February 1851

Honored sir,

Herewith you receive a sketch that generally agrees with your own.[11] Above all, I had to clarify the *musical* form for myself. It is a compelling subject; we will have to cut out everything that is not absolutely essential to the development of the plot—even, I am afraid, the intervention of supernatural forces. Only the ghost of Hus[12] I can imagine is really admissible.

There is so much I would like to discuss with you, but for today I have to confine myself to the most important points:

The oratorio must be appropriate for the church *and* the concert hall.

It cannot last longer than two and one-half hours, including breaks between the parts.

If possible, everything that is simply narrative or reflective should be avoided, and above all the dramatic form should take precedence.

[It should be] as historically accurate as possible, especially where Luther's familiar sayings about strength are concerned.

You never take advantage of the opportunities for choruses. Certainly you know Handel's *Israel in Egypt*? For me, that is the ideal *choral work*.[13] I would like to see the chorus play an equally important role in our Luther oratorio.

Give me double choruses, too, especially in the final numbers of each part.

There must in any case be a solo soprano part. It seems to me that Katharina[14] could be introduced with great effect. And their vows (in part 3) cannot be omitted.

The chorale "Ein' feste Burg," as the point of climax, cannot be introduced before the very end, in the final chorus.[15]

Hutten, Sickingen, Hans Sachs, Lucas Cranach,[16] and the Electors Friedrich and Johann Philipp of Hessen will probably have to be left out—unfortunately![17] If we were to include all these solo parts there would be terrific problems everywhere in the casting; they can all be mentioned in the narrative, though.

I believe it would be very difficult to weave the German Mass into the various parts.[18] But the chorale can be employed in its stead.

Luther's general relation to music—his love for it, which he pronounced in a hundred lovely proverbs—should likewise not go unmentioned. One might consider an alto or a second soprano part [for this purpose].

Otherwise I agree completely with everything you say concerning the metrical treatment of the text and the folklike, old-German character that should be imparted to the verses.

I believe the music should be the same way—effective not so much through artfulness as through conciseness, power, and clarity.—

Honored sir, we are about to undertake something well worth the toil. It will require courage as well as humility. Please accept my gratitude for your receptiveness to my idea. Let us take up and pursue this great endeavor with all our powers.

Yours truly,

R. Schumann

P.S.[19] I might mention the following writings that may be of use:

1. *Martin Luther; ein kirchengeschichtliches Lebensbild* [Martin Luther: a church-historical biography], by Dr. [Carl August] Wildenhahn [Leipzig,] 1851.

2. *Luthers geistliche Lieder und Gedanken über die Musik* [Luther's sacred songs and thoughts on music], newly collected etc., by K[arl] Grell [Weimar,] 1817.

3. Winterfeld's text on the Lutheran chorales.[20]

I can send you no. 2 from here. Would you compare my plan with yours and then send me a *very detailed sketch* of the whole?

—R. Sch.

I devoted all my energies to the project—indeed, I spent several more months of the most intensive work on it—but unfortunately, all came to naught. Schumann envisioned the work too differently for us to be able to achieve our common goal.

As with the opera, I had my own ideas concerning the new disposition of the *form* of the oratorio. I wished to rely upon neither Handel, Bach, nor Mendelssohn[21] but rather to seek my own way along a new path. I rejected the narrative recitative as an impoverished means of linking individual movements; instead I inserted a chorus that simultaneously presented and reflected upon the plot, after the model of Greek tragedy. I did not wish to forfeit the churchlike character, and I still wanted to weave the Lutheran testament of faith into the work via the German Mass.

Though I had reservations about Schumann's singling out *Israel in Egypt,* that did not lessen the task of confining myself to the most essential plot elements and avoiding anything episodical. To me it seemed almost an advantage that the epic form of the oratorio, unlike the musical drama, did not have to avoid lyrical points of repose and reflection but could achieve its musical development through a free combination of lyric and epic expressive techniques. If one gave precedence to the dramatic, one could consequently adhere strictly to the drama—but then the work should be presented on the stage, not in the concert hall.

Schumann's request that the work last no longer than two and one-half hours seemed infeasible. If this were observed, anything not belonging strictly to the plot would have to be omitted, leaving little more than a historical skeleton of my intentions. And I had no inclination to realize this work against my own convictions.

But I still believed I could convert Schumann to my way of thinking, if only I could show him part of my plan realized according to my conception. So I not only drafted a detailed sketch of the entire plan but also fleshed out the first part of the oratorio. My rendition became so involved that the first part alone would have sufficed for a performance lasting an entire evening. But this did not deter me. I rounded off the first part so that it was also self-sufficient, and I presented the whole plan as a "Reformation Trilogy," to be performed over the course of three nights.[22]

I was fully aware that I was not acting according to Schumann's wishes. But nonetheless I was resolved not to pursue the project if I could not persuade Schumann of my position.

His next letter brought me the necessary clarity. He wrote:

Düsseldorf, 13 May 1851

Most honored sir,

Recent weeks have been so frenetic and fragmented by rehearsals, performances, and other undertakings that I could hardly collect my thoughts on anything else. How grateful I am for your missive; the great seriousness of purpose with which you have approached the work only reinforces my conviction that our collaboration can only be productive. But I do not know whether we can continue from this beginning. Just the prelude,[23] however appealing I find its individual ideas, would take up an entire evening—and I cannot warm to the idea of a two-part oratorio[24] presented on different days; I think that would represent an unfortunate course.

So what now? I believe we must either reduce the material down to its simplest components or select just a few of the great events of Luther's life. I also believe we should not allot too much space to the intervention of supernatural beings; I cannot square that with the character of the Great Reformer as we know him, as an upright, self-reliant person.

How difficult it is to resolve this and other such matters in correspondence; how quickly we could accomplish our goal if we could spend some time together, which is what I would hope for. It would deeply pain me to hear that the difficulties that have arisen would cause you to abandon the project. I have already looked forward to moving on with the work this summer. So please be so good as to give me an indication whether you are still interested, and whether we will strive to master the splendid idea that fulfills us.

Many greetings from your truly thankful

R. Schumann.

.

Schumann obviously regretted having to discard my diligently constructed text. But as a composer he had every right to request a text according to his *own* ideas, whereas I, considering my rights as a librettist, would have preferred to sacrifice performances rather than rearrange the text in a form I found contrary. Likewise, I was disinclined to give the libretto to a lesser composer than Schumann. Thus the grand Reformation Trilogy, with which I had hoped to reform the oratorio, remained incomplete and uncomposed.

But I made one last attempt. Always remaining true to my idea, I reduced the sketch to its bare essentials and sent Schumann a second, shorter arrangement. Along with it I enclosed several of my lyric poems, which I offered for Schumann to set. I then received the following answer:

Düsseldorf, 25 June 1851

Honored sir,

In recent weeks several newly begun undertakings, as well as older ones that had to be completed,[25] have prevented me from concentrating as I would have liked on one thing, our Luther text. And for some time yet I will not be able to concentrate on it properly, as I am currently distracted by so many diverse activities. In particular I now see that such an idea, such a work, cannot be carried out through correspondence alone; and so I fall back upon your hopes that you will be able to visit me on the Rhine this fall. Just bring a complete sketch with you then, and that way we will accomplish more in a few hours than we otherwise would in weeks.

Only one thing more I would ask you to consider, which has become increasingly clear to me. Our oratorio must be thoroughly folk-like, something that will be understood by peasants and citizens—as is only fitting for the hero, who was such a great man of the people. I would also attempt to keep my music as much in this character as possible, with as little artifice, complication, and counterpoint as possible, instead achieving its effect primarily through simple, stirring rhythm and melody. I hope you will work with me on this and soon let me hear more, even if you cannot come to visit right away.

Many thanks, too, for the poems; music will soon be written for one or the other. I will gladly take care of the poems for Dr. Müller soon.[26]

But now another question and a favor. It occurred to me that some ballade or another could be easily and effectively arranged as a concert piece for solo voices, chorus, and orchestra. In particular I have been looking at Uhland's[27] *Des Sängers Fluch* [The singer's curse], but I lack a poet who could mold some passages into musical form. In the enclosed version, which naturally will require a good deal of your attention, I have suggested where the original must be retained and where, in no. 2 and in the ensemble of no. 3, it must be changed. I would of course like to retain Uhland's meters and to accommodate his tone as much as possible. If you should have the time and inclination to consider this favor I would be so grateful to you!

In any case I hope to hear from you again soon, with news of how your plans for the fall are taking shape. Best regards to Wenzel; I refer him—and also you—to a book: the collected poems of Elisabeth Kulmann (6th edition):[28] a true spiritual island, risen to the surface in the chaos of the present.

Yours truly,
R. Sch.

·

(On a separate sheet the following sketch of *Des Sängers Fluch* was drafted:)[29]

No. 1. Chorus with solos: "In olden times . . . blossoming comradeship."

No. 2. Duet form (perhaps ten lines in all). An elder and a youth: "Be ready now . . . stone heart."

No. 3. Recitative (soprano): "Already they stand . . . swelled to the brim." Ensemble: Elder, youth, king, queen, chorus (expansively developed).

No. 4. Recitative: "And as if dead of a storm . . . gardens resound."

No. 5. Harps: "Woe unto you!"

No. 6. Chorus: "The old man has called it. . . . That is the singer's curse."

·

This was the third text within a year that was supposed to employ me as Schumann's poet. He had rejected the first; I myself had let the second drop. I felt obligated to bring the third attempt to a successful end in order to justify Schumann's confidence. And I was also fully aware that I could count on little appreciation and still less recognition for my efforts. There is in fact no task more thankless than arranging the works of celebrated poets for musical purposes. Every change, every cut, every addition is decried as sacrilege by the critics. Now, even though the most conservative aesthetician has to understand that such an arrangement *without* alterations is absolutely impossible, the *caeterum censeo*[30] is still always present: the work should have been left unchanged (which, in this case, would mean uncomposed). In this undertaking, of course, I thought I would be somewhat sheltered by Schumann's name, but I was only fooling myself. Yet I was so innocent in the whole undertaking!

There were squabbles, though, concerning its realization. And strangely enough, I was chided precisely for the very proper way in which I proceeded. I wanted to provide as little possible input of my own and therefore selected from Uhland's poems the material for the songs of the harpist and the youth that seemed suitable for the large choral scene that Schumann wanted "expansively developed"; I left the final decision to Schumann himself. Thus three versions of the main scene up to the catastrophe were eventually produced. I allowed myself to add only a tender, fanciful youthful affection between the young man and the queen, in order to provide a motivation for the king's angry outburst. The rose thrown to the youth by the queen in thanks for his songs seemed to me far too innocent a reason for the king's bloody deed. In a stage presentation much more can be said with looks and gestures than with words; and in the short, narrative form of the ballade much is left to the reader's imagination. But where the spoken dialogue alone is supposed to accomplish everything, as in the concert oratorio, the motivation must be carefully established in order to make the course of events as clear as possible.

Precisely this idea pleased Schumann, and that was enough for me. Of course I could not win his complete approval with the first draft. He wrote to me:

Düsseldorf, 18 July 1851

Honored sir,

Today I am allowed the pleasure of writing you only a few lines, for we already have one foot on the train for an excursion to Heidelberg and elsewhere. But I hope to see you soon.[31] Now, there is a possibility that I will be away on 17 August: I have been invited to Antwerp to be a judge for a prize competition in a large song festival; and since the festival promises to be interesting I am rather inclined to attend.[32]

But in any event I will not depart before the 15th. Perhaps there is a possibility that you could be here before the 15th, or that we could meet later, on your return trip? You might apprise me about this with a few lines.

And now, most of all, thanks for the eagerness with which you have taken up my idea. It is a splendid musical subject, and your idea of choosing the singer from other Uhland poems for the recitatives is truly superb. Now of course this produces some ambiguities in the connections between the movements. These, however, can be easily clarified through some instrumental passages linking the speeches of the king, the queen, and the chorus. But then the whole becomes much too long, and the entire lengthy central movement would have to be limited to one song by the youth, one by the old harpist, a duet between the two, and a trio or quartet with the queen and king—after which the king hurls into the crowd his accusation "You have led my people astray!"

All this, however, can be best explained in person; and even though it will be difficult to wait so long, I will do so for the benefit of the work. For today accept once again my gratitude, and let me know soon about your travel plans. With many greetings,

Yours truly,
R. Schumann

Best regards to Wenzel; this spring I composed a fairy tale, *Der Rose Pilgerfahrt*,[33] which we performed a week ago with good success; please tell Wenzel about it, as he always takes an interest in me.

·

I immediately executed the changes Schumann wanted, shortened my text considerably, and searched for new songs for the solo scenes. I postponed my trip to Düsseldorf until Schumann's return from Antwerp and on 22 August received word from him that he was back in Düsseldorf and was expecting me: "I would be pleased if you would come quite soon."

The 3d of September was the long-awaited day on which I would finally meet Schumann in person. I arrived in Düsseldorf during the night and, with pounding heart, made my way to Schumann's residence the next day at 11:00 A.M. His house stood on a wide street lined with chestnut trees, not far from the Rhine. He lived on the second floor; I was led into the music salon, where two grand pianos stood next to each other. Hardly had I been announced before Schumann entered the salon from his study, received me warmly, offered his hand, and said in his soft voice: "Now that's nice, that you've come." I was too moved to fashion much of a reply, and I followed him into his study, on the back side of the house. It had only one window overlooking the courtyard, and was quietly situated, small but comfortable. Before the window there was a writing table upon which manuscripts lay; along with a large desk there was also an elegant cabinet for scores and books, containing a finely bound personal library in exemplary order. Surveying it quickly I saw, in addition to his own works, scores by Bach, Handel, and Beethoven. Portraits of famous musicians adorned the walls. Immediately above the desk hung a portrait of Elisabeth Kulmann.

Schumann seated himself next to me on the sofa, looked at me amicably—and was silent. I had already been advised that he was very quiet; nonetheless, this persistent silence made me increasingly self-conscious. I spoke of anything and everything I thought might interest him—and he was silent, nodding his head in agreement now and then, and probably also interjecting an approving or questioning word occasionally. But he simply let me keep talking.

At last I pulled out my manuscript: my *third* version of the Luther oratorio and my *second* of *Des Sängers Fluch*. This finally got the conversation under way. Schumann wanted me to stay several weeks in Düsseldorf in order to work through the whole thing thoroughly with him. For the time being, I was unable to do so. But I posed a different question: whether Düsseldorf might be a place well suited for me to settle down on a *long-term* basis. I would have liked nothing better than to reside permanently near Schumann. I had not yet established myself anywhere else; so if Düsseldorf could offer me any prospect for a secure occupation, I would decide on the spot to remain there.

But Schumann himself advised me against it. He did not believe I would be able to find anything there that could reward a long-term residence. If I wished to live only from my literary efforts and not a regular position, however, then he would recommend a stay in Switzerland (Zurich or Bern). He had been there again that summer; it was simply all too lovely. If he had his way, he would prefer to reside there permanently. Then he spoke highly of the writings of Jeremias Gotthelf, which he was then reading with particular pleasure.[34]

After a visit of more than an hour I decided it was time for me to go. Schumann dismissed me very warmly and asked me to return that evening. I was with him again at 5:00. We immediately set about discussing my text. Concerning the Luther project I again showed him my ideas for reworking the oratorio that had led me there, and asked him to reconsider my outline. I sensed that probably I was not convincing Schumann. He took the manuscript and placed it on his podium without looking at the first detail. The text for *Des Sängers Fluch*, however, was subjected to strict scrutiny. He suggested cuts and changes and asked me to recommend more song texts by Uhland for his selection, since only some of those already chosen appealed to him.

Then he got up and asked me if I would like to accompany him; he was accustomed to visiting some acquaintances at this time every day in a nearby restaurant. Naturally I went with him, and there Schumann presented me to W. Müller von Königswinter, Robert Franz, Tausch,[35] and some Düsseldorf artists. The conversation was stimulating, unforced, but it touched on nothing of particular interest. I accompanied Schumann back to the door of his house. He asked me to return at the same time the next morning. In the mornings he customarily worked until about noon.

When I entered his study the next day Schumann was working on a score. "Liszt wants to perform my *Manfred* in Weimar," he said. "I am just working on adapting the drama for the stage. If *Manfred* is published, I want to have this abbreviated text released before the score. That way, it can also be performed with the various roles in concert performances."[36]

I thought to myself that he must not have had many stage performances behind him, and that was why he had immediately set about arranging the text for concert performances. I referred to the incidental music to *Egmont* and *A Midsummer Night's Dream* as models.[37] "That would mean a complete reworking," countered Schumann, "and that is not my task. *You* try it sometime; it's not at all easy.[38] I must confine myself to summarizing the drama. I have chosen the translation by Posgazu [*recte* Posgaru] because I prefer it to Böttger's.[39] A performance of *Manfred* poses some problems concerning the scenery. On the stage, the spirits always appear all too concrete. For example, what do you think about the appearance of the ghosts of the elements?"

I answered that I found the way the Dresden Hoftheater was then staging Faust's dream (under Devrient's[40] direction)—with misty scenes merging into one another—most satisfying. This idea seemed to please Schumann, and he asked me to tell him more about it. Then we discussed Elisabeth Kulmann, whom he respected greatly. He informed me that he had recently composed two volumes of Lieder from her poems;[41] then, turning to the poems I had sent him, he encouraged me to send still more. Above all he was seeking texts suitable for female listeners. These, however, were not easy to find, and he would greatly appreciate my special consideration of his request.

At the same time he gave me permission to write a second verse for Eichendorff's[42] "Frühlingsnacht" (Op. 39, no. 12). The poem was just too short, but rather than have the single strophe performed twice (as concert singers usually did at the time) he preferred to develop the poetic ideas further. He wanted me to provide a new strophe.[43]

Then Schumann expressed his wish to compose several more ballades after he finished *Des Sängers Fluch,* which he hoped to begin soon. He was searching for more Uhland texts. I recommended Geibel's[44] *Page und Königskind,* partly because of its fantastic subject and partly because that ballade cycle had the advantage of requiring no further changes in the text. One could compose it exactly as Geibel had written it. Schumann could not clearly recall these ballades, but he did not forget my suggestion; indeed, the following year (June to September 1852) he composed *Page und Königskind.*

Schumann gave me two more months to complete the final version of *Des Sängers Fluch,* and until spring for the Luther oratorio.

When I left him at about 1:00, Schumann invited me to a country outing with his family that afternoon. There I came to know him from the most informal side, as a family man. He was more good-natured and talkative than I would have thought possible after my first meeting. He told his wife of our plans, praised my enthusiasm in following up on his wishes, and encouraged me to try my hand at dramatic works as well. There was still much to be done in opera; but the best preparation for that would first be a suitable drama that I would try to bring to the stage in order to gain experience.

·

It was a beautiful, unforgettable afternoon, the 5th of September 1851. That night I returned to Leipzig, where one of my first efforts was finally to complete *Des Sängers Fluch.* I already knew well enough that it was not easy to satisfy Schumann. But undaunted, I became more determined to win his final approval. At the beginning of October I sent him the manuscript. Not until two months later did I receive the following letter:

Düsseldorf, 7 December 1851

Honored sir,

Once again I bring you *belated* thanks for your last delightful missive. Recent months have been quite hectic. At their end I hoped and very much wanted to be able to give you more definite news about my progress in composing the ballade. But unfortunately, I have been distracted by other projects, and have not even begun. So please accept my many thanks for the zeal you have devoted to the new rendition. Except for a few cuts I think it is very successful, and I can hardly wait to begin on it.

It would please us greatly to see your bride-to-be[45] and yourself here in Düsseldorf. Other than one performance on 11 December, the next concerts will be on 8 and 22 January. At the end of this week we are meeting to determine the programs for these concerts. If you could perhaps let me know by Saturday whether you are still planning a trip to Düsseldorf, and whether Fräulein Eyth could play in a concert on 8 or 22 January, I would inform the directors in the conference and quickly give you the details.

As concerns the Luther project: I am beginning to worry whether we will be able to conquer the task. I feel an urge to write a larger work and would so gladly have devoted the coming year to this one. Will it be possible?

Thank you also for your poems. I hope they will be set to music.

As for what you say about the share of ownership on the text for the ballade: we will discuss that later, as soon as the work is successfully [completed].[46]

Did you hear my overture to *Die Braut von Messina*?[47] I ask because it was *you* who aroused my desire to compose it. I have heard varying accounts of its success. I am accustomed to the majority of the public not understanding my works at the first hearing—especially the better, deeper ones. In the case of this overture, though, I would have expected a more immediate acceptance. But then, no work of any substance can be immediately understood if one has not already studied the score.

Enough for now. I hope this letter finds you in the best of health, and that you let me hear from you quite soon. Please give my cordial regards to Fräulein Eyth.

R. Sch.

·

That was the first time Schumann had spoken freely with me about the worth and success of one of his compositions. This pleased me as a sign of his growing trust. I reported to him right away the very favorable impression that this overture—certainly his best, after *Manfred* and *Genoveva*—had made upon me and other admirers, and I could also reassure him about the general reception of his work. To be sure, I failed to tell him the work had attained only a *succès d'estime* among the general public.

I wanted to postpone the concert trip with my bride to Düsseldorf until the premiere of *Des Sängers Fluch*, since Schumann had already told me during my earlier trip to Düsseldorf that the harp would play a prominent role in the ballade and that its part would be too demanding for the resident harpist, a dilettante. He had remarked that he wanted to write the harp part to be equally well suited for the piano, since it might be played on that instrument more often than on the harp. Sooner than I expected I was surprised and delighted to receive a new letter from Schumann. He wrote:

Düsseldorf, 10 January 1852

Honored sir and friend,

In haste but with great pleasure I write to inform you that a certain harp part could soon fall into the hands of your young lady-friend. The sketch for the piece is finished, and though the instrumentation is a large undertaking, it may be mastered without too long a delay. I have worked with great enthusiasm, and I believe the whole will have a great dramatic effect.

That is one thing I wanted to tell you. And then there is the other— namely, that I am now looking forward most eagerly to our great *reformer* and would like to get to work on that project sooner rather than later. I hope you have not forgotten it entirely.

Many greetings to you; please do not let the good beginning of our collaboration also be the end!

Yours truly,
R. Schumann

On 22 [January] we will premiere *Der Rose Pilgerfahrt* with orchestra. Many greetings to Wenzel.

However gladdening these words, and however much they should have stimulated me to resolve my ideas about the Luther project with Schumann's as quickly as possible, I was so involved with my own affairs at the time that I could not meet his amiable challenge. *Des Sängers Fluch* had taught me that it was not easy to work with Schumann. Even if I had shaped the Luther text completely according to his ideas, I could not have hoped to satisfy him completely all at once. The undertaking had already cost me half a year, and, though well intentioned, I simply no longer had the time for it. I therefore left this question unanswered until later, when things had calmed down, but I did have the pleasure of personally seeing Schumann not long afterward.

In March he came to Leipzig, primarily to give a concert in which his *Manfred* Overture and *Der Rose Pilgerfahrt* were premiered. I hurried back from Dresden to attend this interesting concert. It was a matinee, given for Schumann's benefit in the Gewandhaus on Sunday, 14 March. I had expected that no seats would be left at a concert in Schumann's honor. But the hall was by no means overflowing, and the ovations afforded the composer were, I thought, likewise too modest. This was the first time I heard the *Manfred* Overture, and it moved me so profoundly that I could hardly contain myself. This feeling may have been augmented by the impression Schumann made with his conducting of the work. I had taken a place in the balcony above the orchestra, so that I could see Schumann's face. His mood was extremely serious. Totally immersed in the score, completely oblivious to the public, and paying little attention even to the musicians, he lived in the tones, molding them to his mission: he himself became Manfred. I sensed that he had poured more of his heart into this work than into perhaps any other, as if in it he spoke to us from the depths of his soul. The public found the overture "too serious." Too serious! When a genius stands on the brink of madness; when, as in this *Manfred*, death is longed for as the redeemer of the torments of the soul! And about this time two years later the noble master himself had crossed the border into madness, his lofty spirit forever sunk into darkness! That morning in the Gewandhaus I felt as though I had received a presentiment of Schumann's fate.

Frau Clara Schumann played Chopin's F-minor Concerto, and the bass Behr sang some of Schumann's Lieder.[48] This was all well and good—but I could not escape the grave mood into which the *Manfred* Overture had thrown me. Only *Der Rose Pilgerfahrt* returned me to better spirits. The similarities to *Das Paradies und die Peri* have always hindered the success of this charming work. Peri is a legendary Indian child from the banks of the Ganges; the Rose blossomed on German soil, in a musical idyll. In it, Schumann successfully adopted a popular tone, with which, however, the choruses of elves are not quite compatible. Thus, there is no true unity in the piece as a whole, but here the poet is not without blame.

The poet Moritz Horn[49] was present, and Liszt, Robert Franz, and Joachim[50] were also in attendance. They all sat in the center loge, with Schumann and his wife, for the director of the Leipzig Singakademie and of the Gewandhaus concerts, Julius Rietz,[51] had taken over the direction of this concert. Once again, the success could hardly be called more than a *succès d'estime*. With Schumann the Leipzigers behaved just as coolly and reservedly as they did with all the more modern composers who followed him. One must occasionally admit what our fast-living generation has long since forgotten: how it judged [composers] a quarter-century ago. That can be instructive, and a consolation for the future.

I was not able to greet Schumann until after the concert. He was obviously exhausted, and asked me to come to him at 6:00 that evening (at the home of the Preußer family).[52] Now came the memorable moment when I would meet Liszt in person. Once again, my friend Wenzel arranged the first encounter. Ever genial and tactful, Liszt sent some kind words to me when he learned that I had worked with Schumann. He invited me to accompany him. Robert Franz, Bartholf Senff (the editor of *Signale*[53]), Wenzel, and several others joined us. We ate in a very modest restaurant, and afterward Liszt invited us all to coffee in the Hotel Bavière, where he was staying. Of course the conversation turned to the concert we had just heard. Liszt was particularly sympathetic to the *Manfred* Overture; at the time he was already preparing the dramatic staging of the work, which he invited us to attend in Weimar.[54] Robert Franz was largely unimpressed by *Der Rose Pilgerfahrt*, and generally showed himself rather unsympathetic to Schumann's more recent works. Even the poet Horn, with whom I became better acquainted that evening, was not entirely satisfied with the treatment of his text. Among other qualms, he said that he had conceived the men's chorus "Bist Du im Wald gewandelt" [no. 15, "Have you wandered in the forest"], which has since become so popular, as something completely different, namely as an emotional solo aria. In short, Schumann had not entirely pleased anyone. He may well have learned of this, which certainly would have deeply wounded and depressed him precisely when he needed recognition and cheering up more than ever before.

My visit that evening was short, for I sensed that he was not in a talkative mood. He introduced me to his amiable hosts, who then invited me to a musical matinee they were giving in Schumann's honor in their guest villa the next morning. At this matinee was everyone who was anyone in Leipzig musical circles, a brilliant meeting of artists: the directors and principals of the Gewandhaus; professors of the Conservatory; members of the theater; the poets Adolf Böttger and Moritz Horn, and the like. At the center, of course, were the Schumanns and Liszt. There was much music making; one of the highlights was the new Schumann Sonata in D minor for Violin and Piano (Op. 121), dedicated to David[55] and performed here by David and Frau Schumann. Frau Schumann also performed several solos, but Liszt declined the persistent invitations to perform, offering instead to play some pieces for piano duet with Frau Schumann. From the available music he selected some marches by Schubert.[56] Smiling, Schumann listened to them, and then said to me, as I was standing captivated directly beside the piano: "One can say of Liszt what was said of German noblemen in 1848: he has learned nothing and forgotten nothing."

For the first time I sensed the cleft separating Schumann from Liszt, who had always received him with collegial familiarity and artistic encouragement. Schumann regarded Liszt with a certain skeptical reserve, to which he also subjected himself. The division of musicians into Mendelssohnians, Schumannians, and Lisztians—that is, into Leipzig, Düsseldorf, and Weimar schools—could no longer be disguised; but the battle became public only when the "Wagner question" came under serious discussion in the daily press later that year (1852).[57] A few months later, when I received the opportunity to take a position on the issues, I counted myself among the members of the Weimar school without a moment's hesitation. But on that morning of 15 March I had no idea that my involvement in the musical war, which has continued uninterrupted ever since, was so close at hand. At that point I had yet to hear a Wagner opera—that would be the decisive moment for me.

The entire week of 14 to 21 March was a Schumann week for Leipzig. Everywhere people rendered the great master the respect and attention he deserved and observed all the protocols. But a true following and sincere veneration were granted him only by the inner circle of his admirers (then growing, but still a minority compared with the orthodox Mendelssohnians). The Conservatory of Music presented a soiree in which Schumann's Piano Quintet and First Piano Trio[58] were performed for the composer and his wife and the complete faculty, including Moscheles.[59] In the Gewandhaus concert of 18 March Schumann's latest symphony, in E♭ (the so-called "Rhenish" Symphony), was performed under his own direction. And as a farewell Frau Schumann gave another chamber music matinee in the Gewandhaus, at which Schumann's latest trio (in G minor, Op. 110) and the new violin sonata, among other pieces, were performed. On 23 March Schumann again departed from Leipzig. As far as I know this was the last time he stayed in that city, where he had spent the best years of his artistic life and had dreamed his dream of love with Clara.

I spoke with Schumann several more times before his departure. The most important was our conversation on the morning of 18 March. Once again he spoke earnestly of the Luther project and explained that he did not want to abandon the undertaking until our collaboration had brought it to fruition; he told me not to lose my courage and enthusiasm. He also spoke again of a comic opera, but I responded that I regarded the task as the most difficult of all because of the danger of a trite libretto and because I had no subject to suggest. "Look at Auerbach's *Dorfgeschichten*[60] again," said Schumann, "and see if there is something in them usable for a naive-comic opera libretto. I have already considered doing *Hermann und Dorothea*; that would surely do quite well for a charming, idyllic opera. I wrote the overture for it with great enthusiasm in just a few hours during Christmas (1851).[61] First let us try a fairy tale, something like *Der Rose Pilgerfahrt* in style and scope. But I want to have a truly mad spirit for this one. Just work out a wild and fantastic subject for me soon." I gladly promised to do so, for this was just what I wanted. Moved, I quickly said farewell to Schumann; I had no idea that this was the last time I would see him or speak with him!

There now ensued a period of perhaps half a year with no interaction between us. The reason was my regular involvement with the *Neue Zeitschrift für Musik* (founded by Schumann and taken over by Brendel), which occupied almost all my time.[62] It was Schumann himself, now indirectly, who prompted me to renew my correspondence with him. The son of Carl Maria von Weber, Max Maria von Weber (now Geheimer Regierungs-Rat in Berlin), was then living in Dresden, where he served as the royal director of railroads. I had many dealings at the home of the spirited man, who has since earned a name for himself as an author in his field, as well as the author of his father's biography[63] and a brilliant essayist. I followed with the greatest sympathy the poetic works that launched his career as a writer. In particular I esteemed very highly his epic *Rolands Graalfahrt* [Roland's pilgrimage to the Grail], which I had assisted in bringing to publication. Because of his official position, Weber did not want to divulge his authorship, so I arranged his first contacts with a young publisher. When the small, charming work appeared in 1852, it did not strike the chord in the general public that I had hoped for, but in educated circles it did arouse attention and a lively search for its author.

One day Weber showed me the following letter from Schumann, which had reached him through his publisher:

To the poet of the *Graalfahrt*: an artist, albeit not a member of the poet's guild, permits himself to send his greetings of honor. If he could, he would most gladly surround this poem with music, if it had need of this, if it were not already itself music. One thing is certain: like a pealing bell this poetry will resound throughout the German nation.

If the rumor were true that the poet is the offspring of a master whom musicians count among their greatest and dearest members, then the lines of this artist, who has occasionally encountered you in years past, if only fleetingly, would perhaps be warmly received.

But whoever he is, I thank the poet for the many noble hours of happiness his poem has brought me. May the acclaim beginning to sound from all sides spur him on to new creations.

Düsseldorf, 12 December 1852.

R.S.

·

This was the complete Schumann, seen from his most endearing side: the great artist who received talented young artistic colleagues with the warmest sympathy. Shortly thereafter he provided a splendid new display of this side in his highly regarded article in the *Neue Zeitschrift für Musik* that introduced *Johannes Brahms*.[64]

Schumann's letter made me all the happier because it confirmed my own opinion. I immediately expressed my pleasure by writing to Schumann that his guess had been correct and that I wholeheartedly agreed with his estimation of the young poetic talent. Now the proper subject had also been found for him; for although *Rolands Graalfahrt* could not be set to music, the same poet had earlier completed a most fantastic fairy tale, *Ritter Mond* [Knight moon], which might as well have been written for music. Surely Schumann needed only to express his interest in order to acquire the poet's permission.

Soon I received the following reply:

Düsseldorf, 27 December 1852

Honored sir and friend,

I was pleased to recognize your handwriting on the envelope. It has been so long since I have heard from you! Many thanks for what you said! It would certainly be a great pleasure for me to create something together with your estimable friend, but I hesitate to approach him directly, since the poet might think that my [first] letter to him, occasioned purely by my convictions, was intended to anticipate such an inquiry. Perhaps you could mediate in the matter.

Des Sängers Fluch is at last finished. I postponed the performance because I have no harpist here and I would very much miss that part at the first performance. Might it perhaps be arranged that your wife take over the part next winter? In any case I would at least like to send it to her and hear her opinion about this or that difficult passage.[65]

Hermann und Dorothea is lying dormant;[66] Luther, unfortunately, too. For almost half a year I lay sick in bed with a serious nervous disorder—perhaps the result of overwork. I have felt better for only five or six weeks now. But I still have to observe my plan to devote myself to larger works, to maintain the highest standards in all things. With a bit more treatment I hope to regain my former energy and health soon.

I would also like to hear how you are doing, whether life in Dresden is as you wished? I do not want to give up on *Luther*, and I hope you feel the same!

Hoping to hear from you again soon, I remain with best wishes and greetings,

Yours truly,
R. Schumann

It pained me to have to admit to Schumann that I had abandoned the Luther project, to which he clung so tenaciously. I took up the text once again, but was even more unable than before to rework it according to Schumann's wishes. Since I had become acquainted with Richard Wagner's dramatic-musical poems, I had completely abandoned the concert oratorio. I could still accept only the church oratorio, which in subject and treatment was (and had to remain) far from the stage. I was disinclined to say this openly to Schumann, so I delayed answering for so long—until I suddenly received another letter from him. It read:

Düsseldorf, 21 February 1853

Honored sir,

You seem to have forgotten me! Or have you perhaps not received my last letter, or misread it? I can hardly believe it. It would certainly please me greatly to collaborate with Max Maria. But I hesitate to write to him so soon after my first letter, as I told you.

The occasion for today's letter to you is once again a favor. I recently read Uhland's poem *Das Glück von Edenhall* [The lot of Lord Edenhall], and I believe it is beautifully suited for a musical setting. May I hope for your poetic assistance? If so, I would like to share my further thoughts on the matter with you. At any rate, the task would hardly be as involved as that for *Des Sängers Fluch*. It would make me most happy if you would respond in the affirmative.

How are you doing, honored sir? Will we not soon see you and your wife again on the Rhine? I intend to perform *Des Sängers Fluch* here at the beginning of winter and would hope for your wife's support. I will take the liberty of sending her the harp part as soon as possible.

Thus I ask once again to receive your kind regards; please let me soon hear a response to my proposal.

Yours truly,
R. Schumann

This letter put me in a newly awkward position. Once again a concert ballade! After the many hours of thankless work *Des Sängers Fluch* had cost me, I should not have been taken in by this new project—especially because I saw in it no potential for any substantial effect and, what is more, could not see what or how much reworking would be necessary. Ultimately, however, my respect for Schumann won the upper hand, and I agreed to work on the arrangement. But I also talked Weber into letting Schumann have his fantastic epic *Ritter Mond*. My expectations for Schumann with this subject were great, and, with the poet's permission, I offered my services to arrange it for musical composition. I sent Schumann Weber's original version and the realized sketch of my own rendition as quickly as possible.

I did not wait long for a reply. It came in a package containing Weber's poem, my Luther text, my text to *Des Sängers Fluch*, and the harp part to *Des Sängers Fluch*.

Düsseldorf, 18 March 1853

Honored sir,

With great regret I send the *Ritter Mond* back to you. I find the poetic invention of the poem outstanding, but I believe it is not suited for music. One dare not present the moon as a person, especially a singing one. I regret that you have undertaken such a large effort in vain for me. But in any case I am very thankful to you for having acquainted me with the original material, and I hope you will give my thanks to Max Maria for it.

A local acquaintance[67] arranged *Das Glück von Edenhall* before you kindly consented to do so, and I have even finished composing it. I only hope that you will nonetheless not withdraw your readiness to collaborate on future subjects.

Your Luther sketch is enclosed. I still cling with all my heart to this idea, the realization of which would do you no harm, either. I also enclose the harp part to *Des Sängers Fluch* for your wife. Tell her, with my best regards, that she should point out everything that is not playable. The harp is too difficult an instrument; the composer, creating from his imagination, cannot always find the easiest way of writing for it.

I likewise enclose the complete text to *Des Sängers Fluch*. Everything marked in red crayon is already composed. The passage you are considering is on pp. 10 and 11. If you can introduce rhymes here and there, that would be very much appreciated, but I think it is impossible for us to accommodate the pervasive meter of the ballade.

Thank you once again for all the kindness and goodness you have shown me. May I someday be allowed the pleasure of returning the favor.

With many greetings from

Yours truly,
R. Schumann

Please send the text of *Des Sängers Fluch* back to me.

.

Endearing and engaging though it was, this letter nonetheless annoyed me. So *Ritter Mond* was discarded—and for a reason that I could not accept. After the ancients had personified all the forces of nature and we had accepted their entire mythology without hesitation, I could not understand why romanticism could not claim the right to do the same. It was really rather irrelevant whether the moon was introduced as Selene, Luna, or Ritter; and it could not have appeared more daring to let the moon sing than to present a rose singing and speaking. But nothing more was to be said, for Schumann had declined the offer. I did not know how to find other, more poetic or fantastic subjects for him and thus considered my responsibility of searching for his material discharged.

His additional cuts to my text for *Des Sängers Fluch* also annoyed me. Schumann had simply deleted the large ensemble that sets up the catastrophe (a quartet of the king, queen, young man, and harpist, with chorus)—in my opinion the dramatic climax of the piece—from the grand middle scene, inserting instead a few words that I could neither change nor metrically alter, let alone versify, since they had already been composed. Of course this dampened my enthusiasm for any further efforts. To be sure, I was no less vain about my verses, but the issue here was that the cohesiveness and complete dramatic construction had been destroyed.

So for the moment I put aside my texts and devoted my attention to other pressing jobs, and in this way the year 1853 passed. I heard nothing more from Schumann[68] until suddenly the stunning reports reached us through the newspapers that on 27 February 1854 he had jumped into the Rhine. He had been saved, but was suffering from incurable mental illness.—

There was widespread shock and dismay about the truly tragic fate that had befallen one of our most noble spirits, and in particular I was deeply and permanently affected. I accused myself of having ignored the esteemed master more than I should have in those last months. Now, of course, it was too late! We still hoped for his recuperation in the sanitarium in Endenich, near Bonn. But in vain. On 28 July 1856 the noble, tenacious spirit passed away!

I have never doubted the causes of the mental illness that developed so rapidly in his last years. His system may well have been predisposed early on for this deterioration. But the breakdown could have been postponed for years if Schumann had not been so overworked, if he had taken better care of himself. I believe that the certificate provided by his doctor, Dr. Richarz in Endenich, which was later published by Wasielewski,[69] confirms this opinion. It states: "One of the primary external causes of this illness is excess stress, generally extreme physical activity, [and] I would say, intellectual excess—a danger to which artistic and especially musical creativity is easily susceptible."

The above letters demonstrate that Schumann had an irrepressible compulsion to work, particularly in his last years; catalogs of his compositions testify that he composed just as quickly, or perhaps more so, during these years than earlier. A decrease in productivity, quantitatively reckoned, was in no way evident—though qualitatively viewed there probably was a decline in his invention and freedom of form. Perhaps he forced himself to work more because he could not bear to rest and because he was still occupied with so many plans that he pursued them all the more doggedly as it became increasingly difficult for him to sustain his work.

Some secret, nagging worry may also have contributed to the decline of his noble spirit. The thoughtless fashion in which the directors of the collective *Musikvereine* in Düsseldorf relieved him of his duties as municipal music director in order to install the young Tausch in his position must have deeply wounded him. It was common knowledge that Schumann was not an adept, secure orchestra director — but of course, this was not his vocation. After all, the Düsseldorfers must have considered it an honor to number an artist of Schumann's caliber among their own. They could not abruptly remove the celebrated master from his worthy position; but in Tausch they could qui-

etly provide him with an assistant director, which in any case would
have been useful for Schumann. But Tausch wanted to become an independent music director—and Schumann was left by the wayside![70]

After more than twenty years people suddenly realized that Tausch
could not adequately represent Düsseldorf's musical affairs. Negotiations were initiated with *Johannes Brahms*, of whom Schumann had
prophesied a year before falling ill that this was the musician whose
arrival was necessary.[71] Schumann had anointed him as his legitimate
spiritual heir.

But when the invitation to become Schumann's successor in Düsseldorf reached Brahms, he respectfully declined. Brahms knew too
much of affairs in Düsseldorf; he knew what he was doing when he
declined.

Today, Robert Schumann is one of the favorite sons of the German
nation—more so than he was during his life. It is the same old story,
which remains ever new! Formerly derided as a romantic, he has already become a classicist.

"If his spirit were to come down to us today!" He would probably
smile in his amiable way at the great throng of disciples who now
swear by his name—and at the petty minds who play so merrily in his
domain and sap the strength of his intellectual estate.—

Appendix: An Unpublished Letter From
Robert Schumann to Richard Pohl

Düsseldorf, 6 February 1854

Honored sir,

Your letter has been found. Because it was pasted into my correspondence books it had to be cut into individual leaves. I thank you
for what you report about your other literary undertakings, especially
for the acoustic letters, less so for the Karlsruhe brochure.[72] Since you
now are closer to me through our many years of acquaintance, I always prefer to get straight to the point and tell the truth, as my conscience compels me. I had no idea that you were "Hoplit." For I do not
particularly agree with him and his party's enthusiasm for Liszt and
Wagner. Those whom they take to be musicians of the future I consider musicians of the present, and those whom they take as musicians
of the past (Bach, Handel, Beethoven) seem to me the best musicians
of the future. I can never regard spiritual beauty in its most beautiful
form as "an out-of-date view." Does Richard Wagner have this beauty?
And what of Liszt's genial achievements; where are they hiding? In his

Autograph letter (recto only) from Robert Schumann to Richard Pohl, dated Düsseldorf, 6 February 1854. Mary Flagler Cary Collection, Pierpont Morgan Library, New York (MFC S3925.P748) desk, perhaps? Does he perhaps wish to wait for the future because he fears he will not be understood now? I cannot concur with this enthusiasm for Liszt.

You also mentioned me in your brochure and discussed sympathetically the *Hamlet* Overture.[73] But elsewhere you vented your feelings about me in a fashion that leads me to believe you do not understand me. You speak of an absence of love for which no amount of reflection can compensate. Have you really considered what you wrote there? You speak of a lack of objectivity; have you considered this, too? Are my four symphonies all alike? Or my trios? Or my songs? And are there really two kinds of creativity, one objective and the other subjective? Was Beethoven an objective [composer]? Let me tell you: these are secrets that cannot be revealed with such miserable words. And then you speak of generic hybrids? Are you referring, perhaps, to the *Requiem for Mignon*, the *Nachtlied, Der Rose Pilgerfahrt, Der Königssohn, Des Sängers Fluch,* and the ballades that I still have in manuscript, *Vom Pagen und Königstochter* and *Das Glück von Edenhall*? Certainly I might yet decide to put these things away and intone my Requiem, which likewise still lies in my desk.[74]

My dear Mr. Hoplit! Humor is the main thing, and then, what you miss in my compositions, especially in the Lied "Du meine Seele," is love.[75] I will turn to these two main points in order to get over what you have done to me. And one more: as long as I have written publicly I have considered it a sacred duty to check every word I said most carefully. And now I have the continuing satisfaction, in publishing my collected writings, of being able to leave almost everything unchanged.[76] I am older than you, and through my many years of creating and working can penetrate into these secrets more deeply and clearly. Do not seek them in philosophical expressions or in subtle differences. A fool with a free, inward soul understood more of music than did the shrewdly thoughtful Kant. Now away, with a leap over the cleft that divides us! I prefer Richard Pohl to Hoplit. And this letter is addressed to the former, with old greetings.

R. Sch.

.

Düsseldorf, den 6ten Febr. 1854

Geehrter Herr,

   Ihr Brief hat sich gefunden. Da er in meine Correspondenzbücher eingeklebt war, mußte er in Blätter geschnitten werden. Was Sie mir sonst von Ihren literarischen Arbeiten mittheilen, dafür danke ich Ihnen, namentlich für die Akustischen Briefe, weniger für die Carlsruher Broschüre. Ich gehe immer gern gerade aus und sage dann, [weil] Sie mir durch langjährige Bekanntschaft näher stehen, nach Gewissenspflicht die Wahrheit. Daß Sie der Hoplit waren, das wußte ich gar nicht. Denn ich harmoniere nicht sonderlich mit seinem und seiner Parthey Liszt-Wagnerschen Enthusiasmus. Was Sie für Zukunfts-musiker halten, das halt' ich für Gegenwartsmusiker, und was Sie für Vergangenheitsmusiker (Bach, Händel, Beethoven), das scheinen mir die besten Zukunftsmusiker. Geistige Schönheit in schönster Form kann ich nie für "einen überwundenen Standpunkt" halten. Hat diese denn R. Wagner? Und wofür denn die genialen Leistungen Liszts—wo stecken sie? Vielleicht in seinem Pulte? Will er vielleicht die Zukunft abwarten weil er fürchtet, man versteh' ihn jetzt nicht? Ich kann nicht mit diesem Lisztschen Enthusiasmus harmonieren.

Sie haben auch mich in Ihrer Broschüre genannt und die Ouver-türe zu Hamlet mit grosser Theilnahme besprochen. Aber Sie haben auch an anderen Stellen über mich sich ausgelassen, daß ich glaube, Sie verstehen mich nicht. Sie sprechen von einem Fehlen von Liebe, die keine Reflexion ersetzen könne. Haben Sie sich wohl überlegt, was Sie da geschrieben haben? Sie sprechen von Mangel an Objectivät— haben Sie sich auch das überlegt? Meine vier Symphonien, sind sie eine wie die andere? oder meine Trios? oder meine Lieder? Ueber-haupt giebt es zweierlei Arten Schaffen? Ein ob- und subjectives? War Beethoven ein objectiver? Ich will Ihnen sagen: das sind Geheimnisse, denen man nicht mit so elenden Worten bekennen kann. Dann sprachen Sie von Zwischengattungen! Meinen Sie etwa das Requiem der Mignon—das Nachtlied, die Pilgerfahrt der Rose, den Kö-nigssohn und des Sängers Fluch, und die Manuskriptballaden, die ich noch habe, Vom Pagen und der Königstochter, das Glück von Edenhall —wie das könnte mich ja bestimmen, die Sachen zurückzulegen und mein Requiem anzustimmen, das auch noch im Pulte liegt!

Lieber Herr Hoplit! Der Humor ist die Hauptsache und dann, was Sie an meinen Compositionen vermissen und was namentlich dem Lied "Du meine Seele" fehlt, sei Liebe. Diese beiden Hauptsachen will ich anwenden, um über das, was Sie mir angethan, hinweg zu kom-men. Noch Eins: ich habe, so lang ich öffentlich schrieb, es für eine heilige Pflicht gehalten, jedes Wort, das ich aussprach, auf das Strengste zu prüfen. Ich habe jetzt auch die ständige Genugthuung, bei der neuen Ausgabe meiner Schriften fast alles unverändert stehen lassen zu können. Ich bin älter als Sie, ich blicke durch mein lang-jähriges Schaffen und Arbeiten tiefer und klarer in die Geheimnisse. Suchen Sie's nicht in philosophischen Ausdrücken, nicht in spitzfin-digen Unterscheidungen. Der Kerl mit freiem innigen Gemüth hat die Musik tiefer begriffen, als der scharfdenkende Kant. Nun mit einem Sprung über die Kluft, die uns getrennt, weg! Richard Pohl ist mir lieber als der Hoplit. An den Ersteren ist auch dieser Brief gerichtet, mit alten Grüssen.

R. Sch.

[Source: Mary Flagler Cary Collection, Pierpont Morgan Library, New York]

NOTES

1. C. A. Krebs (1804–80), pianist, conductor, and composer. [Ed.]

2. Like *Genoveva*, the original version, *Leonore, ou l'amour conjugal*, received only three performances (November 1805). A second version was given in 1806; and a third, the version usually performed today, in 1814. [Ed.]

3. Wagner's *Oper und Drama*, published in 1851 and revised in 1868, was later described by Richard Strauss as "the book of all books on music." It was the blueprint for Wagner's ideas on text and musical subjects first realized in the *Ring* cycle. [Trans.]

4. *Die Braut von Messina, oder die feindlichen Brüder* (The bride of Messina) (Tübingen, 1803) includes a lengthy preface on the use and function of the chorus in tragedy. [Trans.]

5. *Zukunftsdrama*, an allusion to the *Zukunftsmusik* associated with Wagner and Liszt. [Trans.]

6. Schiller's *Don Carlos* (Leipzig, 1799); *Wallenstein, ein dramatisches Gedicht* (Weimar, 1800); and *Wilhelm Tell* (Weimar, 1804). [Trans.]

7. E. F. Wenzel (1808–80), pupil of Friedrich Wieck and contributor to the *Neue Zeitschrift für Musik*. [Ed.]

8. Friedrich W. Whistling (1808–61), Leipzig music dealer who published several of Schumann's works. [Ed.]

9. Johann Zizka von Trocnow (1370–1424), hero during the Bohemian wars following the death of King Wenceszlas in 1419. [Trans.]

10. Sketched between 29 and 31 December 1850, orchestrated between 1 and 12 January 1851. Premiered in the Düsseldorf subscription concerts on 13 May 1851. [Pohl]

11. This detailed sketch encompasses four closely written pages. It is carefully worked out but requires too much involved discussion for here. [Pohl]

12. Johannes Hus (1361–1415), Czech priest executed as a heretic for his opposition to ecclesiastical dogma. [Trans.]

13. Schumann enclosed the libretto of Handel's *Israel in Egypt* in his package. [Pohl]

14. Katharina von Bora (b. 1499), a former nun whom Luther married in 1525. [Trans.]

15. Schumann may have recalled here Giacomo Meyerbeer's grand opera *Les Huguenots* (1836), which *begins* with an orchestral overture based on the

chorale, and which Schumann, in a celebrated review, had severely criticized for its theatrical effects as "leading to evil" (*Neue Zeitschrift für Musik* 7 [1837]: 73–75). [Ed.]

16. Ulrich von Hutten (1488–1523) and Franz von Sickingen (1481–1523), advocates of the Reformation who fought in the Knight's War of 1522; Hans Sachs (1494–1576), celebrated *Meistersinger*, prominent figure in Wagner's *Die Meistersinger von Nürnberg* (1868); and Lucas Cranach the Elder (1472–1553), German painter and engraver. [Ed.]

17. I had included these characters in my draft of the libretto. [Pohl]

18. This had been my idea, since I conceived the oratorio in the sacred style. [Pohl]

19. On a separate page. [Pohl]

20. The reference is probably to Carl von Winterfeld, *Der evangelische Kirchengesang und sein Verhältniß zur Kunst des Tonsatzes*, 4 vols. (Leipzig, 1843–47). [Trans.]

21. Pohl was probably thinking of Handel's *Israel in Egypt* (first performed in 1739), Bach's *Christmas Oratorio* (1732), and Mendelssohn's *St. Paul* (1836) and *Elijah* (1847). [Trans.]

22. Perhaps evidence of Pohl's Wagnerian aspirations: Wagner's *Ring* consists of a prologue and three music dramas, to be performed on separate evenings. [Ed.]

23. According to my plan the prelude would constitute the first evening's performance. [Pohl]

24. Including the prelude, there would be three parts. [Pohl]

25. Schumann had composed *Der Rose Pilgerfahrt* (first with piano accompaniment) from early April to mid-May, and then, from mid-May to mid-June, his *Königssohn*. [Pohl]

26. I had asked Schumann to deliver some of my lyric and epic poems to W[olfgang] Müller von Königswinter for his *Rheinisches Album* [Pohl]. Müller von Königswinter (1816–73) was a lyric and epic poet, novelist, and author of a ballade version of the Lorelei legend. [Trans.]

27. Johann Ludwig Uhland (1787–1862), poet, philologist, and literary historian. [Trans.]

28. Jelisaweta Borisnova Kulmann (1808–25), polylingual Russian translator of Milton, Metastasio, and Dante; her own collected poems were published posthumously in 1835. [Trans.]

29. *Des Sängers Fluch* concerns an old man (the harpist) and a youth (the singer), summoned by the king to serenade the queen, who has heard of the elder's musical talent. The old man warns the youth of the king's reputation as a man with a "stone heart" (no. 2), and the two appear before their audience. The youth first sings a folk song that so moves the queen that she falls in love with him; at the king's request for war songs, he is joined by the harpist. In no. 3, their music further arouses the queen's affections for the youth; the king, however, is angered when the music recounts that the harpist's brother had been murdered by the king years earlier. And when the king recognizes the

queen's attraction to the youth he sentences him to death. The chorus sings a lament (nos. 4 and 5), and the old man invokes a curse of famine and drought for the kingdom and of oblivion and a life devoid of music and song for the king (no. 6). [Trans.]

30. *Caeterum censeo* ("I censor the others"), reference to Cato the Elder (234–149 B.C.; also known as Cato the Censor), who, after an official visit to Carthage, ended all his speeches in the Roman senate with the line "Caeterum censeo, Carthaginem esse delendam" ("I censor the others; Carthage must be destroyed"). [Trans.]

31. I had written Schumann that I wished to visit Düsseldorf in August. [Pohl]

32. Robert and Clara traveled to and from the Antwerp competition between 16 and 22 August 1851. [Trans.]

33. *Der Rose Pilgerfahrt* (The pilgrimage of the rose), Op. 112, composed on a text of Moritz Horn in 1851 and published in 1852. [Trans.]

34. Jeremias Gotthelf, pseudonym for Albert Bitzius (1797–1854), Swiss poet and novelist whose works deal predominantly with the condition of the peasant class. [Trans.]

35. Robert Franz (1815–92), composer of songs and sacred works, author of monographs on Bach and Handel; Julius Tausch (1827–95), composer and conductor in Düsseldorf from October 1846, who succeeded Schumann in 1853. On Müller von Königswinter, see n. 26. [Trans.]

36. Liszt premiered Schumann's incidental music to Byron's *Manfred* as a dramatic production in Weimar on 13 June 1852. [Trans.]

37. Beethoven's overture and incidental music to Goethe's *Egmont*, Op. 85 (1809–10); and Mendelssohn's overture and incidental music to Shakespeare's *A Midsummer Night's Dream*, Opp. 21 and 61 (1826 and 1843). [Trans.]

38. I have indeed done this, though only since Schumann's death. My concert arrangement [of *Manfred*] was published by Breitkopf and Härtel in 1858 and is now used everywhere. [Pohl]

39. Posgaru (pseud.) published his annotated translation in Breslau in 1839. Adolf Böttger (1815–70), best known as translator of Byron, also translated Pope, Goldsmith, Milton, and Ossian, as well as Longfellow's *Song of Hiawatha*, and arranged the text for Schumann's *Das Paradies und die Peri*, Op. 50. [Trans.]

40. Eduard Devrient (1801–77), theater historian, librettist, actor, and baritone. He sang in Mendelssohn's revival of Bach's *St. Matthew Passion* at the Berlin Singakademie in 1829 and later became an advocate of Wagner and his ideas on theater. [Trans.]

41. The *Mädchenlieder*, Op. 103, and the *Sieben Lieder*, Op. 104. [Trans.]

42. Joseph Freiherr von Eichendorff (1788–1857), poet, novelist, and critic. His "Im Abendroth" was later used in Richard Strauss's *Vier letzte Lieder*. [Trans.]

43. The next year I wrote the second strophe, which Schumann approved. Later it was published in a new, separate edition of the Lied [Pohl]. On

the Eichendorff *Liederkreis*, Op. 39, see Jon W. Finson's essay on pp. 156–70. [Ed.]

44. Emanuel Geibel (1815–84). He collaborated with Mendelssohn on a libretto for the opera *Die Lorelei*, left unfinished at Mendelssohn's death in 1847, and with Paul Heyse on the *Spanisches Liederbuch*, of which some poems were later set by Hugo Wolf. *Page und Königskind* (Page and king's child) was published as Op. 140 in 1857 under the title *Vom Pagen und der Königstochter*. [Trans.]

45. In Karlsruhe I had become engaged to the harp virtuoso Jeannette Eyth and planned to come to Düsseldorf with her, where she wished to play in a concert conducted by Schumann. [Pohl]

46. Of course I demanded no honorarium from Schumann, but asked that he credit me with the ownership of the text when he sold the piece to publishers. Because publication occurred only after Schumann's death, however, this matter was not discussed further. [Pohl]

47. It had been premiered in November in the Leipzig Gewandhaus. [Pohl]

48. The bass Heinrich Behr (b. 1822) was active in both Bremen and Leipzig; Schumann dedicated the *Husarenlieder*, Op. 117, to him. [Trans.]

49. Moritz Horn (1814–74), actuary in Chemnitz. [Trans.]

50. Joseph Joachim (1831–1907), celebrated violinist; student of Ferdinand David at the Leipzig Conservatory; and friend of Mendelssohn, Schumann, and Brahms (see also n. 35). [Ed.]

51. Julius Rietz (1812–77), cellist, conductor, composer; succeeded Mendelssohn as Düsseldorf's municipal music director in 1835; later served as principal editor of the Mendelssohn *Gesamtausgabe*. There was no Singakademie in Leipzig; presumably Pohl refers to the Leipzig Liedertafel. [Trans.]

52. See p. 298, n. 23. [Ed.]

53. *Signale für die musikalische Welt*, influential music periodical based in Leipzig, published from 1842 to 1941. [Trans.]

54. See n. 36.

55. Ferdinand David (1810–73), violinist, composer, and pedagogue, concertmaster of the Leipzig Gewandhaus Orchestra from 1836. [Trans.]

56. Possibly the *Trois marches héroïques*, D. 602, *Trois marches militaires*, D. 733, or *Six grandes marches*, D. 819. [Trans.]

57. During the latter half of 1852 the *Neue Zeitschrift* ran a long series of articles and editorials on Wagner and "Wagnerismus"; Pohl became a regular contributor under the pseudonym "Hoplit" (see the appendix). [Trans.]

58. Piano Quintet in E♭, Op. 44, composed in 1842 and published in 1843; Piano Trio no. 1 in D minor, Op. 63, composed in 1847 and published in 1848. [Trans.]

59. Ignaz Moscheles (1794–1870), piano virtuoso, composer, and teacher. Schumann dedicated the Piano Sonata in F minor, Op. 14, to him. [Trans.]

60. Berthold Auerbach (1812–82), *Schwarzwälder Dorfgeschichten* (Village stories of the Black Forest), 4 vols. (Leipzig, 1843–53). [Trans.]

61. *Hermann und Dorothea*, Op. 136, published posthumously in 1857, was

inspired by Goethe's epic poem of the same name (Weimar, 1798). Schumann's overture is remembered today chiefly for its liberal use of the *Marseillaise*. [Trans.]

62. On Brendel's editorship of the *Neue Zeitschrift*, see Jurgen Thym, "Schumann in Brendel's *Neue Zeitschrift für Musik* from 1845 to 1856," in *Mendelssohn and Schumann: Essays on Their Music and Its Context*, ed. Jon W. Finson and R. Larry Todd (Durham, N.C., 1984), pp. 21–36. [Ed.]

63. Max Maria von Weber, *Carl Maria von Weber: Ein Lebensbild* (Leipzig, 1864–66). [Trans.]

64. Schumann's last published article, "Neue Bahnen," *Neue Zeitschrift für Musik* 39 (1853): 185–86. [Trans.]

65. The harp part was sent later, but it was never performed during Schumann's lifetime. The first performance took place in 1857 at the [Lower Rhine] Music Festival in Aachen, again conducted by Liszt. [Pohl]

66. Apparently, Schumann either already had an arrangement of the text at this time or was seriously planning one. It is not at all unlikely that he himself undertook the poetic reworking, at least at the stage of sketches. [Pohl]

67. Dr. [Ludwig] Hasenclever [1813–76] in Düsseldorf. The work was composed between 27 February and 12 March 1853. [Pohl]

68. Pohl notwithstanding, there was additional correspondence; Schumann wrote to him on 6 February 1854 (see the appendix). [Trans.]

69. Dr. Ludwig Richarz was the director of the sanitarium at Endenich, where Schumann spent his last years. Richarz's memo on Schumann's illness and death appears in Wilhelm Joseph von Wasielewski, *Robert Schumann: Eine Biographie*, 3d ed. (Bonn, 1880), pp. 298–301. [Trans.]

70. See also p. 297, n. 7. [Ed.]

71. See n. 64. [Ed.]

72. Between July 1852 and August 1853 Pohl authored (first anonymously, then under his own name) a series of "akustische Briefe" in the *Neue Zeitschrift für Musik*, dealing with musical acoustics from physical and philosophical points of view. The "Karlsruhe brochure" probably concerns the reopening on 1 April 1853 of the Karlsruhe Hoftheater, which had been closed for more than five years. [Trans.]

73. Probably the *Hamlet* Overture, Op. 4, by Joseph Joachim. [Ed.]

74. Schumann's Requiem, composed in 1852, was published as Op. 148 in 1864. [Trans.]

75. The song "Myrthen," Op. 25, no. 1, on a text by Friedrich Rückert. [Trans.]

76. Schumann refers to editorial work on his *Gesammelte Schriften* (Leipzig, 1854). [Trans.]

Robert Schumann in Endenich (1899)

EDUARD HANSLICK

TRANSLATED BY SUSAN GILLESPIE

The music critic Eduard Hanslick (1825–1904) played a vital role in Viennese musical life during the second half of the nineteenth century. During a period of some thirty years, from the 1860s to the 1890s, his reviews appeared in the *Neue freie Presse*, where he became identified as the champion of Brahms and outspoken critic of Wagner, Bruckner, and other composers associated with the movement of *Zukunftsmusik*. Hanslick's celebrated treatise on musical aesthetics, *Vom Musikalisch-Schönen*, was published in 1854, the year Schumann was hospitalized at Endenich; it ran to many editions and argued the case for music as an absolute, self-sufficient art. Hanslick found in the music of Mendelssohn, Schumann, and Brahms a distinguished tradition of German instrumental music on which to base his views. His essay on Schumann at Endenich provides a candid view of the composer's last years.

[Source: "Robert Schumann in Endenich, mit ungedruckten Briefen von ihm," in *Am Ende des Jahrhunderts* (Berlin, 1899), pp. 317–42.]

.

Soon half a century will have elapsed since Robert Schumann was installed (24 October 1850) as municipal music director in Düsseldorf. We know from his letters that he felt well and satisfied there during the first two years and only complained about the unaccustomed strain of conducting. We also know, however, that he was increasingly disturbed by a torturous state of nervous excitation that befell him and that he suffered from delusions, was pursued by voices and sounds and, finally, in an attack of overwhelming panic, abruptly left the house and threw himself from the Rhine bridge into the water. Rescued and brought home again, he soon recovered, but this rapid return to his old self did not last. Schumann felt so apprehensive about the nervous excitation that began to cast a veil over his mind that he himself asked to be admitted to a sanatorium. Because his condition in fact made continuous observation necessary, Schumann was brought on 4 March 1854 to the private insane asylum of Dr. Richarz in Endenich near Bonn, where he remained until his death (29 July 1856).

Schumann's condition during his stay at Endenich has been the subject, as I have frequently had occasion to observe, of quite erroneous impressions. It is understandable that the thought of a sanatorium of this kind inspires the most terrible images in most people. But these by no means always correspond to reality. Nothing is more incorrect than to imagine Schumann as a patient in whom every spark of mental ability had been extinguished or every thread that bound him to his surroundings torn asunder, as was the case with the unfortunate Lenau,[1] whose appearance made a lifelong impression on his friends as the most terrible memory. Nothing like this was the case with Schumann. Gentle and friendly, actually more communicative than in many of his healthy days, he conversed with his visiting friends Brahms and Joachim. He played music, read, wrote letters, and composed. His sickness expressed itself not in the alarming forms of exaltation or complete apathy but rather as a profound fatigue, a melancholic lassitude that might now and then cross over into flight of ideas.[2] I cannot forget the beautiful words that Ferdinand Hiller spoke at his friend's grave: "Your tired mind! You had demanded too much of it. Things that may be vouchsafed to a grateful recipient in an hour of grace, you demanded as the right of every moment. For a long time your mind obeyed willingly—and who can say how it came to be in conflict with you? Perhaps it was only a brief spat, of the kind that can occur between the best of friends, and only appeared to our shortsighted eyes as a quarrel, and you are now back on the best of terms and are smiling at everything we are saying about you here, smiling gently and forgiving us for it!"

I think it could only be comforting for all the admirers of this great artist and splendid human being to be given a more comforting description of Schumann's last days. No one can offer a more faithful rendition of this friendlier image than Schumann himself in the letters that he wrote from the sanatorium to his wife, Brahms, and Joachim. As I read these letters, I often felt as if the Schumann of the old days were looking at me with his gentle gaze and speaking in his familiar, quiet, friendly voice. The letters are invaluable contributions to our knowledge of Schumann, profound and deeply felt chords from his heart. It is impossible for the tender love of his wife, of the children, of friends, and, finally, of his art, to be expressed more movingly than in these letters from Endenich. How grateful Schumann shows himself to be for every little sign of love that Clara sends him; how tirelessly he reminds her of experiences they shared in happier days; how eagerly he comments on and praises the compositions of his two younger friends Joachim and Brahms!

Is it not our longstanding duty to transmit this evidence of Schumann's last thoughts and feelings, and with them a transfigured, purified image of the deceased, to the large and devoted community of his admirers? There are seven letters from Schumann to his wife, four to Brahms, and one to Joachim, which I publish here for the first time with the permission of the two last-named friends and of Schumann's eldest daughter, Fräulein Marie Schumann.[3] Half of the letters are available to me as originals, the other half in the form of copies made by Clara and Brahms. I have not permitted myself to make any changes in them, except to supply in brackets occasional words that were evidently omitted in haste.

I will precede the letters to Clara, which follow next, with a few necessary words of explanation.

Schumann's wedding day was 12 September; Clara's birthday, 13 September—this is why in his first letter, dated 14 September, Schumann expresses his joy that his wife wrote to him "on just such a day." The coincidence of important days of the calendar always struck Schumann as significant. Thus, in his second letter, he praises "the joyful message that Clara had given him a boy precisely in June." Schumann's birthday was June 10. The boy whose birth was announced in this way was named Felix,[4] as Schumann wished, in memory of the "unforgettable" Mendelssohn! His godfather was Brahms. Mendelssohn himself had lifted Schumann's eldest son, Ludwig,[5] from the baptismal font. It was a peculiar superstition of Schumann's that it was not a good idea for a child to receive the name of its godparent. Felix Schumann died of pulmonary tuberculosis at an early age and never saw his father. He was poetically inclined; one of his poems, "Meine Lieb' ist grün" ("My love is green"), gained fame through Brahms's setting (Op. 63, no. 5). Ferdinand,[6] Schumann's second son, took part in the campaign of 1870 and died as a result of the privations of the war. The eldest of the three sons, Ludwig, languished for many years in a sanatorium, from which death finally released him in January 1899. As for the daughters, Julie[7] died as the wife of an Italian count. The youngest daughter, Eugenie,[8] lives in London as a piano teacher. The two eldest, Marie (her mother's faithful companion and care giver) and Elise,[9] whose married name is von Sommerhoff, live in Frankfurt am Main.

The variations on a theme in E♭ major mentioned in the first letter have a strange history known only to Schumann's closest friends. One night, early in February 1854, Schumann suddenly rose from his bed and asked for light, since Franz Schubert had sent him a theme that he must write down immediately. On this theme in E♭ major he began to compose variations, as his illness was beginning to overtake him. On the unfortunate 27 February he suddenly leapt up in the midst of writing down the fifth, turbulently emotional variation, ran hatless from the house, and threw himself into the Rhine. Rescued from the waters and brought back home, he immediately sat down at his desk without a word and continued to write the variation exactly where he had left off. The variations have not been published, although the theme has been included in the supplementary volume of his collected compositions.[10] This same theme was given a moving resurrection and transfiguration in the variations for piano–four hands, Op. 23, of Brahms.

The other compositions by Schumann mentioned in the same letter are the ballad cycle *Vom Pagen und der Königstochter*, Op. 140, and the *Konzert-Allegro mit Introduktion* in D minor, Op. 134, dedicated to Brahms. The *Gesänge der Frühe*, the manuscript of which Schumann requested, are not songs but five piano pieces, Op. 123 [*recte* 133], "dedicated to the eminent poetess Bettina."[11] The low-German word *Läuschen*, which occurs in the third letter (and is familiar from Fritz Reuter's *Läuschen un[d] Rimels*,[12] was replaced by Joachim with the word *Ballade* in the printed edition of his *Drei Stücke für Violine und Piano*, Op. 5. "The theme on which you wrote variations" (in the fourth letter) refers to the Variations on a Theme by Robert Schumann, Op. 20, dedicated to him by Clara Schumann. Brahms took the same theme, in F♯ minor, as the basis of his Variations, Op. 9, and dedicated them to Clara Schumann. Schumann mentions these variations by Brahms in the later letters, as well.

The friends about whom Schumann inquired are the composer Woldemar Bargiel,[13] a stepbrother of Clara; the excellent conductor J. H. Verhulst, of the Hague (1816–91);[14] Lindhult, a voice teacher in Cologne; Julius Otto Grimm, Royal Music Director in Münster;[15] and finally Ernst Adolph Becker (not F. A. Becker, as Schumann erroneously identified him in his dedication of the *Nachtstücke*), born 1798 in Dresden, died 1874, examining magistrate in the bureau of mines ("Secretary of Mines") in Freiberg. He was a close friend of Schumann and in particular was his confidant in the tale of his love for and engagement to Clara Wieck. Schumann's "congratulations on the award in Holland" refers to the honorary degree given by the Amsterdam music society "Maatschappij tot Bevordering der Toonkunst."

The "order of the days in August: Clara, Aurora, Eusebius" (in the fifth letter) refers to another one of Schumann's sentimental calendar reminiscences. The name Clara falls on 12 August, Eusebius on 14 August. I have not been able to identify "Aurora" and her special meaning for Schumann.

In the last letter, dated 6 January 1855, Schumann refers to Brahms's Ballades, Op. 10. That he referred to the third Ballade (Intermezzo, B minor, 6/8) as "demonic," whereas Clara saw in it angels drifting through the blue sky, immediately made those in his vicinity anxious, and the plan to have Schumann released from the sanatorium was abandoned. Brahms himself was more inclined toward Schumann's point of view concerning the nature of the piece than toward Clara's.

Letters from Robert Schumann to Clara

Endenich, 14 September 1854

How overjoyed I was, beloved Clara, to see your handwriting! I thank you for writing on just such a day and [I thank] you and the dear children for still thinking of me with your accustomed love. Greet and kiss the little ones! If only just once I could see you and speak to you! But the distance is too great, after all. At least I would like to hear this much from you, how your life is in general, where you are living and whether you are playing as splendidly as you used to, whether Marie and Elise are progressing, whether they are still singing, too— whether you still have the Klems grand piano,[16] where my collection of scores (the printed ones) and the manuscripts have ended up, where our album is, the one that had the autograph manuscripts by Goethe, Jean Paul, Mozart, Beethoven, Weber, and many letters addressed to you and me,[17] and where the *Neue Zeitschrift für Musik* and my correspondence are. Do you still have all the letters and words of love that I wrote you and sent you in Paris from Vienna? Could you perhaps send me something interesting, for example the poems of Scherenberg,[18] a few earlier volumes of my journal, and the *Musikalische Haus- und Lebensregeln*?[19] I am also short of music paper, for sometimes I would like to write down some music. My life is very simple, and I continue to enjoy the lovely view toward Bonn, and, when I am there, the view of the Siebengebirge mountains and Godesburg, which you will also remember, how in the hottest sunshine I was working on the *Page* and had an attack of convulsions. Then, dear Clara, I would like to know whether you have been responsible for my clothing and whether it is you who has sometimes sent cigars? It means a lot to me to know that. Do write me in more detail about the children, whether they are still playing Beethoven, Mozart, and things from my *Jugendalbum*,[20] whether Julie continues to play, and how Ludwig, Ferdinand, and adorable Eugenie are doing. Oh, how I would love to hear your wonderful playing once more! Was it a dream that last winter we were in Holland and you were so brilliantly received everywhere, especially in Rotterdam, and they gave us a torchlight parade, and in the concerts the way you played the E♭-major Concerto, the Sonatas in C major and F minor by Beethoven, Etudes by Chopin, and *Lieder ohne Worte* by Mendelssohn, as well as my new *Concertstück* in D so magnificently? Do you still remember a theme in E♭ major that I heard one night and on which I wrote variations; could you send them to me and perhaps also include some of your compositions?

I have so many questions and requests—if only I could come to you and say them to you directly. If you wish to cast a veil over any of the things I have asked you about, do it. Adieu, beloved Clara and my dear children, and write soon. Your old, faithful

Robert

.

Endenich, 18 September 1854

Beloved Clara,

What joyful messages you have sent me once more, that heaven has given you a splendid boy, and in the month of June! That dear Marie and Elise performed the *Bilder aus Osten*[21] for you on your birthday, to your and my surprise; that Brahms, to whom you should please convey my friendly and respectful greeting, has now moved entirely to Düsseldorf—what joyful messages! If you would like to know what name I prefer above all others, you will probably guess it—the unforgettable one! I was glad to hear that the complete collected works have appeared as well as the Cello Concerto, the Violin Fantasy that Joachim played so magnificently, and the *Fughetten*.[22] Could you, since you have offered so kindly, send me one or the other of them? If you are writing to Joachim, give him my greetings. What have Brahms and Joachim written? Has the Overture to *Hamlet* come out, and did he finish his other one?[23] You write that you are giving the lessons in the piano room. Who are your students right now, and who are the best? Are you not overexerting yourself, dear Clara?

Evening, eight o'clock. I have just returned from Bonn, as always paying a visit to Beethoven's statue and delighted by it. As I was standing in front of it, the organ sounded from the cathedral. I am much stronger now and look much younger than in Düsseldorf. Now I should like to ask you a favor, that you should write to Dr. Peters that he should sometimes give me some money for things I want and you reimburse him. Often poor people ask me [for money], and then I feel sorry. Otherwise my life is not so eventful as before. How different it used to be! Give me news about the lives of our relatives and friends in Cologne, Leipzig, Dresden, and Berlin, about Woldemar, Dr. Härtel; you know them all.

Now I would like to recall some things for you, blissful times gone by, our trips to Switzerland, to Heidelberg, Lausanne, Vevey, Chamonix, then our trip to the Hague, where you accomplished the most amazing things, then the trips to Antwerp and Brussels, then the music festival in Düsseldorf, where my Fourth Symphony was performed for the first time and on the third day my Concerto in A minor, which you played so splendidly, to brilliant applause, the "Rhine" Overture,[24] with less brilliant applause. Do you remember, too, in Switzerland, how the Alps appeared for the first time in all their splendor, the coachman broke into a faster trot, and you felt just a little afraid? I have journals of all our trips, including the ones I made as a schoolboy and student—even better—would you give me the pleasure of sending me a volume of your diary and perhaps a copy of the loving words that I wrote to you in Paris from Vienna? Do you still have the little double portrait (by Rietschel[25] in Dresden)? You would make me very happy with it. Then I have a wish I would like to ask you, to tell me the children's birthdays; they were written in the little blue book.

Now I want to write to M. and E. [Marie and Elise], who sent me such warm greetings.

Adieu, most warmhearted Clara, don't forget me; write soon to your

Robert

·

Endenich, 26 September 1854

What joy, beloved Clara, you have given me once more with your letter and the package and the double portrait. My imagination was very

confused by the many sleepless nights, and now I see you once more
with your noble, serious features.

But what you wrote—gave me the warmest joy. Also what you said
about Brahms and Joachim and both of their compositions. I am surprised that Brahms is studying counterpoint,[26] which does not seem
at all like him. I would like to get to know Joachim's three pieces, for
piano and viola; do you remember the *Läuschen* for violin and pianoforte, that terrible piece? Many greetings to Woldemar, too.

I can remember Laurens's[27] portrait of Brahms but not of me.
Thank you for telling me the children's birthdays; who are to be the
godparents for the littlest one, and what church is he to be baptized
in? Write me more about the children and about yourself, warmly
beloved Clara.

Your
Robert

Endenich, 10 October 1854

Dearly beloved Clara, what a package of joy you have sent me once
again! Your letter, with Julie's; Brahms's composition, on the theme
on which you wrote variations; and the three volumes of the *Wunderhorn* by A. B.,[28] my favorite book, from which I composed many
pieces; and even included "Wenn ich ein Vöglein wär" in *Genoveva*.[29]
Do you remember how Golo sings it more and more boldly and accompanies the verses with different melodies?

Now thank you very warmly for the copy of the little poem that I
wrote to you in Paris from Vienna. I still like the anagram of Roma
(Amor) a lot. Sometimes I wish you could hear me playing fantasies at
the piano; those are my loveliest hours. I must study the variations by
Brahms more closely; I will write to him myself.

Perhaps, through your goodness, I could have another look at the
manuscript of the *Gesänge der Frühe?* What is happening with the publication of the *Concertstück* in D with orchestra, which you played so
beautifully in Amsterdam, and the second Spanish *Liederspiel?*[30]

Beloved Clara, you now have my congratulations for the honor in
Holland;[31] that was the first honorary degree I received. If you are
writing to Verhulst, give him my best. Who is Herr Lindhult? I
thought I saw him once in Düsseldorf; he didn't say much but seemed
to carry a lot within himself. I remember Herr Grimm very well, too;
we were always with him and Joachim in the cafeteria at the railway
station (in Hanover). Give him my greetings and especially Fräulein
Leser, too. I will write to Brahms myself, and to Marie and Julie. My

walks to Bonn continue, and I restore myself with the charming view of the Siebengebirge mountains; do you still remember how we climbed the Drachenfels and ran into a dignified clergyman? We had a hard time going against the current and getting to the island of Nonnenwerth. Now adieu, beloved Clara; greetings to everyone who remembers me.

Your
Robert

·

12 October 1854

I have just received your warm letter with the daguerreotype of little Marie, which still lingers in my memory. My thanks for the cigars, too, as well as the fourth volume of the *Wunderhorn*. I, too, remember the English chess book fondly, and it gives me pleasure to solve some of the unsolved games. I admire the Brahms variations more and more. Would you give him the enclosed letter? I am glad to hear that you have had news from Becker in Freiberg, too, and look forward to some possibility of receiving news from Härtel concerning the thematic index of my compositions.[32] Now I also have to tell you how much your variations delight me, more and more, and I remember your magnificent performance of them, and of mine too. I enjoy thinking about the poem to you, dear Clara, too, among my writings, and of the day in August when . . . the days followed in the order of Clara, Aurora, Eusebius, and I sent you my engagement ring via Becker. Do you remember Blankenburg, where I made you look for a diamond ring in a bouquet of flowers on your birthday, and you lost one of the diamonds in Düsseldorf and someone found it again! Those are blissful memories.

Write me even more, dear Clara, about the children. It was always hard for Ludwig to speak, but I wouldn't have thought this about Ferdinand. And write very soon and always such cheerful news. In old and new love, your devoted

Robert

·

From a letter dated 27 November 1854

The variations by Johannes delighted me on first reading and even more as I have gotten to know them. I will write to Brahms myself later; is his portrait, painted by de Laurens, still hanging in my study? He is one of the handsomest young men as well as one of the most brilliant. It delights me to remember the magnificent impression he made the first time with his Sonata in C major and later his F♯-minor Sonata and the Scherzo in E♭ minor.[33] If only I could hear him once more! I would like [to have] his Ballades,[34] as well.

6 January 1855

Now, my Clara, I would like to thank you most especially for the artists' letters, and Johannes for the Sonatas and Ballades. I know them now. The Sonatas—I remember hearing him play them once—and so deeply moved; everywhere full of genius, profound, moving, the way everything is woven together. And the Ballades—the first one wonderful, quite new; only the *doppio movimento*, the same as in the second one, I don't understand—doesn't it get too fast? The finale beautiful/strange! The second one—how different, full of variety to give rich sustenance to the imagination; there are magical sounds in it. The final F♯ bass seems to lead into the third Ballade. What is the word for it? Demonic—magnificent, and the way it gets more and more secretive after the *pp* in the trio; the latter altogether transfigured and the return and finale! Did this Ballade perhaps make a similar impression on you, dear Clara? In the fourth Ballade, how lovely, that the strange first note of the melody alternates back and forth in the finale between minor and major and then stays ruefully in major. Forward now to overtures and symphonies! Don't you prefer that to organ [music] too, my Clara? A symphony or opera that generates an enthusiastic response and much excitement is the quickest way to move all the other compositions forward, too. He must.

Now give Johannes my best greeting, and the children, and you, my heart's love, remember your long-loving, devoted

Robert

The following letters from Schumann to Brahms and Joachim need only a few introductory comments. As soon as he heard of Schumann's illness, Brahms immediately took up residence in Düsseldorf, in order to be near Frau Clara and her children, comforting and helping her in this difficult time of trial. Schumann had been the first to recognize and acknowledge young Brahms's great talent—now the family had the opportunity to get to know his heart. Brahms was the most frequent and welcome visitor at Endenich; he came once or twice a week to see the patient, who was devoted to him with tender affection. His appearance evidently had a friendly, calming effect on Schumann, with whom he conversed about his relatives and about music, and also played [piano]–four hands. Otherwise the doctor only rarely permitted close friends access to Schumann, who had to be sheltered from every form of excitement. Clara herself was allowed to see him only very shortly before his death, when he could no longer speak. Joachim wrote to me when he sent me the last letter from Schumann: "I visited Schumann three times in Endenich. The first time I had comforting impressions, his look was entirely the old friendly one, the affectionate, profoundly loyal gaze that shines forth from so many of his lines of music, dreaming of beautiful worlds. He spoke much, if hastily, inquired about friends and musical happenings, and showed me alphabetical lists of city names that he had assiduously compiled. When I was preparing to go, he took me aside mysteriously in a corner of the room (although we were not observed) and told me that he was longing to leave there; he had to leave Endenich, for the people there had no idea at all what he meant and wanted. It was like a knife in my heart! On parting he accompanied me a ways along the entrance road and then embraced me. (An attendant had followed at a distance.) The other two times unfortunately every ray of hope vanished; he had deteriorated visibly both physically and mentally. In feverish excitement he leafed through his earlier compositions, reproducing them in truncated form with trembling hands on the keyboard—heart- and ear-rending! The splendid man must have suffered beyond measure."

The compositions by Brahms that were mentioned in Schumann's letters are the Ballades, Op. 10, the Scherzo, Op. 4, the Six Songs, Op. 3, and finally the Variations in F♯ minor, Op. 9, which were already mentioned repeatedly to Clara.[35] The tenth variation (*poco Adagio*) contains the "memory that Clara wrote about," namely a recollection of the theme by Clara Wieck that Schumann had used as the basis of his poetic Impromptus, Op. 5. Along with Brahms, it was Joachim whose creative talents Schumann especially prized. The variations by Joachim that Schumann praised so warmly and characterized so well were published by Breitkopf as Op. 10.

The piano accompaniments to Paganini's Caprices,[36] written down by Schumann in Endenich, are in Joachim's possession in manuscript form. "They are," as Joachim wrote, "in a very simple harmonious mode, very clearly written and logical." We must by no means think in terms of a continuation of the two scores of Studies after Caprices by Paganini for piano by Schumann, Opp. 9 and 10, which are, for the most part free, independent inventions.

Jan Albert von Eycken (born 1822 in Holland), about whom Schumann asked Joachim, worked as an organist at the reform church in

Elberfeld from 1854 until his death in 1868.—Elisabeth Kulmann, whose poems Schumann requested, came from a German family in Alsace, was born in 1808 in St. Petersburg and died there in 1825. Schumann, who had an enthusiastic predilection for her poems (published in 1857 by K. F. Großheinrich), composed the *Mädchenlieder* for two soprano voices, Op. 103, in Düsseldorf, as well as the *Sieben Lieder*, Op. 104, on texts by her.

The poem by Friedrich Rückert that Clara sent Schumann "in the original" was a kind of thank you from the poet for the two little books of Lieder based on Rückert's *Liebesfrühling* that were published by Robert and Clara Schumann (Op. 37). The little-known poem may have a place here on account of its intimate reference to Schumann and as a virtuosic example of Rückert's rhyming art:[37]

An Robert und Clara Schumann

Lang ist's, lang,
Seit ich meinen Liebesfrühling sang;
Aus Herzensdrang,
Wie er entsprang,
Verklang in Einsamkeit der Klang.

Zwanzig Jahr'
Wurden's, da hört ich hier und dar
Der Vogelschar
Einen, der klar
Pfiff einen Ton, der dorther war.

Und nun gar
Kommt im einundzwanzigsten Jahr
Ein Vogelpaar,
Macht erst mir klar,
Daß nicht ein Ton verloren war.

Meine Lieder,
Singt ihr wieder,
Mein Empfinden
Klingt ihr wieder,
Mein Gefühl
Beschwingt ihr wieder,
Mich, wie schön
Verjüngt ihr wieder:
Nehmt meinen Dank, wenn auch die Welt,
Wie mir einst, ihren vorbehält.

To Robert and Clara Schumann

Long, it is long
Since I sang my love's springtime song
In yearning strong
My lonely heart
Echoing its silent part.

Twice ten years
Passed, and now and then I heard
A single bird
Who to my ears
Piped a tone that came from there.

  And now my dear
Along comes, in the twenty-first year,
  A feathered pair
And makes it clear
Not a single note has disappeared.

My songs
You sing again
My feelings
You sound again
My emotion
You move again
You make me young—
How fine—again.
You have my thanks, though the world again
May withhold its own, as it did then.

Letters from Robert Schumann to Brahms and Clara

Endenich, 27 November 1854

My dear Brahms! If only I could come to visit you, see and hear you again and your magnificent variations, or my Clara's, of whose wonderful performance Joachim has written to me. How the whole is so singularly rounded, with the wealth of imaginary brilliance we have come to expect from you, and then bound together in a way I had not expected from you, the theme surfacing here and there, surreptitiously, then so passionately and movingly. Then again the theme completely disappearing, and how magnificent the ending after the fourteenth one, so skillfully constructed as a canon at the second, the fifteenth in G♭ major with the second part so filled with genius, and the last one. And then I must thank you, dear Johannes, for all your friendship and generosity toward my Clara; she always writes to me about it. Yesterday, as you may know, she sent me some volumes of my compositions and the *Flegeljahre* by Jean Paul, to my joy. Now I hope to see something of you, too, in another form, although I treasure your handwriting. The winter is quite mild. You know the environs of Bonn; I always take pleasure in Beethoven's statue and the charming view of the Siebengebirge mountains. In Hanover we saw each other the last time. Only write soon, now, to your admiring and loving

R. Schumann

Endenich, 15 December 1854

Valued friend! If only I could come to you and Clara[38] at Christmas! In the meanwhile, I have received your portrait from my splendid wife, your familiar picture, and recall the spot in my room quite well—under the mirror. I am still elevated by your variations; I would like to hear many of them by you and my Clara; I have not mastered them completely, in particular the second one, nor the fourth in tempo, nor the fifth; but the eighth (and the slower ones) and the ninth—there seems to be a recollection about which Clara wrote to me, on p. 14; where is it taken from? From a song?—And the twelfth—oh, if only I could hear you play it! Clara has also sent me the poem Rückert wrote to us, the original; I am sorry about that, although it gives me great pleasure, since she has removed it from the album. She also wrote me about your Ballades; what works of yours have come out during our separation? Not the Scherzo? I am sure it has. How much pleasure it would give me if I [could] get to know some of your new pieces. Write soon again, dear Johannes, and about our friends, too. I am pleased to hear that they remembered me in Hamburg. [If only I] could see the city, which I saw some time after the fire, once more. Now I suppose you are back in Düsseldorf; we haven't seen each other since Hanover. Those were happy times. I am glad to have the pleasure of my girls Marie, Elise, Julie, and their significant talents. Do you listen to them sometimes? Adieu, my true friend; speak of me and continue to write. Your deeply devoted

Robert Schumann

Endenich, 11 March 1855

Dear friend,

Thank you for the package. The cravat fits me well. And the issues of the *Signale*[39] have given me much pleasure. I already wrote to Clara and Joachim that all that was new to me. How is it that the current volume 1855 is so incomplete? Only [nos.] 6, 8, 10, 11; and I have just now received no. 12.

I am planning to write as soon as possible to Dr. Härtel and offer him some things. I do not know for sure whether the pieces for cello and pianoforte are called *Fantasiestücke*.[40] I am hesitating about one of them, the last, although it seems to me the most significant; it starts in D major, the first trio in A major with wonderful basses (the cello sounded very good, but the violins did not). I wanted to ask you and Clara to have the piece by Fuchs copied and sent to me. Then I would like to inquire of Dr. Härtel about the Ballades and speak to him truthfully, in all modesty, if there is still time. The Scherzo was one of those pieces that had to be published, but one of your most difficult as to tempo. Recently I performed it satisfactorily, the way I wanted to. And the trios! And the finale! Scherzo! Isn't there another Sonata in F♯ minor available—for borrowing, that is? Would you remind Clara about the Caprices by Paganini, that she should send them to me soon, and, if I may ask, music paper (twelve-lined, actually twelve times five-lined). I am looking forward to it very much. The piano reduction for four hands of the *Fest-Ouvertüre mit Gesang über das Rheinweinlied* has now appeared from Simrock in Bonn. My wife wrote to me that she might be able to put together another new volume now. After Op. 123 she would have to start over; but on the back the consecutive numbers.

The walk recently was not far; it should have been much farther. Away from here completely! More than a year, since 4 March 1854, the exact same way of life, and the same view of Bonn. Somewhere else! You and Clara should think about it! Benrat is too close, but maybe Deutz, or Mühlheim.

Write to me soon! You say that I should think of you sometimes, dear Johannes—sometimes from morning to nightfall. So, adieu until we meet again soon,

Your R.

Endenich, March 1855

Your Second Sonata, my dear, brought me much closer to you again. It was completely unfamiliar to me; I live in your music, so that I can

play it more or less right away, straight off the page, one movement after another. For that I bring offerings of thanks. From the
very beginning, the *pp*, the whole movement—there has never
been one like it! The Andante and these variations, and then this
Scherzo, completely different from the others, and the finale, the
Sostenuto, the music at the beginning of the second part, the *Animato*
and the finale—bring a laurel wreath immediately for Johannes,
who is coming from somewhere else. And the Lieder, starting with
the very first one; I seemed to be familiar with the second; but the
third—it has a melody (at the beginning) that nice girls will swoon
over, and the splendid finale. The fourth quite original. In the fifth,
music so beautiful—like the poem. The sixth completely different from the others. The melody/harmony on-rushing, rustling, I
like it.

Next, many thanks for the things you sent, for the Caprices by Paganini and the music paper. Some of them (five) I have already har-
monized. But the work seems harder than my free treatment in the
past. The reason is, the bass so often lies in the violin, in its way. At any
rate my earlier piano solo arrangements would make the work now
much easier. Do you know the variations for pianoforte and viola by
Joachim in detail, dear Johannes? Have you heard them played by
Clara and Joachim, by chance? This is a work that, along with his
overtures, his *Fantasiestücke* for violin and pianoforte, even surpasses
them, pressing ahead into the most varied, fantastical regions. He has
learned secrets of the viola, the pianoforte; the first variation, right
away, I would like to hear played by Joachim—what a melody! The
second one, how different, the viola in lower chords. The fourth, like
a dream. In the fifth, the contradiction—very serious (at the finale an
excellent pedal point). The sixth, odd, on account of the theme in the
bass; the other voices play into it with the beginning of the same melody. The ninth, the tenth (gypsy and Hungarian character, as national
as it is possible to be), and the final variation complete the work, as one
showing the greatest mastery.

In the *Signale* I read that the city administration in Düsseldorf has
announced a competition for a new music director. Who could that
be? Not you? Perhaps Verhulst would be interested, if he were approached. They should do that.

One more plea for the poems of Elisabeth Kulmann and an atlas;
if I am not mistaken, maybe two years ago Herr Schuberth from
Hamburg sent two atlases as a present along with a large number of
other books.

Dear and honored friend, in your last letter you write: "You probably know, a poet does not like to invite guests to a poor table." How do you mean that? Adieu until soon.

Robert

A Letter to Joseph Joachim in Hanover

Endenich, 10 March 1855

Honored master!

Your letter put me in a very happy mood; your great gaps in your artistic education and the so-called violin eye and the salutation—nothing could have amused me more. Then I reflected: Overture to *Hamlet*—Overture to *Heinrich*—*Lindenrauschen* [Rustling linden trees], *Abendglocken* [Evening bells], Ballades—the volume for viola and pianoforte—the odd pieces that you played with Clara in Hanover one evening at the hotel, and as I kept thinking, I came up with the following opening for a letter: dear friend, if only I could have been the third member of the party! Reinecke[41] always used to tell me about the city. I would gladly have flown after you to Berlin, too. Johannes sent me the *Signale* last spring, to my great enjoyment. For everything that occurred during of 20 February [*sic*] was all new to me. And such a musical winter, and the following of 1854–55 never before; such traveling, flying from city to city—Frau Schröder-Devrient, Jenny Lind, Clara, Wilhelmine Clauß, Therese Milannollo, Fräulein Agnes Bury, Fräulein Jenny Ney, J. Joachim, Bazzini, Ernst, Vieuxtemps, the two Wieniawskis, Jul. Schulhoff, and as composer Rubinstein.[42] And then what a great mass of salon virtuosos and other significant figures, such as H. v. Bülow.[43]

I am also very happy that Reinecke has come to Barmen as music director. Barmen and Elberfeld are two musical towns. Do you know, perhaps, whether Van Eycken [*sic*] has been hired in Elberfeld? He plays quite splendidly; in Rotterdam I heard him [play] fugues by Bach, including the B A C H fugues, the first and last one on an organ that was worthy of him. Now I am keeping my eye out for you; come soon, even if it means carrying a torch. That would make me happy. I have a plan to harmonize the Caprices by Paganini, and not in a complicated canonical way like the A-minor variations but simply and therefore [have] written to a certain beloved woman who has them under lock and key. I fear she is worried that it might cause me exertion. I have already worked on a lot of it, and it is not possible for me to remain idle for a quarter of an hour, and Clara always sends me something so that I can amuse myself intellectually.

Thus I delve deeper into Johannes's music. The First Sonata, as the first published work, was one the likes of which had never existed, and all four movements a single whole. In this way one gets more deeply involved in the other works, for example the Ballades, the likes of which also never existed before. If only he, like you, honored friend, would go among the masses, the orchestra and chorus. That would be magnificent.

For today, we would like to close, as we are just reflecting on some people who so frequently move us in sacred hours, and say goodbye for today. May we meet again soon.

Your very devoted
R. Schumann

NOTES

1. The poet Nikolaus Lenau (1802–50), the "German Byron," who attempted to settle in the United States in 1832; he was overtaken by mental illness in 1844 and died in an asylum. [Ed.]

2. As authentic evidence I quote an unpublished letter from the director of the sanatorium, Dr. Peters, to Frau Clara Schumann: "Endenich, 1 April 1854 / I am glad to be able to tell you that the improved condition and more peaceful behavior of your husband has remained stable since Monday. Still very much in need of rest, he spent the greater part of the day, with the exception of the time that he spent, at his own request, taking a walk, napping on the sofa or preferably on the bed. No attacks of fearfulness were observed during this period, nor have the previous aural delusions recurred. On the whole he was gentle, friendly, quite unconstrained, but abrupt when it came to conversation. He has not been violent toward his attendant, as did occasionally occur at first. On the contrary, he was well disposed toward him and expressed his regret that he had earlier caused him considerable upset; yesterday, when he inquired about the date, he made a joke about April Fool's Day. On his walks he often looks for violets. His appearance is better; appetite and sleep are very good." [Hanslick]

3. Marie Schumann (1841–1929). [Ed.]

4. Felix Schumann (1854–78), who died of tuberculosis. [Ed.]

5. Ludwig Schumann (1848–99), who was hospitalized at Colditz. Hanslick is in error here, for Mendelssohn had died in November 1847. Hanslick may be referring instead to Schumann's first son, Emil (1846–47). See also p. 214. [Ed.]

6. Ferdinand Schumann (1849–91), who was confined from 1870 on to an asylum. [Ed.]

7. Julie Schumann (1845–72), who married the Count Vittorio Radicati di Marmorito in 1869; she died of tuberculosis. [Ed.]

8. Eugenie Schumann (1851–1938). [Ed.]

9. Elise Schumann (1843–1928). [Ed.]

10. It was included by Johannes Brahms in the supplementary volume, series 14, no. 9, of *Robert Schumann's Werke*, ed. Clara Schumann (Leipzig, 1893); the first edition of the complete set of variations was issued by Karl Geiringer in 1939. [Ed.]

11. Bettina von Arnim (1785–1859). [Ed.]

12. The German novelist Fritz Reuter (1810–74), who employed the North German dialect of Plattdeutsch in his writings. [Ed.]

13. Woldemar Bargiel (1828–97), a student at the Leipzig Conservatory, who held positions in Berlin, Cologne, and Rotterdam. [Ed.]

14. J.J.H. Verhulst, composer who conducted the Euterpe concert series in Leipzig. [Ed.]

15. J. O. Grimm (1827–1903), composer and conductor, student at the Leipzig Conservatory. [Ed.]

16. J. B. Klems (1812–72), Düsseldorf piano builder. [Ed.]

17. The album was assembled in 1845 by the Schumanns and is now in the Sächsische Landesbibliothek in Dresden. Parts of the album have been published in *Briefe und Gedichte aus dem Album Robert und Clara Schumanns*, ed. Wolfgang Boetticher (Leipzig, 1981). [Ed.]

18. Christian Friedrich Scherenberg (1798–1881), actor and poet. [Ed.]

19. See also pp. 175–76. [Ed.]

20. See Bernhard R. Appel's essay in this volume. [Ed.]

21. *Bilder aus Osten*, Op. 66, for piano–four hands (1848). [Ed.]

22. Schumann's Cello Concerto in A minor, Op. 129, Violin Fantasy, Op. 131, and *Sieben Klavierstücke in Fughettenform*, Op. 126, all of which appeared in 1854. [Ed.]

23. The Overtures to *Hamlet*, Op. 4, and to Herman Grimm's *Demetrius*, Op. 6. [Ed.]

24. The *Fest-Ouvertüre mit Gesang über das Rheinweinlied*, Op. 123, published in piano-vocal score in 1853. [Ed.]

25. The portraitist Ernst Rietschel (1804–61). [Ed.]

26. At this time Brahms was exchanging with Joachim contrapuntal exercises every fortnight. [Ed.]

27. J.-J.-B. Laurens (1801–90), French painter. [Ed.]

28. The collection of German folk tales, *Des Knaben Wunderhorn*, published by Clemens Brentano and Achim von Arnim between 1805 and 1808. [Ed.]

29. The duet between Golo and Genoveva in no. 9 of the second act. [Ed.]

30. The *Spanische Liebeslieder*, Op. 138 (1849). [Ed.]

31. See p. 272. [Ed.]

32. The *Thematisches Verzeichniss sämmtlicher in Druck erschienenen Werke Robert Schumanns*, ed. A. Dörffel, appeared from Breitkopf and Härtel in 1860. [Ed.]

33. Piano Sonata no. 1, Op. 1 (1853), Piano Sonata no. 2, Op. 2 (1853), and Scherzo in E♭ minor, Op. 4 (1854). [Ed.]

34. Ballades, Op. 10 (composed 1854, published 1856). [Ed.]

35. *Sechs Gesänge*, Op. 3 (1854), Variations, Op. 9 (1854). [Ed.]

36. Composed at Endenich between 1853 and 1855 but not published until 1941. [Ed.]

37. In the German, all the verses of each stanza end with the same masculine rhyme. [Trans.]

38. In the letters to Brahms, Schumann often uses the second-person plural (familiar form), a pronoun that may be interpreted to refer to Brahms and Clara together. In these letters, such references are translated "you and Clara." [Trans.]

39. The music journal *Signale für die musikalische Welt*. [Ed.]

40. Presumably the *Fünf Romanzen* for cello and piano (1853; now lost). [Ed.]

41. The composer Carl Reinecke (1824–1910), who studied at the Leipzig Conservatory during the 1840s. For his impressions of Schumann as a teacher, see Carl Reinecke, "Mendelssohn und Schumann als Lehrer," *Neue Zeitschrift für Musik* 78 (1911): 2–4. [Ed.]

42. The singer Wilhelmine Schröder-Devrient (1804–60); pianist Wilhelmine Clauß (1834–1907); violinist and composer Therese Milannollo (1827–1904); violinist Antonio Bazzini (1818–97); violinist and composer H. W. Ernst (1814–65); Belgian violinist and composer Henri Vieuxtemps (1820–81); the Wieniawski brothers Henryk (1835–80) and Jozef (1837–1912); the pianist and composer Julius Schulhoff (1825–98); and the Russian pianist-composer Anton Rubinstein (1829–94). [Ed.]

43. The conductor, pianist, and composer Hans von Bülow (1830–94). [Ed.]

Schumanniana (1925)

FREDERICK NIECKS

Among the earliest critical biographies of Schumann to appear in English was Frederick Niecks's *Robert Schumann*, which was issued first as a series of articles in the *Monthly Musical Record* between 1921 and 1923 as a "supplementary and corrective biography," and then as a book in 1925. The son of a violinist who played under Schumann during the Düsseldorf years, Niecks (1845–1924) studied philosophy in Leipzig before moving in 1868 to Edinburgh, where in 1891 he was appointed Reid Professor of Music at the university. In the closing pages of his biography, Niecks drew upon anecdotal accounts of his father, the violinist Joseph Joachim, and of other contemporaries of Schumann to accomplish a detailed sketch of Schumann's character and celebrated eccentricity—as Niecks put it, of that "dreamy self-obliviousness that seemed an inner state behind a veil." [Ed.]

[Source: Frederick Niecks, *Robert Schumann*, ed. Christina Niecks (London, 1925), pp. 290–94, 298–305.]

If we want to understand a man it is better to listen to his friends than to his enemies. Joachim found it difficult to believe that Schumann should have any enemies, and perhaps he had as few as any man can expect to have; but his ways were at times liable to give offence, and his friendships were not all free from friction. Among the most faithful and comprehending were the Bendemanns, Bendemann[1] even admonishing Schumann on occasion at the risk of offending him. At a party given by the Bendemanns Schumann sat the whole evening by himself in one of the inner rooms—they had several communicating rooms.[2] The pianoforte was in another room, and after playing, Clara joined her husband, who asked, "Who was playing?" "I." "Really?" And she wept. When supper-time came, Clara carried wine and food to him in his corner, and later went to him and said, "I feel unwell, shall we not go?" "But why should we go? It is so nice here." And they remained. At last Bendemann said to Schumann: "Although it is very impolite of a host to say so to a guest, I cannot help saying that you should have taken your wife home before now." Schumann said nothing but was angry. Next day Bendemann received a letter in which Schumann said in an irritated way that he did not need to be told of his wife's excellences, that he was well aware of them. Bendemann apologized, and the friendship was restored. On another occasion Bendemann called to take Schumann out and found him dressing. After fumbling with his tie for some time he called out, "Clara, my waistcoat." And she brought it, and afterwards his coat. Bendemann reproved him for this, but without convincing him. A conversation with Schumann rarely lasted more than ten minutes. As to likenesses, Bendemann said that the Rietschel medallion[3] is excellent; the whistling shape of the mouth, however, was in reality more marked—the artist had toned it down. (The Bendemanns never heard any whistling sound, but Frl. Hartmann stated that Schumann not only shaped his lips as if whistling, but did actually whistle—she had often heard it when sitting next him at table.) There is no painted portrait from life of any importance. Bendemann himself made a drawing from a photograph. The Bendemanns possessed a letter relating to the dedication of the *Bilder aus Osten*; and another, shorter, inviting them to stand godparents;[4] they are neatly written, only here and there indistinct. Bendemann remarked that the handwriting resembled Mendelssohn's.

Frl. Mathilde Hartmann,[5] an excellent amateur singer and friend of the Schumanns, was the first to sing the Rose in the *Pilgerfahrt*.[6] Soon after the first performance Schumann gave her the poem with a kind inscription, and later the pianoforte score with a dedication. She was much at the house, and as Schumann liked to sit next to her at table, Frau Schumann arranged it so. Although he talked little and fragmentarily, sometimes he spoke well—once she heard him talk very finely about painting with a painter sitting opposite him at table. He spoke softly: walked as if he had no bones in his body. Sometimes, after music and supper, there was dancing—Frl. Hartmann had seen him dance with his wife, when he looked like an amiable bear. He was very amiable. "Nobody accompanied me so well, not even his wife."

Herr *Justizrat* Herz (the reader will remember the trying part he had to play in the negotiations about conducting)[7] emphasized Schumann's kindly disposition; he himself had experienced no brusqueness from him. A letter he received from Schumann after the breach exonerated him from all blame. The step taken by the committee was, Dr. Herz said, necessary, and it was taken with all possible delicacy.[8]

Langhans,[9] my master, told me of his visit to Schumann when passing through Düsseldorf on his way to Paris with Japha (another well-known violinist).[10] They called on Schumann and were shown into a dark room; after some time Schumann appeared in the doorway, but having gazed into the room he vanished, shutting the door. After a further wait the two art-disciples asked if they had been announced to Dr. Schumann, and learned with amazement that he had gone out long ago. Langhans and Japha played string quartets with Ruppert Becker[11] and Bockmühl,[12] and when Schumann heard that his quartets had been played elsewhere he was vexed at not having been invited.

And now let us hear the wholly congenial and most loyal friend— Joachim.[13] He described Schumann as of noble appearance, and well-disposed and kindly in manner. If anyone or anything displeased him he simply turned away; he would not engage in exchange of words and argument. When he said, "He is not a gentleman" ("Das ist kein feiner Mann"), it was as much as to say, "I will have nothing to do with him." But he was in general so amiable that it is difficult to understand how he could have enemies. In Düsseldorf he had enemies, which may be ascribed to his distinguished, silent, reserved nature, than which the Düsseldorfers would have resented rudeness less. [This is hardly fair! (Christina Niecks)] Schumann was never witty in conversation, but pleasantly humorous, with a gentle touch of humour ("freundlich humoristisch, so ein leiser Anflug von Humor"). Once the topic of Hauptmann's book *Die Natur der Harmonik und der Metrik* [The nature of harmony and meter], new in 1853, came up.[14] Joachim said he found it difficult to read as he had not enough mathematical knowledge, and had not got beyond the thirtieth page. Schumann replied: "Indeed, did you get as far as that? I stuck at the first pages. It is not musical at all." Schumann had spoken or written to Joachim of a beautiful effect in a passage for the horns in his *Hamlet* Overture,[15] and Joachim inquired afterwards how they had sounded. "They didn't come in." "Perhaps the parts are not right?" "Yes, I saw to that myself." At the rehearsal the horns failed again. Instead of rating the players roundly Schumann turned sadly to Joachim and said, "They don't come in." Schumann never could conduct, Joachim said. In early days he may have beaten time accurately enough, but he made no remarks on the performances. At the rehearsal of *Paradise and the Peri* Clara (at the pianoforte) said: "My husband says that he wishes this passage *piano*"; and he stood by and nodded gratefully. Repetition without indication. If it did not go then, moral indignation. To the drummer in the A-minor Concerto: "Once again; *once* again; once again, you must count." And when the drummer came out with angry words Schumann was angry, and said, "That is impertinent." At a performance of one of his own symphonies he stood dreamily with raised baton, all the players ready and not knowing when to begin. Königslöw[16] and Joachim, who sat at the first desk, therefore took the matter into their own hands and began, Schumann following with a smile of pleasure. Of Schumann's musical sympathies and antipathies Joachim had little to tell me. He did not believe in the supposed antipathy to Haydn, but he remembered that Schumann said of the slow movement of a Haydn sonata for pianoforte and violin that one could no longer play such music. In later life he found all *tempi* too fast, and beat time with his foot, keeping back his wife's pace, for instance. In his last works the strong accentuation is striking, also a certain heaviness.

When Joachim visited Schumann at Endenich he talked about books and music, inquiring specially about Rubinstein, whose compositions were being much praised at the time.[17] Then Schumann led Joachim into a corner of the room, and said: "I cannot stay here any longer. They do not understand me." To Joachim's question whether he wished to go back to Düsseldorf, he answered: "Oh no, that is degradation." At the first visit Joachim thought that improvement might be hoped for; but at the second he thought Schumann's condition hopeless. He was trembling, and when he played Joachim his own compositions with trembling hands it was horrible to hear. When Joachim left, Schumann took his hat and said he would accompany him a little way. But at the door he stopped suddenly, nodded quickly, and said abruptly, "Adieu." Joachim inferred that Schumann imagined that he was being followed by attendants. . . .

Schumann [had] arrived in Düsseldorf on the 2d September, 1850, with his family, and full of joyful expectations; he left it on the 4th of March, 1854, accompanied by his physician and friend, Dr. Hasenclever,[18] and two keepers. Then followed two years of wretchedness in a private asylum at Endenich, near Bonn; after which, on the 29th of July, 1856, death laid his kind hand upon him.

At the time of Schumann's stay in Düsseldorf I was still a little boy; my personal recollections are therefore few and unimportant. I remember very well my father pointing him out to me as he was slowly walking by himself in the public park (Hofgarten). And I still see the quiet face, the protruding rounded lips (as if he were whistling, or pronouncing *O*), and the absorbed, absent look. I must often have seen him conduct, but remember distinctly only one occasion—namely, a rehearsal of a Mass at St. Maximilian's Church on a Saturday afternoon before some great church festival.[19] The organ-loft, the disposition of the chorus and orchestra, the bearing of the conductor, and the light that fell upon the group through the large windows behind them, form a picture indelibly impressed upon my mind. This was one of the occasions on which Schumann became so entirely oblivious of the work he was engaged on that he let his baton fall. With regard to this point, I must, however, caution the reader. For although I seem to remember the circumstance well enough, I still cannot help feeling a little doubtful about it. Memory often plays such curious tricks. It not only combines different events, but also what we have experienced with what we have been told. It is, however, an indubitable fact that Schumann let his baton fall on several occasions. My father told me often how one day at a rehearsal when this had happened, Schumann came up to him as he stood at his desk and showed him a baton with a string attached to it and to his wrist, and said with childlike simplicity and a satisfied and pleased expression on his face and in his voice, "Look, now it can't fall again!"

How Schumann's imagination was always busy is shown by the following occurrence:—At the first rehearsal of a new work of his one of the trombone players left out some notes intended by the composer, either because the passage was not in his part, or because he had made a mistake in counting. Schumann duly noted and pointed out the omission. After the same movement had been played at the second rehearsal, the composer turned to the trombone player in question, who this time had been as silent as on the previous occasion, and remarked: "It is all right now, and sounds very well."

Schumann's absent-mindedness led sometimes to curious encounters and scenes. Let me give two examples. Whilst a pupil of the Leipzig Conservatoire, Dr. Langhans played with some fellow-students a work of Schumann's at one of the evening entertainments of the institution. The composer, evidently pleased with the performance, sent word through Ferdinand Wenzel[20] to the young violinist to come to him. Inexpressibly happy, the youth hastened to the revered master. Imagine his feelings when, on presenting himself to Schumann, the latter remained dumb. After waiting respectfully for a while, the disappointed hero-worshipper ventured to say something; whereupon Schumann made an effort, and asked him: "What country do you come from?" and then relapsed into silence. A more interesting case is the following one. From 1849 to 1854 there existed at Paris a concert society, a "Société Sainte-Cécile," founded and conducted by François Jean-Baptiste Seghers.[21] The advancement of the art, not gain, was the object of all concerned in the undertaking. I have been told by a friend of mine, who was one of the body, that the executants gave their services gratis. M. Seghers and his enthusiastic supporters were especially anxious to make the Parisians acquainted with the best modern works. Among the various new compositions which were brought by them to a first hearing in Paris was Schumann's Overture to *Manfred*. The performance, however, gave rise to disagreements between the conductor and some of the players, among whom the Teutonic element was strongly represented. The question was: What are the *tempi* intended by the composer? To settle the debated points, Carl Witting, who was then preparing to go to Germany, was commissioned to visit Düsseldorf, and in the name of the Société Sainte-Cécile to lay the matter before the composer. Herr Witting arrived at Düsseldorf, called on Schumann, was received by him, and explained to him the object of his visit. When he had ended, and was looking forward to an answer that would set all doubt at rest, Schumann, who was smoking a cigar, said: "Do you smoke?" "Yes," was Herr Witting's reply. But the composer had already become—or, rather, had again become—oblivious of his visitor, for he neither offered him a cigar nor gave him an answer to his questions. After waiting for some time, Herr Witting made another attempt to get the desired information, but with exactly the same result—the words "Do you smoke?" followed by silence. A third attempt elicited as little as the two previous ones, and Herr Witting took his leave of the composer just as wise as when he greeted him on entering.

Although an eloquent writer, and, as Wasielewski relates,[22] occasionally expressing striking ideas in his conversations, Schumann was generally taciturn, and had much difficulty in finding words for what he had to say. "He could not say without breaking down once or twice, 'Ladies and gentlemen, our next rehearsal will be to-morrow at seven o'clock.'" These are my father's words, from whom I have also the following anecdote.

Schumann was in the habit of going in the evening to some restaurant to read the papers and drink a few glasses of beer or wine. He rarely continued to frequent any house for long, as he was sure to meet soon with something that annoyed him. At one time he took into favour Korn's restaurant on the *Hundsrücken*. On the very first evening, after a considerable stay, during which he read the papers, drank several glasses of beer, and ate something, he left without paying. The waiter noticed it, and was on the point of going after him; but the host, though he did not know his guest, would not permit this, being convinced that forgetfulness, not dishonesty, was at the bottom of the singular proceeding. "Let him alone," the host said; "he is a gentleman, take my word for it; he'll come back and pay." Part of the host's prophecy was fulfilled; Schumann came back, but he paid neither the old nor the new reckoning. The host, of course, thought this very strange. His confidence, however, remained unshaken. To satisfy his curiosity he inquired among his other guests if they knew the silent gentleman who sat apart from the rest. Some of them knew the Herr Music Director, and they advised him to send his account to Madame Schumann. This the host did after some time, and forthwith came the money, accompanied with thanks, and the request not to disturb her husband.

The relation between Schumann and his wife must have been very beautiful. We know from his literary works, and, still better, from his letters, how he loved her, and how she inspired him. Those who have lived near them know equally well how she watched over him, placed herself between the outside world and him, and prevented, as far as possible, those rubs which tortured his sensitive mind. Schumann, on the other hand, owing to his self-absorption, may have caused her unwittingly and unconsciously much annoyance, and even inflicted upon her many a severe pang. Of the two anecdotes I shall now tell, the second shows how precious her husband's approval was to Madame Schumann. Dr. Langhans met the composer and his wife at an evening party at the house of the Preussers in Leipzig.[23] It is needless to say that there was music. Among the works performed was Schumann's Quintet, in which Madame Schumann took the pianoforte part. In all this there is, of course, nothing remarkable; but the reader may perhaps think it sufficiently remarkable that the composer, to prevent the great pianist, his wife, from hurrying the *tempi*, beat time on her shoulders.[24] The next anecdote describes a scene which took place several years later at Düsseldorf. Madame Schumann had played at one of the subscription-concerts some unaccompanied solo pieces.[25] Her husband sat not far from her, behind the pianoforte. When she had finished there was a general rivalry among the audience and the musicians on the platform to give expression to their delight, which she, however, heeded little, for she saw her husband motionless and cold. "Have I not played well, Robert?" But there came no response, and she wept whilst the hall was ringing with ecstatic applause.

And now my last anecdote. At Düsseldorf I have often heard that when Schumann was rescued from the Rhine, into which he had thrown himself (on February 27, 1854), he spoke with rapture of the beautiful music he had heard in the river, and was inconsolable that he had not the power to write it down. Whether the story is based on fact, or is a product of the myth-making popular imagination, I cannot tell. The reader will remember the incident related by Wasielewski, namely, that shortly before this occurrence Schumann rose from his bed and asked for a light, as Schubert and Mendelssohn had sent him a theme which he must write down at once.[26] Afterward he wrote five variations on this theme. Brahms made use of it in his Variations for Four Hands, Op. 23.[27]

In the sub-title of these Schumanniana I promised "discussions," which discussions, however, are, strictly speaking, only *a* discussion, and the subject of it is Mendelssohn's opinion of Schumann. That Schumann admired and loved Mendelssohn *cannot* be doubted; it is patent to all that have eyes to see and ears to hear. That Mendelssohn was well-disposed towards Schumann *need* not be doubted; indeed, Hiller tells us (*Mendelssohn: Letters and Recollections*, Cologne, 1878) that Mendelssohn esteemed Schumann highly.[28] What may, however, well be doubted is whether Mendelssohn fully apprehended Schumann's greatness. Few, if any, writers, have dealt with this question in a satisfactory manner. Most of them are so anxious to free Mendelssohn from any possible blame that they rush into all sorts of inconsistencies and irrelevancies. Spitta, in his interesting biography of Schumann (in Grove's *Dictionary of Music and Musicians*) may be instanced. He writes as follows:

"Mendelssohn at first only saw in Schumann the man of letters and the art-critic. Like most productive musicians, he had a dislike to such men as a class, however much he might love and value single representatives, as was really the case with regard to Schumann. From this point of view must be regarded the expressions which he makes use of now and then in letters concerning Schumann as an author. (See *Mendelssohn's Briefe*, ii, 116; Lady Wallace's translation, ii, 97; and Hiller's *Felix Mendelssohn Bartholdy*, Cologne, 1878, p. 64.) If they sound somewhat disparaging, we must remember that it is not the personal Mendelssohn speaking against the personal Schumann, but rather the creative artist speaking against the critic, always in natural opposition to him. Indeed, it is obviously impossible to take such remarks in a disadvantageous sense, as Schumann quite agreed with Mendelssohn on the subject of criticism."[29]

To this statement of the case various objections may be urged: 1) that the passage in Mendelssohn's letter (30 January 1836)[30] alluded to by Spitta proves that the writer misunderstood Schumann's criticism (*Gesammelte Schriften*, vol. i, p. 139[31]); 2) that it is foolish to despise all critics alike, as the judgments of men possessed of the requisite technical and general knowledge cannot but be highly instructive to the artist, especially when the critic is a creative artist like Schumann; 3) that it is difficult to understand how an artist of Mendelssohn's culture could entertain so low an opinion of aesthetics, and not only of the philosophy of art, but also of the theory of art, as we find again and again expressed in his letters. These were deficiencies in Mendelssohn's mental constitution (or were they merely affectations?) which cannot be explained away. Another deficiency was his inability to comprehend Schumann. I look on the matter as an interesting psychological problem. Nothing could be farther from my mind than to accuse Mendelssohn of jealousy, or any kindred abomination. I simply suspect that he was one of the many great creative artists who, by the nature of their genius, were incapable of appreciating their differently gifted contemporaries. Let me point out some of the facts from which I have drawn my inference.

Mendelssohn, writing on [15] March 1835, from Düsseldorf to Frau Voigt,[32] of Leipzig, a friend of Schumann's (see *Acht Briefe*, Leipzig, 1871), remarks: "May I ask you to thank Herr Schumann in my name with friendly words for his friendly present. I should like to be a few days in Leipzig that I might tell him how many things in it are to my mind and please me, and again how other things do not. Indeed I feel certain he would become of my opinion if I could explain to him exactly what I mean. Among my favourites is no. 11 in F minor.[33] Once more please thank him very much, and tell him how much pleasure he has given me."[34] A passage in a letter addressed to Hiller, and written on 15 April 1839, runs thus: "One morning at a rehearsal somebody showed me a number of the *Neue Zeitschrift für Musik* (the editor of which, Schumann, was the whole winter in Vienna) wherein there was news concerning me."[35] This sounds rather distant. But the main fact is that in the Mendelssohn letters, published under the auspices of his family, the name of Schumann does not appear at all, not one of his compositions is alluded to.[36] And yet Mendelssohn wrote to his sister Fanny often and fully about new musical works, and must have heard, or at least got sight of, many of his great contemporary's compositions. For had not Schumann by the end of 1839 written all his important solo pianoforte pieces, in 1840 a large number of his best songs, in 1841 the First Symphony (which Mendelssohn himself conducted),[37] etc., in 1842 the string quartets (dedicated to his *friend* Mendelssohn) and the Pianoforte Quintet and Quartet, in 1843 *Paradise and the Peri*,[38] etc.? I therefore ask, Does not this silence speak with convincing eloquence?

NOTES

1. Eduard Bendemann (1811–89), painter of portraits and historical scenes, student of Wilhelm von Schadow in Düsseldorf, a professor at the Kunstakademie in Dresden, and a close friend of Mendelssohn and the Schumanns. [Ed.]

2. Possibly on 29 March 1846, described by Schumann as a "Matinée bei Bendemann," during which Mendelssohn and Clara performed Beethoven's "Appassionata" Sonata, works by Carl Maria von Weber (with Weber's widow in the audience), a Lied by Schubert, arias by Gluck (sung by Wilhelmine Schröder-Devrient), and pieces from Mendelssohn's incidental music to *A Midsummer Night's Dream*, Op. 61, played as a piano duet. See Robert Schumann, *Tagebücher, Band II: 1836–1854*, ed. Gerd Nauhaus (Leipzig, 1987), p. 399. [Ed.]

3. Ernst Rietschel (1804–61), sculptor. [Ed.]

4. For Emil Schumann, born on 8 February 1846. [Ed.]

5. Mathilde Hartmann (1817–1902), soprano. [Ed.]

6. In Düsseldorf on 5 February 1852. [Ed.]

7. The reference is to the difficulties Schumann experienced while he was municipal music director in Düsseldorf (1850–54). Already in 1851 press reports critical of Schumann's conducting had begun to appear; during the summer of 1852 Schumann's assistant, Julius Tausch, deputized for him; and on 7 November 1853 a committee, on which Justizrat Herz served, proposed to Schumann that he should conduct only his own works. The composer subsequently resigned his position. See Niecks, *Robert Schumann*, ed. Christina Niecks (London, 1925), p. 268. [Ed.]

8. For another view of the events leading up to Schumann's resignation in Düsseldorf, see Richard Pohl's account on pp. 258–59 here. [Ed.]

9. Dr. Wilhelm Langhans, violinist, composer, and writer on music. The young Niecks studied violin with him in Düsseldorf. [Ed.]

10. G. J. Japha, violinist. [Ed.]

11. Ruppert Becker, violinist, son of Schumann's friend C. F. Becker (1804–77), an organist, composer, and music critic who became the editor of the Leipzig *Allgemeine musikalische Zeitung* in 1844. [Ed.]

12. R. Bockmühl, amateur cellist. [Ed.]

13. Joseph Joachim (1831–1907), violinist, conductor, and composer. Studied under Ferdinand David in Leipzig and performed under Mendelssohn; later a close friend of Brahms. [Ed.]

14. Moritz Hauptmann (1792–1868), music theorist and violinist, Thomaskantor at the Thomaskirche in Leipzig, and friend of Mendelssohn. [Ed.]

15. *Hamlet* Overture, Op. 4, composed by Joachim c. 1855. [Ed.]

16. O. F. von Königslöw (1824–98), violinist, pupil of Moritz Hauptmann at the Leipzig Conservatory. [Ed.]

17. Anton Rubinstein (1829–94), Russian pianist and composer. [Ed.]

18. Dr. L. Hasenclever, who arranged the text after Uhland for Schumann's *Das Glück von Edenhall*, Op. 143 (1853). [Ed.]

19. Possibly of the *Kyrie* and *Gloria* of Schumann's Mass, Op. 147, which he directed in Düsseldorf on 3 March 1853. [Ed.]

20. E. F. Wenzel (1808–80), pianist who studied with Friedrich Wieck and then taught at the Leipzig Conservatory. A friend of Schumann, Wenzel contributed to the *Neue Zeitschrift für Musik*. [Ed.]

21. François J.-B. Seghers (1801–81), Belgian violinist and conductor. [Ed.]

22. See Wilhelm Joseph von Wasielewski, *Life of Robert Schumann*, trans. A. L. Alger (Boston, 1871; reprint, Detroit, 1975), p. 188. [Ed.]

23. G. L. Preusser (1796–1860), Leipzig merchant; his wife Emma (1817–68); and daughter Annette (1826–89), to whom Mendelssohn gave an autograph manuscript of the Six Organ Sonatas, Op. 65, in 1846. The party may have been on 14 March 1852 during a visit to Leipzig; Schumann noted in his diary: "Abends Gesellschaft bei Preussers. Musicirt" (Schumann, *Tagebücher, Band II*, p. 432). [Ed.]

24. Speaking of Leipzig, I may quote a passage from Hans Andersen's autobiography which, I think, is little known. It occurs in that part of the book which treats of the years 1840–44: "From Weimar I went to Leipsic, where a truly poetical evening awaited me with Robert Schumann. This great composer had a year before surprised me by the honour of dedicating to me the music which he had composed to four of my songs [Op. 40]; the lady of Dr. Frege, whose singing, so full of soul, has pleased and enchanted so many thousands, [was] accompanied [by] Clara Schumann, and the composer and the poet were alone the audience; a festive supper and a mutual interchange of ideas shortened the evening only too much." I have taken the liberty of inserting a few words which, I hope, the not very idiomatic translator will forgive [Niecks]. Andersen visited the Schumanns in Leipzig on 22 March 1842 (Schumann, *Tagebücher, Band II*, p. 217). Livia Frege (1818–91) was a soprano who sang the title role of Schumann's oratorio *Das Paradies und die Peri* in 1843. [Ed.]

25. During the early 1850s. The programs for several of the concerts are given in Rainer Grossimlinghaus, *Aus Liebe zur Musik: Zwei Jahrhunderte Musikleben in Düsseldorf* (Düsseldorf, 1989), pp. 41ff. [Ed.]

26. Wasielewski, *Life of Robert Schumann*, p. 185; see also Niecks, *Robert Schumann*, p. 287. [Ed.]

27. The theme and first four variations were completed before, and the fifth after, Schumann's plunge into the Rhine River. An edition was published by Karl Geiringer in 1939. [Ed.]

28. Ferdinand Hiller, *Mendelssohn: Letters and Recollections*, trans. M. E. von Glehn (London, 1874), p. 179. The composer and conductor Ferdinand Hiller (1811–85) was a close friend of Mendelssohn and Schumann. He served as municipal music director in Düsseldorf between 1847 and 1850, when, on his departure for a similar position in Cologne, he was replaced by Schumann. [Ed.]

29. George Grove, ed., *A Dictionary of Music and Musicians* (London, 1890), vol. 3, p. 393; *Letters of Felix Mendelssohn Bartholdy from 1833 to 1847*, ed. Paul and Carl Mendelssohn Bartholdy, trans. Lady Wallace (London, 1868). [Ed.]

30. The passage in the 1836 letter, from Mendelssohn to his older sister, Fanny Hensel, concerns the composer's reaction to a review Schumann had written of the *Melusine* Overture, Op. 32: "But as to the fabulous nonsense of the musical papers, about red coral and green sea-monsters, and magic palaces, and deep seas, this is stupid stuff, and fills me with amazement" (*Letters of Felix Mendelssohn Bartholdy from 1833 to 1847*, p. 95). In his review, which appeared in the *Neue Zeitschrift für Musik* at the end of 1835, Schumann had written: "Everyone will think of the gay pictures so favored by youthful fantasy—those legends of life in the marine abysses full of darting fish with golden scales, of pearls in open shells, of buried treasures which the sea has stolen from men, of emerald castles towering one over the other, and so on." Robert Schumann, *On Music and Musicians*, trans. P. Rosenfeld (New York, 1946), p. 203. [Ed.]

31. Robert Schumann, *Gesammelte Schriften über Musik und Musiker* (Leipzig, 1854), which reprints the *Melusine* review. [Ed.]

32. Henriette Voigt (1809–39), pianist, to whom Schumann dedicated the Piano Sonata in G minor, Op. 22. [Ed.]

33. The reference can only be to no. 14, "Estrella," of the *Carnaval*, which is in F minor. The only other early composition by Schumann which contains a no. 11 is the *Davidsbündler*; none of the numbers, however, is in F minor. As the *Carnaval*, although finished in 1835, shortly before the above letter was written, was not published till September 1837, Mendelssohn must have had a manuscript copy. This circumstance would explain the discrepancy with regard to the number of the piece, as Schumann may have subsequently changed the order of succession. The supposition of a slip of the pen on the part of Mendelssohn would, of course, explain the matter equally well. [Niecks]

34. Felix Mendelssohn, *Acht Briefe* (Leipzig, 1871), including his letters to Henriette Voigt (1809–39). [Ed.]

35. Hiller, *Mendelssohn: Letters and Recollections*, p. 136. [Ed.]

36. In a letter to Karl Klingemann of 31 January 1847, Mendelssohn alluded to some difficulties with Schumann but without specifying their nature; otherwise, the relationship between the two composers appears to have been unstrained. See *Felix Mendelssohn-Bartholdys Briefwechsel mit Legationsrat Karl Klingemann in London*, ed. Karl Klingemann (Essen, 1909), p. 320. Schumann's memoirs of Mendelssohn, penned after his death in 1847, display throughout an unreserved, admiring tone. As we now know (see pp. 225–26), after Schumann's hospitalization in 1854 Mendelssohn's brother Paul offered to assist Clara. [Ed.]

37. On Mendelssohn's role in the revision and premiere of the First Symphony, see Jon W. Finson, *Robert Schumann and the Study of Orchestral Composition: The Genesis of the First Symphony, Op. 38* (Oxford, 1989). [Ed.]

38. In 1844 Mendelssohn recommended Schumann's *Das Paradies und die*

Peri to the English publisher Edward Buxton: "I have read and heard this new work of Dr. Schumann with the greatest pleasure . . . and I think it a very impressive and noble work, full of many eminent beauties. As for expression and poetic feeling it ranks very high, the choruses are as effectively and as well written as the solo parts are melodious and winning." Letter of 27 January 1844, in Felix Mendelssohn, *Letters*, ed. G. Selden-Goth (New York, 1945), p. 331. [Ed.]

PART III

Criticism

On Robert Schumann's
Piano Compositions (1844)

CARL KOßMALY

TRANSLATED BY SUSAN GILLESPIE

The composer–music critic Carl Koßmaly (1812–93) was one of the original members of Schumann's *Davidsbund* (League of David), organized in 1834 to combat philistinism in music. Trained in Berlin, where he studied with Mendelssohn's teachers C. F. Zelter and Ludwig Berger between 1828 and 1830, Koßmaly held posts in Bremen and Detmold as a Kapellmeister, and in Stettin, where, after 1846, he served ably as an orchestral conductor. He received some recognition for his Lieder; in 1840, Schumann included one of Koßmaly's Byron settings in a supplement to the *Neue Zeitschrift für Musik*. As a critic, Koßmaly contributed to Schumann's journal and to the *Allgemeine musikalische Zeitung*, where in 1844 he published his review of Schumann's piano compositions, the earliest substantial essay devoted to the composer in the German press. Though couched in somewhat vague language, Koßmaly's review makes several crucial points: that in 1844 Schumann's piano music was not yet widely known; that the music was filled with bizarre mannerisms and technical difficulties that strained the understanding of the listener; that Schumann's more recent piano music revealed a marked stylistic simplification; and, finally, that for all its difficulties the piano music "must be counted among the most remarkable, significant artistic phenomena" of the time.

Responding to Koßmaly's review in a letter of 25 January 1844, Schumann observed: "So much in your essay has deeply pleased me. Concerning some points, you might be of a different mind, I believe, if we could just spend a longer time together. . . . You are the first to write an excellent word about me."[1] In 1856, when news of Schumann's death reached the United States, the Boston-based *Dwight's Journal of Music* ran parts of the essay,[2] which is presented here in its entirety in a newly prepared translation by Susan Gillespie. [Ed.]

[Source: *Allgemeine musikalische Zeitung* 46 (1844): 1–5, 17–21, 33–37.]

Momus may please the clamorous marketplace,
A noble heart prefers a nobler face.[3]

In every art, what is external and superficial is always more readily accepted, and light, traditional works tend to gain a certain validation and recognition more quickly than those that are truly fine and original. This applies to music as well. The composer who can capture and absorb the dominant trend, strike up a popular tune and willingly subordinate his ideas and feelings to the demands of fickle fashion and the changing wishes and desires of the common masses, or kowtow before the graven images of the present era—such a composer will always be more likely to enjoy a profitable result, and to see his efforts crowned with success and fame, than the tone poet who strives, above all, for originality, nature, and truth, who, fearing and despising the conventional and stereotypical, always creates out of the fullness of his own power, means, and abilities, driven by real inner necessity—in short, who wants to be self-contained and self-reliant.

This is an old truth that has long since become a truism, a fact sufficiently affirmed by numerous examples from the history of art of all nations and periods.

One should not conclude from this phenomenon, however, that there is greater aesthetic barbarism or degeneracy of taste in any one particular period of art. This occurs quite naturally and is easily explained by reasons we shall endeavor to elucidate below.

The ordinary and conventional, the average, the things that represent fashion for *tout le monde* and are immediately comprehensible and universally accessible, with their smooth sophistication, their blurred Everyman's physiognomy, and the lightness and ease that always characterize the mediocre (qualities that genius often lacks, precisely because genius bears a greater and heavier intellectual burden)—these things always find everywhere open doors and ears. Understanding them does not require any special mental effort, strain, or significant intellectual investment; we are not jolted out of our comfortable habits, as we definitely are in the case of artistic creations that are quite new and original and flow from the deepest wellspring of individuality, where at first people do not quite know what to make of them and are rendered shy and awkward precisely by what is new and unfamiliar. The more distinctly original these creations are, the greater the embarrassment in which people find themselves as to how they should react to and evaluate them, because the public is still lacking the intellectual means for coming to grips with the works in question and does not yet possess any appropriate standard by which to judge their true value.

Let us recall, for example, the uncertain, not at all favorable reception of *Iphigenie*,[4] *The Magic Flute, Don Giovanni, Figaro*, or the questionable, by no means general success of Beethoven's *Fidelio*, his symphonies, or Carl Maria von Weber's *Euryanthe*, and so forth.

But little by little this uncertainty among the public vanishes; gradually the light of recognition dawns in more and more minds; the mists of undeserved darkness in which the ignorance of the masses has allowed such a work to languish are dispersed by the rays of truth and of the irresistible argument of its greater merit.

This moment of accurate, just appreciation and recognition never fails to come to pass—even if, occasionally, it requires a longer period of time than usual. If a work is truly excellent, then no matter how long it has remained hidden and unknown, sooner or later its hour will come. Every artistic perfection, greatness, or beauty, every aspect of its profundity or genius, however fine it may be, is destined to find an echo in some fraternal human breast, some sympathetically resonating soul somewhere in life and in the world—often where one would least have expected it, beyond the scope of even the most far-reaching expectations.

The same can be predicted, without any particular gift of prophecy, for Robert Schumann's piano compositions, which currently find themselves in an analogous situation with regard to their recognition. In spite of their noteworthy and significant musical merit, they too have become known and recognized only among a small, albeit select and artistically knowledgeable, circle. The broader public has remained relatively untouched, and Schumann's works have not succeeded in reaching the popular masses; while at the same time many an empty, gussied-up mediocrity has been trumpeted in best Jericho fashion as a model of excellence and has gained a certain short-lived celebrity.

For these and related reasons—also because until now no detailed description but only isolated references have appeared in print about Schumann's musical achievements—we have decided to set down our opinions and convictions in a rather lengthy, separate article for the public. In giving practical expression to the principle that has always guided us, namely to promote the good and authentic wherever it may be found and to emphasize it in a way that befits its merit, we are afforded no small pleasure, in expressing our straightforward opinion, in giving the first impulse toward realizing our earlier prophecy —a prophecy that can seem excessively risky or problematic only to those unenlightened about the general evolution of the artistic spirit of humankind and the phases of the masses' intellectual progress.

To gain the proper critical and historical perspective on the subject under review, we may first look back at the musical situation of the past ten or fifteen years, the prevailing tendency in this period, and the most eminent phenomena or achievements in the realm of art. What we find, on the one hand, is an exaggerated predilection for mechanical skill, a preference for execution, excessively cultivated and developed virtuosity, and a bravura that defies all limits and far outstrips all hitherto known difficulties—in a word, a technique that has been driven to the extreme of perfection and is truly astonishing.

On the other hand, we find a more or less significant ebb in actual intellectual and spiritual production, a gradual retreat and drying up of the river of ideas that once flowed so profusely and powerfully, of the actual element of creative power—in short, a lack of natural genius and the disappearance of independent, original spirits.

We do not fail to recognize the manifold advantages of a constantly perfected and expanding technique, the value of technical skill cultivated with moderation and purpose, or the great benefits of continually increasing virtuosity. By virtue of the ever greater perfection and sureness of execution that such virtuosity entails, and of its ever more masterful control over the material means of expression, the sphere of the composer's ideas must perforce be extended, and—since there is less and less that is "impractical" or "unplayable," and the actual "difficulty" itself tends to disappear—he is naturally attracted to entirely foreign, original paths, and is inspired by the greater external freedom and ease, by the wealth of the powers he commands to entirely new, bold, and surprising combinations and to ever greater challenges in their execution.

We oppose only excess and exaggeration—a virtuosity that sees in itself the sole, ultimate aim of art, when, after all, virtuosity should be merely a means to serve the nobler purpose, the soul and spiritual expression in music. The new virtuosity would turn this around, as is unmistakably demonstrated by the so-called compositions of this genre, of whose meager content one may say, with Shakespeare: "His reasons are as two grains of wheat hid in two bushels of chaff."[5]

Following this necessary digression, we would like to reiterate that the foregoing description of the recent and contemporary state of musical affairs is meant in a general sense; there are and have always been exceptions—individuals who strive for higher, nobler goals—even in our own epoch.

These individuals, however, have had little success in counteracting the general abuses and exaggerations of virtuosity, and they have not always possessed a sufficiently forceful originality, nor has their talent mustered enough imposing intellectual strength to make a determined stand against the reigning taste (or lack of taste) and to force it to take a different, more authentic direction.

Under such circumstances it counts for a lot not only to have kept oneself afloat but to have remained in one's own current.

Such recognition must be given, without exception and in unusual measure, to the piano compositions of Robert Schumann. Although they are, for the most part, contemporaneous with the aforementioned tendency—which, we may note in passing, continues along the course of degeneration into ever greater superficiality, banality, and conceit—they have nevertheless remained untouched by the influences of that luxurious mind- and thought-destroying virtuosity; one might more readily reproach them with the opposite error, although this should only be called half an error, and then only in a certain sense, since it actually derives from a strength. Hippel[6] says that some virtues and faults have the same father and different mothers. One thing is certain—servile personalities can never fall into the error that is identified here.

Incidentally, we plan to return to this point again later and address it more fully at that time.

Since our goal cannot be to provide a complete critical dissection of every single work but instead, for the moment, only to encourage closer acquaintance with the composer and to draw greater attention to his achievements, we wish to focus for the most part only on those works by Schumann that are distinguished—at least in our opinion—by their notable originality and sharply characteristic traits. It is precisely these characteristics that most easily engender interesting and important aesthetic and art-philosophical observations, for they allow the richest harvest of all kinds of conclusions and discoveries in the realm of composition and therefore can lead to the essential enrichment and expansion of the knowledge of art. Precisely as a result of their more distinct physiognomy, these compositions are also better adapted for the formation of concrete and accurate judgments.

In all Schumann's compositions for the piano one can sense a constant striving for originality—originality of both form and content, even if the former is not always marked by uniformly fortunate results and the latter often can by no means be called uplifting. One cannot fail to note the powerful, lasting impressions that the study of classical models, such as Sebastian Bach or Beethoven, made on Schumann; on occasion the listener can even identify more recent composers, for example, Franz Schubert, Felix Mendelssohn Bartholdy, or Chopin.

It goes almost without saying that one must speak, in this case, not of actual reminiscences or intentional, slavish imitation but rather of works created in a similar tone and a related spirit—a distinction that is often overlooked by critics who are one-sided, narrow-minded, or self-consciously subjective and prejudiced.

The originality for which Schumann always strives does have a rather disturbing effect at times, when his intention always to be new and striking makes itself all too strongly felt. It annoys us even more, however, when this striving occasionally degenerates into the search for alienating, unheard-of phrases and completely unenjoyable bizarreness. For one thing, such a calculated, premeditated procedure destroys the God-given intellectual spontaneity, the happy lack of affectation, and inexpressibly magic naïveté that are the highest charm of every genuine work of art; it is also a persistent detriment to pure, peaceful, artistic beauty.

This holds true, in particular, for those pieces that belong to [Schumann's] earlier period, almost all of which suffer from confusion and overdecoration. And even if, according to Novalis's[7] dictum, the latter qualities almost always betray a wealth of ideas and a significant, though still disorderly, richness, the same poet states elsewhere that it is usually easier to understand the artificial than the natural and that more intelligence, but less talent, is required to create something simple than something complicated.

One may assume that sometimes Schumann may have created too much of a good thing precisely in order to express a stronger reaction against the commonplace and philistine, out of pleasure in high-spirited opposition or displeasure at shallow, frivolous, and unfocused virtuosity in general; that his work may have been too pithy, dense, and laden with meaning, so that it is often difficult to get through it, as if one were lost in a thick, overgrown forest, the path barred from moment to moment by mighty tree trunks or knotty roots, powerful vines and sharp thorns, and could escape only with difficulty.

But there is yet another probable cause that may have influenced the characteristics criticized above and that we would like to mention in passing.

Following Ludwig van Beethoven's overwhelming, titanlike appearance and the soulful-sounding and characteristic melodies of Carl Maria von Weber, following the compositions of the splendid, abundantly talented Franz Schubert, with their more than earthly glory, and the genuinely poetic and witty overtures of Felix Mendelssohn that illuminated the sky like meteors, it has become fashionable among music critics to speak of a "romantic music par excellence," as of a field that has only recently been opened up to music and must now continue to be cultivated.

"Musical romanticism"—people thought they had hooked some amazingly rare fish in the pond of musical terminology, whereas actually they had only come up with a strange, high-sounding name, a new slogan for something that we have essentially long possessed—admittedly to a lesser degree in some tone poets and a greater in others. Or are we not already surrounded, in Johann Sebastian Bach (see his two Passions, the B-minor Mass, and his keyboard compositions), in Handel's oratorios (*Saul, Samson, Jephtha, Semele*, etc.), not to mention *Don Giovanni* and *The Magic Flute*, by that wondrous, heavenly magic, that musical-romantic spirit, that later pours forth from the mighty symphonies, from *Der Freischütz* and *Euryanthe*, the Lieder with their profound sentiments and ideas, or the *Midsummer Night's Dream* and *Fingal's Cave* [Overtures], by the above-mentioned masters?

Be that as it may, as soon as this concept of "musical romanticism" emerged, in its excessive and exaggerated, one-sided, overly exclusive and hence erroneous form, with a tendency toward everything arbitrary, eccentric, and formless, it was precisely the most important and promising younger talents who came together to form a regular club, the first requirements and responsibilities of which included making up conscientiously for whatever might have been missed previously in the way of "romantic" arbitrariness, unruliness, and extravagance, by swearing a mutual oath to try to be as bizarre, strange, mystically profound, and extravagantly geniuslike as possible.

The idea was to be overflowing at every moment with the rarest perceptions, the noblest, most precious sentiments, so that one was prepared at any moment to utter the greatest profundities and the cleverest maxims and artistic truths, and to toss off the finest, most effusive subtleties as if they were so much dross. At the same time, naturally, things always occurred in such a way and were carefully arranged so that all these splendors were displayed in a fittingly public view.

This was called "new romanticism"; its proponents saw themselves as discoverers, prophets, and bringers of the new light—the romantically privileged new romantics, by the grace of God.

Our author must have been strongly, if only temporarily, infected by this so-called new romantic school. We now intend to prove our assertion, to illustrate and demonstrate its validity by returning to the above-mentioned works, which derive from an early period, and by pointing specifically to the actual compositions that betray the influence of new romanticism.

These include, for example: Allegro in B minor, Op. 8 (Leipzig: Friese [1835]); Symphonic Etudes, Op. 13 (Vienna: Haslinger [1837]); *Konzert ohne Orchester*, Op. 14 (ibid. [1836]); Sonata for Pianoforte, Op. 15[8] (Leipzig: Friese); [and] Fantasy, Op. 17 (Leipzig, Breitkopf and Härtel [1839]).

Much that is original, fine, and spiritually profound may be found in these youthful compositions; they contain many beauties that betray unusual talent, and many superb passages. Many a rare jewel sparkles among the last two works, in particular (Opp. 15 and 17), but they are still diamonds in the rough; they have not yet been cleansed of impurities and are still encrusted with common, less refined minerals and ores.

Along with the overdecoration and confusion that have already been criticized and that are maintained almost throughout, on every page one finds difficulties of the first and most perilous caliber piled up unnecessarily and to such a degree that even the best, most practiced performer, if he does not rank with the professional virtuosos, the Liszts and Thalbergs,[9] must quail before them and despair of achieving even a more or less satisfactory performance.

The richest harvest of wildly proliferating, highly unsatisfying outgrowths of new romantic hypergenius are undoubtedly found in the Fantasy for Pianoforte, which is dedicated to Liszt. Its eccentricity, arbitrariness, vagueness, and the nonclarity of its contours can hardly be surpassed. Here the extravagance of which the composer is so particularly fond sometimes degenerates into bombast and complete incomprehensibility, as the striving for originality occasionally loses its way, becoming overwrought and unnatural. To have recourse to a simile, the composer reminds us of a wealthy, distinguished man who, in the aristocratic conceit of making himself unapproachable, egotistically and stubbornly shuts himself off from the world, digs deep moats around his entire property, causes great hedges of thorn to be planted, warning shots to be fired, and traps to be laid, and so fences in and barricades himself that in the end people cannot help but be discouraged from making his acquaintance. The single and welcome exceptions are the *Davidsbündlertänze* and *Carnaval*. The former, which seem more like first drafts that have been dashed off than completed character pieces, nevertheless distinguish themselves by the variety and originality of their attitude and tone. This is also true of the latter, which are clever and interestingly handled "musical genre pictures" that sparkle with a certain *je ne sais quoi* of genuine French esprit and barbed wit. They are a genuine, fresh, fantastic masquerade, boisterous and colorful, full of high jinks and intrigue. But among the wild crowd of chaotically thronging figures, the tones of wanton pleasure that rise like champagne bubbles—touching and surprising us—there sometimes emerges a single seemingly lost note of gentle, sweet feeling and humoristic fulfillment and constancy.

If we look at Schumann's piano works in the order of their composition, it is interesting to observe how the composer gradually gains in simplicity and increasingly works his way toward spiritual autonomy.[10] Little by little the composer's real nature, his musical subjectivity, emerges more purely, distinctly, and independently, and at the same time one can sense a greater ease and conscious sureness in his treatment of the motives. The previously disturbing and awkward heavy-handedness vanishes, as the composer seeks to rid himself of all unnecessary baggage and incidental material and increasingly restricts himself to what is essential and inevitable. Whereas in the beginning he always wrote in such a difficult manner that—to use Börne's[11] expression—"the axle threatened to break under him," one can now entrust oneself to him with less risk.

Here one must mention the *Kinderszenen*, Op. 15 (Leipzig: Breitkopf and Härtel [1839]), which are unquestionably among Schumann's finest achievements in this genre and which we intend to discuss at some length. Thanks to a half-prophetic, half-poetic intuition and to that mental subtlety that is peculiar, in general, to an objective view of things, the composer has succeeded in immersing himself so completely in certain moods, states, and memorable moments of the child's world and in possessing it musically to such a degree that a thoughtful visitor must feel most intensely moved and vividly impressed by it. How is this unusual effect produced—how is the listener transported into such a perfect illusion? By the truth of the description, the naturalness of the coloration; because the tone poet has become utterly at one with his subject, has lived his way completely into or rather back to it, in a word: because he has most auspiciously achieved the gently naive, genuinely childlike tone that issues forth so sweetly and so free of care.

These *Kinderszenen* are the most convincing proof that even significant, characteristic elements can be pressed into a small space and the confines of a predetermined form, that it is not always necessary to give free reign to one's fantasy and throw oneself into the arms of accident and arbitrariness. Often precisely the most superior artistic minds feel goaded by a kind of noble and refined vanity, and pride themselves in submitting voluntarily to certain laws and rules, for they recognize quite clearly that it only enhances their reputation and increases their merit and triumph to have achieved something great and original thanks to or in spite of conforming to formal limits and constraints.

The *Arabeske*, Op. 18, and the *Blumenstück*, Op. 19, must also receive praiseworthy mention, albeit these works are notable more for their melodic flow, clarity, and songlike attitude than for any particular originality. The latter is somewhat compromised by an occasional family resemblance to Mendelssohn's *Lieder ohne Worte* and John Field's[12] nocturnes and romances. The character of the Fieldian cantilena, with its soft, enthusiastic, delicate, lyrical, almost feminine quality, can be heard unmistakably in both pieces; but one is not troubled by this resemblance. On the contrary, the effect is highly pleasant, because Schumann has understood how to add something that the Englishman [*sic*] never achieved and that raises Schumann far above John Field. This superiority is based on Schumann's harmonic treatment and all the other figures and accompanying forms, which are incomparably sounder, fuller, and more richly varied—in short, more artistically aware and complete—than is ever the case with John Field, where looseness and uncertain or arbitrary combinations almost betray the hand of a dilettante.

The *Humoreske* (Vienna: Pietro Mechetti [1839]) is more significant and autonomous, as is the Sonata in G minor (Leipzig: Breitkopf and Härtel [1839]). We confidently declare both works to be the most significant, outstanding showpieces of the entire collection, with its many fine, original works. In the *Humoreske*, the great variety of content and form, the continual and quick, although always natural and unforced succession of the most varied images, imaginary ideas and sentiments, fantastic and dreamlike phenomena swell and fade into one another, and not only maintain but continually increase one's interest from beginning to end.

One of the most difficult tasks of the aesthetic philosopher will always be to express musical effects in words, to use paraphrase to explain and give recognizable form to what is indescribable and immaterial. Whatever most intelligent, fine, and well-considered thoughts he may offer in this case, they will always appear imperfect, inadequate, cold, and forced compared with their subject.—But this will not deter us from at least making an attempt to sketch the impression that the *Humoreske* made on us, even if the result should be nothing but a half-measure, and an imprecise one at that. If the sketch turns out to be a purely subjective product of individual emotion, if we ourselves depart in our interpretation from the actual intentions of the composer, we will find solace in the general lot of commentators, who are often clever when it comes to discovering a number of things that the artist, in the rush of emotions and fired with enthusiasm, has unconsciously incorporated into his work, but on the other hand may also fail to notice other things that the artist inserted into the work with full awareness and clear intent. In addition, it is quite conceivable that there could be several different interpretations of the same work, each one eminently sensible, appropriate, intelligent, and capable, as it were, of opening some new door to understanding and providing the key to hitherto hidden secrets of the spirit—as Novalis seems to say, among other things, when he remarks somewhere "that a work is all the more interesting, and a genuine expression of personality, the more impulses it gives—the more meanings, varieties of interest, points of view, indeed the more ways it has of being understood and loved." This seems particularly applicable to the above-mentioned composition. If we therefore confess without further ado that we feel as if a completely unique, brisk but bracing freshness emanates from it, as if a pure Alpine breeze wafted over us and we were alternately surrounded by cascading forest streams in a youthful, fresh tumult; if we add that a peculiar, shudderingly sweet feeling of power, of intellectual fullness and health seems to characterize this *Humoreske*, which gradually communicates itself to the listener and fills him with a feeling of satisfaction that is as perfect, blissful, and profound as can be elicited only by those melodies that spring from the deepest, most secret source of the heart and from that genuine enthusiasm which transcends earthly bounds—then we believe that we shall not have missed the truth but instead come rather close to it, even if in our own way.

The G-minor Sonata would offer an even richer prize for commentary as well as significant material for all kinds of discussions and adventurous interpretations; however, we would like to confine ourselves to the observation that the composer made use, in this case, of the existing, traditional sonata form and has adhered to it with almost complete consistency.

What was said above regarding the *Kinderszenen* about the observation of certain limits and artistic laws may be taken to apply as well to the *Humoreske* and the G-minor Sonata; however, one must make the distinction that the plan and scope of the latter two compositions are incomparably broader and more significant, that their forms and dimensions are more fully imagined and larger and in them everything is more developed and worked out (whereas in the first they were sketchier and more hastily suggested), and that in general they reveal a higher, bolder flight of ideas.

The *Nachtstücke*, Op. 23 (Vienna: Mechetti [1840]), must also be mentioned; they are characterized, in their rhapsodic, arbitrary combinations, by something improvisational, something that seems to be borrowed from the moment, the accidental mood.

Also the *Faschingsschwank aus Wien*, Op. 26, a companion piece to *Carnaval*—at least one finds all the same colorful variety and bright, pleasantly effervescent mood. Humoristic heat lightning flits through all its segments, fireworks of wit and gay exuberance dart upward from all sides, and we are surrounded by hissing, mischievous bursts of roguish mockery and the most unrestrained frolicking, for example on pp. 7 and 8–9, where among other things the old-fashioned, narrow-minded and genuinely philistine motive "When grandfather took grandmother," which also appears in *Carnaval*, introduces a grotesque contrast and produces a genuinely comic rococo effect.[13] The musically most substantive of these fantastic images is unquestionably the Intermezzo (no. 4), which of all works in the collection appealed to us most strongly. Still, it is not easy to predict how such an ominous fellow, such a troublemaker and genuine grouch as this one, peering through the visor of his E-minor helmet, could mingle with the cheerful surroundings and turn up in this gay society. His rough, serious, severe tone, which has to cast a sudden deathly pale over all pleasure and good cheer, is certainly not well suited for the "prank" announced in the work's title. Once the listener has happily survived this Intermezzo, he draws as deep and free a breath as if he had been released from an evil spell, and is tempted to shout after it, as Shakespeare's Orlando did after Master Jacques: "I am glad of your departure; adieu, good Monsieur Melancholy."[14]

With this, we may consider our subject closed for the moment and end our discussion. Whether we have succeeded in achieving the impartiality that is essential in the search for and discovery of the truth in all things, and without which even the most enlightened art critic will never be able to offer anything of general validity and thoroughness, is left to the insight of others to decide. In any case, we can assure the reader that we have continually fixed our eye on this goal and have at least striven to reach it with our best efforts and goodwill, so that nothing, certainly, has been intentionally introduced into our work that could render the truth and competency of our statements suspicious or doubtful as a result of an excessively subjective view, private prejudice, or personal preference. Even if these statements may occasionally have taken on a critical cast, and whatever censures we may have occasionally found ourselves compelled to express, this much is certain and can be stated as the overall result of the present consideration: that Schumann's piano compositions must be counted among the most remarkable, significant artistic phenomena of our day, that they are characterized through and through by a great nobility of effort and incorporate many seeds of a new era.

Like everything profound and skillful, like everything serious and deeply personal, they, too, will make their way to the general public only gradually and with effort, and will only slowly win a larger audience and recognition; but then they will all the more certainly exercise a lasting influence on the entire direction of composition and on musical thought in particular. In the foregoing attempt to encourage greater attention for the compositions discussed here—however early or late they may come to enjoy success—we are animated by the conviction, the true interest in having performed a fundamental and useful service to the cause of art.

NOTES

1. F. Gustav Jansen, ed., *Robert Schumanns Briefe: Neue Folge*, 2d ed. (Leipzig, 1904), p. 235. [Ed.]

2. *Dwight's Journal of Music* 9 (1856): 173–75, 181–82. [Ed.]

3. Momus, in classical mythology, was the god of censure and mockery. [Ed.]

4. Either the opera *Iphigénie en Aulide* (1774) or *Iphigénie en Tauride* (1779) of C. W. Gluck. [Ed.]

5. *The Merchant of Venice* 1.1.116. [Ed.]

6. T. G. von Hippel (1741–96), whose writings, indebted to Laurence Sterne, influenced the work of Jean Paul Richter. [Ed.]

7. Novalis, pseudonym for the writer and poet G.F.P. von Hardenberg (1772–1801). [Ed.]

8. Koßmaly must mean either the Piano Sonata no. 1, Op. 11 (1836), or the Piano Sonata no. 2, Op. 22 (1839). [Ed.]

9. Sigismund Thalberg (1812–71), pianist, composer, and rival of Liszt. [Ed.]

10. On this point, see Anthony Newcomb, "Schumann and the Marketplace: From Butterflies to *Hausmusik*," in *Nineteenth-Century Piano Music*, ed. R. Larry Todd (New York, 1990), pp. 258–315. [Ed.]

11. Ludwig Börne (1786–1837), member of the Junges Deutschland movement in Germany. [Ed.]

12. John Field (1782–1837) was born in Ireland but spent most of his life in St. Petersburg and Moscow. A child prodigy as a pianist, he performed throughout Europe and was celebrated for creating the piano nocturne. [Ed.]

13. See also pp. 84ff. [Ed.]

14. *As You Like It* 3.2.311–12. [Ed.]

Robert Schumann with Reference to Mendelssohn-Bartholdy and the Development of Modern Music in General (1845)

FRANZ BRENDEL

TRANSLATED BY JÜRGEN THYM

Exhausted from ten years of strenuous duties as editor of the *Neue Zeitschrift für Musik* (which he had founded in 1834), and also desiring more time for composing, Robert Schumann sold his journal in 1844 to Franz Brendel (1811–68). Under Brendel's editorship the *Neue Zeitschrift* gradually became a mouthpiece of the "New German" (*Neudeutsche*) School, a label coined by Brendel in 1859 to encompass the music of Wagner, Liszt, and Berlioz, among others. Initially Brendel did not set out on such a radical turnabout, although the seeds for the later direction were planted early on in three major articles published in several 1845 and 1846 issues of the journal: "Zur Einleitung," "Robert Schumann mit Rücksicht auf Mendelssohn-Bartholdy und die Entwicklung der modernen Tonkunst überhaupt" (translated here in excerpts), and "Vergangenheit, Gegenwart und Zukunft der Oper." Brendel's attitude toward Mendelssohn and Schumann was ambivalent; neither of them thus far had contributed to a German national opera, "the art form that could best meet the political and cultural aspirations of a united Germany as it was envisioned in the *Vormärz* period leading up to the revolution of 1848."[1] He doubted that either composer would have any lasting significance for the fu-

The translator would like to thank John Rothgeb of the State University of New York, Binghamton, and R. Larry Todd of Duke University for their help in improving the wording of this translation.

ture development of music in Germany—Mendelssohn because of the retrospective and academic tendencies inherent in his music, Schumann because he was meandering between different compositional approaches and lacked a clearly perceived direction. Out of fairness and diplomacy Brendel left open the possibility that the two composers, especially Schumann, might be drawn eventually to the compositional direction he envisioned for the music of the future.[2] [Trans.]

[Source: Franz Brendel, "Robert Schumann mit Rücksicht auf Mendelssohn-Bartholdy und die Entwicklung der modernen Tonkunst überhaupt," *Neue Zeitschrift für Musik* 22 (1845): 63–67, 81–83, 89–92, 113–15, 121–23, 145–47, 149–50. Translated here are the second (pp. 81–83, 89–92) and fourth (pp. 121–23, 145–47, 149–50) parts.]

The work of art, like the living organism, is a unity of different parts; just as the organism divides into a multiplicity of members and organs, all supported by a pervasive unity and all segments of one organism, so the artwork divides into a multitude of ideas and emotional states, all originating in a basic idea and all having this basic idea as their foundation.—Thus, the evolution from lower to higher levels, from lower to higher species in the organic world, is characterized initially by the predominance on the lower level of a unity that lacks rich divisions and a multitude of organs, whereas on the higher level the multitude of differences appears ever more prominent. By analogy, these characteristics occur also in the development of art. For example, in the music of Haydn, Mozart, and Beethoven [we witness] a continuous evolution from a predominant unity, from the prevalence of a basic emotional state (*Grundstimmung*), to ever greater variety, to ever greater differentiation of this basic emotional state. Thus, when Haydn progresses to a richer type of expression, he does so by presenting different shadings of one color rather than different colors. Mozart offers us a rich portrait with the most diversified colors, but the differentiation is part of the general harmony; the basic unity provides a counterweight to the rich divisions and variety of colors and fuses all the individual aspects into one grand, total image. Beethoven, finally, pursues the different emotional states to their ultimate destination; as in the higher organisms, the parts appear in ever more developed, individual shapes. The strength of Beethoven's genius, however, is confirmed in that, after the most powerful struggle, after attending to the most diversified aspects, he is, in the end, able to develop an overriding perspective that controls these parts and forges them into a unity.

Beethoven created the most richly structured totality; he was led in this direction by historical necessity. At the same time this encouraged another characteristic, namely Beethoven's striving for expression as definite as possible. Because of his historical position, more than any of his predecessors Beethoven had to aim in purely instrumental music to express definite emotional states that could also be comprehended verbally. Indeed, the more he progressed in his creations and the more he established his personal voice, the more pronounced this characteristic became, so that we can speak of a progression from the indefinite to the definite as the developmental law of his genius. What we have just specified as the direction for all three masters, what even more comprehensively—in the turn from the epic to the dramatic—can be seen as the general developmental law for art, is repeated here in the individual and particular. We can therefore witness how in Beethoven the word finally struggles free of purely instrumental music, how everything instrumental no longer satisfies him, how he calls for the word, for poems to aid him, and how he links them with instrumental music in order to form an altogether definite impression and to achieve through the word the final precision still lacking in instrumental music. His Fantasy for pianoforte, orchestra, and chorus is proof of this approach, as is his Ninth Symphony, where Schiller's "Ode to Joy" is truly a consequence of the preceding instrumental music: the word serves the music and is called on for assistance in achieving the final definition that is otherwise lacking.

The more Beethoven strove for definite expression—and this now becomes a third perspective—the freer and more courageous the turns his imagination, in a parallel progression, took, and the more it exceeded the laws of a rational, musically logical elaboration. That beautiful balance of fantasy and logic which makes contrapuntal elaboration at once sound like the freest, most expressive invention is magnificent and unsurpassed in Mozart. Beethoven, in his way, achieved greater things, and yet in this regard he took second place to Mozart; his nature did not enable him to achieve his predecessor's unity and integration. In his later works he allowed his imagination an ever less restrained power, so much so that, liberated from the bonds of logic, it often reigned free, leading surely to bizarre and idiosyncratic results.[3]

As a consequence of all this, structure in [Beethoven's] great musical creations—in his symphonies, for example—had become so rich and manifold that initially no intensification seemed possible. Evidently art had reached, at least in this genre, its highest peak. Thus we see that younger composers who followed Beethoven consequently no longer used larger forms but instead were deeply and increasingly engaged in individual emotional states. They tried to turn them into ever more definite expressions; they sought to achieve fixed, self-contained tone paintings; and [in general] they recognized "characteristic" expression as the main goal of their efforts. A definite sentiment was [now] captured in a smaller frame; larger forms for a while fell into disuse, and the etude and similar genres, elevated to the status of character pieces through ever more significant poetic content, attained the widest predominance.

The comprehensive, integral, self-contained totality of the past disintegrates into its constituent parts; individual moods that once were only aspects of a larger whole now become independent and turn into objects of special creations. A particular, individual emotional state becomes the sole content of a piece of music; shorter compositions with different characters are strung together; a poetic idea provides the connecting thread; and coherence through technical means takes second place. Beethoven's quest for concreteness of expression, for the representation of definite psychological states, led to small character drawings with the most definite expressions in the briefest [temporal] space. The unchaining of fantasy completely emancipated earlier forms of elaboration, the earlier type of coherence based on technical means; and both tendencies together caused music to venture out from its immediate realm to representations based on poetic ideas. Here I have arrived at Schumann's artistic beginnings; his earliest compositions are, in the sense indicated here, narratives or cycles of interconnected lyrical poems. The poetic idea is predominant, and the parts are linked not by technical devices but by poetic threads.

The first such work in which Schumann's own voice manifests itself in a decisive, albeit not quite mature, fashion is *Papillons*. Later, of course, he wrote more comprehensive, mature works with a more concise content, a more developed consciousness and a richer treatment of the piano; but the *Papillons* are so characteristic, and I value them so much, that I cannot avoid stressing their significance, especially since, in my opinion, they belong to the more easily accessible works of this kind and thus are a suitable introduction for those still unfamiliar with Schumann's works.[4] The work was called "Butterflies" in order to convey at once its unusual character, its loose, poetic nature, and its desire to be absolved of all strictly musical requirements.

The subject matter, the fantastic image on which the composition is based, is the portrayal of a masked ball—neither a literal representation, of course, nor a tone painting of sequential events but a portrayal of the impressions, of the emotional states during a ball. Only in this way can such a composition be raised from the realm of the tasteless to the level of artistic creation. True, occasionally external events too are portrayed, but on the whole, subjective and objective aspects intermingle in a fantastic way.

Listening to dance music late at night stimulates a special fascination, when the more powerful moods of the day have yielded to nocturnal sensibilities. Aroused by conversation and the spirits of wine, one listens to the music from a distance, perhaps from an adjacent room. Indulging in such impressions, I know almost nothing that could stimulate the fantasy and sentiments more passionately and vigorously, not with beautiful harmonies but in a fantastic way. This emotional state is the basic mood of *Papillons*; it sets the scene, the perspective of the entire composition, and provides, at the same time, an interesting glimpse into Schumann's individuality. I have already noted that the composition does not contain objective portrayals; nor does the composer participate directly in the action. He only reproduces the moods and events of the ball in his imagination and offers fantastic enjoyment. Already the first piece, a slow waltz, articulates this nocturnal fantasy, this dream state, quite decisively; already this miniature displays Schumann's individuality. It is preceded by a brief introduction of four measures, which for me expresses the sentiments one feels upon entering the ballroom. In the second piece the dancers separate; the assembly swirls around in colorful ways. In no. 3 a clown makes an unexpected entry and entertains with a few buffoonlike gestures. A piece of passionate expression in 3/8 meter and a dreamy polonaise lead farther into the center of the scene. In no. 10 the ball music sounds as if from afar; a tender dialogue develops in an adjacent room. The lovers return to the ballroom, the doors are opened, and the dance music again becomes more audible. Then follows a polonaise with a stormy, lively character in the bright key of D major. The whole work is concluded by the "Großvater-Tanz"[5] with the melody of the opening waltz joining in; finally the guests retire, all become quiet, the lights go out, a clock strikes six times (the high A of the descant), the last guest steals away home, and one tone after the other dies away.

Thus Schumann begins in an entirely personal way, taking his own character as a point of departure. But at the same time it was the evolution of music that had necessarily led to such individuality and to such solutions for [musical] tasks. The same principle can also be observed in other spheres, in other artists, only conditioned differently by different individual characteristics.

Following *Papillons* are several works whose ideas are less clearly pronounced: a composition titled "Intermezzi," a set of variations [Impromptus on a Theme by Clara Wieck, Op. 5], and so on. As I remember these works—I intentionally avoided looking at the scores so that the details would not cloud the overall perspective—there is genius in them, but this genius is limited and does not yet manifest itself purely and clearly. Again significant and clear in this respect is the *Konzert ohne Orchester*, which so far appears even less known than Schumann's other works. The compositions just mentioned could be called transitional works, leading to compositions in which the direction first indicated in the *Papillons* finds perfection and completion, in which the fantastic structures appear most successful, and which, taken together, mark the first period of Schumann's compositional achievements: *Kinderszenen, Kreisleriana, Davidsbündlertänze, Fantasiestücke*, and several others.

Kinderszenen—perhaps the best among Schumann's earlier works— no more contain objective portrayals than do *Papillons*. Rather, they [*Kinderszenen*] depict an adult's naive emotional states, reminiscences of childhood, or—more precisely—states outgrown but still preserved in a more developed consciousness. These states appear here separately, and all the images and situations (the most beautiful pieces, "Glückes genug" [no. 5], "Träumendes Kind,"[6] and so on, must be interpreted in this way) are the signatures of a facile sensibility that has preserved a deep inwardness, a world of innocence. The expression is clear and simple; each movement is complete in itself, and the work demands less technical prowess. In the last movement [no. 13, "Der Dichter spricht"] the composer asks—if I interpret him correctly—why we should not turn our thoughts back to this beautiful childhood world and momentarily live in our memories.

In the *Fantasiestücke* I would like to call special attention to two numbers, one titled "Am Abend" [*recte* "Des Abends," no. 1], the other, "In der Nacht" [no. 5]. The first indulges our imagination with blissful pleasures, the light of spring and fragrant blossoms; the second, a powerful night music, brings ghostly, horrifying images and frightful dreams[7]—emotional states contrasting with those of the first piece. Schumann's compositions can often be compared to landscape paintings in which the foreground gains prominence in sharply delineated, clear contours while the background becomes blurred and vanishes in a limitless perspective. They may be compared to fog-covered landscapes from which only now and then an object emerges glowing in the sunlight. Thus the compositions contain certain, clear primary sections and others that do not protrude clearly at all but rather serve merely as backgrounds. Some passages are like points made prominent by the rays of the sun, whereas others vanish in blurry contours. These internal characteristics find their correlate in a technical device: Schumann likes to play with open pedal to let the harmonies appear in blurred contours. For this reason the performing artist must strive in these compositions less for the sharply delineated, rich sound of the modern piano virtuosos, and, in agreement with the idiosyncrasy just described, more for a greater tenderness and a certain murkiness in producing the sound—qualities that, of course, cannot be incorporated into public performances. All these remarks pertain especially to the latter composition.

The *Davidsbündlertänze* reveal the principal sides of the composer's individuality, which are here separated and juxtaposed as opposites: the tender, naive, and heartfelt; and the passionate, stormy, and fantastic. They appear as distinct entities under the names Florestan and Eusebius. We encounter again the naive intimacy of the *Kinderszenen*, turned more toward the medieval and romantic: this is the persona of Eusebius. He is opposed, however, by the passionate and agitated Florestan. This juxtaposition, this division of the composition into opposites, and these vacillations and struggles are deeply significant: they show humor to be the main principle in Schumann's early compositions—the same principle that had already gained ever greater prominence in Beethoven—and they point toward what must be considered the ideal of contemporary instrumental music. Among the younger composers, Schumann wrestles most decisively with the problem of apprehending and articulating this principle, and he does so chiefly in his first period.

But the most beautiful composition of the first stage of development is perhaps *Kreisleriana*. Here everything, excepting the last piece, is expressed clearly and precisely; here the forms have gained the highest degree of transparency, and at the same time the work contains the most magnificent outpourings. I consider this work one of the most beautiful pieces of contemporary piano music, and those who do not yet know it are simply at a loss. The earlier nocturnal humor appears clarified and purified, the excess of fantasy—as far as this is possible at this stage of creativity—has been channeled into the confines of distinct musical structures. Nevertheless, despite these confines the work shows everywhere the most abundant fantasy, animation in the world of fantasy, a fantastic manner that pervades the core of Schumann's individuality. Just as Goethe, for example, in the *West-Ostlicher Divan*[8] imagines being in the Orient, and just as he reproduces those experiences in his imagination (living through them in his imagination, not directly as events affecting him in the real world), so does Schumann appear to us in this work and most of his earlier compositions. They reveal a subject focused entirely on itself, one that lives and breathes exclusively in its own inwardness and only moves outward from this center into the external. This subject is not connected directly and intimately with the external, and it does not experience external circumstances personally and immediately; rather, it appropriates them through fantasy. It is an individuality that expresses only itself and its personal emotional states, but it depicts the world only as far as the Self has been touched by it. It is a subjectivity, evolving ever more concretely as part of the historical process and now manifesting itself to the extreme in a fashion governed by fantasy and humor.

With these and other, similar compositions, which I pass over so as not to become too discursive, we can conclude the discussion of Schumann's first compositional period. I have developed the historical basis and the artistic standpoint that are the conditions for these creations and from which alone they can be comprehended. In addition, I have discussed a few major works and their characteristic features. Now I still need to make some general remarks, pointing out also a few deficiencies of this approach and considering the public reaction so far to Schumann's works.

If fantasy has emancipated itself in the way described above from the intellect—that is, from contrapuntal elaboration—then it is obvious that the intellect, no longer integrated into a higher organic context, appears now as a separate faculty standing in opposition to fantasy. This explains, in addition to essential internal characteristics of the earlier works, one external feature, specifically the *naming* of the pieces. The intellect shows its separateness, shows that alongside the artistically creative consciousness there is, so to speak, [yet] another uninvolved facet, in that it reflects on the piece, adds the last possible degree of precision, confers a title on the piece, and thus connects it with a perfectly definite conception. Nearly all of Schumann's early works carry such names; he was the first to introduce such titles. True, earlier virtuosos occasionally added names to their compositions as well, but there they were merely extraneous titles without precise relation to the content of the music. With Schumann, however, they often serve (as, for example, in *Kinderszenen*) to give final definition to a piece. These titles have met, in part, with strong opposition; critics did not comprehend that they were only the result of reflection about an existing artwork and misunderstood them as the preexistent schema after which the composition was modeled. Considering these titles for what they really are, however, aestheticians cannot raise objections. The titles signify a direction, a stage of development in music.

Schumann wrote another work, similar in approach to *Papillons,* yet larger in scope and also technically more demanding; he called it *Carnaval.* Here the external separation of the intellect is particularly noticeable; here its disconnection affects even the shape of the work. Characters appear in disguise, in musical masks such as Chopin and Paganini as well as the traditional characters of the Italian carnival; in addition, Schumann himself enters in his dual role as Florestan and Eusebius, and the "Großvater-Tanz" returns, but in a strange harmonic parody under the title "March of the Davidsbündler against the Philistines." The work is witty and has beautiful, characteristic features. But because the intellect participated significantly in the composition, that is, extraneously, it also impresses itself on the listener, thereby revealing the shortcomings of this direction as well as the erroneous roads to which it can lead. The work is entirely removed from the realm of spontaneous artistic creation. Wit and cleverness play the principal roles. The composition is interesting as an essay in characterization in instrumental music; it is interesting in its attempt to draw character portraits within the limits of short instrumental movements. But the [listener's] sentiment receives only precious little nourishment; for the most part the intellect is occupied and even functions in the creative process as a separate faculty. Simply because the work, in order to be understood, requires knowledge of and acquaintance with the persons mentioned above robs it of its general impact and removes it from the general human sphere. Liszt selected it, because of its virtuosity, for public performance here several years ago;[9] as far as its content is concerned, in consideration of the peculiarities discussed above, he could not have made a more unfortunate choice. In conclusion I would like to point out the play with several letters of the alphabet—if I am not mistaken, those of Schumann's name—as a characteristic feature of the composition, which provides its individual movements with special links.[10]

These are in my opinion Schumann's most important early keyboard compositions, some of which have already been widely disseminated; but if we consider their inner worth, we soon notice that these works have not yet gained a popularity commensurate with their significance. External and internal reasons explain this phenomenon; in the remainder of this section I shall account for the most important reasons. Although the most significant artistic productions have been discussed in different journals, extremely little has been said about Schumann, who, more than anybody else, requires an introduction. Only his most recent and more elaborate compositions (at least some of them) have been reviewed thoroughly, whereas the earlier works

mentioned here have mostly eluded comment. Schumann's compositions are sometimes extremely difficult, not very rewarding [for the
performer], and far removed from the trappings of virtuosity. The
forms of early virtuosity were elevated by him to a more spiritual type
of expression; the empty passagework vanished with one stroke. The
technical difficulties thus are less audible, and as things have stood
until now—I say "stood," because soon the period of pretentious and
shallow virtuosity will have passed—works of this nature, accordingly,
have not been chosen by virtuosos for concert performance, and for
that reason they were necessarily deprived of a principal outlet. Critical reviews have been equally rare, and thus there has been no occasion to acquaint the general public with Schumann's works.

The essence [of music] is revealed only after extensive and detailed
studies. There are compositions that open up their inner core at first
glance and immediately yield the enjoyment they can offer; others
grant access slowly, after extensive efforts, yet their attractiveness remains undiminished, whereas the former soon lose their power. And
there are still others that combine both sides, works that have an immediate and permanent effect on us; this is particularly true of
Mozart. Schumann's works belong to the second category. Initially,
before the vast amount of notes has been properly understood, everything is chaotic and confusing, and only after the technical aspect has
been conquered does the inner core of the music begin to emerge.
This is a very important point. I know from numerous experiences
that many pianists were intimidated because they could not get a taste
for these works after reading through the scores, and thus were afraid
to put effort into studying the music.

A fourth reason lies in the modern, youthful approach of Schumann's works, a condition that makes the music less accessible to the
older generation. We encounter here the same phenomenon as in the
field of literature, where Heine is appreciated by the entire young
generation, while older people long denied him recognition. Finally,
we cannot conceal the deficiency that Schumann does not always succeed in finding an entirely clear, appropriate expression for his ideas
and that consequently some musicians were repulsed and did not
know how to find their way out of this chaos. Several of Schumann's
compositions merely show striving and struggle and are not free of
blemishes and confusion (less of ideas than of expression). His harmonic peculiarities cause offense as well, and considerable harshness
in the succession of his chords provokes concerns among connoisseurs. But this caveat, justified as it seems to be, needs to be stated
most cautiously. Similar criticism was directed against Beethoven,

even Mozart, and later generations held decidedly different views on this matter. The question is always whether such liberties are justified and appropriate, whether they are caused by inner necessity, or whether arbitrariness and artificial striving is the reason for the novelty. If the harmonic progression is the really suitable expression of a fine artistic mind, then it is justified regardless of what theory says; but if the particular progression is not caused by necessity and if it is not justified by the basic character and unity of the whole, then grammar steps in with its proper rights.

Herewith I may close the second section. The foundation on which Schumann's later creations have been erected, the individuality of his first period of creativity, its strengths and shortcomings, have been discussed, and also the external circumstances that until now prevented recognition of Schumann as the composer who embodies the new ideal of the time. The next installment will give us a chance to discuss the turning point, to study Schumann's later development, and to contrast him with Mendelssohn, the representative of the second principal direction of German contemporary music. Then we will have occasion to understand more precisely two of the most significant personalities and thereby get closer to the goal stated in the prospectus of our journal, namely to penetrate consciously all areas of contemporary music and, as far as possible, pave the way for an epoch of free creativity mediated by criticism.[11] Only a clear orientation can free us from dullness, from the triviality of ephemeral music literature; only [critical] thought can stem this senseless output, this constant repetition of what has already been done, by leading us to recognize what the times need and which direction young talents must take.

Both composers [Mendelssohn and Schumann] became active in an era of a more comprehensive and, in external matters, more intense creative activity. Mendelssohn composed overtures, symphonies, songs, larger piano works, the excellent Piano Trio [probably no. 1 in D minor, Op. 49], [the oratorio] *St. Paul*, and all the other great works that gained him an ever higher recognition in the musical world. Schumann, initially and until most recently, wrote a large number of songs, the symphonies (of which especially the First is excellent), then the [String] Quartets, the Piano Quintet and Piano Quartet, and the *Peri*, his largest composition [*Das Paradies und die Peri*, Op. 50]. All that has been said so far summarizes the major achievements of both composers: Mendelssohn animates traditional forms, infusing them with his individuality; on the basis of tradition, he addresses new tasks. Schumann, on the other hand, emerges from his inwardness; he moves away from the fantastic humor and indulgence in fantasy of his earlier works and comes closer to an objective style and expression. Restless, passionate agitation gives way to a more restrained type of expression, traditional forms replace the self-generated ones, and the quest for definite expression reaches its peak when the composer enters the field of vocal music. Whereas initially and with great insistence he wrote only for piano, as if to limit himself exclusively to this instrument, now he devoted himself with the same eagerness to vocal and orchestral works, and he composed a large number of songs, all written at the same time;[12] some are now in the process of being published, whereas others have already appeared.

Schumann's songs are in a certain sense a continuation of his character pieces for piano, and in several respects their nature is determined by the qualities of those pieces. Their definiteness of expression has now reached its conclusion through the presence of a text. The melodic element has become autonomous in the vocal, whereas the rich piano texture has been retained, often constituting in the accompaniment the most important aspect of the songs. That the [instrumental] composer has written is evident everywhere. It is not the enthusiasm of the vocal composer, and not—or not so much—the desire to express the sentiment of the poem in the vocal part and to concentrate all expression therein, that has been the generating force behind these songs. Rather, it is a general musico-poetic enthusiasm, which strives to capture the content of the songs through exclusively musical means. For that reason the songs are, in part, instrumental pieces rather than songs, even though occasionally they contain some very beautiful vocal melodies. Overall, however, the melodic element recedes; often we find only a declamatory treatment of the voice with the principal expression located in the accompaniment. Another determining factor is that Schumann, in his effort to overcome his inwardness and to ascend to the first level of objectivity, does not always penetrate to decisive clarity and occasionally betrays evidence of fermentation and struggle. Schumann's songs are essentially German Lieder; they are characterized by a deep inwardness, even one-sidedly so. In part they do not satisfy the strict demands of vocal composition, but they are so excellent in this one-sidedness that I consider many of them the most outstanding of the genre and, at the same time, the most outstanding among Schumann's works. Even the poems have been selected with the most excellent [literary] taste, and although not all are suited for musical settings and some—only natural in view of such a quantity—are perhaps not well chosen, the composer has nevertheless always managed to represent something interesting, something truly poetic. There are relatively few declamatory passages in our lyric poetry; instead of the self-contained and the concrete, what is expressed are psychological moods that need to be felt rather than represented externally to an audience; in short, they cannot be declaimed. For this reason, a number of these songs are more suited for private enjoyment than for public performance. They are rich in deep sentiments and beautifully conceived poetic turns, but—and here they deserve the highest praise—they are devoid of superficial material effects; thus, not many of the songs are suited for concert performance. Despite these limitations, which can be viewed only as relative deficiencies, the songs are, as noted, outstanding. If in individual cases blemishes need to be criticized, I would observe first of all that the composer occasionally worked too fast, producing less than significant results. Now I will focus on several of these song editions and point out what appears to me noteworthy, without, however, thereby implying that [just] the songs discussed here are the best. Only the large number of songs required me to deal here in greater detail with just a selection and to reserve discussing other, no less successful, songs for a later occasion.

Just as the composer was able to articulate the simple and naive in *Kinderszenen,* so in the song cycle *Frauenliebe und -leben* he expressed the deepest inwardness, the intimate life of a female sensibility. The heart has been revealed without mediation in these songs; one looks straight into the depths of the soul. An excellent song, for example, is "Helft mir, ihr Schwestern" [no. 5], which is sung with a joyousness that makes the heart burst; it is a composition that immediately and powerfully grips the listener. Less successful—an example of the hasty production mentioned above—is "Er, der Herrlichste" [no. 2], in which the melody of the beginning reappears—psychologically falsely—at a place with an entirely different expression. Beautifully conceived, however, is the conclusion of the cycle with the return of the beginning. I pass over other excellent features of this work.

Several of the earlier piano compositions have already reminded us of an old German quality; this folklike, naive, true-spirited character appears even more pronounced in the Reinick songs. This folklike sentiment is remarkable for a contemporary composer; it appears, indeed, as though once a certain level of sophistication was reached (as is the case of our time), a return took place to the simple and unbroken soil from which the later productions grew. Mendelssohn occasionally arouses similar sentiments, and it is particularly interesting to note that both composers meet in this respect, coming together to such a degree that the authorship of several particular songs, but for minor stylistic differences, could be misattributed. Apart from the fact that these songs are clear manifestations of the historical necessity of such sentiments, they are also evidence for the earlier mentioned rapprochement between both composers. The first and last songs are the best in this collection.

Schumann is a romantic—herein lies the primary explanation for the old German naïveté just mentioned—and his realm of sentiments is therefore closely related to that opened up by the poets of our romantic school. The fantastic opulence of which they dreamed was captured musically by Schumann in his *Liederkreis* on texts by Eichendorff. Most outstanding in this excellent collection are the song in F♯ major and the last, two fine compositions.[13]

The composer penetrates the Geibel texts less deeply; he approaches here the more pointedly vocal and has essentially produced pieces that *can* be sung to an audience. The young boy with the magic horn sings briskly in celebration of life [no. 1]. The romantic humility of the poem "Der Page" [no. 2] is very well captured in the melody. Most beautiful, most captivating [of all] is "Der Hidalgo" [no. 3], with its southern romantic coquettishness.

The *Balladen und Romanzen*, recently published by Whistling in Leipzig [*Romanzen und Balladen*, Op. 49], should also be mentioned. In this collection, "Die feindlichen Brüder," after Heine [no. 2], may again be considered an example of a hurried production; the bass lines are beautiful, but the melody is insignificant. However, "Die beiden Grenadiere," after Heine [no. 1], is excellent and one of the finest of Schumann's songs; the appearance in it of the *Marseillaise* has the most striking effect.

Schumann's evolution from this point onward consisted in continuing and intensifying the later direction just discussed, and the result has been creations in different compositional forms and genres. I will not review these compositions in detail. Since they have just recently appeared or are in the process of appearing, they will be reserved for a special discussion. Here it mostly suffices to introduce the general aspects for those special reviews to be written later. Now I note only that Schumann's individuality, originally confined within narrow limits, experiences in the evolutionary process an ever greater expansion. The sharp edges of his subjectivity are deflected, his ruggedness softens, and the composer descends from the isolation of his former height. In all aspects he shows advancements and expansions that were tremendously difficult for just such an individuality. Just as the later, similar keyboard compositions compared to *Papillons* contain deeper sentiments, greater richness and power of ideas, more developed instrumental treatments, and several other advantages, so do these orchestral and vocal works show growth in comparison with the later piano compositions. But in my opinion, just as Schumann was even earlier occasionally less successful with older forms (e.g., the sonatas) than with the free outpourings of his inner self, so it appears that his expression is also not entirely successful in some of these later works. It seems as though the composer, from his subjective standpoint, is not entirely at home in the objective world and thus occasionally lapses into lack of clarity, even dryness. The First Symphony opens up everywhere wide perspectives, but the intended objectivity of expression is not always reached. As I remember this work—having heard it often, albeit several years ago, in rather cautious, imperfect performances—there is too much detail, too much fantastic abundance. The orchestration is often beautiful, but also frequently blurred without distinct contours. As excellent as the oratorio *Das Paradies und die Peri* must be considered, as rich in content and musical innovation as this work is, the reconciliation of subjective and objective elements, above all a balanced approach in all sections, has not been completely accomplished, and occasionally Schumann seems no longer true to himself when he has to step outside himself. The foundation of Schumann's creativity is his subjectivity, and at the present time he loses unity of style and character when he ventures into the epic realm.

The most successful of his later works are, in my opinion, the more significant songs, the *Peri*, and the Piano Quintet. The string quartets I have not heard often enough to be able to form a definite opinion, but the most recently published piano quartet seems to confirm my reservation expressed earlier.

After freeing himself from the bonds of tradition, Mendelssohn first seized on the fantastic as an area where he recognized his mastery, and he articulated in his *Lieder ohne Worte* an awareness of the mission of the era.[14] Expanding and intensifying his individuality in all directions, he then wrote the grand sacred and dramatic works and the larger instrumental compositions. Mendelssohn is an eclectic, but in the noblest sense of the word. He used what could be learned and considered from the era before him and fused it with what was originally his own and the characteristic features of his talent. All of this, especially his culture, justifies calling him a first-rate talent. True, other great masters with a richer imagination yielded to an unconsciously creative artistic instinct; they wrote works that, because of their liveliness and immediacy of invention (which Mendelssohn does not have to such a degree), made a deep impression, but which also showed the deficiencies that are necessarily the result of such a standpoint. (These deficiencies have to do with too much reliance on the immediate invention, leading to something merely raw and natural as opposed to something purified by artistic consciousness.) In Mendelssohn's music, however, the background of cultivated taste, deliberate calculation, and classical restraint is always evident. Even Mendelssohn's individuality is initially more narrowly confined, but he expanded it through his studies, and whatever he had in him he was able to bring to the highest perfection. His efforts toward that end—unlike Schumann's—were facilitated by his orientation, by nature an objective one. Thus, for the reasons mentioned here, we see in Mendelssohn the possibility of treating successfully tasks that belong to an earlier artistic period, as well as a critique, made manifest especially through his creations, of purely romantic music in its narrow sense—a critique even of artistic styles that indicate a progress in history. Mendelssohn, if I am not mistaken, would assert that everything that was beautiful at one time would remain beautiful for all time in the same manner; that it would always have to evoke the same sympathies even though the all-inclusive beauty, unifying all evolutionary stages, is never brought to appearance in this world but only as a historically determined ideal, shaped by the character of the times and the developmental levels of history. He is the leader of a direction that views art less as an expression of the time and pays homage more to the beautiful in itself. There is no doubt that this standpoint is largely justified, and it must be called misguided to attempt, as today's liberals do, to reduce all poetry and art to a political statement. But it is just as true that art has the function of representing the struggles of history and of articulating the highest principle that provides movement in history. Mendelssohn has the advantages of the older classical direction; through his "classicality" he has become the man of the era, but it is also proper to criticize him for his lack of modern sympathies.

Since this is not the place to discuss Mendelssohn's compositions, I will not name individual works. I want to mention only the [incidental] music for *Antigone*, because it can serve as proof of what has been said and as an occasion to add a few thoughts about contemporary art. It has already been stated, correctly so, that there is something contradictory about dressing up a play from antiquity with modern music, thereby unifying in one work the most extreme contrast—the intimacy of Christian music and the extroversion of the Greek representational principle. Having conceded the undeniable contradiction and even the inadmissibility of the task, I can only laud the composition, even though by nature Mendelssohn is little inclined toward the heroic. Everything in the work is so outstanding, so admirable and ingenious, that a performance enraptures the listener, and one does not become aware of the contradiction, especially since highly poetic words are sung here. It is wonderful to see a work of antiquity brought back to life in this way. We must warn only against an excess of imitation of this experiment; and although we thank the creator of the first such attempt for its extraordinary quality, we reject the imitators. We have already suffered so much at the hand of classical antiquity, we have been so held back in the development of our nationality and language by the all-too-powerful influence that antiquity was permitted to have up to the present time, that we would rather not be inconvenienced by it in the musical arena. If we had a national theater and a firm, sophisticated taste in artistic matters, the influence of the foreign would not cause damage; indeed, it would be welcomed as a symbol of high culture. But under the present conditions everything foreign only distracts from our course of evolution and impedes progress. Moreover, such attempts easily lead to the artificial, as is already partly the case in Berlin, where the attempt was initiated to set the whole of antiquity to music,[15] and where the composition of Horatian odes brought about a regression to a stage of evolution that predominated in the sixteenth century (see Winterfeld, *Der evangelische Kirchengesang*, vol. 1, p. 169[16]), but was fortunately superseded through the later development of our art.

Schumann began with the most decisive inwardness; he was initially unable to appropriate the more objective forms and could create only according to his own individuality. He needed to create everything from within and therefore struggled with expression until he was able to produce the traditional on his own. Thus, if Mendelssohn's music is characterized by the grand, comprehensive perspective and the ability to cope with large tasks, we see Schumann—in this respect inferior to Mendelssohn—occupied primarily with the elaboration of details. In the process, he easily loses the global perspective as a result of the richness of individual passages and reduced concern for clear structure. Mendelssohn takes into account what succeeds; his sensitive knowledge of what is proper prevails. Schumann follows the urge of his inner self; the novelties are more the results of a subconscious drive. Schumann pushes himself; Mendelssohn knows his strength. Looking back to the past, Mendelssohn knows how to articulate his thoughts in concrete terms; Schumann struggles with expression. He subsequently digs deeper, perhaps, and makes new discoveries, but he fails to reach the final and utmost clarity in his less successful works. Mendelssohn, in his less successful works, slips into formalism and mannerism and is noticeably repetitious—in some keyboard works, for example, especially with certain favorite turns and figurations. Schumann writes quickly, now and then all too hastily; Mendelssohn polishes and refines, occasionally perhaps too much. Schumann evokes more immediate sympathy; Mendelssohn gives more the impression of perfection and classical standards—Goethe and Schiller have been characterized in the same way. Mendelssohn dares nothing that is not to the point; Schumann often fails to produce this pointed effect. But in Mendelssohn's works the musical thought is sometimes inspired by knowledge of its effect, as if from the outside, whereas with Schumann it comes from within. The characteristic features of both composers, as depicted here in several principal respects, are the necessary result of the [aesthetic] principles they represent and thus are the necessary consequence.

Through the preceding discussion, I believe, I have articulated the issue that fundamentally concerns the evolution of contemporary art, thereby presenting a detailed description of the program sketched in nos. 1 and 2 of this journal.[17] What remains is to add to these considerations speculations about the future, to develop some practical consequences, and to reach a final judgment in the form of a subjective opinion.

I have described Schumann as subjectivity in its most pointed form, which only gradually absorbs the objective element; Mendelssohn is the opposite. Mendelssohn's task was, by nature, clearer and firmer; he is the most beautiful fruit growing most recently out of the old trunk, and this explains his greater popularity in comparison with Schumann. Within the more narrowly defined boundaries, Mendelssohn has confidently reached the goal of his striving. Because of his clearly pronounced character, he has gained the scepter in the musical life of our time. He is a representative of classicism in our time, but for that reason he is not an expression of the present time in its entirety, less still of future trends. Schumann is forced to strive for his ideal, the ideal of the younger generation, and to struggle for its manifestation. He is not yet finished with it, and his direction is not yet clearly worked out. Both artists are unsuited to establish a school, to attract a circle of younger talents to their shores. Mendelssohn's students would work for the future even less than would the master. Disregarding the benefits they would gain in purely musical, technical terms from such an alliance, I fear that, along with the whole movement, they would degenerate into superficiality and formalism. Schu-

mann's students would lack the essential trait that a greater predecessor could provide: secure and firm guidance toward a clearly
recognized goal. Schumann has changed substantially in the course of
his compositional activity. Perhaps even unconsciously influenced by
external factors and his residence in classical Leipzig, he has approached the objectivity of the opposite movement. But the question
is whether he can reach fulfillment by following this avenue. Would it
not have been possible to transfer the same fantastically humorous
manner of his keyboard works to the orchestra, to imbue orchestral
music (with appropriate modifications, of course) with the spirit of his
piano works? And would such free fantastic emanations not have captured the ideal of the time: to cause technical elaboration to recede in
favor of a spiritual life that is richly dramatic, humorous, and fantastic? Or are Schumann's new, larger works only a second major stage
that will give way to a third, raised to a higher level by the former,
which reconciles and unifies everything? I regard the early piano
works very highly; they were the necessary continuation after Beethoven. Schumann did not earn popularity with them, but there will
come a time when these pieces will find more general recognition,
and for that reason I believe that this point of departure should not
be denied or partly rejected, as seems to be the case, by the composer.

I have pursued the development of the two most significant composers of the younger generation; I have stressed the historic importance and rich talent that both have. Must the result of the discussion
now be that neither can serve as a model, and that, notwithstanding
these first-rate talents of our time, neither can free us from the doubts
of everyday life and give us a firm guarantee for the future of art?

In accordance with the predominance of Protestantism in Germany, which makes the individual become self-reliant and gradually
renounce communal living, a congregation of individuals around a
major center is a rare event, especially in our present time, when the
former aristocracy of the spirit [*Geist*], maintained by the few, is replaced by a republic of spirits. A close, immediate association of
younger talents with the two artists is not possible for these reasons, as
well as for others already mentioned. But when we search for the
reasons why Mendelssohn and Schumann gained their importance in
our time, we see that, besides individual talent, their comprehensive
education, encompassing not only music but literature and aesthetics—and in Mendelssohn's case, also biblical studies— must be viewed
as the decisive factor. That both composers filled their inner worlds
with the spiritual treasures of our people, that they had an eye for the
tendencies of the time, that they were open and sensitive to other

interests, including nonmusical ones—all this is the principal reason for their significance. And in this way—indirectly, that is—they can be a model for budding artists, not through pedestrian imitation but by emulation of the splendid example both have set in our time.

NOTES

1. Introductory note to Susan Gillespie's translation of the portion of Brendel's article concerned with Mendelssohn, in *Mendelssohn and His World*, ed. R. Larry Todd (Princeton, 1991), p. 341. [Trans.]

2. For a more detailed account of Brendel's first year as editor of the journal, see Jürgen Thym, "Schumann in Brendel's *Neue Zeitschrift für Musik* from 1845 to 1856," in *Mendelssohn and Schumann: Essays on Their Music and Its Context*, ed. Jon W. Finson and R. Larry Todd (Durham, N.C., 1984), pp. 21–25. [Trans.]

3. During much of the nineteenth century Beethoven was mostly revered for the music of his heroic period. The works composed in the last decade of his life, especially the piano sonatas and the string quartets, were perceived by his contemporaries and later music critics, as Brendel's comments show, as overly esoteric soliloquies. [Trans.]

4. As will become clear in the course of the discussion, there are generally two ways to gain access to these artistic creations: following Schumann's evolution in an ascending direction, or beginning with the most recent works and then working backward in time. It appears to me less useful to start with individual pieces selected, perhaps, from the middle of Schumann's output. [Brendel]

5. A seventeenth-century dance cited by Schumann in a variety of works as a symbol for the old and obsolescent. It derives its name from the text underlay: "Und als der Großvater die Großmutter nahm" (And when the grandfather took the grandmother). See pp. 84–91. [Trans.]

6. There is no piece of this title in *Kinderszenen*. Brendel most likely refers to either "Träumerei" (no. 7) or "Kind im Einschlummern" (no. 12). [Trans.]

7. Schumann found in his music for "In der Nacht" an association with the myth of Hero and Leander. [Trans.]

8. Goethe's reading of the poetry of the Persian Hafis in the translation by Josef von Hammer-Purgstall inspired him to write poems (collaborating with Marianne Willemer) in an "oriental" manner. The poems were published as *West-Östlicher Divan* in 1819. [Trans.]

9. Liszt performed three concerts in Leipzig on 17, 24, and 30 March 1840—he became very friendly with Mendelssohn and Schumann during that time—and three concerts again on 6, 13, and 16 December 1841. (See Ernst Burger, *Franz Liszt: A Chronicle of His Life in Pictures and Documents* [Princeton, 1989], pp. 122 and 134.) [Trans.]

10. *Carnaval* is indeed pervaded by musical anagrams based on the pitch

names A, S (E♭ in English), C, and H (B in English) as well as As (A♭ in English), C, and H. The letters are derived from Schumann's name and from Asch, the Bohemian hometown of his then fiancée Ernestine von Fricken. [Trans.]

11. Brendel outlined his editorial policy for the *Neue Zeitschrift für Musik* in a double issue (nos. 1 and 2) of the journal on 1 January 1845, his "inaugural address." (See translation of excerpt of "Zur Einleitung" in Jürgen Thym, "Schumann in Brendel's *Neue Zeitschrift für Musik*," pp. 31–32.) [Trans.]

12. Most of Schumann's songs were written during the year 1840, appropriately known as the *Liederjahr*. [Trans.]

13. Brendel clearly singles out the last song "Frühlingsnacht" as a particularly convincing example of Schumann's art of Lied composition. But since "Frühlingsnacht" is in F♯ major, the identity of the other song he praises is unclear. No other song in the *Liederkreis* is in that key. "In der Fremde" (no. 1, "Aus der Heimat hinter den Blitzen rot"), in F♯ minor, was not included in the cycle until the second edition of the *Liederkreis* in 1849. [Trans.] (On the first version of Op. 39, see pp. 156–70. [Ed.])

14. Mendelssohn's *Lieder ohne Worte*, piano pieces with songlike textures and styles, most of which had been published by 1845. [Trans.]

15. Brendel is referring here to an attempt, initiated by the Prussian King Friedrich Wilhelm IV and his artistic counselor Ludwig Tieck, to revive Greek tragedy in the 1840s. (See Eric Werner, *Mendelssohn*, trans. Dika Newlin [London, 1963], pp. 368ff.) Mendelssohn was commissioned to write the incidental music not only to Sophocles' *Antigone* and *Oedipus at Colonos* but also to Racine's *Athalie*. [Trans.]

16. Carl Winterfeld, *Der evangelische Kirchengesang und sein Verhältnis zur Kunst des Tonsatzes*, 3 vols. (Leipzig, 1843–47; reprint, Hildesheim, 1966). [Trans.]

17. See n. 11. [Trans.]

Robert Schumann (1855)

FRANZ LISZT

Schumann's relationship with Liszt figures as one of the most complex professional relationships within the composer's circle. It began auspiciously enough in 1837, when Liszt published a laudatory review of three piano works by Schumann—the Impromptus, Op. 5; the Sonata in F♯ minor, Op. 11; and the Sonata in F minor, Op. 14—in the *Revue et gazette musicale*.[1] The following year Liszt dedicated his Paganini Studies to Clara, and in 1839 Schumann reciprocated by dedicating the Fantasy, Op. 17, to Liszt. By then, Liszt was becoming recognized as the unrivaled piano virtuoso of the age. In March 1840, Schumann traveled to Dresden to cover Liszt's German concert tour for the *Neue Zeitschrift für Musik*, and there the two met for the first time. They then proceeded to Leipzig, where Liszt continued his tour.

Schumann reported to Clara that he felt as if he had already known Liszt for twenty years.[2] In the *Neue Zeitschrift* he wrote glowingly of Liszt's performances,[3] though the tenor of the relationship now began to change. In Leipzig, Liszt became embroiled in several intrigues;[4] and in 1848, at a dinner party in Dresden, matters came to a head when Schumann took offense at some disparaging views Liszt voiced about Mendelssohn. By this time, Schumann had retired as editor of the *Neue Zeitschrift*, which was about to become an organ for the progressive party of "musicians of the future" centered around Liszt and Wagner. By contrast, Schumann was increasingly perceived to be associated with the Leipzig neoclassicism of Mendelssohn.

Notwithstanding the polemic about the future course of German music that raged at midcentury in the musical press, Liszt, for his part, endeavored to treat Schumann respectfully. In Weimar, where he settled as the court music director in 1848, Liszt performed portions of Schumann's music for *Faust* and *Manfred*, and the opera *Genoveva*, and in 1854 he dedicated his new Piano Sonata in B minor to Schumann.[5] But by the time this work was published, Schumann had been admitted to the asylum in Endenich. As a final sign of respect, in 1855 Liszt issued a lengthy series of articles in the *Neue Zeitschrift*,

portions of which are translated here.[6] Hailing Schumann as a visionary, Liszt reviewed Schumann's dual career as music critic and composer, and offered a spirited defense of programmatic music and of
Schumann's use of programmatic titles—for Liszt, clear enough evidence of Schumann's contribution to German music. [Ed.]

[Source: Franz Liszt, "Robert Schumann," *Neue Zeitschrift für Musik* 42 (1855): 133–37
(23 March), 145–53 (30 March), 157–65 (6 April), 177–82 (20 April), 189–96 (27
April).]

I

TRANSLATED BY JOHN MICHAEL COOPER

An exhaustive aesthetic portrayal of an author such as the one just
named would require more than several pages—it would require an
entire book. Therefore, today we do not attempt to underscore the
complete significance of an artistic career, of a name that assumes
such a secure position among the most honorable and honored of our
time. The ongoing interest with which we have observed this planet—
one of the most conspicuous on the present horizon—from its first
appearance would perhaps entitle us to trace its various phases with a
precision appropriate for relating facts deeply impressed upon our
consciousness, so as to render the full recognition due this spirit,
which has productively aspired upward, with the noblest energy. . . .
We would surely regard it as an honor and duty not to hesitate to pay
him the undiminished tribute he may expect from one of his first
admirers and most earnest friends—one who, from the very beginning, grasped the lofty position that had to be accorded him by all
artists who consider themselves representatives of a special class . . .
that concurs with the spirit of progress and the general artistic development of their time. But we believe the time has not yet come when
we might measure the complete compass of his appearance, when we
could say: "Behold, this is what he wanted, strove for, and attempted;
this is what he achieved and attained; here, he did not follow the path
to its final destination; here, he strayed." We shall be able to accomplish this only after the publication of the master's most recent works.
As testaments to his later style (and certainly to the forms that he
eventually chose) they hardly number among the less interesting
items in his oeuvre, whether they approach those principles from
which he distanced himself in the passion of youth or, on the other
hand, reveal a steadfast progress along the path chosen at that time.

Now, whether these works are the flowers of that sunny prime of life or the fruits of autumnal days, we must know them intimately if we wish to trace knowledgeably the causes and effects of the most decisive moments of his artistic life. Even the works now available from his earlier and more mature periods reveal an appreciable difference in their essential emotional content and expression. The question of whether Schumann's earlier or later style is more fortuitous and successful can then be addressed profitably, and answering this question will enable us to draw some conclusions about such an important case. Furthermore, this opportunity may allow us to address some of the most important and vital issues of our art. . . .

Schumann's muse would also be imperfectly represented if one viewed an individual work without considering its position in his works as a whole. His individual works arose less from the need to paint and represent, to chisel and give form to their subjects, than from the need to use the subject as an opportunity to express the feelings residing within him. Only by comparing his different compositions, therefore, can we recognize the significance he attached to a chosen mode of expression and form, and thus grasp the idea of a particular work and estimate the dimensions of its feeling. . . .

In our view a correct judgment of Schumann's music can be neither imagined nor formulated; there is no reasonable examination to which we can subject its merits and deficiencies . . . before we can grasp the two sides of his public persona, the twofold effect he has had on the art of his time: as a creating artist, a sensitive, inspired man; and as a thoughtful writer, a scholarly, cultured mind. For centuries it was as if music and literature were separated by a wall, as if the inhabitants on each side recognized each other only by name. If they even came into contact, they resembled Pyramus and Thisbe: they secretly regarded and touched each other only through the cracks and gaping fissures of the stones piled up between them. Schumann was at home in both lands; it was Schumann who opened a breach for the inhabitants of the divided regions through which at least some intermediaries could force their way. . . .

II

TRANSLATED BY CHRISTOPHER ANDERSON

Because of his literary education, which bestowed upon him as insightful a taste in poetry and prose as in harmony and counterpoint,

Schumann played a dual role in the musical art. This is not the place to decide which role was more important; his talents could converse in two languages—words and tones—with the same clarity, if not intensity. Nor should we consider here whether the successful works produced by these conditions linked great, beautiful poetry to great, beautiful music. Still, the first contribution stands in the foreground. [Schumann's] diligent studies, his keen sense of discretion, probing taste, and practiced tact are adequate proof for us that in him the two arts were fused into one and that, instead of being paralyzed by struggling and striving with each other (as would result from a clumsy, unwieldy combination of the two), their powers were doubled. But in how he united the roles of critic and artist, Schumann exercised his creative gifts twice over. Not content to express his ideas in arid words, he fulfilled the task he posed for the critic when he said: "We admit that we consider the noblest criticism to be that which leaves an impression similar to that left by the object of criticism."[7] "In this sense, Jean Paul[8] could contribute more insight into a Beethoven symphony or fantasy through a poetic counterpart than could those well-known art critics who put a measuring stick to the colossus and assess its value according to its faults." Schumann was able to reproduce with such sensitivity and exactitude those poetic moods and mature contemplations awakened in him by art and its manifestations that one might well say that his rich, ample powers of imagination were reflected just as completely in the pages he offered to readers as in those he offered performers. Therefore, first we turn to [Schumann] the writer; for even if—as we do not wish to imply—his criticism exercised a lesser influence on the art of his time than did the poetic aspects of his musical works, his literary activities are no less significant for our own time, and they familiarize us with an exceptional aspect of such a rarely encountered individuality.

Already Weber recognized the advantages for the musician who did not remain aloof from journalism and the daily press.[9] Schumann proved how correct Weber was in this issue, which even today most of us address only superficially: he founded a journal (the same one to whose columns we dedicate this article) and shortly thereafter assumed its editorship.[10] In order to understand the necessity of these sacrifices . . . we must consider for a moment what led him to this decision. Today we acknowledge him because time has validated not only his conclusions about previous art but also his vision of the inevitable changes in the artist's situation well into the distant future. . . . Those who give the world such far-reaching spiritual vision often risk being ignored and disdained by those who, myopic and nearsighted, refuse to concede the approach of anything they cannot recognize. But why should anyone convinced of their shortsightedness care whether they deny his assertions and mock his undertakings? [Schumann] relentlessly followed a path that would bring him closer to a goal well beyond the horizon of the masses. . . .

We would have wished to establish in just a few words the correctness of Schumann's efforts in assuming the double role of critic and artist. But since the issues considered here have not yet been fully grasped by most of us, we permit ourselves to consider them from two perspectives: 1) *the artist's criticism with regard to the public*; and 2) *its effect on the artist himself*. Thus, first we will demonstrate the disadvantage to the public when criticism is left to those not even conversant in the tools of art,[11] and then we will demonstrate the benefits for the artist's intellectual development when he takes criticism into his own hands.

Art was not born yesterday. Was there criticism in those distant times to which we can trace the beginnings of the arts? Or was it born simultaneously with them, and did it flourish and wither as they did? Does it benefit or harm art, or is it an infirm offspring, a sticky resin on the mighty oak? Or a necessary offspring that maintains the balance between the various powers? Is it like the shadow inevitably cast upon the sea of light by every solid body, or is it the beneficial plow, which tears up and furrows the soil so that it may bear fruit?

All these questions may be answered in the negative as well as the affirmative. There has always been criticism; for in no culture has art ever developed in a fashion unsympathetic to that culture, and never has one art been successfully transplanted from one soil to another, suddenly becoming popular, unless the transplant was first prepared by frequent exchanges and continuing influences, as happened before Greek art was exported to the Romans, before the hegemony of the Italian Renaissance in European culture, before the infiltration of Spanish literature into French. . . .

[But] modern times have seen the development of what appears to be a completely different genre of criticism. This criticism differs from previous ones in the scholarly baggage it carries, and in the pedantic preoccupation of its scalpel-wielding (probably sometimes butter knife–wielding), microscope-equipped analyses, in which it applies to art the laws of anatomy. This criticism speaks in a frightful, hoarse voice, threatens with the switch and rod, and plays the flesh-hungry bogeyman; artists shrink before it like larks before the scarecrow in the wheat field. But we believe it is nonetheless just as significant as the previously named, more general, instinctive varieties of criticism. To recognize this, one need only strip it bare of its frightful garments and see what a hollow, lifeless thing this patchy bundle of rags is, this thing that can instill fear only if one is afraid of ghosts. . . .

Earlier criticism resembled a kind of enveloping atmosphere, an indefinable aura that became more translucent around certain persons and things but, by its very nature, remained intangible and unstable; it eluded a firm grip, like water running between our fingers. But since the press has transformed criticism into a visible manipulator, a concrete manifestation of accumulated power, and since criticism, empowered by the press, has begun to hurl into the world its decrees, judgments, appointments to immortality, and sentencings to exile, it has become *authority*. Criticism has erected a kind of torture chamber where it hourly, or as often as it wishes, strings out selected victims on the torture rack, puts them in Spanish boots[12] and handcuffs, and roasts them as it wishes over a slow-burning fire, pinching, tweaking, skewering them on the stake to mock and whip them, ultimately to drag them through the streets in humiliation. . . .

In view of such facts, in view of such a dangerous condition, will artists continue, from laziness or lack of self confidence, to entrust a job to others who accomplish it with so much less talent, even if with sufficient skill? This would cause substantial damage to both art and artists. We are well acquainted with the scruples that restrain many artists, [who] . . . know only too well how painstakingly one learns the use of the brush, the chisel, and the score, and [who] in noble modesty shy away from the literary use of the quill, a tool they were never taught to use. Out of respect for literature . . . , they have too long accustomed themselves to believe that if one is to appear in print, artistry belongs in prose as well as poetry; they should have rid themselves of this prejudice long ago . . . as if the authors of journal articles had studied, as if they had thought and reflected, as if they possessed the necessary *savoir dire*! The most honest artists could admit to themselves that they understood a hundred times more about the subject than do everyday critics. But even if they realized this, they would not dare reveal themselves [in print], for they fear being slandered if they think they possessed the necessary literary ability. Given the position of the press in our society, one must recognize this clearly as an error, for today it is no longer a momentous step to join the press's ranks. Formerly the book was a rostrum, the pamphlet a stage. The writer became an actor when he addressed the public. But in the nineteenth century, the word *authorship* has lost much of its weight. "Le journal a tué la conversation" ["the journal has killed conversation"], one says in France, where piquant conversation had truly become a powerful art, so that its effect had earned the respect and prestige of political influence. This art is not dead; it is only reshaped, since most educated members of the press—of all standings and nationalities—have gradually come to a general rendezvous. . . .

If the press is now nothing other than a new form of conversation, a new way to express thoughts as they are awakened in us by the daily course of world events, and if they are reflected in our own spirit and views, why should an artist of excellence (synonymous with an ingenious intellect) lack the ability to formulate clearly his ideas and opinions, his feelings and impressions, and in this way contribute to the general conversation in the press? Moreover, if he limits himself to certain specialties, he will always have something informative to say about them. Whoever understands only his *trade* thoroughly will express himself better without any special oratorical art than those ignoramuses who so often inundate the press with their rhapsodic, arty chatter. . . .

It seems as though musicians have realized that the hour has come when it is no longer possible to turn their backs on the breach, to relinquish their intellectual fatherland—with its borders established by criticism—to foreign, profane hands. For about fifteen years, the number of those has gradually increased who, among the musical luminaries of our day, have also dedicated themselves to literary activity. In France, Berlioz swings his scepter, from which often flies the golden flash of his humor.[13] At times, it transforms his imagination into a magic wand; at other times, however, it turns his tiresome impatience into a switch. Wagner is systematically presenting a complete structure of ideas, organized like a ladder, that society strives to comprehend as a pyramid, with its summit occupied by drama.[14] Marx impresses with the noblemindedness of his style and the precision of certain passages that seem to conjure up the genius of the Latin language, while in others the beautiful richness of poetic images clothes his deepest thoughts.[15] Hiller,[16] Halévy,[17] and Adam[18] write with a fine, lively, sharp and witty pen, and Hans von Bülow[19] does not come up short of ink for his scores because previously he used a few drops to express biting, spirited irony. Just as that philosopher made believers out of those who doubted his cause by the example of his own life, the citation of the above names may suffice as proof to those who doubt the possibility that one can unite literary and artistic talent. With Schumann, this union is further enhanced by his contribution that he did not unconsciously give in to the pressures of the circumstances, that he did not merely await the arrival of the most extreme necessity once he had recognized it. [Rather], he affixed the seal of mental and material sacrifice upon the realization of his views. He was not content to be zealous, to preach, to work, to fight for his idea— which in the coming decades will possibly be just as little understood as it was generally twenty years ago. . . .

In his well-considered, pure, and gracious style, just as in his striking, harmonious use of image, Schumann must be numbered among the most significant journalists. He belongs to those who transformed musical criticism into a literary object. [Before him] one seldom had heard in Germany scholarly, intelligent, and accurate writing about music in any more flowery a style than one finds in arithmetic textbooks. Schumann avoided the dryness of the professionals, who had addressed music in such an unattractive style and always exclusively from a technical standpoint: one could easily have been frightened away, even if one were forced to digest such fare in order to become a musician. He knew how to interest the laymen, to whom musical journals had previously offered too much boredom and not enough instruction. Without lapsing into far-reaching dilettante fantasies about our masterworks, without wandering a thumb's breadth from the ground of reality, he excited and refreshed [others] through poetic images. He engaged the imagination and was so admirably instructive that one gladly let oneself be instructed. Just as the iridescent dragonfly and the sparkling hummingbird are miniature masterworks of nature, so was the shortest article from Schumann's pen a model of intellect, color, humor, sobriety, or satire. He was able to impart an interesting turn to the simplest praise or criticism. He could tie together the individual characteristics of his subjects with general perspectives; their subtlety and accuracy often guarantee his criticism a longer life than the discussed work may have or have had. His definitions . . . are so excellent that subjects will always be found for which his advice is useful, just as Martial's epigrams and Horace's satires still reflect the weakness and ridiculousness of those whom they deride. One can best describe the general character of his criticism by conceding that he conscientiously lived up to the words with which he himself defined the task of criticism, like a sacred vow: "[Criticism] knocks the weapon from the hand of fools and the conceited; it spares those with good intentions and educates them; it greets the courageous with vigorous friendliness; it withdraws the dagger in the presence of the strong, and salutes." We must also call upon his words in respect to those times when . . . he not only judged mediocrities too kindly but deemed them worthy of discussion at all, while the present time has already forgotten them, and rightly so: "There are certain things over which one should not lose one word."[20] And further, "But art is served only with the masterful; whoever cannot produce this every-where and at all times has no claim to the name of a true artist."[21] "Whoever does not stand on the heights of the present will usually find himself mistaken about the effect of his accomplishments, and often about the accomplishments themselves."[22] "Do not write any more adagios better than Mozart's. If you put on a wig, do you be-come wiser for it?"[23] It would have been better if his magnanimity, bordering on extravagance, had not misled him into stringing finely cut, delicately conceived diamonds on dull, titleless names: a would-be nobleman's crown has no right to fine jewels. When one hunts ordi-nary beasts, one does not use arrows enameled with gold; one saves them to fight against the "princes of the forest"!—On the other hand, we find moments in which the bitterness of Schumann's censure arises from a lack of approval. But to his credit let it be said that the former mistake occurs more frequently than the latter, and both make only a very small claim against his merits. . . .

III

TRANSLATED BY R. LARRY TODD

When Schumann saw the moment approach when the artist could no longer avoid participating as a general critic of art, and when he must have felt obliged to allow his own voice to be heard among those who had used and abused the right in public, he took a higher vantage point than that of merely being useful to the public, to creative artists in general, and to the artist-writer in particular. . . . He assessed the purpose of music, its current position among the other arts, its histor-ical development up to the present as the result of the past, and its future as determined by the present. In this last he must have asked himself whether in such a society and time seething with so many new elements, music could remain without new interests and tendencies; whether for music, which recently (since scarcely more than half a century) had established for itself a new foundation, it was of the highest significance to clarify the differences between music's own past and present as they related most inwardly to the present and past of the rest of the world.

With his mature, rare, gifted intelligence he considered that this or that art form in this or that land arose and developed not by accident but as the blossoming and climax of a whole series of customs, devel-opmental phases, views, manners of thought, and convictions, so that

. . . with the considerable upheavals of social and cultural conditions, music too had to strike a new path, find a new upturn, and find modern forms for modern contents of feelings, in order to offer the next generations a new garment made of new material. He did not want music (while all society, turning on another axle, felt alienated from the old, more naive, ardent culture) to cling narrowly to the viewpoints of earlier intellectual conditions, the former needs of the public, the antiquated views of art, and to welcome its inevitable fall.

Above all it appeared necessary to him to raze the whole structure by which music for so long had been cut off from the contemporary intellectual movement, to free music at any price from its isolation, to bring music into contact with those forceful, constant air currents, those countercurrents of views and feelings, and, above all, to identify how the Zeitgeist manifested its strivings and ambitions. . . .

Other arts appear to be more closely tied than music to the necessities of life. . . . Thus, when one considers the easier blossoming of [poetry], and the inseparable ties of the other arts to the most unobliging requirements of life, one must doubt whether music can rival the popularity of the sister arts, and one might ask whether music can be entrusted with such a difficult struggle, whether it should not always remain in the shadow of the other arts, as formerly was the case. . . .

Music does not just restrict its most splendid pronouncements to large-scale works for the masses but also responds to the most conflicting requirements of our soul and fills it with all the impressions of which music is capable. None of our most inner feelings remains inaccessible to her; she welcomes them in all forms. Arousing and heartening in a military camp, great and majestic in the church, dramatically stirring, lively, and merry on the stage, entrancing and charming in the ballroom, she shows herself tender, pious, or passionate in lyrical works, mild or piercing in entertaining songs for mixed or male chorus, eloquent and dithyrambic in symphonic poems . . . ; she resounds in the temple as in the forest and is a stranger to no one. . . .

Despite these signs and symptoms of the time, today many are convinced that since Bach and Handel music has moved ever closer to her complete downfall and can deviate no further from the highest expression of the beautiful without entering her aphelion. We can no more foresee the *future of music*, to the extent it continues its development from phase to phase, than Fiesole[24] could imagine Michelangelo, or the Aegean sculptors could Phidias and Praxiteles,[25] or Jan van Eyck could Cornelius,[26] or Josquin Gluck.[27] For our part, we do not believe that this blossoming consists of endless reproductions of the same forms, the same contours and colors. If atmospheric conditions influence the richness, strength, and fruit of vegetation, if plants become fuller and more graceful through cultivation and contact with foreign elements, . . . how could the influences of the social atmosphere, of culture, the contact with new intellectual elements fail to affect the arts? . . . [Predicting] the future of music nevertheless numbers among those problems that certain people gladly compare to making gold; in other words, it amounts to seeking the impossible. But neither mockery nor disbelief, neither burning at the stake nor persecutions of any kind have ever stopped the stream of ideas from surging up to undermine the dilapidated or from fertilizing the earth like the old symbolic Nile. What can one gain from denying progress? Even Galileo—could his retractions conceal the light of ideas beneath the bushel of ignorance? What good did it do to deny the motion of the earth?—*E pur si muove* [And yet it moves]! But since the value of believing in the difficult consists of being sure of the unknown, in the fullness of time those who foresaw and recognized the arrival of certain knowledge within a given term will be honored. In many languages (such as Slavic) the poet and prophet are one and the same word: one calls him a seer [*Seher*]. Schumann was one of those seers whom the mind led beyond the borders of the present, whose beliefs became knowledge, and who, guided in their affairs by their beliefs, were often ignored while they lived but then extolled after they were gone. He inferred from what music had been what it must become and determined from this the future of the artist after he had stopped being what he was. He grasped that neither art nor artists should any longer come and go through the world separated from the life of mankind, . . . as if vegetating and decaying in a hermetically sealed room. He perceived that the silence and seclusion of the first, early period of art had been charitable and purposeful but that her childhood, her maturity, should now hurry forward to embrace the progress of ideas that have formed the moral facet of every civilization. He perceived that music had been summoned to take her place at the big table, that she must penetrate through to the strivings, feelings and opinions, the ways of thinking and the lives of contemporary generations; that art and artists finally had to give up the exclusive habitations of mystical regions, where no tears or raging, no sighs or laments reached, neither cries of joy or victory nor laments and woes of living hearts.[28] This conviction determined and influenced his human life and artistic direction. As a human he felt the need to tie authorship and music together; as a musician, the need to tie the history of music more closely to that of poetry and literature. . . .

Schumann was not mistaken when he recognized among the most important means of attaining this last goal the selection of poetic masterworks for musical texts. He was not mistaken when he considered it hereafter impossible, in composing a cantata or oratorio, to make do with any old canvas that had been prepared haphazardly from historical threads; nor was he mistaken when he considered it necessary to give some instrumental music a firm poetic foundation through the use of titles—as it were, images in perspective. As for his Lieder, we should hardly have to comment that a fine sensibility and practiced taste like his had to be spent on works in an even more discriminating way than Schubert's, and that for his songs he chose only verses whose formal beauty emerged from a feeling that was as capable of heightened expression as the word could give him. It is expecting too much to search among the poems he set for only the most excellent texts; however, we maintain that with him we find the smallest number of mediocre texts, that in his compositions he carefully and steadfastly excluded everything except the melancholy that muffled the strains of his lyre and did not correspond to the graceful, tender, sensitive ideal filled with cheerful innocence, with youthful uninhibitedness and daring. He correctly says: "Why employ mediocre poems, which always must take revenge on music! Weave a garland of music around the head of a true poet—nothing more beautiful; but to waste it on a commonplace face, why bother?"[29]

In his large vocal works he took the trouble to meet the double requirements of his time. First, he was careful to augment the repertoire of concerts, still sparingly in demand given their important position among musical performances and the increasing competition they offered the theater. Also, he tried to avoid stiff biblical subjects, formerly so appropriate, that Mendelssohn knew how to modernize even as their outmoded, antiquated features were becoming increasingly more perceptible. Schumann eluded happily the pedantic meaninglessness that perforce characterized historical and occasional cantatas. To this end he broadened the range of subjects to which music for chorus and orchestra could fill out longer time spans. He transplanted church and theatrical works into the concert hall and thereby discovered poetic terrain no less sublime and pure than that of the oratorio, but not as exclusively religious. He offered the attractions and diversions of opera without requiring their essential dramatic features, so that the lyrical, specially musical element could attain a greater presence. In his *Paradies und die Peri* he led the honorable caravan of the oratorio into Kashmir valleys full of eternally blooming roses and streams springing from Eden, where the eye of Peri and the spirit of Huri gazed. *Der Rose Pilgerfahrt* belongs to those images that one might call visions of poetic mysticism—here, clouds become fragrances, waves moving tones; here, everything is a transparent allegory of an inexpressible feeling, and the symbol charms us like those naive chains of ideas whose puzzles we often pursue with the meaningful questions of childhood. The *Requiem for Mignon* performed the rare service of enriching the consummate creation of a master with a new idea, a fortunately successful stroke. This last lament, this thousandfold sigh repeated above a grave covering so much suffering and beauty, so much yearning and misfortune, is like the final chord of an earthly lot full of painful dissonances. The choral ballads, like *Der Handschuh*, *Des Sängers Fluch*, *Das Glück von Edenhall*, and other works of this kind may be considered more or less successful in their choice of subject matter, but they attest no less to the author's constant striving to acquire the most beautiful trophies of poetry and to relate his name with those of Goethe, Schiller, Uhland, and Moore.[30] This effort is still more evident in his decision—which, we believe, Schumann was the first to take—to compose complete parts of a tragedy, of the most monumental work of our time, *Faust*, without modifying or arranging the text in any way. Although he conceived his music to Byron's *Manfred* for the theater, in which form it was presented only in Weimar,[31] this work will still find attentive audiences in the concert hall and justifiably should be performed with Schumann's other works that enrich our concert programs.

But eliminating all unworthy texts, selecting [only] materials and verses that offer the most suitable drawings for musical colors are not the only means to tie music to poetry. Like vocal music, instrumental music can in its own way have a claim here. Schumann was not the first to propose this idea, but his contribution . . . consists in having understood the idea, endorsed it, defended it in his critical writings, and applied it practically in his compositions with discriminating taste. Berlioz, since his first appearance, had chosen this path with feverish intensity; Mendelssohn . . . gave names to his symphonic pieces that could serve as programs (*Melusine*, *Meeresstille*, *Fingalshöhle*, etc.).[32] Schumann continued this practice and, as a successor of equal stature, went further: he completed some attempts, dared to do more in certain areas, and won broader terrain in this direction. He did not deny pure music its immediate effect; he knew the higher regions of light in our cosmos to which music dared to aspire. . . . Because he treated instrumental music not by imitating Mendelssohn but by competing with him, Schumann proved how deeply aware he was of music's magical power, with which it alone can transport us on the wings of feelings higher than any other inspiration, and with which it allows us to surge into the infinite with no destination, without subject and object, like bodiless essences. . . . But he did not forget that the cult of the beautiful is not limited to a single rite, that not all souls with developed insights can scale certain peaks where they can comprehend without fainting the play unfolding at their feet. . . . And why not approach them as the angels approached the shepherds to announce the happy news of the light in the wilderness? Why not accompany them, as the star showed the holy kings the way to the cradle? Why should instrumental music always do without an accompanying light? Why should she occasionally not make use of a certain poetic foundation? Why should she not indicate the mood, or label it more precisely, with which she wishes to transport the listener? Why should she not specify the particular image, group, or landscape that hovered before the composer, the feeling that ruled him as he created his work? . . . In this respect Schumann says quite cogently: "One has criticized here and there the titles of musical compositions that have been multiplying in more recent times and said, Good music does not require such clues. Certainly not; but music forfeits ever so little through them, and they afford the composer the surest way of preventing obvious misperceptions about the character [of his music]. If poets do it, if they seek to veil the meaning of the entire poem behind a title, why shouldn't also musicians? Just allow the hint to be contained in words clever and fine enough; then one will really be able to recognize the musician's culture."[33] "The Ave Maria of Henselt[34] offers an example of how a well-chosen title may enhance the effect of music. Without that title one would play the piece like an etude of Cramer.[35] But with the Ave Maria [even] the most prosaic person thinks of something. . . . but in finding the correct name for his child the musician has to see what every other artist does: a false name can misfire, however good the music is; an appropriate name can considerably raise one's joy at understanding."[36] "Did not Beethoven in the title to the C-major Overture employ the expression 'written by' instead of 'composed by'?"[37] "There are secret states of the soul [*Seelenzustände*] for which a hint from the composer can lead to faster understanding and must be acknowledged gratefully."[38] He expresses himself still more clearly when he says: "So far as the difficult question of how far instrumental music should go to portray thoughts and events is generally concerned, here we view too much too apprehensively. One certainly errs in believing that composers hastily prepare pen and paper with the intention of expressing this or that in order to depict, to paint. But not infrequently one fixes on occasional impressions and influences from the external world. Unconsciously, next to the musical fantasy, an idea often continues to have its effect, for next to the ear there is the eye, and amid the sounds and tones of the advancing music this constantly active organ defines certain outlines that can be compressed into clear shapes and take form. Now, the more these elements related to the music carry thoughts or images generated by the sounds, the more poetic or plastic the expression of the composition, and the more fantastic or focused the musician's understanding, and all the more will his work be received or comprehended. Why could the thought of eternity not come over Beethoven in the middle of his fantasy? Why could the memory of a great, fallen hero not stir him to compose a work?[39] Why could the memory of one blessed, lapsed time not stir another? Or should we be ungrateful to Shakespeare, who summoned from the breast of a young composer a work worthy of him?[40] Should we be ungrateful to nature and deny that we borrow from her sublime beauty for our works? Italy, the Alps, the image of the sea, a spring twilight—has music not yet informed us about all this? Indeed, even smaller, more specific images lend music such a charming, definite character that one is amazed how music is able to express such things. So a composer related to me that while he was writing down a piece the image of a butterfly on a leaf swimming along in a brook impressed itself on him; this imbued the little piece with the tenderness and naïveté that the image could possess only in reality. In this fine genre of painting Franz Schubert was especially a master, and I cannot omit relating the experience of how once, while performing a Schubert march, the friend with whom I was playing answered my question, whether or not he could see individual shapes before him: 'Truly, I found myself in the middle of Seville more than a hundred years ago, before Dons and Donnas promenading with train dresses, pointed shoes, daggers, etc.' Remarkably enough, our visions were in agreement, including the city."[41]

In his analyses Schumann frequently sought to provide the titles lacking [in compositions]; he succeeded all the more when one considers that the task is a thankless one. In pieces of small dimensions, like Hiller's etudes, or of a certain homogeneity, like Moscheles'[42] compositions, [providing titles] is difficult; in pieces of great dimensions it is dangerous and not too advisable. But [to attempt this] reveals [Schumann's] preference for programs, his lively, inevitably correct critique of titles and of composers' devices that he subjected to examination, never forgetting to account for the success or failure of their applications. Like Beethoven he wrote overtures to great tragedies, to Schiller's *Braut von Messina* and Shakespeare's *Julius Caesar*.[43]

The clue about the character of a piece expressed in a pithy title was closer to him than the idea of an absolute program such as Mendelssohn used in his *Meeresstille*, in which an entire poem formed the foundation of the musical material;[44] nevertheless, Schumann was prepared to explore the matter in more detail: "The idea of underlaying poems with independent music, of finding a series [of poems] and nicely mediating between them and the whole, is an exceptional one worthy of imitation."[45] "The philosophers imagine the matter to be worse than it is: surely they err if they believe that a composer working according to some idea sits himself down like a preacher on a Saturday afternoon, arranges his theme according to the usual three parts, and properly works it out; surely, they err. The creation of the musician is something completely different; and if an image, an idea hovers before him, so he will only feel fortuitous in his work if the idea comes to him in lovely melodies, carried by the same hands that carried the golden pails of which Goethe speaks somewhere. Therefore, keep your prejudices, but at the same time examine and do not let the bungling of the pupil pay for the master."

In no way do we misjudge the evils that go hand in hand with the preference for programs, whether drawn from complete poems or from fragments, from implied or developed prose, from a motto or an epigraph, or only from a title. Through misuse of bad taste programs have often become so laughable that their opponents have a good time citing uncountable misuses and recommending their complete elimination. But if one wanted to reject everything that could be misused, would one not have to begin with music, since on the average she offers infinitely more bad than good, more stupid than intelligent, more trivial than significant? Before he became a musician Schumann was too accustomed to the realm of fantasy, he encountered too often those spirits who inhabit fire and air, and he lived in too close a relationship with those rare, attractive beings who encircle the minds of Hoffmann[46] or Jean Paul not to take his art further in these directions—directions that are perhaps less divine but more diverse, fantastic, visible, and magical than those of an abstract feeling that animates the slumbering waves of an instrument with stormy lamenting or gentle breezes. Meanwhile the unusual balance between his lively enthusiasm, fiery strength of imagination, and well-tempered criticism enabled him to account for the interests our different abilities have in producing works of this kind; he commented quite correctly about one of these: "How the pieces originated, whether from within to without or vice versa, has nothing to do with the matter. . . . For the most part even composers do not know. For one it is this way, for another that way; often an external image passes by, often a series of tones comes again to the fore. If what remains is music and independent melody, one really shouldn't brood but enjoy."[47]

. . . No author before [Schumann] published as impressive a list of works in which program and content came so perfectly together. He borrowed a title from poetry only when his piece was completely permeated with the spirit of the same. Thus, his *Kreisleriana* (Op. 16) splendidly fills out the image of this fantastic romance figure, whom we know like a close friend.[48] And so the *Fantasiestücke* (Opp. 12 and 88) appear to have blossomed in a completely special environment where Jean Paul's and Hoffmann's united breath creates an atmosphere around a little blue star, where mountain peaks of lapis lazuli rise up, where streams of melted diamonds flow, where flowers become female figures, around which silver and golden satellites dance, spinning around like juggler's balls, and where mercurial, iridescent, prismatic sunlight or secret moonbeams shine as happy lovers would like. In the *Nachtstücke*, Op. 23, there shimmer more owls' eyes than stars, we see more sheet lightning than fireflies, we hear more bats and wind howling in decaying bay windows than sighs of love. There, the dry leaves touch the grass like spirits driven around, startled from their rest; wild images thicken the darkness and allow no thoughts of gentle breezes and secretly stolen kisses to arise. In the *Kreisleriana*, Op. 16, the *Album für die Jugend*, Op. 68, and the *Klavierstücke für kleine und große Kinder*, Op. 85, that grace is apparent, that naïveté always striking the proper tone, that spiritual feature that often strangely affects us in children, when their easy credibility makes us smile, when the sharpness of their questions sets us back—a feature also found in the cultural beginnings of people, where it offers that tone of imaginative naïveté that the longing for the wonderful awakens, and that formerly lent all its charm to Aesop's Fables, the *Gnomen-* and *Sylphenmärchen*,[49] and the tales of Perrault ("Bluebeard," "Little Red Riding Hood"), still today the entrancement of youth and among the honored reading of their most lovely memories.[50] With what discrimination [Schumann] allowed the most varied impressions of youth to follow one another; how harmoniously he divided light and shade in the procession of events in the external life of the child as he depicted the child's inwardness! And, to pause for a moment on one generally known work [*Kinderszenen*, Op. 15], how fortuitous the sequence of pieces is! If during the tale of "Fremde Länder und Menschen" [no. 1] one imagines the obedient, blond children's heads turned stiffly toward the narrator's face, in the "Curiose Geschichte" [no. 2] their aroused fantasy is again directed to their surroundings, where the

"Haschemann" [no. 3] then makes a transition to their tumbling and playing. But there is one child whose thoughts roam afar, to the impossible, who wishes to pile joy on joy, game on game. One answers this "Bittendes Kind" [no. 4] with a wise, soft reproach: "Glückes genug" [no. 5]! So the hardly developed souls must learn the difficult truth about earthly inadequacy, whose painful frailty is that we may not drink continually at the well of sentimentality, of the pleasures of the imagination. But this inner maxim is followed by a "Wichtige Begebenheit" [no. 6]. Here the young minds turn from their inhibiting dreams, from their distress caused by the slightest reproach, to the changing circumstances of reality. For some the principal charm again lies in that, stimulated to earnest contemplation, they indulge in precious "Träumereien" [no. 7], in which one can never abandon oneself better than "Am Kamin" [no. 8], by the crackling flame of the hearth. There again commence the wonderful tales full of marvelous adventures, such as the "Ritter vom Steckenpferd" [no. 9], or full of horrors and shivering shudders, when they become "Fast zu ernst" [no. 10] or take fright ["Fürchtenmachen," no. 11]. But now that most gentle, kind spirit, the sandman, descends upon the eyes of the "Einschlummerndes Kind" [no. 12] weary from all the confusing images. Then "Der Dichter" [no. 13] speaks to those at rest, blessing all the little events of the day and raising their significance with his contemplative mind, for they reflect symbolically the great events of mature life and often appear in the same sequence, stimulated by the same impressions. One can say that nearly all Schumann's works conclude with this last quality: each time we imagine ourselves seized by the consecration of a poetic saying, we feel as if the poet, just him and no other, has turned to us and left us after greeting us.—*Papillons* (Op. 2), Intermezzo (Op. 4), *Arabeske* (Op. 18), *Blumenstück* (Op. 19), *Noveletten* (Op. 21), *Romanzen* (Op. 28), *Bunte Blätter* (Op. 99), and *Märchenbilder* (Op. 113) arouse through their names fantastic ideas to which the musical performance completely corresponds. They exhibit the most subtle differences between the gentle gleam of the flower and the butterfly's fluttering around rose cups; between the rapt interest in the narration of the *Noveletten* and the turning, entwining, and unwinding of marvelous arabesques that, continually diverging, nevertheless constantly meet again, between a sentimental romance and the merry impressions of an intermezzo. These differences become clear only through the certain, fine sense of organization, and through the composer who has given each piece such an excellent name that no other is at all applicable. . . . The *Bilder aus Osten* (Op. 66) and the *Waldscenen* (Op. 82) are, with their exceptional grace, full of the rarest distinctions;

they lend the *local color* a certain charm that some will vainly try to reproduce from their external form, instead of pursuing their mystery by divining the feeling that form arouses in mortal hearts. The last two works transport us with poetic truth to the fresh air of northern forests or the glowing soils of the Orient; we see the golden dust that glistened on Naxos when the god of wine was born,[51] or the turquoise heaven with mauve clouds, under which the Thuringian hunter looks after the noble maid. And while such images hover before the eyes of the inspired soul, the soul simultaneously imagines hearing the song of a lark, or the soft step of a hind who dares to come forth from a thicket, or the whispering stirring of that Aegean sea that washed against Athens and Ionia, those two places of cultivation and elegance. And no one will confuse the uproar accompanying the wild hunt with the thunder that announces the approach of a jinni[52] to the Moslem then still the ruler of that sea. The *Davidsbündlertänze* (Op. 6) and the *Ballszenen* (Op. 109) depict easel paintings in which a hundred touches of coquetry, enjoyment, passion, love, blindness, and dizziness are splendidly reproduced as they are aroused by the dance and allowed to overflow, turning incessantly from heart to heart, until all is entwined with the same electric chain of the most charming intoxication. The Viennese *Faschingsschwank* (Op. 16 [*recte* 26]) could serve to illustrate the burlesque journeys of Princess Brambilla,[53] who will be remembered for her adventures; here he depicts with such delightful roguishness and genial comedy the farce of official festivities. *Carnaval* (Op. 9) reveals a colorful masquerade of artists whose groups are treated so directly, so energetically and vividly, that by remarkably reproducing their physiognomies and capturing their most lively gestures it must count among the richest and most successful works of the author and of this genre in general. The *Humoreske* (Op. 20), with its cunning nit-picking, is such a perfect musical equivalent to what the most eccentric English have dubbed *humour* that it can only be characterized and described by this title.

The complete correspondence that Schumann achieved between the ideas contained in the title and their musical coloring cannot be recommended enough as a model. For him a loose connection between certain peculiar rhythms and the memory of certain things was not sufficient. It did not help matters to portray a barcarolle, an Undine,[54] or a fishermaiden with arpeggiations; in his eyes the clanking of wheels did not suffice to paint a lovely miller's daughter;[55] and he certainly was as unenthusiastic about the *Bananier* as he was about the *Mazourka bleue*, the *Caprice savant*, or the *Polka étoile*. Unlike so many others he did not confuse possible mixtures of particular impressions that the different senses feed us or reminiscences of totally different things that affect us in completely similar ways, with a favorite label that one stuck onto a work without pursuing more noble poetic intentions—just as landlords or merchants, who used to choose for their posted emblem a golden angel or a white lion, believed they were cultivating a very fine taste, since, indeed, lions and angels appeared so often in poetic works! And when they advertised a linen store with fluffy cats or a perfume store with a basket of roses, their Pegasus stood on the highest height. But such behavior should not be seen as justifying the existence and appearance of a program, let alone borrowing Christian names or surnames from celebrated persons or famous personalities. The *Paganini-Galops* fit about as well as *Durika*-gloves, as *Lind*-polkas smell like *Lind*—hair cream.[56] No one denies less than we that in the past and present there are celebrities and events that cannot fail to influence the poetic fantasy; we recall only how large Napoleon's mighty shadow loomed in Beethoven's dreams. But passing crazes should not be compared with the tones to which Napoleon inspired Beethoven or with Schumann's marches from the year 1849;[57] rather, such crazes remind us that during the triumphant days of old Rome a parody of her splendor was allowed to be exhibited before the Triumphator.

But it is just as often difficult to find suitable programs (and only those) for music as to be a poet. For our part, we are far from denying the noble distinction that music without any program has, a distinction Goethe expressed in these words: "The merit of art appears most eminently in music, since music has no substance that must be taken into account; she comprises only form and content, and ennobles all that she expresses."[58] But we do not shyly maintain that to fulfill all the requirements of a program a higher level of intellectual refinement is more necessary than to create specific music. Certainly instrumental music can be higher than any other because of its sublime feelings and formal content, and even can attain a height to which no program dares follow; nevertheless, the task of one who ties himself to a program and offers a point of comparison for his creation is no less. Whereas in the former only inspiration and formal perfection are decisive, in the latter one's invention must be continually reconciled with the subject announced at the beginning, a subject everyone knows, the subsequent treatment of which everyone is entitled to follow. . . .

Therefore, we believe we do not expend praise undeservedly on the great musician who concerns us today when we label him the author who in his pianoforte compositions most completely grasped the significance of the program and gave the most splendid examples of its employment. He admirably succeeded in summoning forth musically the effect that the object portrayed and realized through his title would have made on us in reality, by grasping the object with his fine poetic side and thus fulfilling the true requirements of the program. Who would like to decide whether the *Kinderszenen* [and] the *Jugend-album*, with their short but completely sufficient, artistically perfect pieces, would have had the same effect if they had appeared with the outmoded title of Bagatelles or Divertissements? Perhaps then these numerous leaves would not have retained their freshness. . . . One cannot respect too much the conscientiousness with which this master always delivers what he has promised and knows how to discover the noblest and most sympathetic side of his subject without ever abandoning, in detail or on the large scale, his distinctive style, without proceeding at the expense of the intrinsic musical worth, without severing, abducting, and pulling apart the artistic material.

In this discussion of Schumann's significant features . . . many other subjects have been overlooked, in which the honor and recognition due him should be discussed further. But, as we have said, his career should not yet be viewed as finished. We hope that soon he will resume his interrupted work and will be able to enrich the art with numerous [new] compositions. No one wishes this more earnestly and longingly than do we, who have always applauded him with honest admiration and cordial respect.

NOTES

1. Reprinted in a German translation as "Robert Schumanns Klavierkompositionen, opp. 5, 11, und 14," in *Gesammelte Schriften von Franz Liszt*, ed. Lina Ramann, vol. 2: *Reisebriefe eines Baccalaurens der Tonkunst* (Leipzig, 1881), pp. 99–107. [Ed.]

2. Berthold Litzmann, *Clara Schumann: Ein Künstlerleben* (Leipzig, 1902), vol. 1, p. 413. [Ed.]

3. *Neue Zeitschrift für Musik* 12 (1840): 102–3. [Ed.]

4. See Alan Walker, *Franz Liszt: The Virtuoso Years, 1811–1847* (New York, 1983), pp. 347ff.; and Wm. A. Little, "Mendelssohn and Liszt," in *Mendelssohn Studies*, ed. R. Larry Todd (Cambridge, 1992), pp. 111–20. [Ed.]

5. See Alan Walker, *Franz Liszt: The Weimar Years, 1848–1861* (New York, 1989), pp. 156–57. [Ed.]

6. The article was later reprinted, with revisions, in the collected edition of

Liszt's writings. *Gesammelte Schriften von Franz Liszt*, ed. L. Ramann, vol. 4: *Aus den Annalen des Fortschritts* (Leipzig, 1882), pp. 103–85. [Ed.]

7. Robert Schumann, *Gesammelte Schriften über Musik und Musiker* [Leipzig, 1854], vol. 1, p. 72. [Liszt]

8. Jean Paul Richter (1763–1825). [Trans.]

9. The German composer Carl Maria von Weber (1786–1826) may be regarded as a precursor of Schumann: Weber contemplated founding a music journal, wrote several articles for a musical dictionary, worked on a musical novel entitled *Tonkünstlers Leben*, and was active as a journalist. For an edition of Weber's music criticism, see *Carl Maria von Weber: Writings on Music*, trans. Martin Cooper, ed. John Warrack (Cambridge, 1981). [Ed.]

10. Preliminary discussions about the *Neue Zeitschrift für Musik* began in Leipzig during the summer of 1833. The first issue appeared on 3 April 1834, and Schumann assumed the editorship early in 1835. See Leon Plantinga, *Schumann as Critic* (New Haven, 1967). [Ed.]

11. "Of course criticism will always be compromised when it does not come from productive figures" (Schumann, *Gesammelte Schriften über Musik und Musiker*, vol. 1, p. 27). [Liszt]

12. During the Spanish Inquisition, an instrument of torture consisting of two metal bars, placed in front of and behind the victim's legs, that were tightened by means of screws. Goethe referred to Spanish boots in the first part of *Faust*. [Ed.]

13. A prolific writer, Berlioz contributed regularly as a music critic to two periodicals, the *Revue et gazette musicale* (from 1834 to 1861) and *Journal des débats* (1834–63). By 1854 Liszt would have known as well the collection of satirical articles, *Les soirées de l'orchestre* (Paris, 1852). [Ed.]

14. The reference is to Wagner's great essays written during his years of exile in Zurich, including *Art and Revolution*, *Artwork of the Future*, and *Opera and Drama* (1849–51), in which he developed his vision of the new music drama and its *Gesamtkunstwerk*. [Ed.]

15. A. B. Marx (?1795–1866), friend of Mendelssohn, editor of the *Berliner allgemeine musikalische Zeitung* (1824–30), and author of the composition textbook *Die Lehre von der musikalischen Komposition* (1837–45). [Ed.]

16. Presumably the composer and author Ferdinand Hiller (1811–85). [Ed.]

17. J.-F.-F. Halévy (1799–1862), French composer of the opera *La juive* (1835) [Ed.]

18. The French opera composer Adolphe Adam (1803–56); facing bankruptcy in 1848, Adam turned to journalism and wrote articles for *Le constitutionnel* and the *Assemblée nationale*. [Ed.]

19. The German pianist-composer Hans von Bülow (1830–94), who moved to Weimar in 1851 to study with Liszt, under whose guidance he undertook his first concert tour in 1853. [Ed.]

20. *Gesammelte Schriften über Musik und Musiker*, vol. 3, p. 30. [Liszt]

21. Ibid., p. 159. [Liszt]

22. Ibid., vol. 2, p. 63. [Liszt]

23. Ibid., vol. 1, p. 289. [Liszt]

24. Uhieno da Fiesole (ca. 1430–86), Florentine sculptor. [Ed.]

25. The Greek sculptors Praxiteles (385–ca. 320 B.C.) and Phidias (500–431 B.C.). [Ed.]

26. The Flemish painter Jan van Eyck (d. 1441) and the German Nazarene painter Peter von Cornelius (1783–1867). [Ed.]

27. The Franco-Flemish composer Josquin des Prez (ca. 1440–1521); C. W. Gluck (1714–87), composer of French and Italian opera. [Ed.]

28. Those opposed to chromaticism [*Antichromatiker*] should reflect that there was a time when the [dissonant] seventh was perceived as the diminished octave is today, and that through harmonic developments the passions attained finer shades so that music was placed alongside the highest organs of art that offer a written record and signs for all the moods of the soul. [Liszt]

29. *Gesammelte Schriften über Musik und Musiker*, vol. 3, p. 263. [Liszt]

30. *Der Handschuh*, Op. 87, for voice and piano; *Des Sängers Fluch*, Op. 139, for chorus and orchestra; and *Das Glück von Edenhall*, Op. 143, for chorus and orchestra, with texts by Friedrich Schiller and Ludwig Uhland. Thomas Moore (1779–1852), Irish poet whose oriental poem *Lalla Rookh* inspired Schumann's *Paradies und die Peri*. [Ed.]

31. On 13 June 1852. [Ed.]

32. The concert overtures *Die schöne Melusine*, Op. 32 (1833), *Meeresstille und glückliche Fahrt*, Op. 27 (1834), and *Fingalshöhle* (*Die Hebriden*), Op. 26 (1835). [Ed.]

33. *Gesammelte Schriften über Musik und Musiker*, vol. 3, p. 17. [Liszt]

34. Adolf Henselt (1814–89), pianist and composer. [Ed.]

35. Johann Baptist Cramer (1771–1858), German pianist and composer active in England. [Ed.]

36. *Gesammelte Schriften über Musik und Musiker*, vol. 3, p. 73. [Liszt]

37. Ibid., p. 52 [Liszt]. The reference is to the "Consecration of the House" Overture, Op. 124 (*Die Weihe des Hauses*). [Ed.]

38. *Gesammelte Schriften über Musik und Musiker*, vol. 4, p. 43. [Liszt]

39. The reference is to the slow movement, the *Marcia funebre sulla morte d'un Eroe*, of Beethoven's Piano Sonata in A♭, Op. 26. [Ed.]

40. Mendelssohn's Overture to *A Midsummer Night's Dream*, composed in 1826 when he was seventeen. [Ed.]

41. *Gesammelte Schriften über Musik und Musiker*, vol. 1, p. 142. [Liszt]

42. The pianist-composer Ignaz Moscheles (1794–1870). [Ed.]

43. *Die Braut von Messina*, Op. 100 (1851); *Julius Cäsar*, Op. 128 (1851). [Ed.]

44. Mendelssohn's overture was conceived as two orchestral tableaux that depicted Goethe's two poems *Meeresstille* ("Calm Sea") and *Glückliche Fahrt* ("Prosperous Voyage"). [Ed.]

45. *Gesammelte Schriften über Musik und Musiker*, vol. 2, p. 225. [Liszt]

46. E.T.A. Hoffmann (1776–1822), German writer, music critic, and composer. [Ed.]

47. *Gesammelte Schriften über Musik und Musiker*, vol. 3, p. 30. [Liszt]

48. Named after the fictional madcap violinist Johannes Kreisler, who figures in the writings of E.T.A. Hoffmann. [Ed.]

49. In European folklore, gnomes, sylphs, salamanders, and nereids were fairylike creatures that corresponded to the four elements of earth, air, fire, and water. [Trans.]

50. Charles Perrault (1628–1703), whose *Contes du temps passé* (1697) introduced for the first time in print the folk tales "Bluebeard" and "Little Red Riding Hood." [Trans.]

51. In Greek mythology, Dionysus was born on Naxos, the largest and most fertile of the Cyclades Islands. [Trans.]

52. In Islamic mythology, any class of spirits, lower than angels, capable of assuming human or animal form and influencing the course of events for good or evil. [Trans.]

53. Possibly Mariette Brambilla (1808–75), Russian singer and amateur composer, whose celebrated career took her to Odessa, Paris, and London. [Trans.]

54. The water sprite Undine, the subject of E.T.A. Hoffmann's opera *Undine* (1816), based on a fairy tale by Friedrich de la Motte Fouqué. The subject was later treated by Gabriel Fauré, and most notably by Ravel in the opening movement of *Gaspard de la Nuit*. [Trans.]

55. Presumably an allusion to Schubert's song cycle *Die schöne Müllerin*. [Ed.]

56. The references are to the Italian virtuoso violinist Niccolò Paganini (1782–1840) and the Swedish soprano Jenny Lind (1820–87). [Ed.]

57. Four Marches for Piano, Op. 76. [Ed.]

58. From the aphoristic "Betrachtungen im Sinne der Wanderer" at the end of book 2 of *Wilhelm Meisters Wanderjahre* (Weimar, 1829), reprinted in the so-called *Maximen und Reflexionen* in the *Ausgabe letzter Hand* of Goethe's works, ed. Johann Peter Eckermann (Weimar, 1833). [Ed.]

Schumanniana No. 4:

The Present Musical Epoch and

Robert Schumann's Position in

Music History (1861)

ADOLF SCHUBRING

TRANSLATED BY JOHN MICHAEL COOPER

Between 1860 and 1869 a series of twelve articles appeared in the *Neue Zeitschrift für Musik* under the general rubric of *Schumanniana*. The author, Adolf Schubring (1817–93), by profession a judge in the town of Dessau, was the stepbrother of the pastor Julius Schubring (1806–89), who had befriended Felix Mendelssohn during the 1820s and collaborated on the oratorios *St. Paul* and *Elijah* (for Julius Schubring's memoirs of Mendelssohn, see *Mendelssohn and His World*, ed. R. Larry Todd [Princeton, 1991], pp. 221–36). Adolf, declaring himself a *Schumannianer*, undertook in his writings to make the case for a Schumann school, separate and distinct from the "conservative" Mendelssohnians and the "progressive" *Zukunftsmusiker* represented by Liszt and Wagner. The proponents of the new school included three musicians largely forgotten today, Carl Ritter, Theodor Kirchner, and Woldemar Bargiel, but also Johannes Brahms, whom Schubring first met in 1856 and with whom he enjoyed a lengthy correspondence (see Johannes Brahms, *Briefwechsel*, ed. Max Kalbeck [Berlin, 1915], vol. 8; for an insightful study of Schubring's view of Brahms, see Walter Frisch, "Brahms and Schubring: Musical Criticism and Politics at Mid-Century," *19th-Century Music* 7 (1984): 271–81).

In his articles that dealt specifically with Schumann, Schubring treated several topics, including editorial issues in *Das Paradies und die*

Peri and the piano works, and Schumann's use of the seventeenth-century "Großvater-Tanz" (see pp. 84–91). The fourth article in the series, translated here, endeavored to place Schumann at the head of a new epoch in music. Drawing on art histories of the time, Schubring's classification divided music history into three broad epochs, the architectonic, the plastic, and the painterly; each of these in turn subdivided into three periods, the epic, the dramatic, and the lyric. The age of German supremacy in music had dawned in the eighteenth century with J. S. Bach, the last lyric composer in the architectonic epoch and the first epic composer in the plastic epoch. Gluck and Mozart were dramatic composers in the plastic epoch; Beethoven, its last dramatic representative, was followed by the lyric composers Schubert and Carl Maria von Weber. In this scheme Spohr and Mendelssohn figured as transitional figures who anticipated the new painterly epoch, which, Schubring confidently asserted, had recently begun with its first epic representative, Robert Schumann. [Ed.]

[Source: "Die gegenwärtige Musikepoche und Robert Schumann's Stellung in der Musikgeschichte," *Neue Zeitschrift für Musik* 54 (1861): 197–98, 205–6, 213–14.]

If one asks the art historians and aestheticians, they will always say that the present, when they think and write, is a time of the deepest decline in art; at most, they see another feeble sunset on their (narrow) horizon. So it was already in Mattheson's and Fux's[1] day—and yet these were contemporaries of Bach and Handel. Their successors recognized that that sunset had been the dawning of a new, more beautiful day, but already in Mozart's and Beethoven's time the old lament was sounding anew. Are not, then, the complaints of our contemporary aestheticians likewise unfounded? The mere fact that the pictorial arts required thousands of years to develop could easily give us hope that the newest art, that experienced in tones, could not possibly be in a state of decline after just a few centuries. I beg not to be misunderstood when I call music the newest art. I do not deny that the Jews and Egyptians practiced music; nevertheless, Jubal is called the father of pipers and fiddlers.[2] A skill merits the name of art only when imagination elevates it above artisanship,[3] and one can speak of the flowering of an art only after it has become the representative ideal of an entire age. For the Jews and Egyptians, this ideal was architecture: Egyptian history is the history of the pharonic constructions; and the Jewish epic, the Bible, tells of the building and rebuilding of the tabernacles and the Temple. This cannot be disputed any more than can that Greece had its ideal in sculpture; the middle ages, in painting; and pealing Christianity, Catholic as well as Protestant, in music.

In the following sketch, which I dedicate with a cheerful and hopeful heart to musicians, I shall attempt to demonstrate that music is currently in the middle of a natural state of development, and that a new epoch has begun precisely with *Schumann*.

The history of the fine arts shows us an eternal progress from the common and material to the particular and spiritual, from the objective to the subjective; for man was made from *dust* and his spirit aspires to *heaven*.

Of the three fine arts, the first one we encounter in most histories of art is architecture, which, concrete and earthbound, treats colossal masses of material. Then, after the gods had revealed themselves to the Greeks in the beauty of mortal form, the flower of sculpture could blossom. The next steps forward in the development of art became possible only with the advent of Christianity and the recognition that God lives *within us*. This new recognition was first manifested in an increased introspectiveness in architecture and pictorial depiction. The pointed arches of the Gothic cathedral, with its spires reaching heavenward, aptly express this upswing just as the majestic portals at its entrance eloquently invite us to enter. And the creator no longer found his ideal primarily in the beautiful forms of the entire naked body but in facial features, as a mirror of *the inner self*. From here to recognizing that this interior was revealed still infinitely more finely in *color*, the light enveloping the body, was just a small step, which *painting* took. And with this new perspective there began again the progression from the general to the specific, with repercussions for the older arts; medieval architecture and art became, so to speak, painterly. Within pictorial art, which was based upon the measurable in touch and sight, no further progress was readily possible; first, it was necessary to cross the border, to make a fresh attempt in a new, purely subjective domain. This step from the spatial to the temporal world was made by *music*, the art of sounding feelings, which, abandoning everything tangible and visible, sacrificed the ability to present the objective, thereby attaining instead the deepest essence of the soul— pure humanity.

To trace further the influence of music upon the other arts would take us too far.[4] For my purpose suffice it to say that the progress of each art has informed the other arts, just as the fine arts collectively progressed from the general (architecture) to the particular, first typical and then individual (sculpture), and then to the most specialized (painting). Consider the path sculpture has traversed from its architectonic infancy: how it manifested itself in the colossal roads to the Egyptian Sphinx, then in the typical sculptures of Praxiteles, then in the individualistic ones of Peter Vischer, and then in Canova's portraits![5]

Now, if each of the three pictorial arts has had in turn an architectural, plastic, and painterly epoch, then this conjecture, according to the law of progressive introspection, corroborates that music has developed similarly and will continue to do so. And indeed, the history of music, so far as we can survey it up to now, has already met this criterion.

We can distinguish here first of all an architectonic epoch. This is the age of rhythm, of measured tones. The triad rules undisputed, even in melody, which is initially just a purely coincidental accoutrement; only later do particular, defined arabesques, released from the spatial into the temporal sphere (that is, the sphere of movement), assume the guises of canon and fugue and thus lead to true melody. But this arabesquelike embellishment cannot yet achieve the freedom of diatonicism, because it remains fettered to the triad and the self-imposed limitations of the church modes.

Attempts are made to develop *rhythmic* sacred song into the motet and the oratorio; the latter represents the wooden beginnings of opera. Rhythmic elements lead to an early cultivation of the most diverse dances, such as the courante, gigue, gavotte, allemande, chaconne, pavane, passacaglia, and à la burla, which are joined in a bouquet of dances to produce the suite, the first of the larger forms of instrumental music.

In the *plastic* epoch the arabesquelike forms of the canon and fugue recede, and the chorale loses its rhythmic element; melody achieves diatonic freedom; and harmony progresses to the seventh chord. The form of the embellished chorale leads to the *alternativo*[6] and variations; the suite is filled with epic contents (similar to episodes) and from now on appears in the form of the modern sonata (quartet and symphony), in which today only individual movements (such as the minuet and march) survive that recall their lyrical origins. By and large, this age has progressed beyond the crystalline age of arabesques, of simple playing with tones, and has attained the status of characteristic, emotive music.

Finally, in the third epoch, the *painterly* one, diatonic melody and seventh chords are no longer sufficient. Determined to raise the previously neglected *harmonic* element to the level of other elements, this age seizes upon chromaticism (from *chroma*, color) and enharmoni-

cism, upon ninth and eleventh chords and upon a richer instrumentation, in order to attain the *colors* necessary to express its finer grada-
tions. Free at last of crystalline arabesques, the third age no longer
finds even emotive music sufficient but begins to strive for an ethical
content (program music). Western pioneers advance beyond the border, and though they do not yet conquer the neighboring province of
poetry, their forward progress at least enables other colonists to settle
near the border.

So, in music as in the pictorial arts, we observe a progression from
the general and material to the individual, spiritual, and moral. First,
in the *architectonic* epoch: simple rhythmic measurement of the tones;
harmony based on triads, melody bound by the arbitrary restrictions
of the modes; and crystalline, arabesquelike structures. Then, in the
plastic epoch: free, diatonic melodic construction; seventh chords;
characteristic, emotive music. And finally, in the *painterly* epoch: en-
harmonic and chromatic melody; harmony expanded by ninth and
eleventh chords; more colorful instrumentation; and the emergence
of the ethical in program music.

And now, if after all this there remains no doubt that German music
is currently in its painterly epoch, then we must still ask when and
with which composers this epoch began. To discover the correct answer we must examine the two previous epochs still more closely. As is
immediately evident to the attentive observer, these epochs have followed parallel courses: Each began with a cycle of epic artists, followed by dramatists and then by lyricists.

In their *represented contents*, then, we observe the same logical, inevitable progress from the general (epic) to the incipient typical to the
individual (ancient and modern drama), and then to the most subjective (lyric)—just as we have referred to this progress in the *manner of
representation* in the three epochs of architectonic, plastic, and painterly music.

After the great Netherlander stonemasons had extracted musical
cornerstones from the rawest materials, the old Italian and German
masters began constructing majestic musical cathedrals at the beginning of the sixteenth century. Because of the close internal affinity of
architectonic form with epic content (based on a common generality),
during the first, architectonic epoch music was naturally able to attain
something of the classical (that is, valuable for all ages) only within the
context of the epic—and indeed, in the very beginnings of the epic, in
chant and measured chorale. For that feeling of naive, childlike wonder at all the majesty that surrounds us—a feeling that underlies
every epic poem—is first expressed in praising the Creator and the

Creation. "And God saw everything that he had made, and, behold, it was very good."[7] Thus, of lasting significance in this epoch are only the great Italian epic composers Palestrina ([c.] 1524–94), G. M. Nanini, and G. Allegri, and their German contemporaries Senfl (c. 1480–1560), J. Eccard (1553–1611), and Schütz (1585–1672).[8] The last-named already began to move forward from oratorio to opera,[9] and was followed by Keiser, Mattheson, and Telemann;[10] but according to its natural limitations, the opera of the architectonic epoch had to remain an essentially wooden structure. In particular, the Germans were hindered in their cultural development by the great religious war and by the confusion that preceded and followed it. They were surpassed by the Italians, especially in music, so that when, among others, Hasse (1699–[1783]) and Graun[11] strove to make up for lost time, the flowering of architectonic opera and lyricism (beginning with madrigals, also cultivated in Germany, and ending with the embellished da capo arias of Alessandro Scarlatti[12]) was already past. By now the Italians had already entered into the plastic epoch, and this step forward was then taken by [our] heroes Bach and Handel as a new point of departure. From this time on, Germans took the lead in advancing musical culture, and they retain it to this day; therefore, for the plastic and following period I can confine my reflections to German music, which is more familiar to all of us and by itself offers a comprehensive view.

Immediately, we again encounter here three great epic artists: first, Johann Sebastian Bach (1685–1750), who simultaneously is the last lyricist of the architectonic epoch, as vestiges in his embellished arias and dances attest. Bach also continued to inform his creations in the most intimate way with the styles of this period, as is evident from his overwhelming reliance on the architectonic forms of the chorale, canon, and fugue in his masses and oratorios, works otherwise filled with a plastic and epic spirit. What the chorale lost in rhythmic elements, it won back twofold through the emergence of melody, leading from figuration to ornamentation and the freedom of diatonic melody.

Then comes the mighty G. F. Handel (1684 [*recte* 1685]–1759), advancing toward the dramatic, in whose works religious materials (the chorale and strict fugue) recede and the human call for freedom begins to sound. And finally there is Joseph Haydn (1732–1809), who sings of the Creator, the Creation,[13] and good, merry people. Inclined toward the lyrical, Haydn breaks loose from the epic into idyllic. But at the same time—and this is his principal contribution to progress—Haydn fills the old, lyrical form of the suite with epic contents (episodes) and develops from it the sonata (also the quartet and symphony).

In the meantime—old Papa Haydn should have seen it!—the great dramatic period had already dawned, represented by the shining figures of Gluck (1714–87), Mozart (1756–91), and Beethoven (1770–1827). The task of the first was to describe in his dramas *typical* characters in the ancient fashion, without comic elements. Then came Mozart, great as much for his synthesis of French, Italian, and German musical styles as for his inexhaustible versatility in presenting comic and tragic personalities after Shakespearean models. And finally there was Beethoven, who, to be sure, wrote only one opera (ἕνα αλλα λεουτα!)[14] but achieved in it a new degree of unity between the typical and the individualistic, and also filled the available musical forms with dramatic contents—an accomplishment that eluded Mozart (who in this respect did not surpass Haydn's accomplishments). I recall here Beethoven's *Missa solemnis*, the second part of *Christus am Oelberge*,[15] the middle and late symphonies, sonatas, and quartets, and some of the variations. As the last dramatist, Beethoven already began to avail himself of lyricism (*An die ferne Geliebte* and "Adelaide"[16]); indeed, he even approached tone painting, not just sensing its emergence, as had Haydn, the last epic composer, but consciously working toward it. Nonetheless Beethoven cannot be regarded as the proper beginning of the painterly epoch, because he still exclusively employed in his paintings only the old plastic materials.

Then, in the lyric period, Franz Schubert (1797–1828) represented an elevated lyricism: hymn, dithyrambe, and ode. Standing nearest the age of the sonata, he succeeded at filling this form with a lyrical content, partly by drawing upon Hungarian elements; but he was at his greatest in his songs, dances, marches, and lyric piano pieces.

Carl Maria von Weber (1786–1826), who represented pure lyricism, could no longer write sonatas or symphonies.[17] Relying upon folk song, he instead succeeded in bringing lyricism to opera (*Preziosa, Der Freischütz*, and *Oberon*[18]). Where he strove for the purely dramatic (*Euryanthe*[19]) his powers proved insufficient. Rather, the lyrical movements in his operas (including the overtures), the solo and four-voice Lieder, and the dances assure him a lasting place in music history.

Now begins a time of fluctuation—sadly, but natural enough during a time of transition. The artists active during this period—mostly mere talents, or at best, partial geniuses—were so captivated and crippled by the authority of the last epic and dramatic heroes that they were incapable of real progress in music. They erred now in their

materials, now in their techniques. First there was Spohr (1784–
1859), whose proper field was contemplative lyricism—the elegy—
but who devoted most of his energies to the symphony, quartet,
sacred oratorio, and opera.[20] As shown by his predilection for chromaticism and enharmonicism, he sensed that music had to become
painterly. But he did not suspect that painterly music had to begin
anew with the epic—that is, with the modern epic, which mastered
the romantic by setting aside religiosity. And because of this contradiction between the new, painterly means of expression and the old,
plastic content, his works, though often technically masterful, seem
unfocused and unsatisfying.

Then there was Friedrich Schneider (1786–1853), a partial genius
who, in his polyphonic Lieder for men's voices and in several passages
from his numerous oratorios and sacred pieces, exhausted himself by
attempting to restore the religious-plastic epic, whose time was long
since past.[21] And finally there was Mendelssohn (1809–47), who was
the greatest of these three but who likewise vacillated between the
worn-out religious epic (which he relentlessly attempted to reinvigo-
rate artificially by lyrical means) and experiments in [musical] landscape painting. Because Mendelssohn clung to the old, plastic, slate
pencil and did not reach for the painter's rich palette of colors, these
experiments (the *Hebrides* Overture and the "Scottish" and "Italian"
Symphonies[22]) could amount to no more than pencil drawings. Only
when he was purely lyrical and worked with plastic means was Mendelssohn a master of his times (consider many of his solo and four-
voice Lieder, certain *Lieder ohne Worte, Die erste Walpurgisnacht,* or,
above all, his charming elfin dances from the *Midsummer Night's Dream*
and the scherzos of some of his quartets).[23]

From the uncertain vacillation and faltering of these plastic lyricists
we may deduce that the plastic epoch is nearing its end. Even Mendelssohn's and Spohr's hesitant forays anticipate the beginning of the
epic period of the painterly epoch.

Number 52 [*sic*] of the *Allgemeine musikalische Zeitung* for 1848 contains the following communication: "It is said that already as a boy
Robert Schumann possessed a special proclivity and gift for representing in tones feelings and characteristic traits. Indeed, he was supposedly able to portray the personalities of different playmates so
precisely and clearly on the piano that they would burst into laughter
at the accuracy of the portrayal."

Gifted with this painterly talent, the boy Schumann was also fortunate that he could follow his own genius unimpeded by the authority
of an imposing musician (old master Kuntsch, who was soon out-

stripped by his pupil[24]). Introduced into the world of romanticism through Shakespeare, Goethe, Jean Paul, Tieck, Hoffmann, and Byron, he could not be restrained by Heinrich Dorn's music theory instruction, through which he galloped in 1831.[25] Schumann remained free of the pedantic wasteland of old school rules.

Just as J. S. Bach was simultaneously the last lyricist of the architectonic epoch and the first epic artist of the plastic epoch, so Robert Schumann (1810–56) achieved greatness first as a lyricist, following Schubert in imbuing plastic lyricism with romanticism; but he was greater still, and a true reformer, as the first epic artist of romantic tone painting. We marvel first of all at his piano works and the surprisingly magical tones he achieved on this instrument (previously treated as sterile); in his orchestral works, at the wealth of tone colors;[26] in his harmony, at the liveliness and direct freshness; in his melody, an expressiveness intimating the most deeply hidden emotional states; in his rhythm, a versatile, inexhaustible primeval quality—and at how he combined all this as had no previous composer. These are *carmina inaudita prius*.[27] Why Schumann's genius in all its greatness has been recognized by so few until now lies in his ideally realistic truthfulness, in the fresh colors of his images, in the novelty of his ideas. It is not in the *form*, for here Schumann generally adheres to older models, with some broadenings that arise from expansions of the material. Rather, it is in the new *content*, which for most of his contemporaries remained a closed book in Schumann's works. Of course, in a new work everyone reads only what he has already experienced as true, or whatever else has slumbered unconsciously within, waiting only to be stirred.

It is said that in the Siberian glacier there hid a giant antediluvian animal from which an entire village obtained its daily supply of meat for years on end, and which nevertheless appeared to remain undiminished, promising to last for years to come. Musically, *Schumann* is such a mammoth and a Croesus: a hundred average musicians can get everything they need from his works, but he will never be exhausted. He introduces so much new that one is initially bewildered and seeks the reason for this confusion in the tone poet rather than in one's own shortcomings. But later we can pick up the piece that was once angrily tossed aside, and if we have meanwhile undergone new experiences in our lives and souls, we then discover that what was incomprehensible before now expresses our more recent experiences most eloquently. Of course, not everyone is as honest as Zelter, who, having declared Beethoven's *Fidelio* incomprehensible, acknowledged after the second performance that he himself had been the ass.[28]

As important as Schumann is in his lyric works, so fragrant with romantic magic, he is at his greatest in his epic works—not the effete religious epic but the modern, romantic one, which has found its proper form in the romance, ballade, legend, novella, novel, and *Märchen*. In his romances and ballades for one and more voices; in *Das Paradies und die Peri, Der Rose Pilgerfahrt, Der Königssohn, Vom Pagen und der Königstochter*; in the dramaticized legends *Manfred, Faust*, and *Genoveva*; in the painterly [string] quartets and orchestral novels; and especially in his piano tales, which he himself designated romances, ballads, novelettes, fables, *Bunte Blätter*, scenes,[29] *Carnaval, Faschingsschwank, Kreisleriana*, and *Märchenerzählungen*—into all these he has poured his deepest and most innermost self, the blood of his soul. In Schumann's withdrawn, introspective subjectivity, too, lies the reason why he entrusted his deepest feelings to the piano. Here, he can give directly of himself, whereas an orchestral theme necessarily must convey a general character because it may be equally suitable for the violin, trumpet, flute, horn, or cello. I recall that in the first movement of the B♭-major Symphony the theme is even taken up by the Turkish triangle.[30] What is more, Schumann can make entirely different demands upon aesthetically literate piano dilettantes than on average performers of chamber music and thus is not forced to restrain himself in his piano works. Because of their more common, more easily grasped thematic content, the symphonies and works for chorus and orchestra have so far remained better known than the more profound, more difficult piano works of his first period, up through Op. 23,[31] which perhaps will be widely understood only by another generation.

We have recognized the present time in music history as the painterly epoch and Robert Schumann as its first epic composer. All that remains to fulfill the theme of this essay is to peer into the future and to demonstrate that the present is a time of hope. Therefore, I now leave the present, for the danger of getting caught here between the anvil and the hammer is too great.

I have already touched upon the intrinsic affinity between architectonic and epic music; the same affinity exists between plastic and dramatic music and between painterly and lyric music. For the progression from the general to the most specific in the *manner of presentation* (from the architectonic to the plastic and painterly) must correspond to an analogous progression in the *material being presented* (from the epic to the dramatic and lyric). Now since, as is well known, the highest achievements occur when the manner of presentation accords completely with the material being presented, we may conclude that in the *first (architectonic) epoch* the greatest achievements were made by the artists of the *first (epic) period*: the Italians Palestrina, Nanini, and Allegri, and the Germans Senfl, Eccard, and Schütz. Then, in the *second (plastic) epoch* the most significant achievements were made by the tone poets of the *second (dramatic) period*, our heroes Gluck, Mozart, and Beethoven, beside whom stood their contemporaries Paisiello, Cimarosa, Grétry, Cherubini, and Boieldieu[32] in French and Italian music as *dii minorum gentium*.[33] And by the same token we should conclude that in the present, *third* epoch, the painterly, the artists of the still-to-come *third* period—the lyricists—likewise will attain their appropriate greatness. Thus, to use an obvious metaphor: if the architectonic epoch and the distinction of its composers represented a decrescendo ($>$) and the plastic a crescendo and decrescendo ($<$ $>$), then the painterly epoch will probably suggest a continuing crescendo ($<$). Some epic artists will yet follow Schumann (perhaps they are already alive and practicing!); only then will the dramatists arrive and, finally, the lyricists, to whom the present epoch evidently will entrust its greatest achievements. A most comforting prospect, then, even if there is to be only a modest crescendo. Will the painterly epoch then be followed by yet a fourth, perhaps specifically musical, period? Or will the next step forward be taken by another musician who, just as Mozart brought together the German, French, and Italian music of his day (enabling Beethoven to develop German music further), will join the music of these three peoples with, for example, the flowering music of the Hungarians, Slavs, and so on, to form a new foundation? We must leave the answer to our great-great-grandchildren. We can do this in all good conscience because, as is obvious from our sketch of music and its necessary, logical course of development, we are certain that the future remains bright for the painterly period begun by the reformer Schumann.

NOTES

1. Johann Mattheson (1681–1764), influential theorist and chronicler of early eighteenth-century musical life; Johann Joseph Fux (1660–1741), author of the widely circulated treatise on counterpoint *Gradus ad Parnassum* (Vienna, 1725). [Trans.]

2. After Genesis 4.21, where Jubal is the "father of them that play upon the harp and the organ." On the tradition of Jubal as the inventor of music, see James McKinnon, "Jubal vel Pythagoras: Quis Sit Inventor Musicae?" *Musical Quarterly* 64 (1978): 1–28. [Ed.]

3. Hottentots and Samyans can build their huts, too, but that does not make them *architects*. [Schubring]

4. It seems to me that the most recently developed branch of painting, landscape, is one such repercussion of music, and some paintings of the Düsseldorf School deal with a purely musical and lyrical content [Schubring]. Schubring may be referring to the leading representatives of the Düsseldorf Academy and its *Malerschule*, including its founder, Wilhelm von Schadow (1789–1862), and Andreas Aschenbach (1815–1910), Eduard Bendemann (1811–89), Theodor Hildebrandt (1804–74), Julius Hübner (1806–82), and Johann Wilhelm Schirmer (1807–63). [Trans.]

5. Praxiteles, Greek sculptor of the fourth century B.C.; Peter Vischer (?1460–1529), celebrated bronzecaster, creator of the tombstone monument of Emperor Maximilian V in Innsbruch, after a sketch by Albrecht Dürer; Antonio Canova (1757–1822), founder of the "modern" school of sculpture, marking the transition to the classic style of Thorvaldsen. [Trans.]

6. In the eighteenth century, paired movements that were to be played in alternation (e.g., minuets, bourées, passepieds). Schumann designated as "alternativo" the middle sections of his Intermezzi, Op. 4. [Trans.]

7. Genesis 1.31. [Trans.]

8. Giovanni Pierluigi da Palestrina; G. M. Nanini (1543–1607); Gregorio Allegri (1582–1652); Ludwig Senfl; Johannes Eccard; and Heinrich Schütz. [Ed.]

9. On Schütz's lost operas, see Werner Braun, "Das Ballett zum großen Kopenhagener Beilager 1634," in *Heinrich Schütz und die Musik in Dänemark zur Zeit Christians IV.*, ed. Anne Orbæk Jensen and Ole Kongsted (Copenhagen, 1989), pp. 78–79. [Ed.]

10. Reinhard Keiser (1674–1739); and Georg Philipp Telemann (1681–1767). [Trans.]

11. Johann Adolf Hasse; and Carl Heinrich Graun (1704–59). [Trans.]

12. Alessandro Scarlatti (1660–1725). [Trans.]

13. The oratorio *Die Schöpfung* (1798). [Trans.]

14. Literally, "One, and a lion!"—an allusion to the well-known Aesop's fable about the lioness who replied, "Yes, but it's a lion!" to a fox who mocked her because she bore only one cub at a time. Meant, of course, is Beethoven's *Fidelio*, given in its first version in 1805, its second in 1806, and its third in 1814. [Trans.]

15. The Mass in D major (*Missa Solemnis*), Op. 123, composed in 1819–23 and published in 1827; and the oratorio *Christ on the Mount of Olives*, Op. 85, on a text by F. X. Huber, composed in 1803–4 and published in 1811. [Trans.]

16. *An die ferne Geliebte*, Op. 98, song cycle on texts of A. Jeitteles; "Adelaide," Op. 46, text by F. von Matthisson. [Trans.]

17. Actually, Weber composed not only two symphonies (J. 50 and 51, published in 1812 and 1839) but also four well-known piano sonatas (no. 1 in C, 1812; no. 2 in A♭, 1816; no. 3 in D minor, 1817; and no. 4 in E minor, 1823). For a reevaluation of the sonatas, see Michael C. Tusa, "In Defense of Weber,"

in *Nineteenth-Century Piano Music*, ed. R. Larry Todd (New York, 1991), pp. 152–68. [Trans.]

18. *Preciosa*, incidental music after P. A. Wolff, premiered in Berlin on 14 March 1821; *Der Freischütz*, opera on a libretto by Friedrich Kind, premiered in Berlin on 18 June 1821; and *Oberon*, opera on a libretto by James R. Planché, premiered in London on 12 April 1826. [Trans.]

19. *Euryanthe*, opera on a libretto by H. von Chézy, premiered in Vienna on 25 October 1823. [Trans.]

20. Ludwig Spohr, violin virtuoso and Kapellmeister in Kassel (1842–59), composed ten symphonies, numerous chamber works, and four sacred oratorios as well as fifteen violin concertos. His oratorio *Die letzten Dinge* (1826) was one of the nineteenth century's most popular before Mendelssohn's *St. Paul* (1836). [Trans.]

21. Schneider composed numerous masses and sacred vocal works as well as nineteen oratorios, of which *Das Weltgericht* (1819) was the most popular. [Trans.]

22. The *Hebrides* Overture, Op. 26; Symphony no. 3 in A minor ("Scottish"), Op. 56; Symphony no. 4 in A major ("Italian"), Op. 90. [Trans.]

23. Mendelssohn released six volumes of *Lieder ohne Worte* ("Songs without Words") during his lifetime, and another two were published posthumously. Schubring also refers to the secular cantata after Goethe, *Die erste Walpurgisnacht*, Op. 60, and the overture and incidental music to Shakespeare's *A Midsummer Night's Dream*, Opp. 21 and 61. [Trans.]

24. Johann Gottfried Kuntsch (1775–1855), organist of the Marienkirche, Zwickau, from 1802. Schumann studied composition with him beginning at age ten and in 1845 dedicated to him the Six Pieces in Canon for Pedal-Piano, Op. 56. [Trans.]

25. Schumann began lessons in figured bass and counterpoint with the theorist Heinrich Dorn (1800–1892) in July 1831, but the lessons ceased in April 1832. [Trans.]

26. Schubring's opinion of Schumann's orchestration differs considerably from later conventional wisdom; see, for example, Weingartner's views on pp. 375–84. [Ed.]

27. "Strains unheard before." Probably from Horace, *Odes* 3.1.2–3. [Ed.]

28. *Fidelio* received its Berlin premiere in October 1816, when Zelter probably heard it. [Ed.]

29. Either the *Kinderszenen*, Op. 15 (1839), the *Waldscenen*, Op. 82 (1850), or the *Ballszenen*, Op. 109 (1853). [Trans.]

30. The Symphony no. 1, Op. 38; Schubring is referring to mm. 181–85, where the triangle takes up the rhythm of the principal subject. [Ed.]

31. The *Nachtstücke*, composed in 1839 and published in 1840. [Trans.]

32. Giovanni Paisiello (1740–1816), Domenico Cimarosa (1749–1801), A.-E.-M. Grétry (1741–1813), Luigi Cherubini (1760–1842), and Adrien Boieldieu (1755–1834). [Ed.]

33. "Deities of lesser nations." [Ed.]

On Schumann as Symphonist

(1904–1906)

FELIX WEINGARTNER

The rise to dominance of Wagner's music and of Wagnerian criticism in the second half of the nineteenth century led to a new appraisal of Schumann's work and of his impact on German music. The *Zukunfts-musiker*, those "musicians of the future" who rallied around the artistic creeds of Wagner and Liszt, now found Schumann's music deficient on several grounds, including his inability to compose a successful opera (*Genoveva*, his sole completed opera, was withdrawn after only a few performances; see p. 235); his continuing preoccupation with classical forms and traditional genres, a characteristic that was now ascribed to the deleterious influence of Mendelssohn; and his deficiencies as an orchestrator.

This last point was explored in considerable detail by the brilliant conductor Felix Weingartner (1863–1942), who had studied at the Leipzig Conservatory of Music in 1881 and then had met Liszt in Weimar in 1883, before assuming a series of positions in Danzig, Berlin, Munich, and Vienna, among other places. In 1897 Weingartner published his study of the development of the symphony after Beethoven, in which he labeled Schumann a "poet of the piano" who, in matters of orchestration, "left about everything to be desired." According to Weingartner, Schumann's scoring was inevitably too full and of a monochrome quality.[1] The symphonies impressed as piano works poorly transcribed for the orchestra, which did not take advantage of the versatility and colors of the modern orchestra. In his *Rat-schläge für die Aufführungen klassischer Symphonien*, Weingartner went so far as to offer specific suggestions for revisions, including thinning out the winds and strings and observing fastidious, precise applications of dynamics. To illustrate Weingartner's retouchings, we include here his ideas for the exposition of the first movement of Schumann's Third Symphony (the "Rhenish"). [Ed.]

[Sources: Felix Weingartner, *The Symphony since Beethoven*, trans. M. B. Dutton (Boston, 1904), pp. 27–34 (slightly altered), a trans. of Weingartner's *Die Symphonie nach Beethoven* (Leipzig, 1897); and Weingartner's *Ratschläge für die Aufführungen klassischer Symphonien* (Leipzig, 1906), pp. 84–86.]

The first and the most peculiarly subjective of the romanticists, if we turn now from the objective, classical romanticist Weber, is Robert Schumann. His individuality was diametrically opposed to Mendelssohn. Highly gifted as Mendelssohn was in mastery of form, was Schumann in inspiration. The former was a perfect artist, even in his early years; the latter pressed impetuously forward, ceaselessly struggling for something new and more perfect than his last endeavor, until gloomy fate fettered the power of his spirit. In the first period of his works we meet Schumann only as a pianoforte composer. Poetical pictures give rise to his compositions: he entwines the name of his youthful love in a theme and writes variations on it;[2] the motley scenes of the carnival give him the inspiration for one of the most spirited pianoforte pieces that we possess; Hoffmann's imaginative tales cause him to write *Kreisleriana* and the significant Sonata in F♯ minor; he represents "the two souls that dwell within his breast" by two personalities, "Florestan" and "Eusebius," and ascribes his works now to the one, now to the other. Violently abused by the critics and musicians who belonged to a guild, he formed, with friends sharing his opinions, the "Davidsbündler league" and dances roughly about on the toes of the Philistines. I may as well say at once that Schumann achieved his greatest significance as a pianoforte composer, as the poet of the pianoforte, one might almost say. Here he possessed the sincerity of the great masters; here he is just what he is, with no pretense of being more. Now, daring conceptions speak to us from these works, and we meet, even today, the offerings of his rich imagination with unabated delight. His treatment of the pianoforte is also original and thoroughly adapted to the nature of the instrument as well as to the musical thought, while, on the other hand, his management of the orchestra leaves, as we shall see later, almost everything to be desired.

At the age of thirty-one he first turns his attention to the greater forms of music, among others to the symphony.[3] Mendelssohn's brilliant figure moving with playful ease through all the domains of music was the shining ideal in Schumann's early life and works,—much to the latter's disadvantage. In the attempt to imitate Mendelssohn, to attain the same finish,—in the endeavor, as I might say, to be classical,—his own originality suffered severely without his being able to reach his model.[4] Throughout his life the spirit of romance and fantasy forced its way into his works, but no longer as it did in his youth. A strange and to a certain extent ingrafted element,—that very Mendelssohnian polish which he struggled in vain to acquire,—robs his later works of that spontaneity which charmed us so in his first compositions. His talent, which bore in smaller forms such precious fruit, became, without growing richer, pulled in this way and that into greater dimensions, and therefore thinner and more threadlike; he was required to yield more than he possessed. His productivity and versatility were nevertheless astonishingly great, even in the second period of his creative work, for there is hardly a musical form which he did not attempt. Since he, apparently in consequence of his being a freethinker, was averse to writing oratorios with biblical text, he accordingly chose secular poems, even fragments from Goethe's *Faust*,[5] for his compositions which are sort of halfway between operas and oratorios. Besides numerous songs, many of which are among our very best, Schumann wrote concertos, chamber music of all kinds, melodramas, one opera, and, as is to be expected from such a versatile artist, also symphonies. I suppose many of you will now look upon me as a heretic when I openly acknowledge that I count Schumann's symphonies as in no wise among his most important works.

In his pianoforte pieces the invention of little, but very expressive, themes, which he knew how to vary and use in an ingenious manner, is very characteristic. In his great symphonies he does not succeed with these themes and themelets, however warm and beautiful the feeling may have been from which they sprang. If you examine his orchestral pieces closely, you will find that he was often forced to repeat single bars or groups of bars in order to spin out the thread further, because the theme in itself is too small for such continuation. Sometimes even the theme itself is formed through the repetition of this and that phrase. On account of these copious tonic and consequently rhythmical repetitions, his greater pieces for the orchestra become naturally monotonous. One can retaliate that the theme of the first movement of Beethoven's C-minor Symphony is much smaller than Schumann's themes. Here is the real difference between the two: in Beethoven's work, after the first entrance of the theme, consisting of four notes, a simple melody, which makes use of the original theme only for rhythmical framework and not really for its own spinning out, arises over the pause of the first violins and the repetition of the theme in A♭–F, and evolves from itself up to the second subject (entrance of the horns in E♭ major). But in Schumann's works the melodious flow of the composition is preserved only by the repetition of themes as such, and the taking refuge in phrases which do not grow out of the subject. This weakness of Schumann's is most apparent in the first movements and in the finales of his symphonies, which—with the exception of the finale of the B♭-major Symphony, which is graceful in its principal theme, but not important—are conventional and noisy. Involuntarily we ask ourselves why we must always rejoice at the end of this symphony, while in Beethoven's works in a similar case the thought never arises? The reason is that in the latter's works the rejoicing follows with psychological necessity from the conquered grief, as in the C-minor or the Ninth, or is already contained in the elementary ground voice of the entire work, as in the Seventh Symphony. In place of the great, broad adagio of the Beethoven symphony appear in Schumann's pleasing, melodious, lyrical intermezzi, which are much better suited to the pianoforte than to the orchestra. In the main, a Schumann symphony is more effective played as a pianoforte duet than in a concert hall. The reason lies in a circumstance which the most unconditional admirers of Schumann can scarcely avoid recognizing,—namely, he did not know how to handle the orchestra, either as director or as composer. He worked almost always with the full material but did not take the pains to elaborate the parts according to the character of the separate instruments. With almost childlike stupidity he expected to obtain fullness and strength by doubling the instruments. Therefore, the instrumentation is heavy and inflexible; the color gray against gray; the most important themes, if played according to his directions, sometimes cannot be heard; and a true forte is about as impossible as a true piano. Whenever I see the players working with all their might, and compare, as a conductor, the labor of the rehearsals and the performance with the final effect, there comes over me a feeling similar to that I have toward a person in whom I expected to find mutual friendship and was disappointed. No sign of life gleams in this apathetic orchestra, which, if given even a simple Mendelssohnian piece to play, seems quite transformed. Schumann's symphonies are composed for the pianoforte, and arranged— unhappily, not well at that—for the orchestra. To be sure, in these works there are flashes of genius, beautifully deep and moving passages that recall the earliest period of the composer's work, as for example the introduction to the B♭-major Symphony, which promises great power. The middle movements up to the first trio of the Scherzo, which is quite meaningless and makes Schumann's weakness most frightfully apparent, are more important than the first. In my opinion, the *Adagio espressivo* of the C-major Symphony, with the real ascending and descending figure for the violins, is the best movement in all of his four symphonies.

Schumann, as an orchestral composer, appears quite different when he conceives some poetical inspiration that is congenial to him, as for instance Byron's *Manfred*.[6] Then he loses his desire to be classical; he dares to be what he is, the imaginative romanticist leaning toward the supernatural and the mysterious. In this mood, which was closely akin to his nature, he succeeded in writing a piece of music that can with all justice be called classical. That wonderfully planned and unusually lofty overture to *Manfred*, in which piece he was also more fortunate in his orchestration, is his only piece of orchestral music which can be compared with that he wrote for the pianoforte. From the rest of the *Manfred* score, we can see that under certain circumstances even an artistic absurdity, like the melodrama, may be of overwhelming effect if a great spirit wanders within its precinct. I am thinking here above all of "The Conjuration of Astarte."[7] This scene, if well performed by actor and orchestra, leaves in its overpowering effect no wish unsatisfied, least of all that Manfred might actually sing. This would be worse than composing the dialogue in *Fidelio* and *Der Freischütz*.[8] I have no idea here of championing melodrama, which is rising up again in these days, and which is even cultivated and defended by Wagnerians.[9] It would be equally foolish to condemn, for instance, "The Conjuration of Astarte" merely because it is melodrama. Especially today, when the disintegrating mind more frequently than ever lays hold upon works of art, and a number of art principles,—the same in German as art condemnations,—which for the most part have arisen through a misunderstanding, or a senseless echoing, of Richard Wagner's prose works, are vaguely ringing in everybody's heads, ready to trip up the first independent composer, it cannot be strongly enough advised that each one shall strengthen within himself the ability to accept without prejudice the impressions offered him. It will then be much simpler to distinguish between true and false, for art principles are dead and unfruitful; it is only the work or the art of genius that is pulsating with life, let it express itself as it will. Therefore Wagner's explanation of the Ninth Symphony, and the place he assigned to this work in history previous to his dramas, will never be convincing, while his conducting of this symphony in 1872 created new pathways in the art of conducting, and its effect has been productive of large results.[10]

Schumann, who always supported all ideal effort most loyally and zealously, after showing a brief interest in the greatest of his contemporaries, in whose glory he should have participated, turned from him first indifferently and then hostilely. Those who love Schumann should try to erase from their memories his small grumblings over *Tannhäuser*.[11] He turned from Wagner to herald a young musician, just coming into public notice through his pianoforte sonatas, with the spirited cry that here was the future messiah of music. This young musician was Johannes Brahms.[12]

Symphony No. 3 in E♭ Major, Op. 97 ("Rhenish")

TRANSLATED BY R. LARRY TODD

This symphony bears the title "Rhenish," though it was not so labeled by the composer himself. Colorful scenes draw by us, which one can easily relate partly to the romantic element of the Rhenish world of sagas and partly to the merry, happy disposition of the people who reside there; in the lovely fourth movement the mood awakened by the sublime image of the Cologne Cathedral appears to be reflected musically.[13] As with the First and Fourth, I recommend that this symphony be performed without interruption between the individual movements.[14] The sense of passing through various landscapes along the river is better preserved, the release of one mood into another takes effect uninterrupted, as when the more or less strong applause disturbs it four times.

The first movement actually may be conducted in strong downbeats for complete measures, but the director will do well to count out the three quarter notes now and then, for example in the first two bars, then again on p. 3, bars 6 and 7 and bars 10–15.[15] More often it will suffice to mark the first and third quarter notes. But in all cases the orchestra must avoid falling into rushing; marked rhythm is an especially strict requirement for performing this movement.

P. 1, bar 6. Trumpets and timpani make a $\diagdown$ and play the following measures up to the *sf* on p. 2 *mezzo forte*.

P. 1, bar 7. The horns make a $\diagdown$ up to the *mf*.

P. 2. The third and fourth horns pause for the first two measures. Both enter (like the first and second) *mf* in the third bar and make a crescendo in bars 4 and 5 to the *sf*.

P. 2, bars 9, 10, and 11. From the second quarter the winds pause completely and reenter only in bar 12. The strings begin with the second quarter of bar 9 *mf* and make a crescendo from here to *ff*. In bar 11 the horns (the second on the lower D) begin piano and follow with a crescendo. Through these and similar interruptions in the winds (which Schumann allows to play almost without pause) the colors of the orchestra achieve a greater variety, and that wearisome— and, in Schumann's symphonies, continuous and unvaried—sound is avoided. The following entry of all the winds has a renewed freshness after the three-bar pause. That the octave doubling is lost in the winds above through the pauses in no way disturbs the melodic flow.

P. 2, bar 12. Trumpets and timpani *ff* $\diagdown$ with the following *mf*.

P. 3, bar b. The entire orchestra begins this bar *p*.

P. 3, bars 7, 11, and 12. The oboes pause in these measures, but play in bars 8–10. In the tenth bar flutes and clarinets make a diminuendo with the violins. In bar 11 all play *p*.

P. 3, bars 14–15. Violins and violas crescendo, which can be supported by a scarcely noticeable broadening of the tempo.

P. 3, bar 23. A sudden *p* in the entire orchestra, to facilitate the following crescendo. Of course, the timpani nevertheless begin in bar 24 *p*.

P. 4, bars 2, 3, and 4. Here it is advisable to let the first violins take

the higher octave, thus , and then again in unison.

P. 4, bars 17, 18, and 19. Just like the similar bars on p. 2.

P. 5, bar 4. Complete orchestra *fp* $\diagup$.

P. 5, bar 6. The first oboe converts the first eighth (G) into a quarter and then pauses during this and the following bar.

P. 5, bars 7 and 8. $\diagdown$ *mf* $\diagup$.

P. 5, bar 12, all players *mf*, two bars later diminuendo.

P. 5, bars 20, 21, and 22. All violins *pp* instead of *p*.

P. 5, bars 23–31. Both oboes pause. If the tempo here drags a bit, the tempo primo resumes with all its force at rehearsal letter C. Already the upbeat in the trumpets and timpani should be *f*.

P. 6, bar 5. Trumpets and timpani *mf*.

P. 6, bars 24–28. The oboes pause and reenter in bar 29. At letter D a very fresh tempo.

P. 7, bar 4. Clarinets, bassoons, horns, trumpets, and timpani enter *p* with a following crescendo.

P. 7, bar 10. Trumpets and timpani *mf* $\diagup$, the next bar *f*.

P. 7, bars 15, 16, and 17. Third and fourth horn double the first

and second, thus:

P. 7, from bar 23 to p. 8, bar 2. The winds pause from the third

quarter, play only the two forte chords, , then

pause again and reenter on the third quarter of the last bar (p. 8, bar 2). To improve the clarity I recommend allowing the cello in the first bar (p. 7, bar 23) to enter with an accent on the third quarter, likewise the violins and violas on the third quarter of the next to last bar of this page.

P. 8, bar 3. From the third quarter horns, trumpets, and timpani *mf* up to the third quarter of bar 6. It is better to delete the previous *sf* in these instruments.

P. 8, bars 12–14. These bars are performed with a strong ritenuto. The bassoons pause three bars before the double bar. The previous B should be as in the clarinets (♩𝄾 instead of ♩·).

NOTES

1. Recent research has suggested that the perceived problem of imbalance in the symphonies had more to do with the increased size of late nineteenth-century orchestras than with Schumann's ineptitude: "It seems incredible that Weingartner did not imagine an alternative means of achieving proper balance in Schumann's orchestration: reducing the proportions of the ensemble to resemble those for which the composer so meticulously fashioned his . . . [symphonies]. If we adopted this practice, orchestras playing Schumann would not exceed Mendelssohn's . . . optimistic maximum ensemble of around fifty players. The relatively low or middling tessitura for the more colourful wind parts could then be distinguished amidst the frequent string doubling, and the fullness Schumann hoped to achieve would be preserved." See Jon W. Finson, *Robert Schumann and the Study of Orchestral Composition: The Genesis of the First Symphony, Op. 38* (Oxford, 1989), pp. 140–41. [Ed.]

2. The *Abegg* Variations, Op. 1, in which the theme (A–Bb–E–G–G) is drawn from the name of Schumann's acquaintance. [Ed.]

3. The First Symphony ("Spring"), Op. 38, of 1841. Weingartner was unaware of Schumann's earliest orchestral efforts, including the Symphony in G minor (1832–33), of which he completed three movements. [Ed.]

4. Here Weingartner appears to echo the views of Franz Brendel, for whom the musical developments of Mendelssohn and Schumann were diametrically opposed. In his 1845 comparative essay in the *Neue Zeitschrift für Musik*, "Robert Schumann mit Rücksicht auf Mendelssohn-Bartholdy," Brendel had compared the two in these terms: "Mendelssohn strives from the external inward, trying by means of what is accepted and generally recognized to arrive at self-knowledge and poetry. Schumann strives from the internal outward, beginning with his original personality: hence the law of his development is to mold this originality into the accepted forms and genres and gradually take possession of them." See Franz Brendel, "Robert Schumann with Reference to Mendelssohn-Bartholdy and the Development of Modern Music in General," trans. Susan Gillespie, in R. Larry Todd, ed., *Mendelssohn and His World* (Princeton, 1991), p. 344; and also pp. 317–37 here. [Ed.]

5. *Szenen aus Goethes Faust* (1844–53). [Ed.]

6. Incidental music to Byron's *Manfred*, Op. 115 (1848–49). [Ed.]

7. No. 10 ("Die Beschwörung der Astarte") from the second part of Schumann's *Manfred* music, from act 2, scene 4, of Byron's poem. [Ed.]

8. The references are to two melodramas (dramatic settings with spoken dialogue set against instrumental music) in Beethoven's *Fidelio* (no. 12, act 2) and Carl Maria von Weber's *Der Freischütz* (no. 10, the finale of act 2), the celebrated "Wolf's Glen" scene. [Ed.]

9. Liszt composed several melodramas, as did the younger Czech composer Zdeněk Fibich. Weingartner is probably referring to Engelbert Humperdinck's *Königskinder* and Richard Strauss's *Enoch Arden*, two melodramas from 1897, the year *Die Symphonie nach Beethoven* appeared. [Ed.]

10. On 22 May 1872 Wagner conducted a performance of Beethoven's Ninth Symphony in Bayreuth, to celebrate the laying of the foundation stone for the new festival theater, which opened in August 1876 with the premiere of Wagner's *Ring*. The Ninth Symphony figures prominently in Wagner's prose writings, including the novella *Eine Pilgerfahrt zu Beethoven* (1840), "Zu Beethoven's Neunter Symphonie" (1846), and "Das Kunstwerk der Zukunft" (1850). [Ed.]

11. On 22 October 1845 Schumann wrote in a letter to Mendelssohn concerning *Tannhäuser*: "And now we can see the whole score in print, fifths, octaves, and all. It is too late now to alter and scratch out, however much he may wish it. The music is no fraction better than *Rienzi*, but duller and more unnatural, if anything. If one says anything of the sort it is always put down to envy, and that is why I only say it to you, knowing you have long been of the same opinion." By 12 November he had altered these views: "I must take back one or two things after reading the score. It makes quite a different effect on the stage. Much of it impressed me deeply." Karl Storck, ed., *The Letters of Robert Schumann*, trans. Hannah Bryant (London, 1907), pp. 250–51, 278. [Ed.]

12. The reference is to Schumann's celebrated "Neue Bahnen" ("New Avenues") article, which appeared in the *Neue Zeitschrift für Musik* in October 1853. [Ed.]

13. See also pp. 98–99. [Ed.]

14. Of course, in Schumann's Fourth Symphony, Op. 120, the four movements are connected and intended by the composer to be performed without interruption. [Ed.]

15. The page and measure numbers refer to the standard edition in Clara Schumann, ed., *R. Schumann: Werke*, series 1 (Leipzig, 1881). [Ed.]

Index of Names and Compositions

List of Contributors

Christopher Anderson is a doctoral student in the performance practice program at Duke University. He holds a graduate degree in organ, has studied at the Stuttgart Hochschule, and is currently researching the music of Max Reger.

Bernhard R. Appel, of the Robert-Schumann-Forschungsstelle, Düsseldorf, is a contributor to the *Robert-Schumann-Gesamtausgabe*. He has edited Schumann's *Missa Sacra*, Op. 147, and the Requiem, Op. 148, among other works, and has published extensively on Schumann and romantic music.

Leon Botstein is President of Bard College, where he is also Professor of History and Music History. He is the author of *Judentum und Modernität* (Vienna, 1991) and *Music and Its Public: Habits of Listening and the Crisis of Modernism in Vienna, 1870–1914* (Chicago, forthcoming), as well as Music Director of the American Symphony Orchestra and Editor of *Musical Quarterly*.

John Michael Cooper is Associate Professor of Music History at Illinois Wesleyan University. He has published articles on Mendelssohn and Richard Strauss, among other topics, and is currently preparing *Felix Mendelssohn Bartholdy: A Guide to Research* for the Garland Composer Resource Manuals series.

John Daverio is Associate Professor of Music and Chairman of the Musicology Department at Boston University. He is the author of *Nineteenth-Century Music and the German Romantic Ideology* (New York, 1993) and has published articles on a variety of nineteenth-century topics. He is currently writing a study of the life and works of Robert Schumann.

Jon W. Finson is Associate Professor of Musicology at the University of North Carolina, Chapel Hill, where he is also Associate Chair for Academic Studies. He has published articles on Schumann, Brahms, and Mahler and is the author of *Robert Schumann and the Study of Orchestral Composition: The Genesis of Op. 38* (Oxford, 1989) and *The Voices That Are Gone: Themes in Nineteenth-Century American Popular Song* (New York, 1994).

Susan Gillespie is Vice President for Public Affairs at Bard College. She has contributed translations of music-historical essays, reviews, letters, and memoirs to each of the previous volumes published in conjunction with the Bard

Festival. Her translations of essays by Theodor W. Adorno have appeared in *Grand Street*, *Raritan*, and *Musical Quarterly*.

rd Nauhaus has been affiliated with the Robert-Schumann-Haus in wickau since 1970 and its director since 1993. He has edited Schumann's diaries and household account books and Clara Schumann's compositions, including her Piano Sonata in G minor. In 1986 he was the recipient of the Schumann prize from the city of Zwickau.

Nancy B. Reich is the author of *Clara Schumann: The Artist and the Woman* (Ithaca, N.Y., 1985), a biography that has been translated into German, Japanese, and Chinese. She has written and lectured on women musicians of the nineteenth century and has served as Visiting Professor of Music History at Bard College and Williams College.

Michael P. Steinberg is Associate Professor of Modern European History at Cornell University and Associate Editor of *Musical Quarterly*. He is the author of *The Meaning of the Salzburg Festival* (Ithaca, N.Y., 1990) and has translated Hermann Broch's *Hugo von Hofmannsthal and His Time* (Chicago, 1984) and Aby Warburg's *Images from the Region of the Pueblo Indians of North America* (Ithaca, N.Y., forthcoming).

Jürgen Thym is Professor of Musicology at the Eastman School of Music, University of Rochester. He has published works on Schumann, Arnold Schoenberg, and the German Lied and is co-translator of Johann Philipp Kirnberger's *The Art of Strict Musical Composition* and Heinrich Schenker's *Counterpoint*.

R. Larry Todd is Professor of Music at Duke University. He has written extensively about nineteenth-century music, especially that of Felix Mendelssohn-Bartholdy. Among his recent work is *Mendelssohn: "The Hebrides" and Other Overtures* (Cambridge, 1992) and the edited volumes *Mendelssohn Studies* (Cambridge, 1992) and *Mendelssohn and His World* (Princeton, 1991).